Computers as Cognitive Tools

TECHNOLOGY IN EDUCATION SERIES

Edited by
Raymond S. Nickerson

Nickerson/Zodhiates • Technology in Education: Looking Toward 2020

Larkin/Chabay • Computer-Assisted Instruction and Intelligent Tutoring Systems: Shared Goals and Complementary Approaches

Bruce/Rubin • Electronic Quills: A Situated Evaluation of Using Computers for Writing in Classrooms

Ruopp • LabNet: Toward a Community of Practice

Schwartz/Yerushalmy/Wilson • The Geometric Supposer: What is it a Case of?

Lajoie/Derry • Computers as Cognitive Tools

COMPUTERS AS COGNITIVE TOOLS

Edited by
SUSANNE P. LAJOIE
McGill University

SHARON J. DERRY
University of Wisconsin—Madison

1993

LAWRENCE ERLBAUM ASSOCIATES, PUBLISHERS
Hillsdale, New Jersey   Hove and London

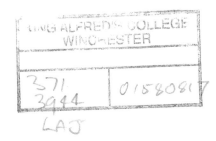
Lawrence Erlbaum Associates, Inc., Publishers
365 Broadway
Hillsdale, New Jersey 07642

Library of Congress Cataloging-in-Publication Data

Computers as cognitive tools / edited by Susanne P. Lajoie, Sharon J. Derry
   p.   cm.
   Includes bibliographical references and index.
   ISBN 0-8058-1081-1. — ISBN 0-8058-1082-X (pbk.)
   1. Computer-assisted instruction—United States. 2. Artificial
intelligence. I. Lajoie, Susanne. II. Derry, Sharon J.
   LB1028.5.C5722 1993
371.3'34—dc20   93-16902
                                           CIP

Printed in the United States of America
10 9 8 7 6 5 4 3 2 1

Contents

Preface

Susanne P. Lajoie
McGill University

Sharon J. Derry
University of Wisconsin—Madison

Writing this preface means that we are putting closure to a project that has been on our minds for some time. It gives us the opportunity to communicate why we think this book is important and how our ideas have evolved throughout the writing process. Two conferences stimulated the development of this volume, the American Educational Research Association (AERA) meeting in 1990 and the NATO conference on adaptive learning environments that was held in Calgary in the summer of that same year (see Jones & Winne, 1992). At the AERA meeting we organized a symposium on Computers as Cognitive Tools, which drew a large enthusiastic audience. The NATO conference brought computer scientists together with instructional and cognitive psychologists for the purpose of bridging gaps between theory and practice in the field of artificial intelligence and education. Discussions at these conferences revealed that the intelligent tutoring movement, long dominated by the student modeling paradigm, had both supporters and detractors. This observation, along with new perspectives on thinking and learning introduced by the situated cognition movement, led us to conceptualize this book and our introductory chapter on theoretical camps in the design of computer-based learning environments.

Theoretical camps are described to stimulate thinking about how researchers situate themselves within general theoretical perspectives and conduct research or develop computer-based learning environments within these perspectives. We do not want to give the impression that these so-called camps are rigid classifications or that any one theoretical camp is superior to another. We highlight the facts that these theoretical camps are evolving and that several contributors belong to more than one. But movement from one camp to another does appear to represent meaningful theoretical reorientation, as well as transition in the design of computer systems that vary in terms of the type of assistance provided to learners. Our original intent in producing this book was to provide readers with exemplars of the types of computer-based learning environments represented by the full range of our camping analogy. We did not attempt to provide a comprehensive examination of all the possible uses of computers in education, but we did purposefully invite contributors who we thought would reflect the theoretical philosophies with which we were concerned, as well as a wide range of practical applications. Accordingly, our contributors address a variety of computer applications to learning ranging from school-related topics such as geometry, algebra, biology, history, physics, and writing, to the more technical domains of electronics and avionics. The exemplars that we have selected are highly varied in terms of the instructional philosophies that guide their design, the types of assessment methods that are employed, and the forms of "cognitive tools" that are embedded within systems to help facilitate and evaluate learning.

The discussants, Alan Lesgold and Susan Chipman, add their respective viewpoints on the various issues involved in conducting empirical research using computers in the classroom. One topic they address is whether computer systems of the type described in our volume will ever have widespread impact on traditional education. Lesgold's optimism on this issue is tempered by Chipman's more pessimistic outlook. We leave it to the readers to decide.

We hope that this volume will provide food for thought for researchers who use computers as tools for enhancing learning. *Computers as Cognitive Tools* is appropriate for a variety of individuals, cognitive scientists, educational psychologists, computer scientists, teachers, and students. We would like to thank the contributors for their diligence in meeting all the deadlines and for making a significant impact on our understanding of the use of computers as cognitive tools. We would also like to thank Richard Lehrer for suggesting we produce this volume.

REFERENCES

Jones, M., & Winne, P. (1992). *Adaptive learning environments*. New York: Springer Verlag.

A Middle Camp for (Un)Intelligent Instructional Computing: An Introduction

Sharon J. Derry
University of Wisconsin—Madison

Susanne P. Lajoie
McGill University

The impetus for editing *Computers as Cognitive Tools* was spurred by questions currently being addressed by researchers in the fields of AI and cognitive science as to "what is good pedagogy and what types of computer systems will enhance learning?" These questions point to answers that may be realized in practice, for the use of advanced computer technology in the classroom is no longer just a researcher's fantasy. Even though state-of-the-art technology always precedes availability in a typical classroom or training environment, we see progress in that researchers are bridging the gap between theory and practice by testing computer systems outside of the laboratory. However, along with this progression has been a theoretical shift that is sometimes misconstrued as the continental divide of AI and education. Presiding on the mountain range that has resulted from this shift is an imaginary camp where researchers take a middle-road theoretical stand on pedagogical principles that guide the design of computer learning environments. Two imaginary camps on opposite sides of this mountain range are often theoretically opposed in terms of their philosophies regarding how computers can be used to facilitate instruction. One camp attracts model builders; the other shelters many non-modelers. Model builders represent what might be regarded as the traditional intelligent tutoring system (ITS) paradigm (if such a young science can have a tradition), which is based on assumptions that students' thinking processes can be modeled, traced, and corrected in the context of problem solving, using computers. Researchers camping with non-modelers are in opposition, either because they do not believe it is feasible to construct adequate cognitive models, or because better or more cost-effective alternatives exist. One alternative is that students can be stimulated to monitor and diagnose their own learning and problem-solving performance through the use of well-designed cognitive tools.

We present our fictitious camping analogy, not for the purpose of pigeonholing our colleagues and pitting them against one another, but rather as a way to alert the reader to some interesting philosophical differences represented in the range of approaches described in our volume. We acknowledge, however, that many of our contributors would not voluntarily align themselves with only one camp. Indeed, it is often the nature of the research enterprise to visit many!

To Model or Not to Model, That is the Question.
(And if one models not, is AI necessary at all?)

We focus on an interesting issue that tends to discriminate camps, their differing degrees of allegiance to the concept of a student model. Narrowly speaking, student modeling refers to the programming techniques and reasoning strategies that enable an instructional system to develop and update an understanding of the student and her performance on the system. More broadly defined, student modeling also includes the processes that actually utilize the system's knowledge about the student as a basis for diagnosing student problems and for selecting instructional approaches that best fit current diagnoses. Considerable debate surrounds this issue of whether strategies for student modeling should continue as a major agenda item for researchers and developers of advanced computer-based instruction. For example, this debate was aired at a recent NATO Advanced Study Institute on computer science and instructional technology, which took place in Calgary, Canada (Jones & Winne, 1992).

The student modeling issue was a major focus of the intelligent tutoring systems (ITS) movement of the 1980s. In fact, a majority of the research devoted to finding useful applications for AI in education can retrospectively be interpreted in terms of what we choose to call the "student-modeling paradigm." Essential characteristics of this paradigm are best illustrated by the prototypical model-tracing method pioneered and popularized by the CMU group (Anderson, et al., 1985), briefly summarized next.

The CMU model-tracing method is based on a theory of learning that assumes that procedural knowledge can be represented in the form of productions. A further assumption is that tutors that assist students in acquiring procedural knowledge should possess a "generic" student knowledge model that contains the desirable productions that an expert problem-solver would execute, and may as well contain incorrect, buggy productions that a novice learner might employ. To develop a tutor, cognitive research must be conducted to aid in specification of both the expert production model and the common buggy, novice productions. These are incorporated into the tutor system as an executable knowledge base. A student's performance on the system can then be *diagnosed* by matching each performance step taken by the student to a production that could be fired by the generic student model under the same constraints and conditions. The system determines whether an expert procedure has just been executed, or whether the student matches a particular novice move. Specific "canned" feedback messages are selected, dependent upon which production in the generic model is matched. Thus, corrective feedback is given immediately so that students are directed toward the expert's solution path and are not permitted to founder or randomly explore the problem space.

In many respects, the CMU approach has been impressively successful in practice. Tutors based on the model-tracing method now exist for a variety of procedural domains, including geometry, programming, physics and algebra. Recently, Schofield et al. (1988, 1989) studied the effects of a large-scale implementation of CMU's geometry tutor within actual classroom settings. Using both experimental and anthropological methods, the Schofield team documented numerous instances of positive learning and behavior changes, for both teachers and students, that could be attributed directly to use of the geometry tutor in classroom instruction. For example, student motivation increased substantially and discipline problems were minimized. In addition, classrooms became more student-centered, with teachers naturally shifting away from traditional roles as lecturers and disciplinarians, and embracing roles as facilitators and mentors engaged in shared problem solving with students.

In the face of such positive recent evidence, it is particularly interesting and timely to consider the arguments of researchers who have chosen to reject or ignore the student modeling paradigm (diSessa, 1985; Papert, 1989; Soloway, 1990; Self, 1988). Without regard to our opinion of their validity, we note that some of these arguments are represented in this volume and summarized here:

1. In complex problem-solving domains, the student model cannot possibly specify all solution paths that a student might take. In order for the model-tracing approach to work, the tutor must constrain the student to follow solution paths that the machine can recognize. Thus, the model-tracing approach confines and hinders the student, who should instead be encouraged to explore and experiment with any solution strategy.

2. It is impossible to determine all the possible "buggy" productions that a student might exhibit, and so an accurate and complete diagnosis of buggy procedures is impossible (Soloway, 1990).

3. "Canned" text cannot capture essential features of good tutorial dialogue; thus, the use of AI in education must wait until we have solved important natural-language issues (e.g., Fox, 1988a, 1988b).

4. Intelligent diagnosis by the tutor is not advisable anyway, since students should be encouraged to reflect upon and diagnose their own performances.

5. Student modeling is difficult to implement in a technical sense. Because development of intelligent systems is expensive and difficult, and since the need for intelligence in CAI can be questioned anyway, perhaps we should regard AI in education as a long-term research goal rather than a practical reality for current

use. At the current time, limited classroom resources might better be spent on unintelligent computing (Nathan et al., 1990; Reusser, this volume).

6. The model-tracing approach is applicable only to procedural learning (Glaser & Bassok, 1989). However, schools should focus on more important types of learning, such as higher-order problem solving and critical thinking.

THE STRUCTURE OF THE VOLUME

Our volume examines a sample of recent work in the instructional technology field to help determine what alternatives to the traditional model-tracing paradigm are now emerging and why. Within the chapters of this volume, the movement forward takes various forms, ranging from development of new model-tracing diagnostic systems on the one hand, to the deliberate elimination of intelligence from educational computing altogether on the other. To the extent that some authors continue to focus on constructing, perfecting or evaluating systems based on student modeling, diagnosis, and tutorial intervention, we see their work as building largely on a so-called 'traditional' ITS paradigm and contributing substantially to the perpetuation and evaluation of the model-builder camp. But we also have included in our book chapters describing instructional systems that clearly are not intelligent tutors and that emerge from a somewhat iconoclastic camp of non-modeling system builders, who have rejected many theoretical assumptions underlying the ITS approach, and have embraced, instead, a constructivist vision of the learner as social "tool user." Finally, we see in our volume a number of 'middle-road' projects that exemplify especially interesting and complex marriages of both modeling and nonmodeling perspectives and technologies. Such marriages, we believe, represent important dialectical mergers that help reconcile theoretical differences between camps and that, in fact, define a new mainstream for instructional technology research in the coming decade.

Section I: Model Builders

Research on student modeling continues to be very relevant and important for a number of reasons. One consideration is that the process of model development itself has value because it can add substantially to our scientific understanding of expertise and learning. Another point is that there are endless possible designs and approaches for student model construction, although only a few variations on the model-tracing methodology have actually been described in detail and used on widespread basis. New developments in computational reasoning (e.g., Bayesian expert system methodologies, fuzzy reasoning techniques, neural network approaches), as well as recent trends in cognitive instructional psychology (e.g., situated cognition, radical constructivism, semiotics) provide bases for highly innovative reconceptualizations of the student modeling enterprise. In sum, the final verdict on the efficacy of student modeling is far from being "in." At the current time we still possess far too little knowledge about possible variations in model design and the extent to which different types of modeling components can represent "value added" to an instructional system.

Although the ITS movement of the eighties spawned development of many pioneering systems, most of these required years of development and a relatively small number were actually finished and used. Surviving systems are just now being tried in actual classroom or training situations, and even these continue to be revised as data become available. Experimental studies with these systems, such as the study reported in this volume by Shute, will hopefully tell us much more about the value of incorporating theoretically-based intelligent student models into advanced instructional technology.

Three chapters in the first section represent substantial investments of energy and faith in the student modeling enterprise. Koedinger and Anderson build upon the model-tracing diagnostic approach, extending it to the development of a new geometry tutor that reifies implicit planning. As their chapter title implies, they provide valuable guidelines for helping those interested in designing model-based intelligent tutors. The assumption that student models are necessary clearly underlies the chapter by Lepper, Woolverton, Mumme, and Gurtner, which describes basic research pertaining to tutorial modeling of motivational states. They also provide practical insights that may encourage and help model builders to incorporate motivational indicators into their student modeling programs. The chapter by Derry and Hawkes provides their most detailed description to date of how fuzzy pattern matching is employed to detect primitive-level student errors in an algebra word-problem tutor. They also illustrate how primitive error indicators can be combined in pattern-matching equations to produce higher-order diagnoses, including diagnoses of motivational states.

Section II: Nonmodelers

Chapters in the second section offer an interesting contrast to those in the student modeling section. Here we showcase projects in which choices were made to either reject or ignore the ITS assumptions that student models, tutorial control, and diagnostic feedback are necessary components of effective computer-based instruction. From this view, the appropriate role for a computer system is not that of a teacher/expert, but rather, that of a mind-extension "cognitive tool." Thus, little or no artificial intelligence is incorporated into these instructional systems, because planning and decision-making control over the learning process is largely relegated to system users.   This philosophy is most clearly elaborated in chapters by Reusser and by Salomon, and is illustrated in practice in the contributions by Lehrer and by Teasley and Roschelle. The Reusser chapter in particular supplies an interesting contrast to the Derry and Hawkes work, since the systems described in those two chapters are theoretically and conceptually similar, although one represents a student modeling approach while the other does not. Researchers in this camp are apt to describe their work in terms consistent with currently-popular trends, such as cognitive apprenticeship (Collins, Brown, & Newman, 1989), situated cognition (Brown,Collins, & Duguid, 1989), and constructivist theory (von Glasersfeld, 1990). We note, however, that these framing assumptions also work reasonably well for the model-based systems discussed in our first section. As pointed out by Derry and Hawkes, the presence of an intelligent modeling capability within a system does not necessarily imply that any particular instructional strategy or philosophy be built upon it. A tutor may use its knowledge of students in different ways. However, a distinguishing feature of the non-modeling forms of instructional technology is that they assign little in the way of instructional decision making to the computer system itself. Rather, "tutoring" is understood to be an artifact of the social classroom environment in which the system is situated.

The arguments of Section II are neo-Piagetian in flavor. In Piagetian psychology, a major function of schooling is to help the student develop metacognitive self-regulation over the processes of learning and problem solving. The most sophisticated form of self-regulation occurs when students exhibit a general tendency for conscious, reflective surveillance of thought, manifested in the ability to discuss and critique one's own problem-solving strategies and knowledge models (Brown, 1987). Nonmodelers (Reusser, for example) argue that "unintelligent" cognitive tools supplied by computer technologies can serve as powerful catalysts for facilitating development of generalized self-regulatory skills, provided they are appropriately deployed within a social classroom environment that promotes reflection, discussion and critique during problem solving. Good computer-based cognitive tools can support such social problem-solving processes by providing physical representations of abstract strategies and concepts, making them tangible for inspection, manipulation, and discussion, thereby encouraging generalized metacognitive awareness and self-regulatory ability.

Vygotsky (1978) believed that self-regulatory capability must be transferred from mentors to students through a specialized form of tutorial-like social interaction which has come to be known as "cognitive apprenticeship" (Collins et al., 1989). From a more traditional tutorial perspective, cognitive apprenticeship is seen as the sharing of problem-solving experiences between a novice and a mentor, the mentor being either a teacher, a more advanced peer, or a computer. A dialogue occurs, exposing the thinking processes underlying the problem-solving interaction. The mentor supplies general direction and encouragements, but supports, or "scaffolds" (e.g., Palincsar, 1986), only those aspects of the problem solving that are clearly too difficult for the novice to manage alone. In early learning, hints and assistance from the mentor enable the novice to successfully execute a task that would be beyond the student's current capabilities if working alone. Importantly, higher-order strategies and control processes are modeled through the mentor's guidance. As the student's problem-solving abilities improve, the mentor gradually fades support, encouraging the student to think independently using strategies and control processes previously modeled.

Much of the theoretical framing offered in chapters of our second section generalizes the cognitive apprenticeship model to complex group interactions involving multiple novices and mentors representing various stages of cognitive development and sophistication. The computer is the focus of group attention, but it promotes shared problem solving without controlling it directly. The teacher is only sometimes present as a controlling agent, and the interaction is not calibrated to the individual student. Thus, for any individual student, the appropriate level of scaffolding, modeling, and fading may or may not emerge. And while there is explicit acknowledgement that the classroom context is a powerful determinant of successful implementation (see Salomon), design of the mentorship strategy supplied (sometimes serendipitously) by the instructional environment is not an apparent, driving concern for the non-modelers. By contrast, model builders see the need for designing mentorship capability into the computer system itself.

Section III: Bridging Differences in Opposing Camps

Between the traditional ITS (model builders) and the more iconoclastic non-modeling positions, there are researchers who believe that cognitive apprenticeship, constructivist learning, and computer-based cognitive tools go hand-in-hand with student modeling. This group of researchers continues to adhere to the faith that through the application of AI, computers can and should serve part of the cognitive mentorship function without giving over total control of the learning and assessment process to system users (teachers and students). In identifying several of our contributors with a fictitious middle-road camp, we focus on examples of how AI-based systems are departing from the traditional student modeling approach.

In the context of Section III we also will mention again several chapters that appear as examples of model-building projects in Section I, perhaps challenging the very efficacy of drawing a distinction between ITS model builders and their middle-road colleagues. That projects described in Section I also belong in Section III can be attributed to the fact that projects with historical roots in traditional ITS are now evolving into something new. We accept this messiness as an interesting fact of life. It points to the adaptibility of the ITS approach.

Clearly, middle-ground researchers share strong affinity with model builders. Yet criticisms frequently levied against the more traditional ITS work are that student models have been too restrictive to accommodate social constructivist views of education, but that it is technically difficult to pre-specify all possible problem constructions that a student might pursue in an exploratory problem-solving session. Responses to these concerns are found in chapters by Derry and Hawkes (Section I) and by Lajoie (Section III), which describe alternative experimental computational approaches to modeling. The Derry and Hawkes system, although traditional ITS in its emphasis on modeling, is non-traditional in its premise that student models need not be accurate or precise in order to provide useful instructional information. To allow the student flexibility in creating problem solutions, their system satisfices with a fuzzy model of student performance, which may vary in accuracy and precision dependent upon what patterns are observed in the student input. Another alternative to traditional student modeling, as used in Lajoie's work, is to have multiple levels of "correct" solution paths and to provide feedback conditional upon which path is selected.

We framed the chapter by Lepper et al. within a traditional modeling approach, placing it in Section I. But this work also represents a significant shift of interest away from purely cognitive diagnoses characteristic of the traditional ITS paradigm. Their interest lies in modeling of students' affective states. Both Derry and Hawkes and Lajoie believe that their computational approaches offer promise for implementing such motivational diagnoses. Some degree of metacognitive diagnosis also should be possible with their methods.

A very different approach to metacognitive modeling is illustrated in the Section III chapter by Schauble, Raghavan, and Glaser. Schauble et al. describe a graphical trace notation that is constructed dynamically by the computer based on the student's actions in the context of the Smithtown microworld. Rather than confining the student or usurping the diagnostic function, their trace notation encourages self-reflection and discovery of knowledge about one's own problem-solving strategies. Such metacognitive reflection devices based on a student model are designed to encourage the development of higher-order thinking skills that may be generalized across problem solving domains.

In sum, student models are now being developed to consider the cognitive, metacognitive and motivational states of the learner and to encourage reflection on higher-order thinking strategies. Yet, what makes certain projects fit better than others into the middle-ground camp exemplified by Section III is that their designs embrace both modeling and the sentiments typically associated with the developmental/constructivist approaches championed by their nonmodeling colleagues. Nonmodelers do not necessarily reject the importance of diagnosis per se, but believe that using a computer to model student performance is either too complex or confining or encourages pedagogical strategies that usurp high-order thinking. They tend to replace the student model with the notion that the computer can *afford* opportunities for learners to diagnose their own actions. This affordance is made possible by cognitive tools in the computer environment as well as by the community of learners who share this experience.

Consider that cognitive tools are objects provided by the instructional environment that allow students to incorporate new auxiliary methods or symbols into their social problem-solving activity that otherwise would be unavailable. When tools are well-designed, tool use by student communities can help them perform and grow beyond their current developmental capabilities (Vygotsky, 1978). Influenced by this philosophy, developers in our book are employing a wide variety of innovative tools designed to enhance cognitive, metacognitive, and motivational development.

The cognitive tools incorporated into systems described by this book assist in all stages of problem solving, ranging from tools that help learners conceptualize problem representations (Derry & Hawkes; Koedinger & Anderson; Reusser) to those that are more deliberately designed to assist learners in reviewing and reflecting upon the entire problem-solving process (Katz & Lesgold; Lajoie; Schauble, Raghavan & Glaser). Some cognitive tools are available that promote the development of procedural knowledge by allowing practice of skills that would not frequently be required in the real world or that would be unsafe to practice outside of the computer environment. These include tools that permit simulations of actual work situations, such as taking measurements on circuit cards, troubleshooting an electronics device, or using laboratory facilities in a hospital (Katz & Lesgold; Lajoie; Schauble, Raghavan & Glaser; Shute). Such simulations allow learners to experiment with tools that might not be available to them otherwise, and provide learners with opportunities to formulate and test hypotheses, and to revise them when necessary. Finally, an important type of tool is one that provides a gateway to whatever knowledge is required in the context of a particular problem-solving situation, such as the on-line library that can be accessed through Lajoie's Bioworld system.

Such tools "scaffold" students' thinking process in the widely-understood sense described by Palincsar (1986). In accordance with the apprenticeship philosophy, such scaffolding should be faded as the learners' problem-solving skills develop. In systems that combine intelligent modeling with the apprenticeship philosophy, one function that can be served by the student model is to decide when and how much to prompt or fade tool availability. Furthermore, the mind-extension tools of intelligent systems support assessment. For as students select and employ tools in actual problem solving, intelligent systems observe patterns in tool use and draw inferences regarding students' developmental growth. Thus, in middle-road approaches, cognitive tools become an integral part of the student modeling process itself.

In sum, when we join the notion of model tracing in a computer-based environment with appreciation for creative mind-extension cognitive tools and for how a community of learners can facilitate learning, we create a camp where AI technologists and social constructivist learning theorists are equally at home. We feel this trend is best represented within our volume in the Section III chapters by Katz and Lesgold, Lajoie, and Schauble, Raghavan and Glaser.

Concluding Comment

Our intent in editing this volume was to highlight and illustrate several important and interesting theoretical trends that have emerged in the continuing evolutionary development of instructional technology. A framework was developed based on the notion of two opposing camps, one evolving out of the intelligent tutoring movement, which employs artificial-intelligence technologies in the service of student modelling and precision diagnosis, and the other emerging from a constructivist/developmental perspective that promotes exploration and social interaction, but tends to reject the methods and goals of the student modelers. While the notion of opposing camps tends to create a sometimes (but not always) artificial rift between groups of researchers, we have resorted to these camps because they represent a distinction that is inherently more interesting and informative than the relatively meaningless divide often drawn between "intelligent" versus "unintelligent" instructional systems. Between opposing camps we find researchers who are enthusiastically assimilating and accommodating the wisdom and creativity of their neighbors, perhaps forming the look of technology for the future.

REFERENCES

Anderson, J. S., Boyle, C. F., & Reiser, B. J. (1985). Intelligent tutoring systems. *Science, 228,* 456–468.

Brown, A. L. (1987). Metacognition, executive control, self regulation, and other more mysterious mechanisms. In F. Weinert & R. Klewe (Eds.), *Metacognition, motivation and understanding, (pp. 65–116).* Hillsdale, NJ: Lawrence Erlbaum Associates.

Brown, J. S., Collins, A., & Duguid, P. (1989). Situated cognition and the culture of learning. *Educational Researcher, 18(1),* 32–42.

Collins, A., Brown, J. S., & Newman, S. E. (1989). Cognitive apprenticeship: Teaching the craft of reading, writing, and mathematics In L. Resnick (Ed.). *Knowing, learning and instruction: Essays in honor of Robert Glaser (pp. 453–494).* Hillsdale, NJ: Lawrence Erlbaum Associates.

diSessa, A. (1985). A principled design for an integrated computational environment. *Human-computer interaction, 1,* pp. 1–47.

Fox, B. A. (1988a). *Repair as a factor in interface design* (Technical Report). Boulder: Institute for Cognitive Science, University of Colorado.

Fox, B. A. (1988b). *Robust learning environments: The issue of canned text* (Technical Report). Boulder: Institute for Cognitive Science, University of Colorado.

Glaser, R. & Bassok, M. (1989). Learning theory and the study of instruction. *Annual Review of Psychology, 40,* 631–666.

Jones, M., & Winne, P. H. (1992). *Adaptive Learning Environments.* Heidelberg: Springer-Verlag.

Nathan, M. J., Kintsch, W., & Young, E. (1990). A theory of algebra word problem comprehension and its implications for unintelligent tutoring systems (ICS Technical Report #90-02). Boulder: Institute for Cognitive Science, University of Colorado.

Palincsar, A. S. (1986). The role of dialogue in providing scaffolded instruction. *Educational Psychologist, 21,* 73–99.

Papert, S. (1980). *Mindstorms: Children, computers, and powerful ideas.* New York: Basic Books.

Roschelle, J. (1990, April). *Mental models from computer models: How do students do it?* Paper presented at the Annual Meeting of the American Educational Research Association, Boston.

Schofield, J. W., Evans-Rhodes, D., and Huber, B. R. *Artificial intelligence in the classroom: The impact of a computer-based tutor on teachers and students.* (Technical Report No. 3) Learning Research & Development Center, University of Pittsburgh, Pittsburgh, PA.

Schofield, J. & Verban, D. (1988). *Barriers and incentives to computer usage in teaching* (Technical Report No. 1). Learning Research & Development Center, University of Pittsburgh, Pittsburgh, PA.

Self, J. (1988). *Bypassing the intractable problem of student modelling. ITS-88* proceedings. Montreal: University of Montreal.

Soloway, E. (1990, July). *Interactive learning environments.* Paper presented at the NATO Advanced Studies Institute, Calgary.

von Glasersfeld, E. (1988). An Exposition of constructivism: Why some like it radical. *Journal of Research on Mathematics Education Monograph,* No. 4, 19–30.

Vygotsky, L. S. (1978). *Mind in society: The development of higher psychological processes* (M. Cole, V. John-Steiner, S. Scribner, & E. Souberman, Eds. and Trans.). Cambridge, MA: Harvard University Press.

MODEL BUILDERS

1

Reifying Implicit Planning in Geometry: Guidelines for Model-Based Intelligent Tutoring System Design

Kenneth R. Koedinger
John R. Anderson
Carnegie Mellon University

This chapter addresses the problem of how basic cognitive science research can be translated into effective "cognitive tools" for learning. We present a set of guidelines that have been used to design a second generation Intelligent Tutoring System (ITS) for geometry and are intended more generally to aid the design of other computer or noncomputer based learning environments. Similar efforts (Anderson, Boyle, Corbett, & Lewis, 1990; Anderson, Boyle, Farrell, & Reiser, 1987; Collins, Brown, & Newman, 1989) have focused on how cognitive theories or principles can be generally applied to instructional design in any domain. In contrast, this chapter illustrates how cognitive science *methodologies* can be used in the instructional design process and we focus on a particular class of domains, ones where instructional innovations may pay off most. Although instructional innovations can certainly benefit from the application of general instructional principles, a large share of the instructional benefit often derives from insights (of researchers or teachers) into the particular instructional domain itself. This chapter describes a set of methodologies intended to help instructional designers gain such insights.

This approach is intended to apply to, and in fact to help identify, a particular class of *enigmatic domains*. These are domains that students find particularly mysterious, for example, geometry proofs and algebra word problems, such that even well-motivated students have difficulty (Koedinger, 1991 provides an operational definition of enigmatic domain). We elaborate a methodology for designing instruction, particularly computer-based instruction, for such domains.

A key point is to emphasize how empirical studies and cognitive modeling of skilled problem solvers can uncover *implicit planning:* thought processes of successful students that are not represented in the notation of conventional instruction. In turn, this model of implicit planning can be used to help design novel instruction. We present a detailed example in the domain of geometry where we have built a second generation cognitive model and ITS for geometry proof problem solving. We illustrate how this model has driven the design of ANGLE (A New Geometry Learning Environment).

A second point is to provide some general guidelines for translating a cognitive model of implicit planning into design specifications for the components of an ITS. Given a cognitive model of skilled problem solving, designing the expert component (i.e., the subject-matter knowledge) of an ITS is straightforward as it can simply be the computer implementation of this model. In the case that a novice model is also available, the expert component can be supplemented with buggy rules to provide the tutor with knowledge of students' common mistakes. These are the essentials of the model-tracing approach in which the tutor is designed to follow the student's problem-solving efforts relative to a cognitive model of ideal and buggy behavior (Anderson, Boyle, & Reiser, 1985).

Translating a cognitive model into design specifications for the interface and tutoring components of an ITS is not as straightforward. We take the model-tracing approach a step further here by providing some guidelines for how a cognitive model of skill can be used in the design of the interface and tutoring components. It is the role of these components to reify and articulate aspects of the model so as to communicate them to students. The guidelines we propose are a generalization of the model-based approach taken in the development of ANGLE. There are 5 steps:

1. Identify the *execution space.*
2. Look for *implicit planning* in verbal reports.
3. Model this implicit planning.
4. Use the model to drive tutor design.
5. *Test* the tutor implementation.

We turn now to description of the development of ANGLE. This description comes in 5 subsections following the 5 steps in the guidelines for model-based tutor design we are proposing. In the following section we generalize these steps in 5 parallel subsections.

ANGLE: A 2ND GENERATION TUTOR FOR GEOMETRY

The Geometry Execution Space

Geometry proof problem solving is hard. For a typical geometry proof, the search space of possible geometry rule applications (i.e., definitions, postulates, and theorems) is quite large. To get an idea of the size, we performed a detailed analysis of a typical problem (this problem appears in Figs. 1.4–1.7). Of the 27 definitions, postulates, and theorems that are introduced prior to such a problem in a traditional curriculum, 7 can be applied at the beginning of this problem. Some of these rules can be applied in more than one way yielding 45 possible inferences that can be made from this problem's givens. Using the results of these inferences, essentially as new givens, we did the same thing over again and found that 563 inferences can be made at this second layer. At the third layer the options really explode as there are more than 100,000 possible inferences. The number of options continues to increase at further layers—at minimum it takes 6 such layers of inferences to reach the problem goal.

For a student to be effective at solving geometry proof problems, he or she must have a method for dealing with this complexity. Many methods are possible as illustrated by the variety of artificial intelligence programs and cognitive models that have been developed for this domain (Koedinger & Anderson, 1990 provide a review). While these previous models differed in the general search strategies and domain specific heuristics they employed, most were built on top of the same underlying problem space representation—one that has the formal geometry rules as operators.[1] We call this problem space the *execution space* and, in general, we define the execution space for a domain as a problem space made up of states that correspond with the steps that problem solvers conventionally write down or *execute* in solving a problem in the domain. The preceding analysis illustrates an exhaustive search of the execution space in geometry.

To more effectively search this problem space, model builders have incorporated more sophisticated search strategies and included more domain specific heuristic knowledge. The search strategies have ranged from backward search in Gelernter's (1963) original "geometry theorem proving machine" to an opportunistic bidirectional search (works both forward and backward) in Anderson, Boyle, and Yost's (1985) cognitive model of skilled geometry students. The heuristic knowledge has ranged from using the problem diagram to reject goal statements that are clearly false (in Gelernter's model) to the addition of specific contextual features that predict the relevance of a rule (in Anderson et al.'s model). Despite these improvements, the key point is that the underlying problem representation has remained the same.

As the definition of execution space suggests, this problem representation is a reflection of the way geometry proofs are conventionally written, for example, in traditional geometry textbooks. Although such textbooks do not explicitly describe a problem-solving method for doing proof problems, the implied method is search in the space of formal rules. One indication of this method is the way traditional textbooks are organized around formal rules: introducing a rule, illustrating it, providing exercises with it, and then on to the next. A second

---

[1]See Newell (1990) or Newell and Simon (1972) for a review of the problem-solving terminology used here.

indication is that the steps in example problem solutions correspond with geometry rules. It seems quite natural then, for students reading such a text (and cognitive scientists, for that matter) to view their problem-solving task as one of searching for an appropriate rule to apply at each step in the problem.

In summary, early geometry problem-solving models assert heuristic search in the execution space as a psychologically plausible characterization of geometry problem solving. Similarly, traditional geometry instruction can be interpreted as implicitly making the same assertion. This assertion is a good first approximation as evidenced, for example, by the Anderson, Boyle, and Yost (1985) cognitive model and its use in the Geometry Proof Tutor which has been shown to be an effective instructional device (Anderson, Boyle, Corbett, & Lewis, 1990).

However, when we took a closer look at the behavior of skilled geometry problem solvers, we found that their mode of attack is distinctly different from the approach of these earlier models. Instead of making local heuristic decisions within the execution space, skilled problem solvers focus their search by initially developing a global solution plan using a representation that is more abstract (and more compact) than the execution space. They were bringing informal perceptual and conceptual knowledge to bear in their initial planning and were leaving the formal details for last. It seemed important to be able to characterize this knowledge both as a goal in and of itself and for pedagogical purposes.

Evidence of Implicit Planning: Step-Skipping

We have referred to the kind of planning we observed in skilled subjects as *implicit planning* to emphasize that it occurs in a problem space that is not explicitly represented in the notation of conventional instruction. In other words, implicit planning is (informal) planning in a problem space other than the (formal) execution space. The identification of implicit planning in a domain provides a first step in the design of novel instruction in that it indicates a kind of thinking which is not supported by or taught in current instruction.

A key piece of evidence for implicit planning in geometry was the observation that in their initial attempt at a problem solution skilled subjects were not thinking about every step in the execution space solution. Instead, they developed a solution sketch in which numerous execution steps were skipped. Consider the protocol in Table 1.1 of a skilled subject solving the problem shown in Fig. 1.1.

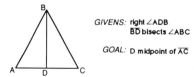

GIVENS: right ∠ADB
$\overline{BD}$ bisects ∠ABC

GOAL: D midpoint of $\overline{AC}$

FIG. 1.1. A geometry proof problem solved by a skilled problem solver whose verbal report is shown in Table 1.1.

TABLE 1.1
A Verbal Protocol for a Skilled Subject Solving the Problem in Fig. 1.1

		Planning Phase
B1:	We're given a right angle–this is a right angle,	Reading given: rt <ADB
B2:	perpendicular on both sides [makes perpenedicular markings on diagram];	Inference step 1: AC⊥BD
B3:	BD bisects angle ABC [marks angles ABD and CBD]	Reading given: BD bisects <ABC
B4:	and *we're done*	Inference step 2:ΔABD = ΔCBD
		Execution Phase
B5:	We know that this is a reflexive [marks line BD],	In this phase, the subject refines and explains his solution to the experimenter.
B6:	we know that we have congruent triangles; we can determine anything from there in terms of corresponding parts	
B7:	and that's what this [looking at the goal statement for the first time] is going to mean...that these are congruent [marks segments AD and DC as equal on the diagram].	

The left side of the table contains the protocol and the right side indicates our coding of the subject's actions.

At the point where he said "we're done," this subject had developed a correct solution sketch for this problem in only 13 seconds. He plans this solution sketch without looking at the goal statement (see Koedinger & Anderson, 1990 for an explanation of this curious behavior) and in the remainder of the protocol he elaborates the solution sketch, reads the goal statement, and explains how it is proven. His words "we're done" indicate his realization that the two triangles ABD and CBD are congruent and that therefore he knows everything about the whole problem—as he explains later: "we can determine anything from there in terms of corresponding parts."

Figure 1.2 shows the 7-step execution space solution to the problem. Apart from the givens and goal, the statements which the expert mentioned while solving this problem are numbered in Fig. 1.2, while the skipped steps are circled.

Consistent with the evidence that verbalizations are accurate reflections of working memory states (Ericsson & Simon, 1984), we conclude that the expert only makes certain key inferences in his search for a solution while skipping other, apparently minor inferences.[2] A person following the implicit message of the traditional curriculum would work in the execution space (as do previous

---

[2]Ericsson and Simon (1984) stipulate that this claim is true only for verbal reports of problem solving that are given concurrently with problem solving. These are the kind of protocols we collected.

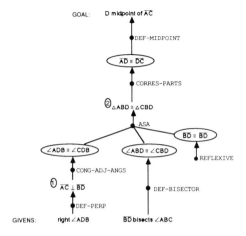

FIG. 1.2. The final solution for the problem shown in Fig. 1.1. The givens of the problem are at the bottom and the goal is at the top. The lines represent inferences with the conclusion at the arrow head, the premises at the tails, and the justifying geometry rule at the dot in between. The statements Subject R mentioned during planning (see Table 1.1) are numbered while the ones he skipped are circled.

problem solving models) and require at least seven thinking steps to come up with a solution plan.[3] In contrast, this subject came up with a solution plan in two thinking steps. It became clear to us that this subject (and our other skilled subjects; see Koedinger & Anderson, 1990) were bringing to bear a different kind of knowledge than that involved in heuristic search of the execution space.

DC: A Model of Implicit Planning in Geometry

Based on these observations, we tried to design a model of expert geometry theorem proving that would be both more powerful and more like skilled humans than previous systems. The model we came up with, the Diagram Configuration model (DC), is briefly summarized here. DC has one major knowledge structure, diagram configuration schemas, and three major processes: diagram parsing, statement encoding, and schema search.

The core idea of the DC model is that experts have their knowledge organized according to diagrammatic schemas which we call *diagram configuration schemas*. These are clusters of geometry facts that are associated with a single prototypic geometric image. Figure 1.3 shows two diagram configuration schemas.

The *whole-statement* and *part-statements* attributes of a schema store the facts that are associated with the geometric image stored in the *configuration* attribute. The configuration is a prototypic configuration of points and lines which is commonly a part of geometry diagrams. In Fig. 1.3, the configuration on the left is a prototype for any set of lines that form two congruent triangles with a side in

---

[3]More than seven thinking steps would result from pursuing blind alleys or arriving at a longer final solution.

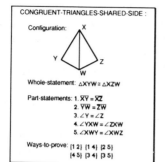
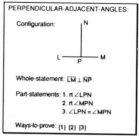

FIG. 1.3. Two examples of diagram configuration schemas. The numbers in the ways-to-prove indicate part-statements. Thus, in the CONGRUENT-TRIANGLES-SHARED-SIDE schema {1 2} means that if the part-statements $\overline{XY} = \overline{XZ}$ and $\overline{YW} = \overline{ZW}$ are proven, all the statements of the schema can be proven.

common. The whole-statement is the geometry statement that refers to the configuration as a whole. The part-statements refer to properties of the parts of the configuration. The whole-statement of the CONGRUENT-TRIANGLES-SHARED-SIDE schema refers to the two triangles involved while the part-statements refer to the corresponding sides and angles of these triangles. The *ways-to-prove* are used to determine whether inferences can be made about a configuration. They indicate subsets of the part-statements which are sufficient to prove the whole-statement and all of the part-statements. For example, the first way-to-prove of the CONGRUENT-TRIANGLES-SHARED-SIDE schema, {1 2}, indicates that if the part-statements $\overline{XY} = \overline{XZ}$ and $\overline{YW} = \overline{ZW}$ have been proven, the schema can be proven—that is, all the other statements of the schema can be proven.

Our basic proposal is that skilled problem solvers plan in terms of these schemas rather than the statements of geometry. The problem solver tries to establish that various schemas are true of the diagram associated with a problem. Establishing one schema may enable establishing another. Because there are a small number of schemas possible for any particular problem diagram, the search space of schemas is much smaller than the execution space.

DC does a type of instance- or model-based reasoning by treating the problem diagram as a specific instance or model (Johnson-Laird, 1983) of the abstract problem statement indicated by the givens and goals of the problem. This use of the diagram as a model allows DC to do some inductive reasoning to aid in the solution of what is nominally a deductive problem. DC induces relationships that look true in the problem diagram (this involves measurements of relative sizes of segments and angles) and uses these relationships to constrain the search space, which would otherwise include many syntactically well-formed statements that are clearly not true in the model.

The logic of this trick relies on the fact that since the diagram is an instance of the proof being constructed, any relationship that can be proven will appear true in an accurately drawn diagram. As a concrete model, the diagram has the advantage of making important relationships clearly apparent (visible in this case) whereas they are only implicit in abstract statements. These perceptual cues have the effect of allowing the problem solver to avoid lots of semantically impossible or irrelevant inferences that may appear relevant when trying to syntactically apply the formal execution space rules.

We can explain the subject protocol in Table 1.1 in terms of the DC model as follows. In B1, he reads the first given and as he marks it in the diagram, he recognizes an instance of the PERPENDICULAR-ADJACENT-ANGLES schema. Since this given satisfies one of the ways-to-prove of this schema, the schema's properties (i.e., the whole-statement and part-statements) can be proven. Correspondingly in B2 the subject says "perpendicular on both sides" which, though not technically well-formed, essentially expresses the three part-statements of the PERPENDICULAR-ADJACENT-ANGLES schema in one neat phrase. In B3, he reads the second given, encodes it as $\angle ABD \cong \angle CBD$, and marks this in the diagram. At this point (or possibly before) he makes a perceptual recognition that two of the triangles in the diagram look congruent and share a side, that is, he identifies an instance of the CONGRUENT-TRI-ANGLES-SHARED-SIDE configuration. Thus, this schema is cued and considering the ways-to-prove, he sees that a part-statement of the PERPENDICULAR-ADJACENT-ANGLES schema ($\angle ADB \cong \angle CDB$) and the encoding of the second given ($\angle ABD \cong \angle CBD$) satisfy one of them ({4 5}). Because he knows he can prove all the properties of this schema and since this schema constitutes the whole diagram, he is able to say "we're done" at this point without reading the problem goal.

Evaluation of DC.   In Koedinger and Anderson (1990), we established the empirical accuracy of DC by showing that it does a good job of accounting for the steps that subjects mention or skip in their verbal reports of proof planning. We also demonstrated its computational efficiency by illustrating how much smaller the schema space is than the execution space. For example, in contrast to the greater than 100,000 states in the complete execution space for the problem discussed on p. 17, the complete DC space for this problem contains only 8 states.

A Point About Learning.   It is important to consider whether the DC model and the method of skilled subjects is distinctly different from that of search in the execution space. One competing hypothesis is that what we've observed in skilled subjects is the result of a skill acquisition process (e.g., ACT*'s composition, Anderson, 1983; or Soar's chunking, Newell, 1990) which has chunked together execution space operators into *macro-operators*. If this were the case, that is, if it were necessary to learn the execution space operators first before learning schemas, then training students in the execution space (as the traditional curriculum implicitly does) would be appropriate. However, we not believe this to be the case.

Although it is true that DC's schemas can be *represented* as a number of execution space macro-operators, there is good reason to believe that schemas are not actually *derived* (learned) from execution operators. In Koedinger and Anderson (1989, 1990) we argued that, among other things, there is too much regularity in the kinds of steps experts skip to be accounted for by a macro-operator type mechanism. The number of possible ways of syntactically combining execution space rules into macro-operators is far greater than the relatively small number of schemas that correspond with expert step-skipping. Macro-operator learning mechanisms cannot explain this limited, but sufficient, set of schemas in a parsimonious way.

The observation that DC schemas correspond with the perceptual structure of geometric objects has led us to propose that, in contrast to macro-operator learning. DC schemas are the result of an inductive learning mechanism that acquires expert operators directly from interactions with the learning environment and not so much from modifying and combining previously acquired operators. This inductive learning mechanism must be capable of identifying categories of percepts (configurations) and attaching the corresponding formal properties (whole-statement and part-statements) to these percepts.

Further support for this proposal comes from data collected in our first evaluation of ANGLE (summarized on p. 33). The hypothesis that DC schemas are learned from an earlier execution space representation predicts that step skipping will not be apparent in novices, but will only emerge as enough expertise is acquired. In contrast to this hypothesis, we found evidence that novices are also occasionally skipping steps quite early in the skill acquisition process.

DC Summary.   In the next section we describe how DC has been used as the expert component for a second generation ITS for geometry called ANGLE. We end this section by comparing DC with the expert component of the first generation Geometry Proof Tutor (GPT). See Table 1.2. In GPT's expert component, the knowledge was organized around the *formal rules* of geometry. These formal geometry rules appeared as parts of production rules that also contained context cues to indicate likely situations in which the formal rule would be usefully applied. The productions implement a bidirectional heuristic search strategy that has a local view in that decisions are only made about the next formal step in the proof (either forward or backward). In contrast, ANGLE's expert component is organized around informal knowledge of geometric percepts (configurations) and associated concepts (part-statements and ways-to-prove). It searches a different

TABLE 1.2
Differences Between GPT's and ANGLE's Expert Components

	Knowledge	Strategy
GPT Expert	Formal rules	Local heuristic search
ANGLE Expert	Percepts & concepts	Global planning

problem space that takes a more global planning view where each decision typically involves many proof steps. We describe how these different cognitive models lead to different tutoring systems in the following section.

Tutor Design: From DC to ANGLE

In this section, we discuss the design of ANGLE and in particular, how its major components, the expert, interface, and tutoring component have been influenced by the cognitive model of problem solving described earlier. The expert component is the subject-matter knowledge of the tutor, the interface component determines how the student interacts with the system, and the tutoring component provides the verbal advice the system gives the student.

Table 1.3 summarizes a methodology for model-based tutor design that indicates a way to translate from a cognitive model of problem solving into design specifications for the interface and tutoring components of an ITS. Given a model of successful students' implicit planning, one needs to find ways to communicate the knowledge representations and cognitive processes that make up this model.

The interface component provides an implicit form of instruction in that students can learn through their perception and interaction with it. Thus, one avenue to teaching the problem-solving model is to invent interface *notations* and *actions* that reify the underlying representations and processes of the model. Interface notations should mirror the model representations such that students can begin to internalize these representations through repeated perception and use of the notations. Similarly, interface actions should mirror the model pro-

TABLE 1.3
Ways to Communicate a Problem-Solving Model in an ITS

	Representations	Processes
Interface	Notations	Actions
Tutor Advice	Vocabulary	Hints and Explanations

cesses such that students can learn these processes through repeated performance of these actions.

Whereas the interface component provides an implicit form of instruction, the tutor component provides a direct way to instruct students on the representations and processes of the problem solving model. Both ANGLE's tutoring messages and the off-line text materials use specific vocabulary to directly articulate the schema representations used in DC. Similarly, the content and order of ANGLE's *hints* and *explanations* have been designed to articulate the problem-solving processes (e.g., diagram parsing, abstract planning) incorporated by DC.

Reifying the Model Through Interface Notations and Actions.   The ANGLE interface includes a number of examples of notations that reify representations in the DC model. The most prominent and important are icons for representing the generic schema categories and for representing student-selected instances of these schemas (see Fig. 1.4). These icons provide a concrete image to which students can attach the related conceptual knowledge about the part-statements

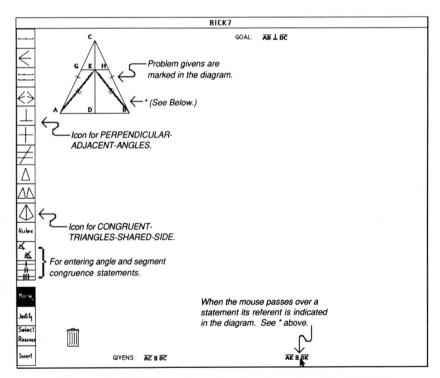

FIG. 1.4.   The ANGLE interface at the start of a problem. The italicized annotations are not part of the interface.

and ways-to-prove. In particular, they reinforce the perceptual character of schemas.

Following GPT, ANGLE incorporates a graph representation of proofs in contrast to the two-column format of traditional geometry instruction. Figure 1.5 illustrates a complete proof plan represented in the proof graph notation, while Fig. 1.7 illustrates the complete proof after execution. This proof graph notation is important because it reifies the search process:

1. by explicitly indicating how a correct solution must be a chain of steps linking the givens to the goal,

2. by allowing the entering of subgoals as possible future links in the solution chain, and

3. by explicitly indicating dead-end solution attempts which are a common part of problem solving even for experts.

Collins and Brown (1990) discuss how this type of "spatial reification" provides a vehicle for learning through reflection.

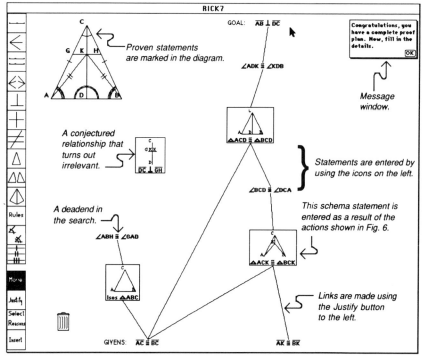

FIG. 1.5.   A completed proof plan. The student performed some extra steps that aren't relevant to the solution. The italicized annotations are not part of the interface.

Following a conventional notation used on paper, ANGLE uses hash marks in the diagram to indicate part-statements that have been proven (see, for example, segments AK and BK in Fig. 1.5). These markings reify an efficient equivalence class representation of segment and angle congruence in contrast to the more cumbersome binary relationships of the formal notation. For example, to indicate that 3 angles are all congruent to each other using the hash mark notation, one can mark all three with the same marking—the marking serves as a token of the equivalence class containing all three angles. In contrast, the formal notation requires three binary statements to represent this situation, for example, $\angle 1 \cong \angle 2$, $\angle 2 \cong \angle 3$, and $\angle 1 \cong \angle 3$.

Finally, as a further aid to the acquisition of schemas, ANGLE highlights a schema within the problem diagram whenever the mouse passes over the corresponding schema instance icon in the proof graph. This is intended to reinforce the relationship between the schema and the rest of the diagram. This is a kind of dynamic notation that cannot be feasibly employed with paper and pencil.

Whereas interface notations were created to reify representations in the DC model, interface actions were designed to reify processes. Following the major processes in DC, ANGLE interface actions are broken down into (1) diagram parsing actions, (2) planning actions, and (3) execution actions. The grain size of parsing and planning actions is designed to emphasize schemas, while the focus on statements and rules is left for execution actions.

The *diagram* parsing actions are those done in order to enter schemas. First the student selects a schema type and then indicates the lines within the diagram that make up an instance of this schema. Figure 1.6 shows the entry of an instance of the CONGRUENT-TRIANGLES-SHARED-SIDE schema. This particular way of constructing a statement, as opposed to the way a student constructs one in GPT or on paper, is meant to reinforce the relationship between the schema instance and the problem diagram in which it is embedded.

The *planning actions* are those done in order to justify schemas and part-statements. To some extent these actions are more elaborate than those made in a two-column proof on paper: In ANGLE, the student must explicitly indicate the premises that lead to a conclusion (that is, by drawing the lines between them), while in the typical two-column proof these links are only implicit. On the other hand, the planning actions are for the most part less elaborate than those required for a two-column proof. Certain details required in a two-column proof can be left out while constructing a plan. Students can omit (a) certain statements usually required in a complete proof, for example, the reflexive statement $\overline{CK} \cong \overline{CK}$ in the first inference in Fig. 1.5, and (b) the rules or "reasons" that usually appear in the right column of a two-column proof.

After a proof plan has been discovered (as shown in Fig. 1.5), the student can fill in the details that were left out in the proof plan by performing *execution actions* which include adding new statements and inserting rules. Figure 1.7 shows the final result of adding all the details to the proof plan in Fig. 1.5. The

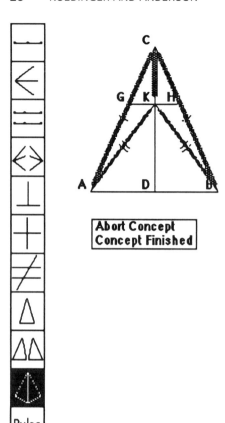

FIG. 1.6. Selection of an instance of the CONGRUENT-TRI-ANGLES-SHARED-SIDE schema: $\triangle$**ACK** $\cong$ $\triangle$**BCK**. This method of schema selection is intended to reify the diagram parsing process.

idea of the separation of planning and execution is that, just as in DC, the student need not worry about the details while searching for a plan. When a plan is found, he need only fill in the details along the path that leads to the goal.

Any tutor interface (or notational scheme for that matter) is implicitly taking an instructional stance about what things are difficult and/or important to learn and what things are not. Three important aspects of the instructional stance taken by ANGLE's interface are worth making explicit: (1) learning about the logical linkages between proof steps is difficult and important, (2) learning the details of proof execution is less important and perhaps less difficult than learning proof planning, and (3) learning how to parse geometry diagrams into particular chunks (DC-schemas) is difficult but it is important for successful search in a vast problem space. The first point is shared by GPT's interface, but not by the two-column notation used on paper. The last two points are special to ANGLE's interface.

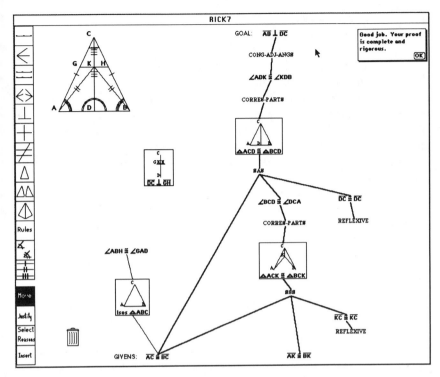

FIG. 1.7.   The final, detailed solution in the execution space. The dark links indicate execution inferences while the lighter links indicate planning inferences. Note that the planning inferences that are not relevant to the solution are not executed.

Articulating the Model Through Tutor Vocabulary and Hints.   While the interface component was designed to reify model representations and processes with interface notations and actions, the tutor component was designed to articulate model representations and processes with the vocabulary and explanations employed by the tutor.

In supplemental text materials, schemas are explicitly presented to students in a format similar to that shown in Fig. 1.3. We decided to call schemas "concepts" as this word is much more familiar to most students. In addition to talking about "concepts," the vocabulary of the schema slot-names, "configuration," "part-statement," and "ways-to-prove" are an explicit part of both the tutor advice and the supplementary text materials.

The content of the feedback ANGLE gives when students make logical errors (i.e., an illegal justification attempt) was also designed to help students learn the schema representation. This logical error feedback first enforces the constraint

(1) that only part-statements of a schema can be used to prove it. When this constraint has been satisfied the tutor then checks (2) that the part-statements the student selected match one of the ways-to-prove. In this way, students can learn that when trying to prove a schema, they need not consider any statements besides the part-statements of that schema.

One straightforward way of communicating model processes is through the content of the hints the tutor provides. ANGLE's hints for entering a particular schema explicitly direct the student toward diagram parsing (a key process in the cognitive model). The hint to enter a CONGRUENT-TRIANGLES schema, for example, encourages careful diagram parsing by asking students to count the triangles in the diagram.

Besides the content of hints, a less obvious way of communicating model processes is through the order in which hints are given. In other words, the order in which hints about appropriate problem-solving steps are given should correspond with the order of these steps in the cognitive model. Following through on this design guideline results in one of the biggest differences between ANGLE and the first generation GPT.

Consider the situation in Fig. 1.8. If a student were to ask for help from GPT at this point, it would focus on using the corresponding-parts rule to make the inference from $\triangle$BCD $\cong$ $\triangle$YZW. The message would be something like "Notice two triangles which are congruent. Think about what this tells you." This is not necessarily a bad hint. But, it lacks a strategic context that might help the student decide which of the six corresponding parts it might be useful to prove. We've observed students blindly following this advice, proving nonessential parts congruent (e.g., $\angle$CBD = $\angle$ZYW), getting the advice again, proving another set of nonessential parts congruent (e.g., $\angle$CDB $\cong$ $\angle$ZWY), and so on. Eventually, they stumble upon the right corresponding parts, in this problem both $\overline{DC}$ $\cong$ $\overline{WZ}$ and $\angle$DCA $\cong$ $\angle$WZX are useful, and only then will GPT start giving advice towards proving $\triangle$ACD $\cong$ $\triangle$XZW.

ANGLE approaches this situation more strategically, that is, starting with $\triangle$ACD $\cong$ $\triangle$XZW and moving back to the enabling part-statements $\overline{DC}$ $\cong$ $\overline{WZ}$ and $\angle$DCA $\cong$ $\angle$WZX. If the student needs help, ANGLE would first provide *schema selection hints* to encourage her to look in the diagram for triangles that she might prove congruent. The student is advised toward entering $\triangle$ACD $\cong$ $\triangle$XZW as an island subgoal. See Fig. 1.9.

Next, she should work on finding part-statements which she can prove from $\triangle$BCD $\cong$ $\triangle$YZW and which are relevant to this goal. If she has trouble, ANGLE provides *part-statement justification hints*. In this situation, the most general such hint would suggest: "Look for OVERLAPPING concepts. That is, look for a part-statement which appears both in $\triangle$ACD $\cong$ $\triangle$XZW and in a concept you've already proven."

Figure 1.9 shows the addition of the necessary part-statements. If the student has trouble here, ANGLE would provide a *schema justification hint* that would

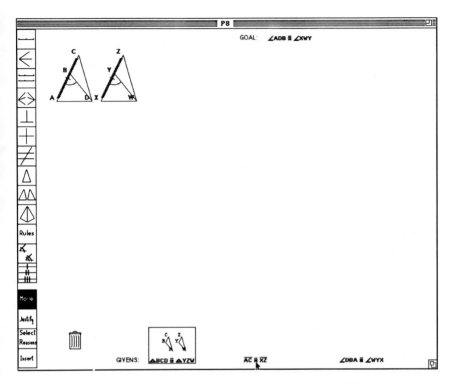

FIG. 1.8.   The context for a strategic hint. The next hint will focus on the selection of the △ACD ≅ △XZW schema and only then, will the hints focus on part-statements that follow from △BCD ≅ △YZW. These hints suggest to select those part-statements which will help to prove △ACD ≅ △XZW.

work her toward finding the appropriate premises ($\overline{DC}$ ≅ $\overline{WZ}$, ∠DCA ≅ ∠WZX, and the given $\overline{AC}$ ≅ $\overline{XZ}$) with which to justify △ACD ≅ △XZW.

ANGLE Summary.   Table 1.4 presents contrasts between the first generation GPT and the second generation ANGLE along the dimensions of tutor design discussed before: interface notations and actions to reify model representations and processes and tutor vocabulary and hints to articulate model representations and processes. While the interface notations of GPT focus on the formal rules of geometry, ANGLE's notations focus on diagram configuration schemas. The interface actions of GPT reify rule application by breaking it down into three steps: selecting premises (the if-part), typing the rule name, and entering the conclusion (the then-part). In contrast, ANGLE's interface actions are at a larger grain size reifying the processes of diagram parsing and schema justification and search. In the tutor component, GPT's messages exclusively use the vocabulary

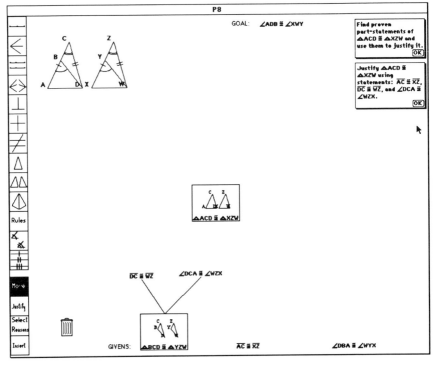

FIG. 1.9. The needed part-statements have been added. Both a general hint and the bottom out hint for the next step are shown in the message windows in the top right. The focus is on justifying △**ACD** ≅ △**XZW** using the proven part-statements.

TABLE 1.4
Contrasts Between the Interface and Tutor Design of GPT and ANGLE

| | Interface Component | | Tutor Component | |
	Notations	Actions	Vocabulary	Hints
GPT	Rules	Premise Rule Conclusion	Traditional	Local only: Execution steps
ANGLE	Schemas	Diagram parsing Schema search	"concepts" "part-stmts" "ways-to-prove"	Global: Schemas Local: Rules

of the traditional curriculum, while ANGLE's messages (and supplementary text materials) make choice use of novel vocabulary to articulate crucial aspects of the schema representation. Lastly, GPT's hints articulate its underlying model of heuristic search in the execution space and thus, they are at the grain size of formal geometry rules (execution steps). In contrast, ANGLE's hints articulate the processes in DC and thus, start at the larger grain size of schemas and then move to the more detailed grain size of rules.

Testing the Tutor Implementation: A Formative Evaluation of ANGLE

This section describes some of the results of our first empirical study of ANGLE. The central goal of our empirical evaluations of ANGLE is to test the hypothesis that the development of more accurate and powerful cognitive models of problem solving can lead to major improvements in the instruction of problem solving, particularly within the context of intelligent tutoring systems. In this study, we compared GPT and ANGLE—two tutors for the same domain whose primary difference is the cognitive model that underlies them. While the cognitive model underlying GPT is a reasonably good one, it has some flaws. It does not do a good job of capturing the more strategic abilities of effective problem solvers. The DC model improves on GPT's model by providing a sound explanation of these abilities. The question is: can this improvement lead to more effective instruction?

ANGLE is still in an early development stage. In particular, the current implementation of the feedback scheme and the wording of the feedback messages are only a reasonable first pass attempt. It takes iterations of usage and redesign to get a good sense for how to make them most effective. ANGLE represents about 1.5 person-years of effort. This study was its first extensive trial. In contrast, GPT represents about 10 person-years of effort and has been through at least 2 major iterations of study and redesign.

Method Summary.   30 high school students were paid to participate. To reduce the amount of declarative instruction in geometry and focus on proof problem solving, we required these students to have just completed a high school geometry course. They came in the lab for six 2-hour sessions and started with pretesting, then worked with either GPT or ANGLE for 8 hours of tutoring, and finished with posttesting. Half the students worked with GPT, the other half with ANGLE. Given the relatively short training time, a subset of the geometry curriculum was used involving the topics of perpendicularity and triangle congruence. It covered 8 rules in the execution space and 4 schemas in the diagram configuration space.

Two versions of the tests (A & B) were used to counterbalance test order. Here we report on the results of one of the four tests given—the proof construction test which provides the most direct measure of students' proof performance. Both the A & B versions of the proof test had four proof problems on it, the first item was of medium difficulty (about the difficulty of the problem in Fig. 1.1: 5 execution steps or 2 schemas in the shortest solution), the second two were difficult (8 execution steps, 3 schemas) and the last was very difficult (10 or 11 execution steps, 4 schemas). A detailed overall score was taken by giving one point for each correct execution step (32 points for version A, 31 for B). In addition to the test results, both tutors collected detailed on-line data of student-tutor interactions.

Overall Results: ANGLE About Equal to GPT.   On the proof test, ANGLE subjects went from a mean pretest performance of 11.0 to a posttest performance of 19.6, while GPT subjects went from 11.9 on the pretest to 23.6 on the posttest. Consistent with the previous results of GPT, both groups showed significant learning ($p < .001$), however, there is no significant difference on posttest performance ($p > .13$). At this early stage of development, ANGLE appears to be matching up with a proven tutor. However, there is room for improvement and this study helped identify some weaknesses in the implementation of ANGLE that we can remedy.

Better Instruction of Planning Than Execution.   In addition to the overall score reported earlier, the proof tests were also scored using a planning measure where subjects got one point for every correct "schema step" in this solution. Schema steps are those that uniquely indicate a schema (e.g., whole-statements). Using this measure we find that ANGLE subjects went from a mean score of 5.5 to 9.7 (on a scale of 12), while GPT subjects went from 5.9 to 10.0. The trend in favor of GPT in the overall score disappears in this planning score. To better understand what was going on here, we counted the number of skipped steps in the proof solutions—that is, cases where the subject had a correct schema step but some of the corresponding execution steps were missing. We found that while skipping about the same number of steps on the pretest, ANGLE subjects skipped significantly more steps on the posttest, 3.5 to GPT subjects' 1.0 ($p < .001$). In other words, although they were planning equally as well, ANGLE subjects are making more execution errors on the posttest.

This result is not surprising given that the development of ANGLE to this point has primarily focused on tutoring facilities for planning. ANGLE's tutoring facilities for execution actions were rather minimal and these results would seem to indicate that such minimal execution tutoring is not sufficient for efficient instruction of proof execution skills.[4]

---

[4]It should be pointed out that proof execution skill (i.e., skill at the formal details of proofs) is not necessarily a primary instructional goal. Some educators are more concerned with more informal, but accurate, reasoning along the lines of DC's conceptual planning.

On-Line Tutor Data: Too Much Flexibility?   The on-line tutor data provided additional pointers to areas where ANGLE can be improved. From observations during the study, it appeared that ANGLE subjects were floundering more often and for longer periods than GPT subjects. This observation was corroborated by the fact that in the fixed 8 hours of training GPT subjects finished significantly more problems than ANGLE subjects, 48.5 to 39.1 respectively ($p < .05$). The number of problems completed was highly correlated with posttest performance ($r = .73$) suggesting that this factor is an important one in learning. Part of the problem with ANGLE seemed to stem from the greater flexibility and complexity of its interface relative to GPT's.

The ANGLE interface was more complex both because it had more types of actions to learn (necessary to implement the distinction between planning and execution), and because it allowed more alternative sequences of actions. Although the ideal sequence of actions is to start by alternating between diagram parsing and planning actions and then finish with a series of execution actions (i.e., following the DC model's approach), ANGLE allowed students to perform diagram parsing, planning, and execution actions in any order. While providing such flexibility seemed like a laudable implementation goal, the interaction of this flexibility with certain other implementation decisions had some negative consequences.

Bottom-out Hint Problem.   One of the more serious problems involves a decision all ITS designers must face: What to do if the student is really stuck and the hints the tutor is giving are not helping. Many ITSs, including ANGLE and GPT, follow a general-to-specific hinting strategy where the first hint in a particular context is very vague, not giving too much away, and if the student still has trouble, the hints get progressively more specific. Eventually they *bottom-out* at the most specific hint. In both ANGLE and GPT, bottom-out hints are given only after the student has made numerous logical errors or requests for help (4 or 5 on average) without making any progress, that is, performing a legal step. One type of bottom-out hint that guarantees continual progress toward the solution is to have the tutor do the next step for the student.[5] This is the approach taken in GPT. In ANGLE, we took the slightly less extreme approach of telling the student what to do next without actually doing it.

Unfortunately, students were not always able to translate ANGLE's bottom-out hints into the appropriate actions and because of the flexibility designed into ANGLE, students were not forced to perform them. In turns out that this situation arose quite often—bottom-out hints were given on 23% of the 561 problems solved.[6] The fact that students often did not immediately perform the suggested

---

[5]At the other extreme, an ITS designer might decide that in a classroom situation it is sufficient to direct the student to the teacher, for example, "You seem to be having a lot of trouble. Please ask your teacher for help."

[6]Some of the early protocol data was lost. Students actually solved 586 problems.

next step is measured by two statistics. Since ANGLE repeats the bottom-out hint if the student continues to have trouble, one relevant statistic is the number of times a particular bottom-out hint was repeated on average. Bottom-out hints were repeated about once (0.97) on average. The second statistic is more telling and leads to a more dramatic result. It is the amount of time that is spent between the time the bottom-out hint is first given and the time the student performs the suggested next step. Because there is more than one solution to these problems, it is possible for the student to finish the problem without ever performing the suggested next step (this happened for only 8% of the bottom-out hints given). In the cases where students do end up eventually performing the suggested next step, about 75 seconds elapse on average. Multiplying this by the number of bottom-out hints given, we find that the students in this study spent almost one half hour on average (26.6 minutes) between being told what to do next and actually doing it. (26.6 minutes is about 6% of the total 8 hours of tutor instruction.) Recall, that bottom-out hints are given only after the student has already given evidence of floundering (e.g., 4 or 5 logical errors or requests for help) and thus, this period of time might be characterized as extreme floundering.

It is possible, on the other hand, that some useful work is going on during this time. For example, the student may be pursuing alternative paths, working out details, or entering future subgoals. Nevertheless, the student ends up needing to perform the suggested action and this statistic clearly indicates a big discrepancy between the way we expected the student-tutor interaction to go and the way it actually did.

One straightforward remedy to this problem is to do what is done in GPT and have the bottom-out hint provide the next step for the student. Another alternative is a simple "interface tutor" that will kick-in after bottom-out hints are given and guide the student in performing the suggested action.

The Whole-statement Encoding Problem.   One of the difficulties encountered in thinking about how the ANGLE interface should reify the problem solving model involved the process of *whole-statement encoding* in which the DC model converts whole-statements that appear in a problem given or goal into the corresponding schema. The question was whether and how this whole-statement encoding process might be reified in ANGLE interface actions.

Here again, we opted for flexibility in the interface. On the one hand, whole-statements that appeared in the givens or goal could be treated, for the purposes of making justifications, just as if they were schemas. This is a short cut in which the whole-statement encoding process is left implicit. Alternatively, the student could enter the corresponding schema and link it to the whole-statement, and thus explicitly perform the whole-statement encoding process. The interface responded by putting the schema (whole-statement plus configuration instance) in the given or goal position that the whole-statement had occupied. An example of the result is shown in Fig. 1.8 where the given on the left, which originally appeared simply as $\triangle BCD \cong \triangle YZW$, has been encoded as the corresponding schema.

Although the student was free to do it either way, in the case that the student needed help at this point, the tutor suggested that they explicitly perform the whole-statement encoding step. Two problems arose. While the interface actions to perform this step were the same as those necessary to select and justify any schema, the effect was different (i.e., the schema replaces the whole-statement to which it was linked). Understanding this interface operation was another thing for students to learn that may have distracted them from learning geometry.

A second problem was the unanticipated awkwardness that sometimes resulted from the way the schema hint templates got applied to this situation. Whereas the majority of these hints read just fine, one of them, the bottom-out hint for justifying a planning action, turned out to be particularly awkward. Since schemas were referred to in the hint messages using the same label as the label for the whole-statement, the justification bottom-out hint message, which has the generic form "Justify ⟨ the desired schema ⟩ using statements: ⟨ the necessary statements ⟩," ended up as "Justify ⟨ whole-statement ⟩ using statements: ⟨ whole-statements ⟩." For example, if the whole-statement $\triangle ABD \cong \triangle CBD$ appeared as a given and the corresponding TRIANGLE-CONGRUENCE-SHARED-SIDE schema (labeled $\triangle ABD \cong \triangle CBD$) had been entered, then if the student happened to need a bottom-out hint, it would read "Justify $\triangle ABD \cong \triangle CBD$ using statements: $\triangle ABD \cong \triangle CBD$."

This proved a bit confusing to students. Many of the cases where a student never performed the step suggested by a bottom-out hint were cases where the student got this hint, didn't know how to implement it, and was eventually able to perform a different step (i.e., one that involved skipping the whole-statement encoding step) with no help from the tutor.

Clearly one way to remedy the problems experienced with the whole-statement encoding step would be to improve the associated hint message. Another possibility would be to remove the flexibility, the option to skip the whole-statement encoding step, and always require the student to perform it. The idea of the whole-statement encoding step was to encourage students to begin problem solving by recognizing any statements in the givens or goal that refer to schemas (i.e., any whole-statements). However, from watching students, this recognition of given or goal statements in the diagram does not appear to be a great difficulty, especially in comparison to the difficulties that arose from allowing and sometimes encouraging the explicit whole-statement encoding step.

Thus, perhaps the best remedy might be to simply eliminate the need to explicitly perform whole-statement encoding. In addition, whenever a problem given or goal is a whole-statement, the tutor should display this statement as a schema complete with the diagram configuration.

Planning Before Execution Not Enforced.   Following the cognitive model, ANGLE's feedback scheme always suggests planning moves first and only suggests execution moves once a complete plan has been found. However, consistent with the effort to make the system flexible, ANGLE allows students to integrate planning and execution. In fact, students rarely completed planning before beginning execution. One measure of this is the percentage of inferences that occurred after execution began, but before planning was finished. Thus, for example, if all the planning is done first this percentage should be 0. Instead, 47% of students' inferences were in this mixed stage. Students' tendency to mix planning and execution was not quite significantly correlated with posttest performance ($p = .06$). However, the pattern is that the students who began execution early scored better on the post-test. This is probably a reflection of students' prior familiarity with the execution space and the good students' better facility with it.

These data indicate that to accurately test the efficacy of teaching the DC model, it seems important to sacrifice some flexibility in the interface and enforce the planning first approach of the cognitive model. Only after completing a plan would students to allowed to begin proof execution.

Study Conclusions: Lessons Learned.   Getting the student-tutor interaction right requires careful and lengthy user study that goes beyond informally watching a few students work with the system for a couple of hours. While we knew prior to the study that ANGLE's tutoring schemes were not perfect, we did not anticipate certain problems like the trouble students had understanding and implementing the bottom-out hints. The lesson is that such problems are necessarily a part of the development process and that tuning the interface and tutoring components is equally as important as following through on the implications of a cognitive model.

A second lesson from this initial evaluation is that the curriculum we used was too small (only 8 geometry rules and/or 4 schemas). This is important because a key difference between the problem solving method ANGLE teaches and the one GPT teaches is that ANGLE's method is more effective in the large search space of geometry rules (the execution space). By limiting the curriculum, the size of the search space is effectively reduced and if it is small enough, the search benefits of ANGLE's method become negligible. With a larger curriculum, then, we are more likely to see a difference between ANGLE and GPT.

GUIDELINES FOR MODEL-BASED TUTOR DESIGN

In this section, we recast the research agenda carried out in the development of ANGLE to this point, generalizing the key steps and presenting them in the form of guidelines for tutor design. Certainly there are other theoretically motivated routes to successful tutor design, not to mention getting there by good intuitions or serendipity. These guidelines are provided as one possible route that may (1) be directly applied in some domains or (2) be used as a departure point for developing related approaches in other domains.

The approach can characterized in five steps:

1. Identify the *execution space*.
2. Look for *implicit planning* in verbal reports.
3. Model this implicit planning.
4. Use the model to drive tutor design.
5. *Test* the tutor implementation.

We discuss the significance of each step, illustrate it in the context of this project, and suggest how it might be generalized to other domains.

Identify the Execution Space

This step sets the stage for step 2 where one looks for underlying problem solving processes that are effectively hidden in current instruction. First, we need to know what aspects of the problem solving process are revealed, at least implicitly, by current instruction. This is the task of identifying the execution space. The execution space for a domain is the problem space most directly induced from the way problem solution steps are conventionally written down.[7] In other words, the operators of this space correspond one-to-one with the written problem steps.

As discussed earlier (see p. 17), the execution space operators for geometry are the various definitions, postulates, and theorems that appear as the "reasons" in the steps of the conventional two-column proof format. The execution space operators for algebra equation solving are the various rules (e.g., You can add the same number to both sides) for manipulating equations. In physics problem solving (e.g., the kind analyzed by Larkin, McDermott, Simon, and Simon (1980), the execution space operators might be the relevant physics formulas.

Another potential guide to the operators of the execution space is to look at the units of knowledge that are provided to students in their textbooks or lectures. Quite often, these units of knowledge correspond with the written problem steps. For example, the traditional geometry curriculum is organized around presenting and illustrating the very same rules that appear as reasons in two-column proof solutions. A similar situation is apparent in algebra and physics.

---

[7]Newell and Simon (1972, p. 144) referred to a "basic problem space" and gave examples of one in a number of domains. It is evident from their examples that what they meant by a basic problem space has some similarity to what we mean by an execution space. However, they did not provide the kind of operational definition we provide here for the execution space.

TABLE 1.5
An Example Solution in the Domain of Algebra Equation Solving

3x - 13	=	2(x - 3)	
3x - 13	=	2x - 6	Distribute
3x - 13 - 2x	=	- 6	x's to left side
3x - 2x	=	- 6 + 13	Num's to right side
	x = 7		

A straightforward way to model problem solving in these domains is as a heuristic search in the execution space—the trick is to find appropriate operator selection heuristics. From the perspective of a student, to the extent that the execution space provides a good characterization of skilled problem solving, his or her learning job is made easier. By definition, execution operators can be induced fairly directly from the steps of worked out examples and may be supported by verbal descriptions in textbooks and lectures. For example, consider algebra equation solving. An example worked out solution is shown in Table 1.5.

In this domain, the execution operators can be fairly directly induced from the steps in worked out examples like that in Table 1.5. This claim is supported by the fact that an early machine learning program did exactly that (Neves, 1981). In addition, the general difference-reduction heuristic turns out to be an effective means of selecting operators. Because this domain independent weak-method works in this domain, extra domain specific heuristics do not need to be learned.

While heuristic search in the execution space is a straightforward candidate for modeling problem solving in a domain, it may not be the problem space that skilled problem solvers typically use. The next step is to see if it is or not.

Look for Implicit Planning

The purpose of this step is to identify the nature of skilled problem solving in the domain and in particular, to see whether or not it deviates from heuristic search in the execution space. To do so, one can collect concurrent verbal reports (Ericsson & Simon, 1984) of skilled subjects solving problems in the domain. As Ericsson and Simon point out, subjects should not explain what they are doing, but merely report what they are thinking. To the extent that heuristic search in the execution space provides a good model, subjects' successive verbalizations should correspond with successive states in the execution space.

However, subjects' verbalizations could deviate from the execution space in a number of ways:

1. Multiple execution steps might be *aggregated* into a single verbalization.

2. Successive verbalizations may *skip* steps in the execution space.

3. Verbalizations may not specify an execution state in full detail, but rather only indicate some *abstract* feature(s) of it.

Regularities in such deviations suggest "thinking steps" that are not represented in the execution space. From the perspective of the student, these thinking steps are an implicit part of the planning process which, in contrast to the execution operators, cannot be directly induced from worked out examples. In other words, when there is implicit planning in the thinking of skilled problem solvers, there may be aspects of a successful problem solving method which are hidden in the traditional curriculum.

In the second Section we showed that skilled geometry problem solvers skip steps in execution space (item (2) above) while developing an initial proof plan. The knowledge that allows them to do so is hidden in the geometry curriculum. While it is possible to induce *some* execution operators from successive steps of worked out geometry proofs in a similar fashion to Neves' (1981) program for Algebra, this induction is not possible in general (see Koedinger, 1991 for an example). Furthermore, it is not possible to apply a general weak-method like difference-reduction or means-ends analysis to effectively perform operator selection in the execution space of geometry. There is just not much information in the syntactic differences between a goal state in geometry, like $\overline{AB} \perp \overline{DC}$, and a given state, like $\overline{AC} \cong \overline{BC}$, that could help in operator selection. As the step-skipping in the verbal reports reveals, successful search in geometry involves operators other than those in the execution space.

One may find no evidence for implicit planning in a domain, in other words, skilled subjects may work in the execution space. This seems likely, for example, in the domain of algebra equation solving. In such a case, building a tutor for this domain may be inappropriate. Conventional instruction may be adequate. In other words, finding no implicit planning would suggest that the conventional written display of problem solving steps corresponds fairly well with the thought steps necessary for successful problem solving in that domain. In this case, well-motivated students may not have much trouble in inducing the necessary operators. An ITS based on a model of skilled problem solving will not be much different from conventional instruction and thus, will be unlikely to help much. In fact, an ITS for algebra equation solving developed in our lab has been compared with a conventional classroom and although students learn with this tutor, they do not learn significantly better or faster than students in a normal classroom (Anderson, et al., 1990). A field test of the RAND Algebra Tutor had similar results: Students using the tutor learn, but no better than students in the control classes (Stasz, Ormseth, McArthur, & Robyn, 1989).

Model this Implicit Planning

If evidence for implicit planning is found, the question becomes what is the knowledge that is responsible for the non-execution space inferences? Generalizations for how to come up with a model of implicit planning are difficult to come by. The diagram configuration schemas described on p. 21 evolved from an initial attempt to apply ideas about abstract planning and abstract problem spaces

(Newell & Simon, 1972; Sacerdoti, 1974). In particular, the first attempt at a model was based on applying the idea of equivalence classes as a way to collapse nearby problem states into one. Diagram configuration schemas evolved through a generalization of the equivalence class idea and the incorporation of perceptual categories as the organizational element.

In the case of aggregation or step-skipping verbalizations (types (1) and (2) above), it is possible that the implicit planning knowledge is the result of composing execution operators. On p. 23, we summarized the arguments against a macro-operator interpretation of the genesis of diagram configuration schemas. These arguments (see Koedinger & Anderson, 1990) suggest some general criteria for distinguishing macro-operators derived from execution operators from operators that merely bear a macro-operator relationship with the execution operators.

In the case of verbalization type (3), the abstract problem space ideas are likely to be relevant. For example, Newell and Simon's (1972, p. 152) augmented problem space for cryptarithmetic provides a model of such verbalizations (e.g., abstract features of states like "the number must be even").

Use the Model to Drive Tutor Design

Once an accurate model of implicit planning has been developed the challenge is to find a way to communicate this model to students. This issue was discussed on p. 24. As people seem to learn best by doing, directly communicating a method to them doesn't usually help much. By design a model of implicit planning contains problem-solving processes that are not reflected in the notation of the current curriculum. Thus, it is necessary to invent new notations which reify the previously hidden representations and processes. These notations can be the basis for interface design. For example, diagram configuration schemas became the basis for the icons in ANGLE's concept menu and for the representation of concept instances in the proof graph. In addition, the computer medium affords the possibility of inventing *novel actions,* which can more directly reify the processes of the model. For example, the interface actions for selecting a schema instance from the problem diagram reify the diagram parsing process (see Fig. 1.6).

The goal of the design of tutoring strategies and messages should be to support and articulate the problem solving method. In ANGLE, the tutoring strategy of focussing on concepts as the grain size for next step advice is intended to support the approach of the DC method of searching in the space of schemas (see p. 30 and Figs. 1.8 and 1.9). The use of terms like "concept," "part-statement," and "ways-to-prove" is intended to articulate crucial aspects of this novel notation.

Test the Tutor Implementation

Although cognitive models can guide the design of the interface and tutoring components, there are still many decisions to be made in the process of implementing these guidelines. There is little theory available to guide these implementation decisions, though some guidelines have been proposed (e.g., see Chabay & Sherwood, 1992). Thus, it is crucial to test and tune an ITS implementation. What seems right intuitively may not be effective. In addition, because of the great complexity of such systems, all possible interactions cannot be anticipated. Long periods of use by multiple students is the only way to "shakedown" possible unanticipated interactions.

Two examples from the formative evaluation of ANGLE are most notable. First, there was the problem with bottom-out hints and more generally, with the conflict between interface flexibility and user confusion. Intuitively it had seemed that learning would be facilitated by both (1) always requiring students to enter proof steps even in the case that the tutor has told them what to do, and (2) always allowing students the flexibility to ignore hints, for example, if they had something else they wanted to do. However, it turned out that students did not use this flexibility effectively and often engaged in long periods of floundering as a result of ignoring or not fully understanding a bottom-out hint.

Second, there was the problem with whole-statement encoding. Here again, there were well-motivated goals to (1) maximize the student's involvement, that is, by not doing the whole-statement encoding step for them, and (2) allow flexibility, that is, allowing students to either explicitly perform or skip this step. However, the result was, on the one hand, added complexity to the interface with little or no added instructional impact and, on the other hand, an interaction with the generic hinting scheme that resulted in a confusing tutor message. It is unanticipated problems such as these that make experimental testing a very necessary part of ITS design and instructional design in general.

CONCLUSION

We have presented a 5-step guide to employing cognitive science methodologies in the design of novel instruction. The guidelines are aimed at domains where learning from examples/cases and from problem solving is apt to be more effective than an emphasis on reading texts and listening to lectures. Thus the steps focus on the nature of examples and problem solving:

• Step (1) "Identify the execution space" provides a method for analyzing worked-out solution examples in current instruction to see what kind of problem solving approach (including representations and strategies) is implied by these examples.

• Step (2) "Look for implicit planning" provides a method for deciding whether this implied problem solving approach is a reasonable characterization of the thought process of skilled problem solvers.

• Step (3) "Model this implicit planning" provides a method for developing a more accurate characterization of successful problem solving—in the case that the characterization implied by current instruction is wanting. As such, these guidelines are focused on domains that students find particularly difficult (for good reason) and for which instructional innovations can show the greatest payoff.

• Step (4) "Use the model to drive tutor design" provides a method for translating the cognitive model developed in step 3 into novel interface representations and actions as well as tutoring messages and strategies that can help make previously hidden thought processes more visible to students.

• Step (5) "Test the tutor implementation" is a recognition that no design guidelines are 100 percent prescriptive—there is no guarantee, even if the guidelines are followed exactly, that a system will be effective.

While much can be learned by testing instructional systems in the lab (not only about the effectiveness of the system but also about the nature of cognition), there is also much to learn from testing these systems in the classroom. We are currently preparing for a field test of ANGLE in a Pittsburgh high school in the spring of 1992. Although this chapter focuses specifically on the design of computer-based learning tools, we would be amiss if we did not mention an equally important issue, that is, the instructional context in which computer-based learning tools are placed and, in particular, the role of the teacher. The impact of the classroom use of LOGO, for example, has been shown to depend critically on teachers providing an effective instructional context to support learning with LOGO (Klahr & Carver, 1988; Lehrer, Littlefield, & Wottreng, 1991; Lehrer, Randle, & Sancilio, 1989). A number of researchers and teachers have offered different perspectives on the role of the teacher, and the social context more generally, in the classroom success of the Geometry Proof Tutor discussed earlier (Epstein & Hillegeist, 1990; Shofield, Evans-Rhodes, & Huber, 1990; Wertheimer, 1990). We are paying to close attention to such issues in our preparations for the field test of ANGLE.

ACKNOWLEDGMENTS

This research was supported by Grant 86-17083 from the National Science Foundation and by a James S. McDonnell Foundation Postdoctoral Fellowship to the first author.

REFERENCES

Anderson, J. R. (1983). *The architecture of cognition.* Cambridge, MA: Harvard University Press.
Anderson, J. R., Boyle, C. F., Corbett, A., & Lewis, M. (1990). Cognitive modelling and intelligent tutoring. *Artificial Intelligence, 42,* 7–49.

Anderson, J. R., Boyle, C. F., Farrell, R., & Reiser, B. J. (1987). Cognitive principles in the design of computer tutors. In P. Morris (Ed.), *Modelling cognition*. New York: Wiley.

Anderson, J. R., Boyle, C. F., & Reiser, B. J. (1985). Intelligent tutoring systems. *Science, 228*, 456–468.

Anderson, J. R., Boyle, C. F., & Yost, G. (1985). The geometry tutor. In *Proceedings of the International Joint Conference on Artificial Intelligence-85*. Los Angeles: IJCAI.

Chabay, R. W., & Sherwood, B. A. (1992). A practical guide for the creation of educational software. In J. H. Larkin & R. W. Chabay (Eds.), *Computer-assisted instruction and intelligent tutoring systems: Shared goals and complementary approaches*. Hillsdale, NJ: Lawrence Erlbaum Associates.

Collins, A., & Brown, J. S. (1990). The computer as a tool for learning through reflection. In H. Mandl & Lesgold (Eds.), *Learning issues for intelligent tutoring systems*. New York: Springer.

Collins, A., Brown, J. S., & Newman, S. E. (1989). Cognitive apprenticeship: Teaching the crafts of reading, writing, and mathematics. In L. B. Resnick (Ed.), *Knowing, learning, and instruction: Essays in honor of Robert Glaser*. Hillsdale, NJ: Lawrence Erlbaum Associates.

Epstein, K., & Hilligeist, E. (1990). Intelligent instructional systems: Teachers and computer-based intelligent tutoring systems. *Educational Technology*, November, 13–19.

Ericsson, K. A., & Simon, H. A. (1984). *Protocol analysis: Verbal reports as data*. Cambridge, MA: The MIT Press.

Gelernter, H. (1963). Realization of a geometry theorem proving machine. In E. A. Feigenbaum & J. Feldman (Eds.), *Computers and thought*. New York: McGraw-Hill.

Johnson-Laird, P. N. (1983). *Mental models*. Cambridge, MA: Harvard University Press.

Klahr, D., & Carver, S. M. (1988). Cognitive objectives in a LOGO debugging curriculum: Instruction, learning, and transfer. *Cognitive Psychology, 20*, 362–404.

Koedinger, K. R. (1991, August). On the design of novel notations and actions for thinking and learning. In *Proceedings of the International Conference on the Learning Sciences*. Charlottesville, VA: Association for the Advancement of Computing in Education.

Koedinger, K. R., & Anderson, J. R. (1989). Perceptual chunks in geometry problem solving: A challenge to theories of skill acquisition. In *Proceedings of the Eleventh Annual Conference of the Cognitive Science Society*. Hillsdale, NJ: Lawrence Erlbaum Associates.

Koedinger, K. R., & Anderson, J. R. (1990). Abstract planning and perceptual chunks: Elements of expertise in geometry. *Cognitive Science, 14*, 511–550.

Larkin, J., McDermott, J., Simon, D., & Simon, H. A. (1980). Expert and novice performance in solving physics problems. *Science, 208*, 1335–1342.

Lehrer, R., Littlefield, J., & Wottreng, B. (1991). *Seeding Mindstorms with LogoWriter: Using LOGO in the elementary classroom*. Fontana, WI: Interactive Education Technologies.

Lehrer, R., Randle, L., & Sancilio, L. (1989). Learning pre-proof geometry with LOGO. *Cognition and Instruction, 6*, 159–184.

Neves, D. M. (1981). Learning procedures from examples. Doctoral dissertation, Department of Psychology, Carnegie Mellon University.

Newell, A. (1990). *Unified theories of cognition*. Cambridge, MA: Harvard University Press.

Newell, A., & Simon, H. A. (1972). *Human problem solving*. Englewood Cliffs, NJ: Prentice-Hall.

Sacerdoti, E. D. (1974). Planning in a hierarchy of abstraction spaces. *Artificial Intelligence, 5*, 115–136.

Schofield, J. W., Evans-Rhodes, D., & Huber, B. R. (1990). Artificial intelligence in the classroom: The impact of a computer-based tutor on teachers and students. *Social Science Computer Review, 8*(1), 24–41.

Stasz, C., Ormseth, T., McArthur, D., & Robyn, A. (1989, March). *An intelligent tutor for basic algebra: Perspectives on evaluation*. Paper presented at the annual American Educational Research Association meeting, San Francisco.

Wertheimer, R. (1990). The geometry proof tutor: An "intelligent" computer-based tutor in the classroom. *Mathematics Teacher*, April, 308–317.

2

A Comparison of Learning Environments: All That Glitters . . .

Valerie J. Shute
Armstrong Laboratory, Brooks Air Force Base

Computerized learning environments can be characterized by the amount of learner control supported during the learning process. This dimension can be viewed as a continuum ranging from minimal (e.g., rote or didactic environments) to almost complete learner control (e.g., discovery environments). Two differing perspectives, representing the ends of this continuum, have arisen in response to the issue of the most optimal learning environment to build in intelligent tutoring systems (ITS). One approach is to develop an environment containing assorted tools and allow the learner freedom to explore and learn, unfettered (e.g., Collins & Brown, 1988; Shute, Glaser, & Raghavan, 1989; White & Horowitz, 1987). Advocates of an opposing perspective argue that it is more efficacious to develop straightforward learning environments that do not permit "garden path" digressions (e.g., Anderson, Boyle & Reiser, 1985; Corbett & Anderson, 1989; Sleeman, Kelly, Martinak, Ward, & Moore, 1989). This disparity between the positions becomes more complicated because the issue is not just which is the better learning environment; but rather, which is the better environment for what type(s) of persons, a classic aptitude-treatment interaction question (Cronbach & Snow, 1977).

Many kinds of learner characteristics (e.g., incoming knowledge and skills) affect what is learned in an instructional setting. This chapter focuses on another individual differences measure, *learning styles*. Baron (1985) defines styles as, ". . . general behavioral dispositions that characterize performance in mental tasks; they are intellectual personality traits" (p. 366). Thus, learning styles may be seen as reflecting different *approaches* to learning and may include such traits as being holistic versus analytic, verbal versus spatial, reflective versus impulsive, or exploratory versus passive (e.g., Baron, 1985; Glushko & Cooper,

1978; Hunt & MacLeod, 1979; Kyllonen & Shute, 1989; Pask & Scott, 1972; Pellegrino, Mumaw, & Shute, 1985).

To illustrate individual differences on one of these style dimensions, exploratory versus passive disposition, compare the following hypothetical persons. After receiving a new word-processing program, **A**nn immediately loads the program onto her computer, tosses aside the manual, and learns the new knowledge and procedures by trial-and-error. In contrast, **B**ob studies the accompanying manual, reads it cover-to-cover, and only then loads the software onto his computer. After 2 weeks, both are using the new word-processing program with comparable efficiency. Which method is better? Which should be supported by a tutor's learning environment? Is there a trade-off between learning time and quality of learning? These questions become very important when developing computerized instructional systems.

This chapter systematically explores the possible interaction between learning environment and learner style on various learning outcome measures. This experimental method has, in the past, been referred to as aptitude-treatment interaction (ATI) research (see Cronbach & Snow, 1977) where aptitudes are defined in the broadest sense of a person's incoming knowledge, skills, personality traits, and so on. The point of ATI research is to provide information about initial learner states that can be used to select the best learning environment for a particular student. To justify such an approach, evidence is needed that individuals do perform better or worse under different learning conditions (or environments).

ATI research was very popular in the 1960s and 1970s, then popularity declined. The main reason contributing to the decline was that the older ATI research typically involved studies conducted in classroom environments. Data were confounded by many extraneous variables (e.g., personality of the teacher, instructional materials, classroom dynamics) making ATIs hard to find and difficult to interpret. The current study circumvents this problem of "noisy data" by using a rigorously controlled learning environment.

An ITS instructing basic principles of electricity was used as the learning task, manipulated to yield two learning environments. These environments differed only in the type of information provided by the tutor to the student. I posited that active, exploratory learning behaviors would facilitate knowledge and skill acquisition, especially in conjunction with the environment supporting inductive learning behaviors. Less exploratory behaviors were hypothesized to be better suited to the structured learning environment.

Learning Task.   The intelligent tutoring system used in this study taught basic principles of electricity: Ohm's and Kirchhoff's laws. It was originally developed at the Learning Research and Development Center, University of Pittsburgh (Lesgold, Bonar, Ivill, & Bowen, 1989) and then modified extensively at the Armstrong Laboratory, Human Resources Directorate. In particular,

I created the two learning environments, developed learning indicators, rewrote the feedback, established the mastery criterion, and modified the interface. Subjects learned by solving problems presented by the computer. They also could read definitions about concepts that were written in a hypertext structure (i.e., nested concepts within concepts), but that was optional. Another optional activity included using a meter with positive and negative leads to obtain readings from different parts of a circuit (e.g., measuring voltage drop, current). Additionally, learners were free to change component values (e.g., increase a resistor's value) to see the effects on the circuit.

The two environments differed solely in terms of the feedback provided to learners. In both environments, following the solution of each circuit problem, learners were informed of the correctness of their solution. I called the first environment "rule application" because after the "right" or "wrong" feedback was given, the computer presented the relevant rule. Subjects then applied this rule or principle in solving subsequent problems. To illustrate, the computer would comment, *"Great! (or Sorry!) You are correct (or incorrect). The principle involved in this kind of problem is that current is the same before and after a voltage source."* Thus the principle was explicated after each problem solution (for both correct and incorrect responses) until learners reached the mastery criterion, which I set as three consecutively correct answers for a given problem type.

I labeled the second learning environment "rule-induction." Here, the correctness of the problem solution was again provided to learners, in conjunction with the relevant variables in the problem, but not their relationship(s). For learners in this environment, the computer might respond. *Great! (or Sorry!) You are correct (or incorrect). What you need to know to solve this problem is how current behaves—both before and after a voltage source.* The inductive environment thus required subjects to generate for themselves the relationships among variables during the solution of problems.

The curriculum consisted of a set of basic principles. Some of these principles were: (1) The current at one point in an uninterrupted wire is equal to the current at another point in an uninterrupted piece of wire, (2) The current before a resistor is equal to the current after a resistor in a parallel net, (3) Voltage is equal to the current multiplied by the resistance ($V = I*R$). There were a total of 26 different principles or "problem types" to be learned.

Problems were generated by the computer based on each of these principles. Each problem was unique to each individual, not preprogrammed, based on the particular subject's response history. For example, if a student needed more work on current flow across resistors, the system would generate a problem satisfying specific constraints such as it must be a "current problem" involving at least one resistor, perhaps requiring a more quantitative solution, and so forth.

Figure 2.1 shows an example of the main screen. On the screen's left, a parallel circuit is depicted with various component values. The upper right of the

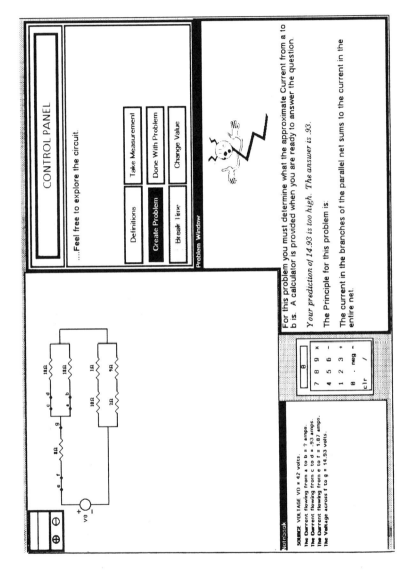

FIG. 2.1. The main screen of the electricity tutor (rule-application environment).

screen presents the learner with his or her main options (e.g., look at definitions, take a measurement on the circuit). Problems are presented in the lower right quadrant of the screen with feedback given in the same window. In this problem, the student was supposed to determine the current (in amps) from points a to b. The values from c to d and from e to f were given. A notebook present at the lower left of the screen allowed for the storage of information. If a student chose to explore the circuit, he or she could store new information in the notebook and compare it to the old data. Finally, an on-line calculator was always available for the solution of more complex, quantitative problems.

Optional (Exploratory) Behaviors. Some individuals like to control what they do and when they do it during the learning process. In this tutor, in addition to solving a problem, there were three different elective activities: viewing definitions, taking measurements on a circuit, and changing circuit component values. The first exploratory behavior was declarative (i.e., looking up terms and definitions) while the second and third activities were procedural. That is, taking measurements and changing components actually required the learner to *do* something to the circuit rather than more passively reading definitions.

If the subject chose to see *definitions,* the screen would clear and a menu of items would appear: ammeter, ampere, charge, circuit, current, ohm, resistance, resistor, parallel circuit, series circuit, voltage, voltage source, and voltmeter. Selecting any of these terms would cause a large window to open that would contain three parts: a relevant diagram, a definition (formal), and an explanation (informal). Bold-faced words would appear within the definitions and explanations. Selecting a bold-faced word would move the learner to the related concept (see Fig. 2.2). In come cases, simulations were available for the learner to run: (a) Comparison between current flow in a series versus a parallel circuit (see Fig. 2.3), and (b) Comparison between voltage drop in a series versus a parallel circuit. A dynamic display would appear on the computer screen illustrating how current (or voltage) operated differentially in the two circuit types, presented side-by-side.

Following problem solution, a subject could elect to *take measurements* on the circuit. For instance, Fig. 2.4 shows what happens when someone chose to measure the voltage drop across a resistor, from point g to point h. Positive and negative leads allow the learner to meter on two parts of the circuit and obtain a reading. Subjects could employ either the voltmeter (giving readings in volts) or the ammeter (giving readings in amps). This option was available at all times. However, if the subject had not yet answered the immediate problem, he or she was not allowed to take measurements that would yield the answer. For example, if the problem to be solved involved "current across a resistor in a series circuit," the learner could only take a voltage reading. After the problem was solved, then it was possible to obtain readings for both voltage and current.

Another optional activity involved changing component values. Again, after

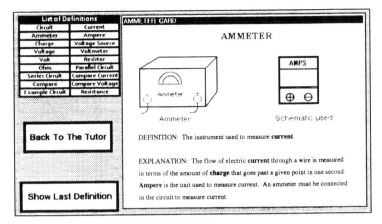

FIG. 2.2.   Example of a definition (ammeter).

solving a problem, a component value (i.e., voltage source or resistor) on the circuit could be modified. Subjects could then observe how that particular change effected other parts of the circuit. To make a change, the subject would button on, for instance, the voltage source. He or she would then type in the new value (e.g., from 76 volts to 55 volts). Results from the changes appear automatically on the screen and in the notebook (see Fig. 2.5).

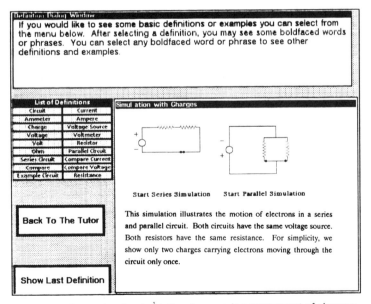

FIG. 2.3.   Example of a simulation (comparing movement of charges in series and parallel circuits).

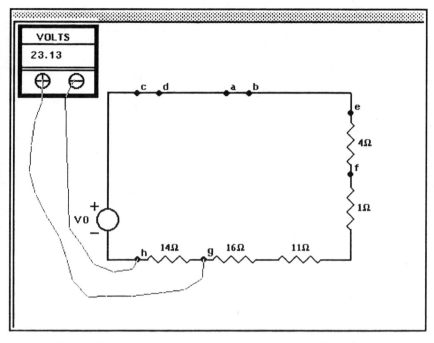

FIG. 2.4.   Using the voltmeter on a circuit to obtain a reading between two points.

Notebook	Old
SOURCE VOLTAGE VO = 55 volts.	76
The Current flowing from a to b = ? amps.	?
The Current flowing from c to d = 1.19 amps.	1.65
The Voltage across g to h = 16.74 volts.	23.13

FIG. 2.5.   The on-line notebook after the voltage source was changed (from 76 to 55 volts).

The computer tallied data on subjects' use of these elective activities. At a global level, I distinguished two kinds of exploratory indices. I computed the first one, "declarative exploration," as the time spent looking at definitions divided by the total time spent on the tutor (because time-on-tutor differed for everyone). The second index was "procedural exploration." This too was a proportion involving the time spent using a meter plus the time spent changing a component's value divided by the total time on the tutor.

Subjects.   There were 309 subjects (84% males, 16% females) who completed this study on the acquisition of basic principles of electricity. Each subject participated for 7 days (45 hours). All subjects were high school graduates (or equivalent) with a mean age of 22 and an age range from 18 to 28. Subjects were obtained from two local temporary employment agencies and none had any prior electronics instruction or training. All subjects were paid for their participation.

Subjects were tested in groups of 15–20 at Lackland Air Force Base, Texas. They occupied individual testing stations and all instructions, testing, and feedback were computer administered with proctors available to answer questions. The ITS was administered on Xerox 1186 computers with standard keyboards and high resolution monochromatic displays on 19″ monitors. On the morning of Day 1, subjects were given a brief orientation to the electricity study and then randomly assigned to one of two learning conditions.

Pretests.   Two pretests were included in the study to assess individuals' incoming domain-related knowledge. The first pretest measured **declarative knowledge** of different electrical components and devices involved in electronics. The concepts that were covered included: ammeter, ampere, charge, circuit, current, ohm, parallel circuit, resistance, resistor, series circuit, volt, voltage, voltage source, and voltmeter. This test included multiple choice and true/false questions. An example multiple choice item from the test asked: Which statement is most true about a *voltage source*? (a) It supplies electricity to a circuit, (b) It cannot store electricity for later use, (c) It does not have to be a physical device, (d) It is necessary to measure the current flowing through a circuit, or (e) It restricts the amount of current going through a circuit. Some example true/false items were: A parallel circuit requires two voltage sources, Unlike charges are attracted to one another, and Resistance is measured in amps.

The second pretest measured **conceptual understanding** of Ohm's and Kirchhoff's laws. These questions did not require any computations. Half of the items in this test contained pictures of circuits along with the questions, and the other half did not have pictures. To illustrate a question without a picture: If current was measured before and after a resistor in a series circuit, would the measurement before the resistor be *higher, lower,* or *equal to* the measurement after the resistor? The questions with circuits were similar, but referred to actual points on the circuits.

Posttests. I developed a four-part criterion test battery to measure the breadth and depth of knowledge and skills acquired from the tutor. The four-part battery was administered on-line at the end of the tutor. The first two tests in this learning outcome battery were identical to the two pretests discussed earlier (i.e., declarative knowledge and conceptual understanding).

The third posttest assessed the degree to which procedural skills were acquired. This test involved the **application** of Ohm's and Kirchhoff's laws in the solution of different problems. These questions did require computations in order to solve them. An on-screen calculator was provided to help solve these items. There were two types of questions, half with accompanying pictures of circuits and the others without pictures. Each question corresponded to a principle of Ohm's or Kirchhoff's laws. Problems with pictures displayed a circuit and the subject was required to compute what the reading was at some point for some component. The subject was required to apply the correct formula (e.g., $V = I*R$). Two of the three values were given and the solution required computing the unknown value. An example test item was: If the resistance in a circuit is 16 ohms and the current is 30 amps, then what is the voltage?

The fourth posttest in the criterion battery measured a subject's ability to **generalize knowledge and skills** beyond what was explicitly instructed by the tutor. The subject was required to generate or design circuits to do specific things. Thus, the test required not only a functional understanding of the laws and principles, but also the ability to compute solutions to novel problems. An example item from this test is included in Fig. 2.6.

In summary, the four tests were designed to measure different aspects of electronics knowledge and skill acquisition, from declarative knowledge understanding to quantitative understanding and ability to apply and transfer Ohm's and Kirchhoff's laws.

Learning Efficiency. I defined two learning efficiency measures. Because instruction in this tutor was self-paced, subjects could take as long as they needed to complete the curriculum. Some subjects were faster acquiring the new material, and others were slower. So the first index was defined as total *time on tutor*. The tutor was also open-ended as far as the number of problems generated per principle. That is, the number of problems a person received was a function of how many problems were needed to reach the mastery criterion (i.e., correctly solving three consecutive problems) per principle. Thus the minimum number of problems that would be created for a given principle was three. So the second learning efficiency index was defined as the total *number of problems* received. Although these two efficiency measures are somewhat related (i.e., it generally takes longer to complete the tutor if there are more problems to solve) they measure slightly different aspects of learning efficiency: speed and accuracy.

Hypotheses. In an earlier study, Robert Glaser and I (Shute & Glaser, 1990) found that individuals demonstrating systematic, exploratory behaviors (e.g.,

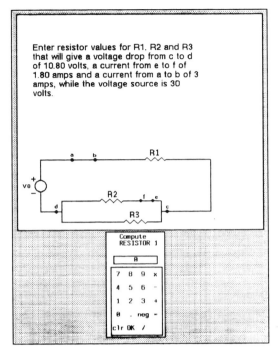

FIG. 2.6.   Example test item from posttest 4: Generalization of knowledge and skills.

recording baseline data before any changes were made, limiting the number of
variables changed in an experiment) were significantly more successful in a
discovery microworld than those individuals evidencing less systematic behaviors. On the basis of this finding, I believed there would be a main effect of
exploratory behavior on outcome where "more exploratory" would be associated
with "better outcome" across criterion measures. Furthermore, I hypothesized
this main effect of exploratory behavior to be even more pronounced in the rule-
induction environment which supported inductive activities. In other words, I
predicted that learners evidencing a lot of exploratory behaviors (procedural and
declarative) should perform better on the outcome measures if they learned from
the inductive environment than if they learned from the application environment.
Conversely, less exploratory learners would benefit from the structured, application environment rather than the inductive environment.

RESULTS

Learning Outcome.   The first criterion I investigated was learning outcome,
defined as the percent correct scores on the four posttests. Although I originally

created these tests to measure different facets of knowledge and skill acquisition, they turned out to be significantly correlated with one another: Posttests 1 and 2 ($r = .33$), 1 and 3 ($r = .76$), 1 and 4 ($r = .58$), 2 and 3 ($r = .41$), 2 and 4 ($r = .44$), and 3 and 4 ($r = .66$). Because of this interdependence among the test data, as well as a desire to keep analyses fairly simple, I computed a factor analysis (principal components) on the four posttest scores and a single factor was extracted, accounting for 65.1% of the posttest variance. The factor scores were saved for each individual (postfac) with loadings per test as follows: Posttest 1 (.85), Posttest 2 (.62), Posttest 3 (.90), and Posttest 4 (.84). Similarly, I computed a factor analysis (principle components) on the pretest data and one factor was extracted (prefac) accounting for 60.2% of the pretest data. Factor loadings for the pretests on this factor were both .78.

The composite learning outcome measure, postfac, was then examined as a function of learning environment and exploratory behavior—declarative and procedural. In addition, I wanted to look at the results of *just* the exploratory behaviors and environment on learning outcome without confounding the results with incoming knowledge (prefac correlates highly, .61, with postfac). By holding incoming knowledge constant (i.e., included as an independent variable in the regression equation), I can isolate the influence of specific behaviors on outcome.

I computed a multiple regression analysis using postfac as the dependent variable. The independent variables included: prefac, learning environment, procedural exploratory behavior (i.e., the proportion of time spent using the meter and changing components in relation to the total time on the tutor) and declarative exploratory behavior (i.e., proportion of time spent viewing definitions in relation to the total time on the tutor). Also the two interactions between the exploratory behaviors and environment were tested.

Results from this analysis showed that 42% of the variance of the outcome factor could be accounted for by these few variables (multiple R = .65). Not surprising, there was a main effect of prefac whereby individuals with more incoming domain-specific knowledge performed better on the outcome measures than those with less incoming knowledge: $t_{(1,299)} = 13.03, p < .001$. But there was no significant main effect of learning environment on learning outcome ($t_{(1,299)} = -1.83, p = .07$). As seen in Table 2.1, the pretest and posttest factor scores were similar (i.e., close to the mean of 0) in the two learning environments so neither environment showed a distinct learning advantage. But there was a slight advantage of the rule-application environment over the induction environment. There was a significant main effect of procedural exploratory behavior predicting the outcome factor: $t_{(1,299)} = -2.16, p < .05$. In this case, high procedural exploratory behaviors were associated with poor outcomes. There also was a significant main effect of declarative exploratory behavior on outcome: $t_{(1,299)} = 3.57, p < .001$. But here, the proportion of time allocated to reading definitions was a positive predictor of learning outcome. Finally, and of greatest interest, there was a significant interaction involving procedural (but not

TABLE 2.1
Summary Statistics of Learning and Behavioral Indicators by Environment

Variable	Mean	SD	Min	Max
Rule-Application (N = 152)				
Behaviors				
METER (minutes)	74.14	46.54	4.23	208.13
CHANGE (minutes)	9.45	9.39	0.00	40.00
DEFINITIONS (minutes)	13.21	9.43	0.68	46.62
TIME (MINUTES)	656.21	222.74	311.38	1230.58
METER + CHANGE (minutes)	83.59	51.03	4.23	220.63
PREFAC (factor score)	0.08	1.06	-1.82	3.41
Proportions				
METER = CHANGE / TIME	0.12	0.05	0.01	0.29
DEFINITIONS /TIME	0.02	0.01	0.0	0.08
Criteria				
POSTFAC (factor score)	0.08	1.06	-1.81	2.75
TOTAL PROBLEMS	140.16	45.95	79.00	291.00
TIME (hours)	10.93	3.71	5.19	20.51
Rule-Induction (N = 154)				
Behaviors				
METER (minutes)	82.14	52.81	4.30	243.48
CHANGE (minutes)	9.41	9.07	0.00	51.43
DEFINITIONS (minutes)	12.96	8.53	0.00	43.60
TIME (minutes)	687.60	201.74	382.52	1219.33
METER + CHANGE (minutes)	91.55	55.94	10.47	243.48
PREFAC (factor score)	-0.07	0.93	-1.57	2.33
Proportions				
METER + CHANGE / TIME	0.13	0.07	0.01	0.31
DEFINITIONS /TIME	0.02	0.01	0.00	0.06
Criteria				
POSTFAC (factor score)	-0.08	0.93	-1.81	2.58
TOTAL PROBLEMS	151.73	51.18	89.00	337.00
TIME (hours)	11.47	3.37	6.38	20.32

declarative) exploratory behavior and learning environment predicting learning outcome: $t_{(1,299)} = 2.44, p < .02$.

To illustrate this interaction, expected values were computed from the regression equation for four groups of subjects: Individuals one standard deviation above and below the average "procedural exploration" score in each of the two learning environments. These results can be seen in Fig. 2.7. Error bars are included in the plots of these expected values—approximate standard error measures for each group (i.e., square root of mean-square error divided by N). As can be seen in the figure, subjects who spent a large proportion of time engaged in procedural exploratory behaviors performed much better on the posttests (postfac) if they had been assigned to the rule-induction environment than the rule-application environment. But subjects showing fewer exploratory behaviors

Posttest
Factor
(expected values)

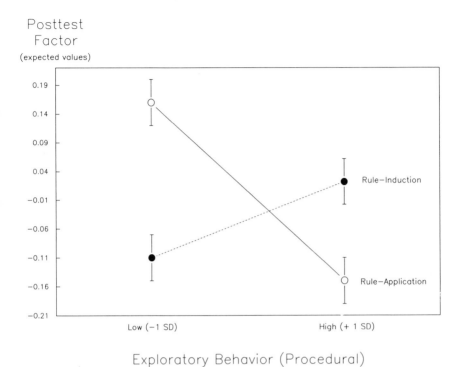

Exploratory Behavior (Procedural)

FIG. 2.7.   Interaction of procedural exploratory behavior and learning environment on posttest factor score (expected values).

learned much more if they had been in the rule-application environment rather than the rule-induction environment.

Learning Efficiency: Time on Tutor.   Similar to the preceding analyses with the outcome data, I computed a multiple regression analysis using time on tutor as the dependent variable and the same predictor variables as above (viz., prefac, learning environment, procedural and declarative exploratory behaviors, and the two interactions between behaviors and environment), and accounted for 26% of the efficiency variance (multiple R = .51). Again, prefac was included in the equation to control for differences in incoming knowledge that might impact learning rate. There was a significant main effect due to prefac: $t_{(1,299)} = -8.38$, $p < .001$ (i.e., more incoming knowledge associated with less time on tutor). There also was a significant main effect of environment on efficiency $t_{(1,299)} = 2.93$, $p < .005$. Individuals in the rule-application environment completed the tutor in less time than did those in the rule-induction environment. There also was a significant main effect of procedural (but not declarative) exploratory behavior on learning efficiency: $t_{(1,299)} = 4.34$, $p < .001$. In this case, using the

Hours on Tutor

(expected values)

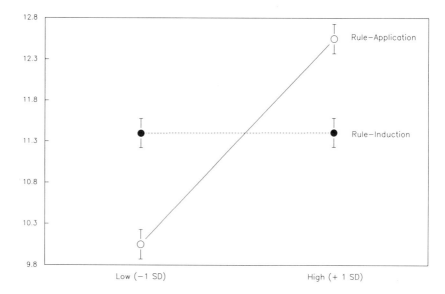

Exploratory Behavior (Procedural)

FIG. 2.8.   Interaction of procedural exploratory behavior and learning environment on total time on tutor (expected values).

on-line exploratory tools was costly in terms of tutor completion time, and despite this increase in time, there was no payoff in increased outcome. On the contrary, from the results with postfac, above, we see that procedural tool usage was associated inversely with learning outcome factor. Finally, there was a significant interaction involving procedural behaviors and learning environment on learning efficiency $t_{(1,299)} = -3.43, p < .001$.

To illustrate this interaction, I computed expected values from the regression equation for four groups of subjects: Individuals one standard deviation above and below the mean procedural exploration score in each of the two learning environments. The results seen in Fig. 2.8 were as follows: Procedural exploratory behaviors were unrelated to hours on the tutor for individuals in the rule-induction environment, but positively related for the rule-application environment (where more behaviors = more time on tutor).

Learning Efficiency: Total Number of Problems Required.   A final regression analysis was computed using total number of problems as the dependent variable and the same set of predictor variables as used above. About one third

(33%) of the variance was accounted for by the set of independent variables (Multiple R = .58). There was a significant main effect due to prefac:$t_{(1,299)}$ = -8.61, $p < .001$. More incoming knowledge, again, was associated with fewer problems required to reach mastery criterion. There was a significant main effect of environment on efficiency $t_{(1,299)}$ = 3.63, $p < .001$. Similar to the findings using time on tutor as the dependent variable, individuals in the rule-application environment required fewer problems, overall, compared to individuals in the rule-induction environment. And there was a significant main effect of declarative (but not procedural) exploratory behavior on number of problems: $t_{(1,299)}$ = -2.89, $p < .005$. People who looked at many definitions required fewer problems to reach criterion, so it was a facilitative activity. There was also a significant interaction involving procedural behaviors and learning environment on learning efficiency $t_{(1,299)}$ = -3.15, $p < .005$.

Expected values from the regression equation for four groups of subjects were computed: Individuals one standard deviation above and below the mean procedural explore score in each of the two learning environments. These results can be seen in Fig. 2.9. The depicted interaction shows that procedural exploratory

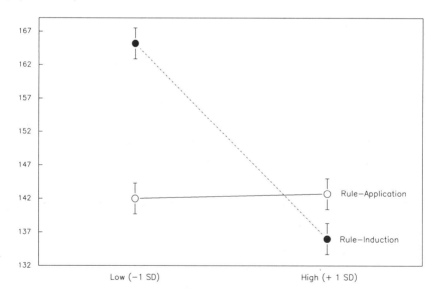

FIG. 2.9. Interaction of procedural exploratory behavior and learning environment on total number of problems needed (expected values).

behaviors were unrelated to number of problems required for individuals in the rule-application environment, but was significantly related for the rule-induction environment (i.e., more behaviors associated with a reduction in number of problems needed to reach mastery).

Within-tutor Analyses

The procedural exploratory index used in the foregoing analyses was computed as total time spent metering and changing component values divided by total time on the tutor. But sometimes total measures can be misleading (e.g., see Shute, 1989). A more refined way of looking at these data is to examine them across similar problem types or time (see Shute & Kyllonen, 1990). To accomplish this goal, I defined 26 new proportions corresponding to each of the 26 principles in the curriculum (rather than just the single proportion). These were computed as the amount of time spent metering and changing values divided by the amount of time spent on each principle.

I computed a factor analysis with varimax rotation on the 26 by 26 covariance matrix of proportions (i.e., time metering plus time changing values divided by total time for each principle). The varimax rotation converged in four iterations yielding a two factor solution. The two extracted factors accounted for 94.2% of the variance of these proportions. Table 2.2 shows the descriptions of the factors, along with associated principles and respective factor loadings.

Factor scores for the two factors were saved for each individual and then used in subsequent analyses. Relationships between factor scores and the criterion measures can be seen in Table 2.3, separated by environment.

In the rule-application environment, the data suggested that early on during the course of learning (factor 1 data, principles 1–9), the proportion of time spent engaging in procedural explorations was not significantly correlated with either posttest factor score or time on tutor.[1] During later learning of the more difficult concepts (factor 2 data, principles 10–26), higher proportions of procedural explorations were negatively correlated with the outcome and efficiency measures (i.e., lower posttest scores and longer time on tutor).

On the other hand, in the rule-induction environment, we see a different pattern of correlations. Early learning (factor 1 data) showed that higher proportions of procedural behaviors were *positively* correlated with outcome and efficiency measures (i.e., higher posttest scores, less time on tutor, and fewer problems to reach mastery). But later on, there was no correlation among the proportions and the learning measures.

The last analysis examines whether an individual's *initial* exploratory data can ultimately be used to predict learning outcome and efficiency measures differen-

---

[1]There was, however, a significant correlation between this proportion and number of problems required where higher proportions were associated with fewer problems.

TABLE 2.2

Factor Analysis Solution With Descriptions and Loadings for Each of the Two Factors Underlying Procedural Exploratory Behaviors

---

Factor 1: These are the first nine principles in the curriculum—simple Kirchhoff's problems involving current flow and voltage drop in series and parallel circuits.

Principle 3 (loading = .927):	The current is the same before and after a resistor.
Principle 4 (loading = .926):	The current before a resistor is equal to the current after a resistor in a parallel net.
Principle 5 (loading = .905):	The current in the branches of the parallel net sums to the current in the entire net.
Principle 6 (loading = .886):	The current in a component is lower than the current for the entire net.
Principle 2 (loading = .881):	The current is the same before and after a voltage source.
Principle 7 (loading = .852):	Voltage drop is lower across any single component of a series net than across the whole net.
Principle 8 (loading = .790):	Voltage drops across components of a series net sum up to the voltage drop across a whole net.
Principle 9 (loading = .730):	Voltage drop is the same across parallel components.
Principle 1 (loading = .683):	The current at one point in an uninterrupted wire is equal to the current at another point in an uninterrupted piece of wire.

Factor 2: This factor is characterized by principles representing later, more difficult problems: Ohm's law (i.e., the interrelationship among voltage, current, and resistance) and the integration of Kirchhoff's and Ohm's laws.

Principle 26 (loading = .958):	Voltage drop is the same across any component as it is across the whole parallel net.
Principle 25 (loading = .958):	Voltage drop is the same across parallel components.
Principle 24 (loading = .957):	The current in a component is lower than the current for the entire net.
Principle 23 (loading = .957):	The current in the branches of a parallel net sums to the current in the entire net.
Principle 22 (loading = .952):	The current before a resistor is equal to the current after a resistor in a parallel net.
Principle 21 (loading = .947):	Voltage drop is the same across any component as it is across the whole parallel net.
Principle 20 (loading = .938):	Voltage drop is the same across parallel components.
Principle 19 (loading = .926):	The current in a component is lower than the current for the entire net.
Principle 18 (loading = .918):	Current is the same across a resistor.
Principle 17 (loading = .905):	Current in the branches of a parallel net sums to the current in the entire net.
Principle 16 (loading = .886):	The current before a resistor is equal to the current after a resistor in a parallel net.
Principle 15 (loading = .867):	Current is the same before and after a resistor.
Principle 14 (loading = .850):	If the voltage goies up or down and the resistance stays the same, this implies that the current will go up or down with the voltage.
Principle 13 (loading = .833):	Current is equal to voltage divided by resistance (I = V/R).
Principle 12 (loading = .805):	When the current goes up or down and resistance stays the same, this implies that the voltage should also go up or down.
Principle 11 (loading = .761):	Voltage is equal to current multiplied by resistance (V = I*R).
Principle 10 (loading = .705):	Voltage drop is the same across any component as across the whole parallel net.

63

TABLE 2.3
Correlations Among Procedural Factor Scores and Criterion Measures, Separated by Learning
Environment

	Rule-Application Environment (N = 152)		
	Postfac	*Time*	*Problems*
Factor 1	.17	-.13	-.28**
Factor 2	.23*	.35**	.14

	Rule-Induction Environment (N = 154)		
Factor 1	.37**	.21*	-.38**
Factor 2	.07	.12	-.18

Notes. * $p < .01$; ** $p < .001$. Factor 1 = Early problems (principles 1-9) in the curriculum dealing with Kirchhoff's law, and Factor 2 = More difficult problems (principles 10-26) involving Ohm's and Kirchhoff's laws.

tially by environment. This has implications for generating decision rules for matching learners to environments. Rather than using factor 1 data (which consisted of the first nine principles in the curriculum), I was interested in testing whether exploratory behaviors, evidenced during learning the first principle, by itself, could predict any outcome or efficiency measures. The data used in this analysis included the amount of time a person spent in procedural explorations while learning principle 1 divided by the total time spent learning principle 1 (PEB1). The other independent variables included in the regression equation were: prefac, learning environment and PEB1 by environment interaction.

Results showed that these independent variables significantly predicted postfac (Multiple R = .62). There was a significant main effect due to prefac (t = 13.5; $p < .001$), where more incoming knowledge was a positive predictor of posttest performance. There was also a significant main effect due to learning environment (t = -2.3; $p < .05$) where the rule-application environment was associated with higher outcome performance. Finally, and of most interest, the interaction between exploratory behavior and environment was significant (t = 2.2, $p < .05$). Higher procedural proportions were associated with greater outcomes in the rule-induction environment, but not the rule-application environment. A graph of this interaction may be seen in Fig. 2.10.

The interaction term did not significantly predict time on tutor, but did predict total number of problems (t = -2.3, $p < .05$). A graph of this interaction may be seen in Fig. 2.11. Thus, the interaction between very early exploratory behaviors and learning environment may be used as a valid predictor of learning outcome and efficiency.

Posttest
Factor
(expected values)

Principle 1 Data Only

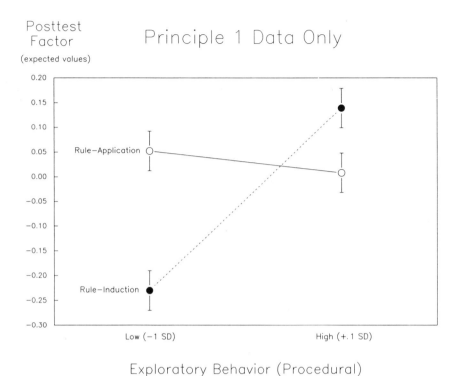

Exploratory Behavior (Procedural)

FIG. 2.10. Principle 1 data only—Interaction of procedural exploratory behavior and learning environment on posttest factor score (expected values).

DISCUSSION

In summary, I used an intelligent tutoring system with two different learning
environments as a complex but controlled learning task to investigate possible
learner style by treatment interactions. This represents a new generation of ATI
research, more rigorously controlled than ATI research conducted during the
1960s and 70s. The learning environments (or treatments) in this study were
identical, differing only in the feedback provided to the learner. After problem
solution, whether correctly or incorrectly answered, one environment directly
stated the relevant principle and the learner applied it in the solution of related
problems; the other environment required the learner to induce the relevant
principle, providing only the variables involved in the rule, but not their rela-
tionship(s). Findings showed that when learner styles (exploratory behaviors)
were matched to environment, learning was superior compared with mismatched

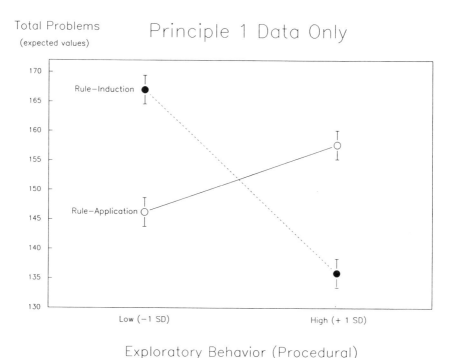

FIG. 2.11.   Principle 1 data only—Interaction of procedural exploratory behavior and learning environment on total number of problems needed (expected values).

conditions. This suggests a new approach to student modeling using "new" ATI methodology (computer-administered learning tasks) and focusing on cognitive tool use as the behavior to model. This contrasts with, for example, modeltracing which records and diagnoses low-level productions underlying the learning process.

The first environment, rule-application, was straightforward and clear—all information necessary to solve a problem was presented to the learner. Subjects in this environment had no tenable need to engage in exploratory, extracurricular behaviors. On the other hand, the rule-induction environment required active participation in the learning process because the tutor only gave learners parts of a principle. Subjects had to come up with the conceptual glue (functional relationships) themselves, by any means they could. Thus, it was believed that the inductive environment would support (if not actively promote) the use of exploratory behaviors so that learners could obtain information needed to solve the problems. But results showed no significant differences between environments for either procedural or declarative exploratory learning behaviors (see Table 2.1). The mean procedural proportions were .12 and .13 in the rule-application and rule-induction environments, respectively. And the mean declarative proportions were .02 and .02 in the rule-application and rule-induction environments, respectively. Thus the two learning environments did not produce different profiles of exploratory behaviors.

In either environment, several different reasons can possibly explain an individual's exploratory behaviors. First, a learner unable to solve the problem being worked on may grope for something that he or she can do instead ("floundering" basis for the behavior). Another person may employ the tools after carefully designing an experiment involving the systematic manipulation of a circuit and taking controlled meter readings. This use of tools may ultimately supplement current understanding and yield other valuable insights ("methodic search for knowledge" reason for behavior). And finally, another person may simply use the on-line tools for fun and diversion ("playful curiosity" basis for behavior). The floundering basis may be associated with cognitive deficits while the methodic search basis may be associated with cognitive surfeits. Playful curiosity could be associated with either/neither.

If exploratory behavior simply reflects cognitive ability, in the rule-application environment, where there was no actual need to explore (the system presented the rule to learners), we would expect to see negative correlations between tool usage and cognitive ability. But in the rule-induction environment, applying exploratory behaviors may denote methodic (and perhaps necessary) knowledge searches. If that were the case, we would expect positive correlations between explorations and cognitive ability. Although not reported, I did compute these correlations and found no significant correlations between procedural exploratory behaviors and cognitive ability—overall and when the data were separated by environment.[2] Moreover, there was no significant correlation between tool usage and prefac (domain-specific incoming knowledge), overall and separated by environment. The degree to which an individual engages in exploratory behavior seems to be unrelated to cognitive ability and unrelated to incoming knowledge.

Although this chapter focuses on investigating possible interactions between exploratory behaviors and environment on outcome measures, some of the main effects turn out to be significant and illuminating; they will be discussed first.

Learning Environments.   Was one environment more successful than the other in promoting knowledge and skill acquisition for the subject matter of basic electricity? Individuals in the rule-application environment, overall, took significantly less time to complete the curriculum and required significantly fewer problems to reach mastery compared to subjects in the rule-induction environment. But sometimes a large investment of time may actually result in greater

---

[2]The cognitive knowledge and skill measures that I examined in relation to exploratory behavior (procedural) included: working memory capacity, information processing speed, associative learning skill, inductive reasoning skills, procedural learning skills, and general knowledge.

gains or outcomes (e.g., the race between the tortoise and the hare). This was not the case in the present study. As a matter of fact, just the opposite was found. Not only did subjects in the rule-application environment learn the material more efficiently (i.e., take less time and require fewer problems to complete the tutor), they also had slightly higher (albeit nonsignificant) posttest factor scores than subjects learning in the rule-induction environment.

Tool Usage (exploratory behaviors).   The next main effect involves exploratory behaviors and their impact on learning. A considerable amount of effort is expended by ITS designers and programmers creating multifarious "bells and whistles" in their systems. The point, of course, is to entice learners (as well as teachers, fellow researchers, and so on) with alterative and entertaining ways to learn. This tutor was no exception. Some very impressive features and capabilities were built into the tutor. For instance, an individual could use an on-line meter (voltmeter or ammeter) to obtain readings from different parts of a circuit. One could change a component's value (e.g., voltage source) and see the ramifications on the circuit. Finally, a person was free to peruse the on-line hypertext dictionary of terms. Which, if any, of these "bells and whistles" were important to learning? Did using these tools (and consequently engaging in exploratory behaviors) actually help or hinder learning? A significant negative main effect was found for procedural exploratory behavior in relation to posttest factor scores and time on tutor (where more procedural tool usage was associated with lower posttest factor scores and more time to complete the tutor). However a positive (facilitative) main effect was found between declarative exploratory behavior and both posttest factor scores and total number of problems needed to reach mastery. These data imply that using the on-line dictionary was a positive behavior but using the fancy meters and changing circuit values were, in general, negative behaviors.

There are several possible explanations to account for these findings: (1) Disruption of procedural skill acquisition; (2) Problems associated with using gross indicators in data analyses (e.g., overall procedural exploratory behavior proportion); and (3) Need to additionally consider other variables in the equation (e.g., learning environment, degree of tool usage). Each of these are discussed in turn.

Disruption of Proceduralization.   Many cognitive psychologists have shown that successful skill acquisition depends on sustained and consistent practice opportunities (e.g., Ackerman, 1988; Anderson, 1987; Schneider & Shiffrin, 1977). If a person focuses on problem solution, then proceduralization is facilitated. But when that person departs from problem-solving activities and goes off to, for example, engage the on-line tools (for whatever reasons), that detracts from, and thus disrupts the compilation process. Referencing the dictionary may be an exception to this disruption because information found in the dictionary directly relates to relevant variables and their relations. Furthermore, there are limited garden paths available to traverse with the dictionary (18 terms defined in all). On the other hand, there are unlimited ways of manipulating circuits (e.g., successively increase a resistor value by one ohm).

Problems Using Total Counts, or "Gross Indicators" in Analyses. In dynamic learning situations spanning a duration of time, examining one variable defined as the sum of actions can be deceptive, especially when viewed in relation to other variables. For instance, Shute (1991) reported findings from a study employing a Pascal ITS as the learning task. One variable defined the total number of hints a person requested from the tutor. This gross indicator correlated with learning outcome (r = −.64), implying that hint-asking was, overall, a very unsuccessful behavior. But this was disturbing because one main feature of ITS's is their ability to provide individualized help when needed. When these data were analyzed across time (rather than using the gross count), asking for hints had much higher negative correlations with outcome during latter stages than the earlier stages of learning.[3]

A factor analysis computed on the data from the current study showed a clean two factor solution (i.e., Factor 1 = first nine principles, and Factor 2 = remaining principles). This breakdown allowed the data to be globally examined across time (i.e., early vs. later learning). Like the data from the Pascal study discussed earlier, findings with these separated data showed that, in fact, procedural exploratory behaviors were positively correlated with outcome measures early on (significantly so within the rule-induction environment, and the trend present in the rule-application environment). But later usage of these same tools was negatively correlated with outcome and efficiency measures, only within the rule-application environment, however. So, the simple main effects involving exploratory behaviors should be qualified (e.g., by time data).

Need to Additionally Consider Other Variables in the Equation (e.g., learning environment, degree of tool usage). The interaction hypothesis tested was whether individuals with above average exploratory behaviors would perform better in the rule-induction environment than the rule-application environment. Conversely, less exploratory individuals were believed to do better in the more didactic, rule-application environment than the more taxing rule-induction environment. The basis for this belief is that when learning environment is matched to certain characteristics of the learner, then performance is optimized (e.g., Pask & Scott, 1972). In fact, all three dependent measures (i.e., posttest factor score, time on tutor, and total number of problems required), showed significant learner

---

[3]This pattern of correlations between hints and outcome over time was seen even after cognitive process measures were partialled out of the hint-asking variable (e.g., working memory capacity, processing speed, general knowledge).

style by environment interactions. Each told the same basic story, but there were some subtle differences.

Posttest Factor Scores.   This disordinal interaction was straightforward: Two opposite trends defined the correlations between exploratory behavior and posttest score. A positive linear trend expressed the relationship between exploratory behavior and outcome in the rule-induction environment (more is better), while a strong negative trend defined the relationship between exploratory behavior and outcome in the rule-application environment (more is worse). On the basis of these results, active explorers would do better on the outcome tests if learning from the inductive environment. But less exploratory folks should, unequivocally, be assigned to the straightforward application environment (see Fig. 2.7) to achieve their best posttest scores.

Time on Tutor.   The significant interaction depicted in Fig. 2.8 showed that high explorers progressed through the curriculum in significantly less time if assigned to the rule-induction environment (again signifying a match between learner and environment). And low explorers completed the tutor much faster if assigned to the rule-application environment (another match). Now consider the slopes of the regression lines. High and low explorers in the rule-induction environment spent approximately the same amount of time on the tutor (11.4 hours, flat slope). Within the rule-application environment, though, a person's exploratory level really influenced learning efficiency (steep slope). A low explorer appropriately placed in the rule-application environment completed the tutor, on average, about 2.5 hours faster than a high explorer inappropriately assigned to the rule-application environment.

Total Number of Problems.   The significant interaction shown in Fig. 2.9 supports the previous findings that low exploratory subjects assigned to the rule-application environment perform better on the tutor than low exploratory subjects assigned to the induction environment (i.e., require fewer problems to reach mastery). And high explorers in the inductive environment require fewer problems to complete the tutor compared to high explorers in the application environment. For this criterion measure, the rule-application environment showed no difference between high vs. low explorers in terms of the number of problems required (about 142 per group, flat slope). But the influence of exploratory behavior on number of problems was particularly striking within the rule-induction group. A difference of 30 problems separated subjects due to matched or mismatched condition. That is, low explorers who found themselves stuck in the rule-induction environment required 166 problems, on average, to complete the curriculum while high explorers, appropriately assigned to the inductive environment, required only 136 problems to reach mastery.

The main conclusion from these findings is that learning outcome and efficiency may be optimized by considering an individual's learning style in the assignment of person to learning environment. But here is the catch: We would like to develop some decision rule(s) for optimal placement of individual to environment. We have seen that a person's exploratory level impacts outcome performance differentially by learning environment. And we can obtain data about a person's exploratory level during tutor interactions. Then how can we make a priori decisions regarding placement? One solution is to *not* make *a priori* decisions. Instead, we could use early tutor data in the decision rule, providing these data showed some predictive validity. In fact, exploratory behavior data, tallied during the initial learning phase (principle 1 data only), *were* shown to be significant predictors of learning data in this study. The early behavior by environment interactions were shown to be significant predictors of learning outcome and efficiency (postfac and total number of problems).

In practice, the learner-to-environment assignment would work as follows: All individuals would initially be assigned to a default learning environment. Results from the study reported in this chapter suggest that, for instructing basic principles of electricity, the default environment should be rule-application because it displayed a distinct advantage over the inductive environment in terms of learning time and number of problems needed for attaining mastery (as well as a marginal advantage of posttest factor scores). Persons would then proceed through the tutor, and information on their explorations would be tallied in real-time. After the first principle was mastered, they would either be switched to the rule-induction environment if exploratory behavioral level was greater than average, else they would remain in the rule-application environment. Decision rules can, of course, be made even more comprehensive with the inclusion of additional conditionals. For example, some other ATI results reported by Shute (1992) suggest that considering an individual's associative learning abilities can inform decisions about which learning environment is the more suitable.

These findings have a direct implication for instruction (e.g., ITS design issues). As psychologists and educators concerned with instruction, our goal should be to maximize learning for as many individuals as possible. Results from this research provide information about which learning environments are more suitable for which learners, and why. In this study, we saw that low exploratory individuals learned efficiently from structured learning environments (rule-application) while high exploratory individuals learned best from freer learning environments (rule-induction). The reason "why" is due to the match between learner and environment characteristics. Furthermore, exploratory behavior does not appear to be simply an artifact of aptitude: the correlations between this learning style measure and various cognitive process measures were zero.

This study also addressed the issue of the utility of various "bells and whistles." Preliminary evidence suggested that, for many learners, all that glitters is not gold. In other words, simply having many and dazzling on-line tools in the environment without requirements for their use may be a wasted effort. Directed tool use may actually have positive effects on learning outcome and efficiency, but that was not tested in the current study. In conclusion, an ITS can potentially increase its effectiveness and progress toward the goal of optimizing learning by adapting to an individual's particular learning style. Learning environments are easily modified while learner attributes (e.g., styles, aptitudes) are less easily altered.[4] However, comparing the relative flexibility of styles to aptitudes, Baron (1985) argues that learning styles are considerably more modifiable than aptitudes (processing components). So, these data can provide a point of departure for building more adaptive learning environments.

ACKNOWLEDGMENTS

I sincerely thank the many people who worked with me on this project. Pat Kyllonen, Ray Christal, Bill Tirre, Scott Chaiken, and Lisa Gawlick-Grendell provided me with many valuable suggestions, from conceptual to analytical, during the conduct of this research. Roy Chollman, Rich Walker, Janice Hereford, Wayne Crone, and Linda Robertson-Shule provided excellent support and assistance in different aspects of the massive data collection job. Finally, I would like to thank the creative and industrious programmers on this project: Tony Beauregard and Kym Costa, as well as the original programmers at LRDC.

The research reported in this paper was conducted as part of the Armstrong Laboratory, Human Resources Directorate—Learning Abilities Measurement Program (LAMP). This study represents basic research funded by the Air Force Office of Scientific Research. The opinions expressed in this article are those of the author and do not necessarily reflect those of the Air Force.

Correspondence concerning this paper should be addressed to Valerie J. Shute, Armstrong Laboratory, Human Resources Directorate, Cognitive Skills Assessment Branch, Brooks Air Force Base, Texas, 78235.

REFERENCES

Ackerman, P. L. (1988). Determinants of individual differences during skill acquisition: Cognitive abilities and information processing. *Journal of Experimental Psychology: General, 117*, 288–318.

Anderson, J. R. (1987). Skill acquisition: Compilation of weak-method problem solutions. *Psychological Review, 94*, 192–210.

Anderson, J. R., Boyle, C. F., & Reiser, B. J. (1985). Intelligent tutoring systems. *Science, 228*, 456–462.

---

[4]However, I am not at this time claiming that exploratory behavior is a trait (i.e., relatively stable individual characteristic). It is probably more a "propensity" and potentially modifiable. More research is needed in this area.

Baron, J. (1985). What kinds of intelligence components are fundamental? In S. F. Chipman, J. W. Segal, & R. Glaser (Eds.), *Thinking and learning skills* (Vol. 2, pp. 365–390). Hillsdale, NJ: Lawrence Erlbaum Associates.

Collins, A., & Brown, J. S. (1988). The computer as a tool for learning through reflection. In H. Mandl & A. Lesgold (Eds.), *Learning issues for intelligent tutoring systems* (pp. 1–18). New York: Springer-Verlag.

Corbett, A. T., & Anderson, J. R. (1989). Feedback timing and student control in the Lisp intelligent tutoring system. In D. Bierman, J. Brueker, & J. Sandberg (Eds.), *Proceedings of the Fourth International Conference on Artificial Intelligence and Education* (pp. 64–72). Springfield, VA: IOS.

Cronbach, L. J., & Snow, R. E. (1977). *Aptitudes and instructional methods: A handbook for research on interactions.* New York: Irvington.

Glushko, R. J., & Cooper, L. A. (1978). Spatial comprehension and comparison processes in verification tasks. *Cognitive Psychology, 10,* 391–421.

Hunt, E., & MacLeod, C. M. (1979). The sentence-verification paradigm: A case study for individual differences. In R. J. Sternberg & D. K. Detterman (Eds.), *Human intelligence: Perspectives on its theory and measurement* (pp. 89–104). Norwood, NJ: Ablex.

Kyllonen, P. C., & Shute, V. J. (1989). A taxonomy of learning skills. In P. L. Ackerman, R. J. Sternberg, & R. Glaser (Eds.), *Learning and Individual Differences* (pp. 117–163). New York: W. H. Freeman.

Lesgold, A. M., Bonar, J., Ivill, J., & Bowen, A. (1989). An intelligent tutoring system for electronics troubleshooting: DC-circuit understanding. In L. Resnick (Ed.), *Knowing and learning: Issues for the cognitive psychology of instruction.* Hillsdale, NJ: Lawrence Erlbaum Associates.

Pask, G., & Scott, B. C. E. (1972). Learning strategies and individual competence. *International Journal of Man-Machine Studies, 4,* 217–253.

Pellegrino, J. W., Mumaw, R. J., & Shute, V. J. (1985). Analyses of spatial aptitude and expertise. In S. Embretson (Ed.), *Test Design: Contributions from psychology, education, and psychometrics* (pp. 45–76). New York: Academic Press.

Schneider, W., & Shiffrin, R. M. (1977). Controlled and automatic human information processing: I. Detection, search, and attention. *Psychological Review, 84,* 1–66.

Shute, V. J. (1989). Individual differences in learning from an intelligent tutoring system. *Technology and Learning, 3,* 7–11.

Shute, V. J. (1991). Who is likely to acquire programming skills? *Journal of Educational Computing Research, 7,* 1–24.

Shute, V. J. (1992). Aptitude-treatment interactions and cognitive skill diagnosis. In J. W. Regian & V. J. Shute (Eds.), *Cognitive diagnosis and automated instruction.* Hillsdale, NJ: Lawrence Erlbaum Associates.

Shute, V. J., & Glaser, R. (1990). A large-scale evaluation of an intelligent discovery world: Smithtown. *Interactive Learning Environments, 1,* 51–76.

Shute, V. J., Glaser, R., & Raghavan, K. (1989). Inference and discovery in an exploratory laboratory. In P. L. Ackerman, R. J. Sternberg, & R. Glaser (Eds.), *Learning and individual differences* (pp. 279–326). New York: W. H. Freeman.

Shute, V. J., & Kyllonen, P. C. (1990). *Modeling individual differences in programming skill acquisition* (Tech. report no. AFHRL-TP-90-76). Air Force Systems Command, Brooks Air Force Base, TX 78235-5601.

Sleeman, D., Kelly, A. E., Martinak, R., Ward, R. D., & Moore, J. L. (1989). Studies of diagnosis and remediation with high school algebra students. *Cognitive Science, 13*(4), 551–568.

White, B. Y., & Horowitz, P. (1987). *Thinker tools: Enabling children to understand physical laws* (Report No. 6470). Cambridge, MA: Bolt, Beranek, and Newman.

3

Motivational Techniques of Expert Human Tutors: Lessons for the Design of Computer-Based Tutors

Mark R. Lepper
Maria Woolverton
Donna L. Mumme
Stanford University

Jean-Luc Gurtner
University of Fribourg

For most of recorded history, formal education consisted largely of individual tutorials. From Plato's *Republic* through the Age of Enlightenment (Locke, 1693; Rousseau, 1762), education was imparted, to the select few who could afford the service, via one-to-one interactions with professional tutors. Only in the past century or two has compulsory education become a common practice.

With the advent of universal schooling came a significant revolution in the nature of formal education occasioned by the rise of the modern classroom environment, in which a single teacher is charged with the simultaneous instruction of a large group of students (Dreeben, 1968; Jackson, 1968). Under the press of numbers, extended individualized instruction was largely supplanted by other, group-based teaching methods. Personal tutoring became a luxury available only to the wealthy or the greatly disadvantaged.

Within the last few years, however, interest in tutoring has been rekindled. With the rise of increasingly sophisticated computers of the sort described elsewhere in this volume has come the possibility of a renewed individualization of instruction. Computer-based tutors can provide cost-effective, yet personalized and individually responsive, alternatives to large-scale classroom teaching (Cuban, 1986; Taylor, 1980). Indeed, the ideal of an immediately responsive, individually targeted computer tutor was stated quite poetically by Suppes (1966), in the earliest days of computer-assisted instruction: "One can predict that in a few more years, millions of school children will have access to what Philip of Macedon enjoyed as a royal prerogative: the personal services of a tutor as well-informed and responsive as Aristotle" (p. 206).

Although early computer-based tutors did seem to provide a cost-effective supplement to traditional classroom instruction in many domains (e.g., Kulik,

Bangert, & Williams, 1983; Lepper & Gurtner, 1989; Niemiec & Walberg, 1987), they remained a far cry from an Aristotle at every desk. As the power and sophistication of computer systems available for educational purposes has increased dramatically in recent years, however, instructional possibilities have multiplied. With the advent of modern diagnostic modeling and "intelligent" tutoring systems in particular (e.g., Anderson, Boyle, & Reiser, 1985; Dede, 1986; Larkin & Chabay, 1992; Ohlsson, 1986; Sleeman & Brown, 1982; Wenger, 1987), the ideal of a computer-based tutor as capable as a human at identifying, and presumably correcting, each student's idiosyncratic misunderstandings seems attainable.

As these systems have become more sophisticated, however, the gap between their obvious intelligence (both in capturing the dynamics of expert understanding and in diagnosing the particular deficiencies in understanding of specific individual students) and their evident limitations as pedagogues has become increasingly apparent. In contrast to the strong, principled models of expertise and diagnosis embedded in these systems, the decisions such programs make regarding even basic issues of pedagogy have remained largely ad hoc and underdeveloped (Dede, 1986; Lepper & Chabay, 1985, 1988; Ohlsson, 1986).

Moreover, there is remarkably little direct guidance to be gained regarding these issues from the current educational literature. Perhaps because tutoring has been sufficiently infrequent in our schools in this century, until recently virtually no empirical research has specifically examined the dynamics of one-to-one tutorials. Research on effective teaching has instead concentrated on the standard classroom, focusing on issues of group-based instruction and classroom management (Collins & Stevens, 1982; Shulman, 1986).

Even among the small group of investigators who have recently begun to examine the actions of actual human tutors as a potential source of information relevant to the design of effective computer tutors (e.g., Fox, 1989; McArthur, Stasz, & Zmuidzinas, 1990; McKendree, Reiser, & Anderson, 1984; Putnam, 1987), the focus of analysis concerning expertise in tutoring has remained largely limited to the study of cognitive issues. Questions of motivational, affective, or social goals and strategies, and the interaction of these factors with cognitive goals and strategies, have remained virtually unaddressed.

In the present chapter, therefore, we address some of these understudied pedagogical issues regarding effective tutoring practices, drawing on our own recent research analyzing the goals and strategies of expert human tutors. In particular, we focus on a set of issues that are not commonly addressed in current computer-based tutoring systems, but which appear critical to successful human tutors—the motivational, affective, socioemotional side of effective tutorials.

The expert tutors described here represent the best of four different samples of tutors that we have studied. We cite examples of their comments during actual tutoring sessions, as well as during stimulated-recall interviews that took place after the sessions. The data encompass three types of elementary school mathematics activities. A first group of tutors (first studied by Putnam, 1987) worked with second graders on addition with carrying. Two other groups of tutors worked with 4th, 5th, and 6th graders on one of two mathematics games for the computer— "The Factory" (Kosel & Fish, 1983) or "Darts" (Dugdale & Kibbey, 1980). A final sample of tutors taught complex word problems to 3rd and 4th grade students. Our choice of expert tutors for each sample was based on both objective (e.g., learning) measures and independent ratings of tutors' overall effectiveness. (For all four samples, we found that there was unanimous agreement across several independent raters in identifying the most expert tutors.) Each of the tutors cited here has been identified by a letter. Tutor A was drawn from the addition sample. Tutors B and C were drawn from the Factory sample. Tutor D was drawn from the Darts sample. Tutor E was drawn from the word problems sample.

BACKGROUND

Implicit in the design of many current computer tutors is a conception of the tutoring process derived from a purely cognitive analysis of teaching. In this analysis, the student is seen as possessing limited, and often systematically erroneous, information that leads him or her to make predictable errors in task performance. From a careful study of these errors, an intelligent tutor can thus diagnose the conceptual difficulties and misunderstandings of any given student. Once these systematic difficulties, or "bugs" in the student's program have been accurately diagnosed, the tutor's remaining job would seem to be to provide the information necessary to disabuse the student of his or her wrong ideas and to displace them with correct information and algorithms (Dede, 1986; Sleeman & Brown, 1982).

Such an analysis has many strengths and has led to the design of quite sophisticated computer tutoring systems. It remains, however, an exclusively cognitive analysis; issues of student affect, motivation, and attention are simply not considered in such models. Instead, such models presume, in many senses, an attentive and motivated learner—a learner anxious to improve his or her performance and eager to hear diagnoses about what he or she is doing wrong. That students may not care about learning the material, that they may not want to hear a detailed litany of their errors, that they are bored or frustrated, or that they are alienated or phobic are not possibilities contemplated by such models.

Such a stance contrasts sharply with that of expert human tutors. In both general interviews about their philosophies of tutoring and in specific commentaries regarding their own actions in actual tutoring sessions, our best tutors appear to devote at least as much time and attention to issues of motivation and affect as they do to issues of information and cognition. Especially when working with remedial students, these tutors frequently describe their greatest challenge not as one of deciding what the child needs to be taught, but as one of deciding how to convey what does need to be taught in a manner that will not further discourage or distress these learners. From these interviews and a detailed analysis of the actual responses of these tutors in working with students in tutorial sessions, we have begun to build a model of the performance of expert human tutors, at least for the area of early mathematics instruction.

The central tenet of this model is that expert and demonstrably effective human tutors' actions in working with individual students are derived from a simultaneous consideration of two complementary "diagnostic models" that the tutor constructs and continuously revises regarding the specific student with whom he or she is working—one cognitive and one affective. On the cognitive side, we see the tutor as trying to diagnose and monitor—though often in a less highly precise and systematic fashion than computer-based diagnostic systems— what the student knows and does not know, and what major misconceptions may underlie the student's errors. On the affective side, we also see the tutor as trying to diagnose and monitor, although in an even less precise and deterministic fashion, the socioemotional state of the child. In particular, we believe that it makes a great difference to effective human tutors whether the student seems attentive or distracted, interested or bored, or confident or anxious about his or her performance.

Thus, we see tutors as attempting to pay simultaneous and continuous attention to both the cognitive and the affective state of the learner, and we view their pedagogical decisions—ranging from which problem to present next to how to respond to a particular mistake or grimace—as depending on these concurrent cognitive and affective models of the student. If so, cognitive and motivational considerations may, in different circumstances, bear one of three relationships to one another.

Frequently, for instance, the pedagogical implications of these two parallel models of student affect and student cognition will prove entirely congruent with one another, each suggesting the same action by the tutor.[1] Following a successful series of trials at a given level of difficulty, for example, both a cognitive and a motivational analysis might suggest the wisdom of moving on to problems at a higher level of difficulty and complexity. Both motivational and cognitive considerations may similarly lead tutors to ask leading or challenging questions, to present abstract ideas within familiar or interesting contexts, or to provide praise for exceptional accomplishments.

In other situations, a second case may obtain: Cognitive and affective considerations may prove at variance with one another, implying contradictory actions

---

[1]Similarly, McArthur, Stasz, and Zmuidzinas (1990), in their examination of the techniques of three experienced algebra tutors, note that "many tutorial actions appeared to fulfill a motivational function while also accomplishing some other [informational] purpose" (pp. 207–208), although they choose to limit themselves to the study of informational goals and techniques of their tutors.

by the tutor. In a previous paper (Lepper, Aspinwall, Mumme, & Chabay, 1990), for example, we highlighted one important class of situations in which these two factors appeared to have been seen by expert tutors as in conflict with one another. At least when working with remedial students, these tutors seemed to view a majority of the situations in which they had to decide how to respond to student errors as involving such a conflict. As a result, the strategies and techniques that our expert tutors used to respond to the mistakes and misunderstandings of remedial students were quite different from those a naive analysis might have suggested.

Consider the student who has made an error that clearly reflects some evident and systematic misunderstanding of the material in question. How should a tutor respond? Conventional wisdom and traditional "learning theory" might recommend that effective responses to student errors include the following steps: (a) identify the response as incorrect for the learner (i.e., provide knowledge of results), (b) give the learner the correct answer (i.e., offer corrective feedback), (c) provide the learner with an explicit "diagnosis" regarding his or her misunderstanding(s) that produced the errors (i.e., highlight the points at which the student's performance diverged from a correct procedure), and perhaps (d) demonstrate for the learner the correct solution process.

Such an approach is highly efficient, in that it involves the straightforward presentation of the information that the learner would require to correct his or her erroneous understanding of the material. It is also an approach frequently underlying the design of computer-based tutoring systems (Dede, 1986; Sleeman & Brown, 1982). Elements are evident in tutoring systems that provide feedback of the following sort (Attisha & Yazdani, 1984):

Your answer is wrong.
Possible causes of error:
1. You multiplied the number in the multiplicand by the number beneath it in the multiplier, and you wrote down the carried number, ignoring the units number.

Our experienced human tutors, by contrast, made little use of any of these strategies. Thus, they virtually *never* provided the answer to a problem, and only in a tiny fraction of cases did they even provide any sort of overt diagnosis of a student's difficulties. In fact, they most often did not even explicitly label a student's incorrect answers as errors. Rarely did they make direct suggestions to the learner about how to proceed, much less demonstrate the correct solution procedure themselves. Instead, they responded to student errors more indirectly. They hinted at the existence of problems with statements prompting reconsideration (e.g., "So, you think it's *126?*") or requesting an explanation ("Now tell me *how* you got that *6?*"). They asked leading questions designed to draw students' attention implicitly to the location of errors (e.g., "Now *which* column is the *one's* column?"). Moreover, these tutors persisted in their reliance on such indirect feedback, asking as many as half a dozen "unsuccessful" questions one after another, rather than simply telling the child directly what the error was or how it could be corrected.

Such strategies, we believe, derive directly from a conflict between cognitive and affective considerations. For these expert tutors, in a nutshell, exactly those things that one would do to present information to students most efficiently about the existence and sources of their errors and misconceptions are, at least for unconfident remedial students, precisely the same things that seem likely to further undermine these students' sense of competence and control. That our expert tutors proved highly successful in motivating and teaching their pupils despite the apparent inefficiency of their approach attests to the wisdom of their practice.

As one highly effective tutor articulated the issues to us in commenting on her response to a student's clearly wrong answer:

> Tutor C: And always there's the problem of language. . . . You don't want to say, 'Yours is totally wrong.' [You try to] couch your terms in a way that they don't feel like they've done something wrong. You know, they've created a nice picture, but it's not exactly what you were trying to get at. . . . so they feel bolstered in what they are doing, whether it's turning into the right answer or not.

Finally, there is a third possibility—that cognitive and affective considerations will frequently prove neither congruent nor in conflict with one another, but that the two factors may prove simply independent of one another. Given a particular problem, for instance, questions of how to interest a child in its solution may often prove orthogonal to traditional cognitive concerns. Tutors may coax, cajole, reassure, or challenge their pupils, to elicit more effort or increased attention from those students. In these cases, we can see the importance accorded to affective and motivational factors by expert human tutors in the actions they take and the statements they make, as well as in the alternative actions and comments they avoid making.

In each of these three cases, however—whether cognitive and affective goals seem mutually supportive, in direct conflict, or simply orthogonal to one another—the protocols of successful human tutors that we have examined have led us to believe that there are four major motivational or affective goals to which tutors attend, at least in working with difficult or remedial learners. These four goals are: (1) confidence—to enhance the learner's level of confidence or self-efficacy, (2) challenge—to produce an appropriate level of challenge for the learner, (3) control—to maintain in the learner a sense of personal control, and (4) curiosity—to elicit from the learner a high level of curiosity.

Each of these motivational goals is of importance to experienced tutors both in an immediate and in a long-term form. That is, our tutors not only want the learner to feel challenged and curious during the tutoring session, so that he or she will be actively involved and attentive during the session. They also want the learner to leave the tutoring session with a more general sense of challenge and curiosity about the topic, so that he or she will be likely to seek out further opportunities to tackle and to learn about the topic in the future. Each of these four goals has been identified in previous work as important to the development of an intrinsic motivation to learn (Lepper & Malone, 1987; Malone & Lepper, 1987). In the following sections, we examine some of the strategies that expert human tutors appear to employ to accomplish these goals with their students.

CONFIDENCE AND CHALLENGE

Confidence and Challenge as Tutorial Goals

Consider, first, the linked motivational or affective goals of confidence and challenge. Expert human tutors, we are suggesting, have as salient top-level motivational goals both to enhance their students' perceptions of self-efficacy and self-confidence at the activity in question and to keep their students feeling constantly challenged by the material they are presenting. Their reasoning, in both cases, is straightforward and has received support in educational and psychological research.

That people will prefer an optimal level of challenge in the activities they undertake is one of the most widespread postulates in the study of human motivation. Thus, within the domains of effectance motivation (e.g., Harter, 1978; Kagan, 1972; White, 1959), perceived competence (e.g., Deci, 1975; Lepper & Greene, 1978; Weiner, 1979), flow states (Csikszentmihalyi, 1975), and self-efficacy (Bandura, 1977, 1986; Schunk, 1983), runs a central common conviction—that activities that provide an intermediate level of perceived challenge for the individual will stimulate interest and investment. Activities that are either trivially easy or impossibly difficult will be of little intrinsic interest and will instead generate boredom or anxiety, respectively.

There is substantial agreement, moreover, on what makes an activity challenging for an individual (Malone, 1981; Malone & Lepper, 1987). First, for an activity to prove challenging, it must provide goals to the person, the attainment of which remains uncertain. Challenging activities, in addition, must provide performance feedback concerning goal achievement and must engage the self-esteem of the individual. We are challenged, in short, by activities that we perceive as meaningful tests of some ability or accomplishment that we value and at which we hope for, but are not certain of, success.

Note that the concept of challenge inherently involves the relationship, or discrepancy, between two subjective variables—the difficulty of success at the activity as perceived by the individual and that individual's estimation of his or her own abilities. Obviously, what is challenging for one person may prove virtually impossible, or exceedingly trivial, for another. Indeed, in the course of learning, we may expect that what was once seen as challenging or even intimidating for a person will subsequently be viewed by that same person, following the acquisition of relevant improved skills or additional knowledge, as boring and banal. Similarly, what is central to one person's self-image and self-worth may be seen as irrelevant and trivial to another.

That the promotion of feelings of challenge in the student is a prominent goal of our expert tutors is illustrated in their spontaneous comments during stimulated-recall interviews, in which they were asked to view and explain their actions in interviews immediately following the actual tutoring sessions. For example:

> *Tutor B:* I just felt he would enjoy the challenge, even if it were a really tough one. Even if he got a really hard one, I thought he would enjoy struggling with it, and had the tools to struggle effectively.

The significance of bolstering the student's confidence in his or her ability seems equally salient in these same interviews with our best tutors. For instance:

> *Tutor B:* I'm concerned about her confidence. I don't want her to feel like she's failing. . . . I want to make sure she leaves feeling O.K., because her confidence was pretty low. I really want to bolster her.

The existing research literature suggests, moreover, that the pursuit of such affective goals should indeed have beneficial consequences for instruction (Lepper & Malone, 1987). Across a wide array of activities, for example, increases in levels of self-efficacy, perceived personal competence, and academic self-esteem have been shown to predict school grades, test performance, and other indicators of academic success (e.g., Bandura, 1977, 1986; Dweck, 1986; Schunk, 1984, 1985; Weiner, 1979). Correspondingly, feelings of challenge have been linked, in a variety of domains, to measures of learning and academic success (Gottfried, 1985; Harter, 1982; Weiner, 1979).

Thus, it should not be surprising that we find a concern with these same factors characteristic of demonstrably successful expert human tutors. Less obvious and more interesting is the question of how these superlative tutors achieve these lofty goals.

Strategies for Enhancing Confidence and Challenge

How is it, then, that our expert tutors seek to accomplish these primarily affective and motivational goals? We find, in the protocols of their successful tutoring sessions, evidence of several general sorts of strategies, both for evoking a sense of challenge in the selection and presentation of problems and for enhancing the student's sense of confidence in his or her own capabilities in solving such problems. A preliminary analysis and categorization of the general strategies and

TABLE 3.1
Strategies for Enhancing Challenge and Confidence

Maintain a Sense of Challenge

Modulate Objective Task Difficulty

1. Select appropriately difficult problems for the student

    (a) Proceed generally from easier to harder problems as the student's skills increase
    (b) Modulate the difficulty level of individual problems presented as a function of the student's current level of understanding

2. Provide scaffolding for the student

    (a) Decide whether, when, and how to intervene in problem solving to forestall or to correct errors
    (b) Break down the problem so as to decrease the size of steps required for successful problem solution
    (c) Increase or decrease the specificity of hints provided to the student as a function of the student's difficulty at a particular point

Modulate Subjective Task Difficulty

1. Emphasize the difficulty of the task
2. Challenge the student directly
3. Engage in playful competition with the student

Bolster Self-Confidence

Maximize Success

1. Maximize success directly

    (a) Praise the student after success
    (b) Express confidence in the student after success

2. Maximize success indirectly

    (a) Comment on the difficulty of the task before or after success (i.e., make success seem like even more of an accomplishment)
    (b) Emphasize student agency after success (i.e., portray the student as an independent problem solver)
    (c) Engage in playful competition with the student after the student has been successful (i.e., indicate how the student has "out-smarted" the tutor)

Minimize Failure

1. Minimize failure directly

    (a) Reassure and commiserate with the student after failure
    (b) Redefine success vs. failure (i.e., emphasize partial success or closeness to desired solution)

2. Minimize failure indirectly

    (a) Comment on the difficulty of the task before or after failure (i.e., provide task difficulty as a attribution for failure)
    (b) Make excuses after failure (i.e., provide explanations which remove responsiblility for failure from the student)
    (c) Provide indirect feedback (i.e., ask questions and provide hints rather than explicitly label an answer as incorrect)

---

the specific techniques that expert tutors use both to challenge students and to bolster their self-confidence are presented in Table 3.1.

Maintaining a Sense of Challenge

Consider, first, the techniques by which expert tutors seek to keep students feeling challenged by the problems they have been presented. Here, an initial distinction contrasts strategies that involve the manipulation of the actual or "objective" level of challenge presented to the learner with strategies that seek to influence only the learner's "subjective" perceptions.

Modulation of Objective Task Difficulty. In a first category are techniques that involve the manipulation of the actual level of challenge provided by the activities the tutor creates for the learner. Given the cognitive model that we believe expert tutors generate concerning their students' knowledge of, and misconceptions concerning, the topic, it is possible for expert tutors to combine their knowledge of the subject matter in general and their model of a specific student in particular to select problems that will provide an appropriate level of challenge for that student. The general goal is to select problems that will prove difficult, but not impossible, for the learner.

Of course, it will often be difficult, even for experts, to predict exactly how much difficulty a given problem will pose for a particular learner. Hence, "midcourse corrections," once a student has begun to work on a difficult problem, for example, may be necessary. These alterations in the objective difficulty level of a specific problem for the learner commonly take one of two forms of additional "scaffolding" of the task for the learner by the tutor. One involves interventions by the tutor, designed either to forestall, or to correct immediately, any error the tutor deems likely to prove unproductive and to make problem solution unlikely for the child. The other involves the breaking down of complex problems into simpler component subproblems designed to provide a more appropriate level of difficulty for the learner.

Thus, we see our best tutors differing from their less successful counterparts in several respects. At the level of problem selection, our most successful tutors are both systematically progressive and highly responsive to the learner. In general, their strategy is to increase task difficulty across problems, one step at a time, but only when they are sure that the student is ready to advance. Although this may seem almost a trivial and self-evident point, it is worth noting that we have observed other equally experienced but less effective tutors proceed through a tutoring session either drawing problems from a wide range of objective difficulty levels essentially at random or proceeding through a predetermined progression of problems absolutely independent of the learner's performance, comments, or actions.

We also believe that our most effective tutors display a much more nuanced model for responding differentially to student errors as a function of their estimates of the learner's current cognitive and affective state. Thus, they will sometimes seek to forestall errors, sometimes intervene as soon as errors occur; at other times they may allow errors to occur so that they may later be "debugged" or they may ignore certain errors entirely. Exactly when they do which is too complex an issue to permit discussion here, but the basic point is that all of these choices involve complicated tradeoffs between both cognitive and motivational considerations about when and how to provide new information and assistance when the student makes errors. In the next sections, by contrast, we examine a number of simpler strategies that appear designed almost exclusively to accomplish motivational goals—strategies that seem intended to alter not the objective difficulty of the task for the learner but the perceived difficulty of the task by that learner.

Modulation of Subjective Challenge.   Obviously, in the end, the experience of being challenged is subjective, and even given a specific activity at some objectively fixed level of difficulty, there remains a considerable range through which students' perceptions of the difficulty of the task, relative to their perceptions of their own abilities, can be manipulated. Equally obviously, strategies for manipulating a learner's sense of challenge may focus on perceptions of the task itself, on perceptions of one's own competence, or on a combination of both. Our best tutors seem to be masters at each of these sorts of motivational techniques.

A first point at which such considerations frequently assume prominence occurs when each new problem is presented. For our best tutors, this is characteristically a point at which any of several strategies for highlighting challenge may be employed. At the most direct level, the tutor may simply comment upon the difficulty of the upcoming problem.

Tutor D: Now this is level three. What's gonna happen is, it's gonna get more difficult.

Tutor E: O.k. Let me try you on another one. I'm gonna change the numbers and make them bigger.

Tutor A:
T: Now I'm going to give you one that you haven't had before, o.k.?
S: O.k.
T: This is really hard.

We should note that such comments are not intended simply to serve the largely cognitive function of providing accurate information to the learner, in order to allow him or her to better prepare for the problem to follow (cf. Leinhardt, 1987). Certainly, our tutors describe their use of these comments, in subsequent interviews, as serving primarily motivational ends.

Tutor A: There's a reason why I say it's a harder one. . . . The reason I do that, if they fail, or if they can't do it, **they haven't lost face**, because I've told them it's hard beforehand. . . . Down here, she said it was too hard, and then she did it. But, by doing that beforehand, you've given them an out.

Even more compelling evidence of the motivational function of these remarks, however, is that fact that they often involve the tutor's telling "white lies" to the student—for example, telling the learner that a coming problem is going to be more difficult even though it is of objectively equal or even less difficulty than the previous problem—a response that would be difficult to generate from a purely informational analysis of the tutoring process.

Moreover, comments on the difficulty of an upcoming problem are clearly part of a larger motivational strategy on the part of our successful tutors. Frequently, for example, mentions of the apparent difficulty of a new problem are followed by friendly, but quite direct, challenges to the student.

Tutor A: I'll give you a harder one this time. I hope you are ready for it.

Tutor E: If I make the numbers really big, can you solve it then?

Tutor A: I don't know, do you think you can do this one?

In some cases, these exchanges become part of a regular and recurrent form of playful competition in which the tutor (slightly dishonestly) presents himself or herself as trying to trick and trip up the student, but in which the student can now "get" the tutor by correctly solving the problem.

Tutor A:
T: You really want it hard?
S: Yes.
T: Oh, Sally. Then I have to correct it.
S: I know. Then it will be hard for you to correct it. (chuckle)

Tutor E: I'm gonna change the numbers here, and I hope they're not screwy like the last one [I made up]. Gotta keep thinking. You're making it harder for me. I don't know whether I can keep up.

At the same time, the strategic character of these techniques is also apparent from the fact that our best tutors are quick to step back from their claims about the difficulty of a problem the moment that it appears their comments may have been *too* successful. If, for example, a student's response to a direct challenge or a comment on the difficulty of an upcoming problem reveals that he or she has lost confidence in his or her ability to solve that problem, expert human tutors seem quick to seek to bolster that student's self-confidence or to reassure him or her.

Indeed, the best of our tutors can be seen clearly modulating the level of perceived challenge, as an exquisitely responsive function of the learner's responses. Consider the following excerpts:

Tutor E:

T: So if I change these numbers, you can still solve the problem?
S: Uh-huh.
T: Alright, I'll do that just to see. (looks at S to interpret reaction) Then Sean gave him 6 candy bars and now he has 12. Can you do that one? You can use the pencil if you want.
S: 6. (answers immediately, solving correctly in head)
T: Six, o.k. If I make the numbers really big, can you solve it then?
S: I don't know. Maybe.
T: You're not sure, eh?
S: No.
T: O.k. Like here's a hard kind.
S: I might have to write it down.
T: O.k., well that's alright, you can write it. Then Sean gave him 25 candy bars. Now Sean has 40 candy bars.

Tutor A:

T: (takes paper and starts writing problem) Ok, now I'm going to give you a harder . . .
S: Ummm, that is hard.
T: That is hard?
S: Yes, it looks very hard.
T: It does look hard, doesn't it? Do you think you can do it?
S: Yes, I can.
T: Shall I ask you where to start, or can you remember?
S: This side. (points) (solves problem correctly)
T: Boy, you were right, you could do it.

In short, expert human tutors seem to invest a great deal of effort to see that their pupils feel appropriately challenged during the tutoring sessions. In doing so, they hope to insure that their students will be attentive to the problem and willing to accept instruction from them. In order to do so, they tailor their own statements and actions quite precisely to the comments and reactions of the students they teach.

Bolstering of Self-Confidence

In addition to this concern with maintaining an immediate sense of challenge, expert human tutors also show great concern for protecting and enhancing the learner's confidence in his or her own abilities. Here, their basic strategies are straightforward and hardly surprising—to maximize successes and to minimize failures. The specific techniques that they use to accomplish these ends, however, are in some cases fairly subtle.

Avoidance of Direct Negative Feedback. Of course, we have already touched, in earlier sections of this chapter, on two strategies designed to protect the learner's sense of self-efficacy. The first and most obvious involves an important set of prominent omissions from the pedagogical repertoire of expert tutors that would appear to be the result of these tutors seeking not to undermine students' confidence in their abilities. It is for this reason, as noted before, that we believe our successful tutors so rarely employ direct negative feedback, provide the learner with overt diagnoses of his or her misunderstandings, or even explicitly label errors as such, but instead rely so heavily on hints and other, more indirect forms of feedback.[2]

"Attributional Inoculation" Techniques.   The second set of already discussed practices relevant to the maintenance of students' feelings of self-confidence in their abilities involves a further consequence of tutors' attempts to challenge their pupils. Thus, the general strategy of identifying (even sometimes erroneously) coming problems as difficult or tricky not only highlights the immediate challenge posed by the problem, but it also serves to "inoculate" the learner against subsequent failure on the problem in question. By providing the learner with an "excuse" for failure in advance, initial comments on the difficulty of the task can take some of the sting out of a possible later failure to solve the problem. Conversely, such initial forewarnings of anticipated difficulties can make potential eventual successes at the problem all the more sweet (and, presumably, more informative about the learner's ability).

Tutor E: (gives new problem to student) Now, that may be a little harder, because it's been a minute since we've done that [type of] problem.

Indeed, in a number of cases, this additional strategic advantage of introducing problems as difficult is made explicit by corresponding comments by the

---

[2]This apparent avoidance of overt negative feedback may seem at least superficially at variance with McArthur, Stasz, and Zmuidzinas's (1990) observation that "for every student error we recorded, there was a remedial response" (p. 209). The critical distinction here, however, hinges on the concept of *direct* negative feedback, and it is simply impossible without additional analyses on their original protocols to determine whether there is any conflict here or not. That is, many of McArthur et al.'s categories under both the topics of "performance assessment" (e.g., "grain of truth" and "do more assess") and "remediation" (e.g., "try again," "suggest right procedure," and "change original problem") appear to involve the delivery of precisely the sort of *indirect* negative feedback techniques that our tutors most commonly employ. In both their case and ours, it is not that these indirect techniques are difficult for students to decipher; these techniques, however, do present negative feedback in a manner that appears to us less likely to undermine students' feelings of confidence and control.

At the same time, in the absence of directly comparable codings, we do not mean to assert that there may not be differences in goals or strategies between McArthur et al.'s tutors and ours. Certainly, it seems a reasonable working hypothesis that the techniques of effective tutors may differ as a function of large differences in the age of the students being tutored or the nature of the subject matter being examined.

tutor *following* the pupil's actual success or failure at the task. Thus we see our successful tutors both using attributions of student failures to task difficulty as a means of keeping students from drawing negative inferences about their own abilities and using continued playful competition after success to emphasize the value of the student's accomplishment.

Tutor D:
S: I'm confused about how you figure that out.
T: Yeah. That's why that's tricky, right. By the way, let me tell you—fractions are not easy things to understand. In fact, you know about the Egyptians, the people who made the pyramids—they were I guess pretty smart people to make the pyramids.
S: (nods)
T: They had a strange feel for fractions, too. Fractions for them were very difficult, so fractions are not easy.

Tutor A: You remembered, and I was trying to fool you. . . . I didn't get to fool you.

Although such an "attributional inoculation" strategy may appear transparent, once it has been explained, it is worth noting that it had not been noticed in the preceding two decades before its mention in our previous report (Lepper et al., 1990). Instead, the quite extensive literature on attributional "retraining" (e.g., Dweck, 1986; Foersterling, 1985; Weiner, 1979) had until that time suggested that a teacher might best directly model those theoretically preferred attributions in which the student's failures are attributed to a lack of effort or a poor strategy. Indeed, there is considerable evidence that the use of such a retraining strategy by a teacher can have significant positive effects on the learner's subsequent motivation and persistence at the task. In a controlled experimental comparison, however, the effects of the more indirect attributional inoculation strategy displayed by our expert tutors proved to have even more powerful positive effects on these same motivational measures (Lepper et al., 1990).

Direct Maximization of Success.   Other common strategies for directly maximizing the impact of success on the self-confidence of the learner have a similar character. Our best tutors do, for instance, sometimes praise the successes of their students, but they do so less often than many of their much less successful counterparts. These effective tutors also seem more likely to use indirect forms of praise, indicating success by noting that the student seems ready to move to a more difficult problem, by reminding the successful student of the difficulty of the problem he or she has just solved, by emphasizing the learner's own agency or responsibility for his or her success, or by explicitly marking the amount of progress already made in the tutoring session.

Tutor B: Great job. That was a particularly hard one.

Tutor C: You did that one without any help.

Tutor A: Boy, ready for a second page. We filled that one up.

Direct Minimization of Failure. Finally, our expert human tutors also spend a fair amount of time directly minimizing the impact that they believe unalloyed failure might have on their students' feelings of confidence. Some of these strategies seem quite unexceptional. It should surprise nobody, for example, to find that our effective tutors will frequently reassure students after failure or will commiserate with them in such as way as to appear to share the blame or responsibility for an error having occurred.

Tutor B: I thought it was right last time, too. I get mixed up between the thin and the thick.

Other strategies for minimizing failure may seem a bit more unexpected. Thus, on the one hand, we see these tutors frequently making excuses for a student's failure.

Tutor B: I think I just didn't explain very well what I wanted you to do.

On the other hand, we even see these tutors redefining what constitutes success and failure, so as to be able to "accentuate the positive" in the learner's performance. Hence, we see objectively wrong answers described by highly effective tutors as being a good first step, a close approximation, or an excellent guess.

Tutor D: Ah, perfect! Except that you missed it.

Tutor B: O.k., you're absolutely right, if we were going to do it like that.

Tutor B: You've certainly got the right idea, but the only problem is that that's a thin stripe.

In sum, our expert tutors sought hard to maintain or increase their learners' self-confidence, even in the face of objective difficulties with the problems provided. In doing so, our best tutors stressed and highlighted the successes of the learner, while minimizing the failures of the learner through overt reassurances, the provision of exculpatory excuses, and even the redefinition of what constitutes "right" and "wrong."

CURIOSITY AND CONTROL

Curiosity and Control as Tutorial Goals

If a first pair of motivational goals, then, includes challenging students and bolstering their confidence, a second pair of affective goals shared by our effective human tutors involves the attempt by tutors to evoke curiosity and a sense of personal control in their pupils. Both curiosity and control are seen by our tutors, and in the research literature, as components of intrinsic motivation. As a result, both are seen by tutors as likely to produce greater attention to the activity and a more active and deeper involvement in learning from the activity.

In some sense, of course, curiosity is the most direct form of intrinsic motivation for learning (Hunt, 1961, 1965). Students who, for their own satisfaction, really want to learn the material and to know the answers to problems posed by a tutor should be those who learn that material best. Theorists who have discussed curiosity as an obvious motivation for learning have commonly suggested that curiosity will be stimulated by some intermediate, optimal, level of discrepancy or degree of incongruity between people's prior expectations and their current observations and experiences (e.g., Berlyne, 1960, 1966; Hunt, 1961, 1965; Kagan, 1972; Piaget, 1951, 1952). More recently, Malone (1981; Malone & Lepper, 1987) has suggested that cognitive curiosity will be aroused when people encounter information or evidence that implies that their current knowledge or understanding is incomplete, inconsistent, or even merely inelegant. This is, of course, the essence of the "Socratic Method" and related instructional strategies that seek to reveal systematically the inconsistencies and the lacunae in the pupil's knowledge structure (Collins & Stevens, 1982).

There are, however, at least two sources of cognitive curiosity. The first, highlighted earlier, is discussed by Malone and Lepper (1987) as a "structural anomaly" process, in which forcing learners to confront the limitations in their knowledge leads them to seek a better understanding of the topic. The second, discussed by Malone and Lepper (1987) as a "spreading interest" process, involves a rather different mechanism though which existing interests spread to related topics and concepts. Here, curiosity should be stimulated by connecting current problems to actors or activities or settings of intrinsic appeal or by placing problems in a context of inherent interest to the learner. This second process, then, is more closely related to discussions of the benefits of "contextualization" (Bruner, 1966) and "personal relevance" (Davis-Dorsey, Ross, & Morrison, 1991; Ross & Anand, 1987; Ross, McCormack, & Krisak, 1986) for learning.

Again, tutors' spontaneous comments during stimulated-recall interviews following their tutoring sessions reveal their concern with these motivational issues and illustrate both approaches.

Tutor C: I don't know whether I'd do it with each problem, but at least with a lot of problems, after they've successfully done it once, I'd say, 'O.k., now can you think of another way to do this?' If you've got time to work on those skills of discovery on the part of the student . . . then they just get more involved and more excited about it, instead of just regurgitating what the teacher comes up with.

Tutor E: I was afraid that he would be reacting negatively to the very idea of word problems, and in order to counteract that, I wanted to think of content or guess at content that would be motivating, and that was one reason for trying to think up my own examples. I saw it as more than a matter of just using different numbers all the time in a word frame. . . . Because a lot of the trick here is to get these tied into experiences that are as familiar as possible, because the darn problems are so arbitrary.

Yet a final cornerstone in traditional analyses of the sources of intrinsic motivations for learning involves the concept of personal control. Here, the basic notion is that people inherently seek a sense of self-determination and personal control over the events in their lives (Condry, 1977; deCharms, 1968; Deci, 1981; Deci & Ryan, 1985)—that people seek, in deCharms' (1968) terms, to experience themselves as *Origins* of their own actions and choices, rather than *Pawns* of external forces beyond their control. Although the link between control and learning may seem less direct than for challenge or curiosity, some have argued that it is *the* fundamental wellspring of intrinsic motivation, from which motivations encompassing curiosity, challenge, and confidence may all be derived (Deci, 1981; Deci & Ryan, 1985).

Once again, the interviews with our expert tutors confirm the importance for them of these issues of promoting a sense of personal control in the learner.

Tutor B: It was also important for me that he was in control. . . . Because the object for me as tutor is to get him to be able to do things on his own. It is important for him to know that he can do things without me, that he's got control of this session.

Tutor C: Just to empower them a little bit, because kids in classes often feel like they're just cogs in a wheel, and when you're doing it one-on-one, you've got the opportunity to let them feel in control, and I think that's important. I like to give them that control.

Empirical evidence, in addition, clearly documents the relationship between a sense of personal control and learning (e.g., Crandall, Katovsky, & Crandall, 1965; Dweck, 1986; Dweck & Elliott, 1983).

It would be hard to argue that provoking curiosity in learners and providing them with a sense of personal control are not laudable goals; the difficult question is, of course, how they might be achieved. In the following section, we examine the specific strategies that our best tutors seem to use in trying to accomplish these goals.

Strategies for Enhancing Curiosity and Control

As with challenge and confidence, we believe that it is possible to identify a number of distinct and complementary classes of methods that excellent tutors use to accomplish these motivational and affective goals. Table 3.2 provides a preliminary categorization, and an implicit conceptual analysis, of the strategies

TABLE 3.2
Strategies for Enhancing Curiosity and Control

Evoke Curiosity

---

1. Make use of "Socratic" methods

    (a)   Select problems that themselves pose, or will later permit the tutor to ask, "leading" questions
    (b)   Ask "telling" questions regarding problem solution, requiring further thought or articulation following successful performance

2. Make use of "associative" methods

    (a)   Present problems in real contexts that show how the knowledge being taught might be put to use by people whom the students know, like, or respect
    (b)   Present problems in fantasy contexts that allow students to identify with popular characters or interesting situations

---

Promote a Sense of Personal Control

---

1. Increase objective control

    (a)   Offer real choices in situations in which the tutor is not certain what would be best for the student (e.g., choices about additional help, using a particular strategy, or moving on to harder problems)
    (b)   Offer instructionally irrelevant choices (e.g., choices over which color pen or paper to use, which manipulatives to employ, or which names to give characters in a word problem)
    (c)   Allow students to offer their own ideas and suggestions and comply with reasonable ones
    (d)   Transfer control physically from the tutor to the child

2. Increase subjective control

    (a)   Use an indirect feedback style (e.g., ask questions and provide hints rather than give answers)
    (b)   Create an illusion of control by pretending to offer the student a choice or pretending to comply with a request
    (c)   Emphasize overtly the student's own agency in the situation

---

and techniques that expert tutors use to evoke curiosity and to enhance feelings of personal control in the learner.

Evoking Curiosity

Consider, then, the problem of evoking curiosity in the student. Here, as with the maintenance of a sense of self-confidence in the learner, a first evident set of strategies for promoting curiosity has already been mentioned in our prior discussion of our expert tutors' careful avoidance of directly giving their pupils the correct answer to problems they are having difficulty with, but instead offering them hints or asking them questions designed to get the students themselves to recognize and correct their own errors. Beyond this avoidance of responses likely to limit or undermine curiosity, however, our most effective tutors also display responses actively designed to promote curiosity as well.

"Socratic" Methods. A first set of techniques by which tutors seek to provoke curiosity in children involves the use of leading, rhetorical, and skeptical questions of the sort traditionally identified with the Socratic Method. The point of these techniques, of course, is to lead the student to "discover" for himself or herself the shortcomings, inconsistencies, and other difficulties that characterize his or her own current understanding of a problem or a subject. The effective use of such techniques, moreover, involves responses at two levels.

First, the stimulation of curiosity in this sense involves the selection of appropriate problems for the student that will permit the tutor to ask the relevant leading questions. Frequently, tutors will seek to create pairs of problems, for example, that involve either two seemingly dissimilar problems that turn out to be closely related or to require similar solutions, or two seemingly similar problems that yield different results or involve different processes. Then, as these problems are posed to students, it is possible to ask them explicitly to compare and/or contrast the different problems, to predict the outcomes or answers for each, and the like.

> *Tutor A:*
> S: Writes 137 + 77 (presented verbally) with 77 on bottom. (solves correctly)
> T: Absolutely right. How would you write it if you wanted to put the 77 on top?
> S: Like this. (writes correctly as requested)
> T: Do you think it'll come out the same as this [previous problem], or not?

In addition, however, the stimulation of cognitive curiosity in this sense also involves the production of "telling questions" regarding any problem solution. Thus our best tutors seem especially likely to ask students further questions about their work, even when they have already given a correct answer. These tutors are likely, for example, to ask successful students a hypothetical or counterfactual question about their performance or their solution to the problem under different conditions.

> *Tutor E:*
> T: So what number does Peggy have to have so that Adrianna has 2 more?
> S: It might be 6 [correct answer].
> T: Would the 6 work? Suppose Peggy had 6. Does that fit the problem?
> S: Yeah.
> T: Why?

They may, similarly, ask their students directly for alternative ways to solve or present or represent the same problem they had just correctly completed, especially when that alternative may be more elegant or effective.

Tutor C: Now is there a way to solve that problem in fewer steps?

Both sets of techniques have been discussed in some detail, though in largely cognitive terms, in previous research (e.g., Collins & Stevens, 1982). In similar fashion, research on "generation" effects (e.g., Slamecka & Graf, 1978)—that is, the greater memorability of associations generated by subjects themselves—might be used to provide a cognitive justification for these methods. At the same time, there is no evidence that either affect or cognition is primary here; these effects described in the cognitive literature could just as well be the result of motivational differences. Our discussions with effective tutors certainly suggest that they view these techniques as simultaneously serving both cognitive and motivational functions.

"Associative" Methods.   Complementing these Socratic methods, then, is a second set of techniques that seek to enhance curiosity by associating problems to be solved with liked or admired actors, or objects, or stories. These strategies, involving variations in the context in which purely abstract problems are embedded, come in two forms. In the first, problems are presented in real contexts in which the knowledge being taught might be put to use by people whom the students might know, or like, or respect.

Tutor E: I come from Canada, and up in Canada, there's a lot of snow and they play hockey all the time. There's a hockey team in the town where I lived that's always doing better than the team from next door. This year, 1990, they won 6 games. I'll call the other team the neighbors' team. This year they won 4 games. So the question is: How many more games did my team win than the neighbors' team?

Closely related is a second method which involves similar use of interesting fantasy contexts as frames into which abstract problems can be embedded. This technique, which has been shown experimentally, to increase motivation and learning (Lepper & Cardova, in press; Parker & Lepper, 1992), is illustrated by the following exchange.

Tutor B:
T: The object of the program here is to make a factory. . . . We're going to be putting together an assembly line. You'll be the worker; I'll be the supervisor.
S: [Later . . .] (solves problem correctly)
T: You're a hero! Great. The customers loved it. We're still in business. More orders are coming in. . . .

Note, once again, that it is also possible to construct a more cognitive analysis of these techniques, based on the literature on context dependence in everyday learning (e.g., Lave, 1988; Rogoff, 1990; Rogoff & Lave, 1984), which documents that people frequently perform quite successfully in concrete and familiar contexts tasks that they would be unable to solve in the abstract. As before, however, it is also equally possible to view these "cognitive" phenomena themselves as having motivational origins. Indeed, the considerable distance between the actual everyday life of our young California pupils and either hockey in Canada or working in a factory may argue for a motivational interpretation of the preceding examples. Certainly, our tutors see these strategies as serving both affective and cognitive functions simultaneously.

Promoting a Sense of Personal Control

Finally, let us turn to the last of our major categories—the strategies by which exceptional tutors seek to maintain and enhance a student's feelings of personal control. Such an objective, it is worth noting, is itself an enormous challenge for tutors, because the tutoring situation is inherently a context in which the relationship between tutor and tutee is highly asymmetric and in which the student has relatively minimal actual power. Nonetheless, we do see tutors both giving their students objectively more control and working hard to give their students a greater subjective sense of personal control.

Increasing Objective Control. Certainly, the most obvious strategy for giving students a greater sense of control is to increase their actual control over the tutoring session, by providing them with a variety of choices. The potential problem with such an approach, on the other hand, is that it permits the student to make "bad" (i.e., instructionally inefficient or dysfunctional) choices. Were students offered complete control over which problems to attempt, for example, they might either intentionally (e.g., in order to avoid having to think hard) or inadvertently select problems that would prove either too easy or too difficult to promote effective learning. Indeed, the large literature on "learner control" in computer-assisted instruction clearly illustrates that even highly motivated adult learners may often make poor decisions about how to spend their own study time (e.g., Steinberg, 1977).

One important way in which our expert tutors appear to deal with this conundrum is to provide students with real choices primarily in situations in which these tutors believe that any choice made will not impede effective instruction. In part, this means explicitly offering choices to the student in situations in which the tutor is not certain what would be best for the student. Our best tutors frequently offer students choices, for instance, about whether they would like additional help from the tutor at some specific point, about whether they would find it helpful to use a particular strategy (e.g., to use manipulatives or to employ a particular representation of a math problem), and about whether they feel ready for a harder problem. In part, this also means tutors allowing students to offer their own ideas and suggestions and tutors responding to reasonable student suggestions and requests.

Tutor A:
T: Do you want another one with zeroes in the middle like that? You did that [one].
S: Why don't you try to do a harder one?
T: Oh, harder?
S: Because I did that one.
T: All righty.

In similar fashion, our best tutors are also likely to offer students frequent choices over "instructionally irrelevant" aspects of the tutoring session. These tutors, for example, are especially likely to give students choices over details of instruction, like which color of pen or paper to use, which manipulatives to employ, what names to give to characters in a word problem, and the like. Such choices, they appear to believe, provide significant motivational benefits, without running the risk of allowing children to make "poor choices" that might disrupt instructional goals.

Tutor E:
T: How many candy bars did Joe have in the beginning?
S: (lengthy pause)
T: I have a suggestion. Let's say these chips are candy bars. Do you like blue, white, or yellow?
S: Blue.
T: O.k. Let's get some blue chips and solve this problem.

In passing, we should note that, although the provision of choice to the student should generally enhance feelings of control, there are probably some limits on this effect. In fact, we believe it is likely that there is some optimal, intermediate level of choice that will be maximally motivating. Thus, if students were confronted with more choices than they could reasonably discriminate or evaluate, they may simply devalue the importance of choice and experience frustration, rather than satisfaction, as a result.

Finally, there is one other strategy that our expert tutors seem to use to promote a sense of control in their pupils. It involves the overt, physical transfer of control from the tutor to the child. Often, at the beginning of a tutoring session, a tutor may exercise a high level of control in order to focus on a limited set of problems. In math, for example, our tutors often begin by themselves writing out the problems to be given to children, in order that difficulties in writing will not compound other conceptual problems. Later, when the child has overcome other problems, the tutor may begin asking the child to write the problems himself or herself. In such situations, our most effective tutors are likely to highlight the symbolic "passing of control" from tutor to student.

Tutor B:

S: (looks at new problem) That's simple. (solves problem correctly)
T: Alright! I have to go on vacation for a couple of weeks. You take over the show. You can choose easy or medium [level] problems while I'm gone, o.k.?
S: O.k. Let me try a medium.

Increasing Subjective Control.   Even when the objective level of control the student has over the sessions is controlled, and relatively low, there remain strategies that expert tutors use to try to enhance students' *perceptions* of personal control. As is well documented in the social-psychological literature, it would seem to be the perception or experience of control, at least as much as actual control, that leads to motivational and affective benefits (e.g., Langer, 1975; Seligman, 1975; Taylor & Brown, 1988).

As in the previous cases of challenge and curiosity, we have already discussed one aspect of tutors' attempts to produce a sense of control in students, in our prior description of the indirect feedback styles of our best tutors. Indeed, the methods by which our tutors present negative feedback to students could almost be used as archetypes for the use of what Deci and colleagues (Deci, 1975, 1981; Deci & Ryan, 1985; Deci et al., 1982) have called "informational," rather than "controlling," feedback—the type of feedback that, in Deci's research, is commonly shown to lead to enhanced intrinsic motivation.

Other techniques that tutors use to promote a subjective sense of control, even in the face of minimal objective control, involve attempts to highlight what Langer (1975) has called an "illusion of control." Thus, we find our most effective tutors will sometimes pretend to offer the student a choice, or will pretend to comply with some request by that child, proceeding all the while as they had previously planned. Or, these tutors may ask a child if he or she is ready for a more difficult problem, but change only the description of the problem (as being either at the same level or more difficult) and not the problem itself as a function of the child's answer.

Tutor B:

S: (has been working on easy level problems) I want to try a harder problem.
T: You want to try a hard or a medium?
S: Medium. I'll do medium.
T: That's a good choice.

Finally, we should also note one last strategy that our expert tutors use to promote a sense of student control—namely, to emphasize the student's own agency in the situation. This last tactic involves, partly, the use of feedback directly stressing the child's agency in producing a successful outcome or, especially, in correcting his or her own work prior to feedback from the tutor.

Tutor A: Catch yourself every time, huh?

Tutor B: You figured that out really well.

Similarly, our best tutors are likely to highlight and stress verbally the "passing of control" from tutor to student, as discussed above. This last strategy may also include cases in which the child is treated by the tutor as an assistant or a collaborator, to whom the tutor turns for assistance in solving some problem.

Tutor B:
    T: So this is all pretty familiar to you?
    S: Yeah, that's easy.
    T: Well, I'm wondering if maybe you can do me a favor. I want you to help me through a couple of these problems. Now, I can do 'em, but I can't [explain them].
    S: Yeah.
    T: Let's just pick one like this one. Can you talk me through this one?

HUMAN TUTORS AND COMPUTER TUTORS

Expert human tutors, it would appear, devote at least as much time and attention to the achievement of affective and motivational goals in tutoring, as they do to the achievement of the sorts of cognitive and informational goals that dominate and characterize traditional computer-based tutors. Given the pedagogical success of these effective human tutors, the obvious question arises: Can these human motivational goals, and the tutorial strategies they spawn, be effectively incorporated into the design of future computer tutors?

Before we turn to this question, however, it may be worth noting explicitly some potentially significant limitations on our analysis of the aims and procedures of effective human tutors. As noted earlier, our observations and interviews all involve tutors working in the domain of elementary mathematics with a captive audience of children from the primary grades. We believe that this is an important domain and population. As cross-national comparisons of children in this country with their peers in Japan, Taiwan, and Korea have repeatedly demonstrated (e.g., Song & Ginsburg, 1987; Stevenson, Lee, & Stigler, 1986; Uttal, Lummis, & Stevenson, 1988), American children have fallen dramatically behind in mathematics achievement. These differences are apparent and statistically significant as early as first or second grade; they are overwhelming by the time students are in the sixth grade. Nonetheless, it seems highly likely that our analyses will be most clearly applicable to this particular context, and less so to very different student populations or areas of study.

Clearly, on the one hand, early mathematics is a domain in which the predominance of explicit algorithms, exact answers, and clear comparisons may leave weak students especially prone to feelings of relative inferiority and low self-confidence, making these considerations more salient. It may likewise be that mathematics is a topic normally taught in such an abstract and "decontextualized" manner that techniques that make problems more vivid and concrete may become especially important. Plainly, on the other hand, the specific strategies that prove most effective with elementary-school children may not be the most effective for more advanced students. Young children, for example, may be especially susceptible to the use of fantasy or playful competition, whereas older students may find these techniques silly or dishonest.

Even more critical, in this respect, may be the difference between students who, like our tutees, are *being required* to participate in a tutoring session and those who *have chosen* to seek out tutoring on their own to help them improve in some area of endeavor. For students in this latter category, for instance, indirect feedback or a sense of control may be considerably less crucial to the success of the interaction. They, more like our hypothetical "robot learner," may want only "the facts" (i.e., the information about the nature of the errors they are making that would permit them to improve their performance) presented to them as directly and efficiently as possible.

Finally, although we have had room here to sketch only the barest outline of an analysis, it seems quite likely that expert tutors will employ at least somewhat different specific strategies for different students. In particular, we would expect tutors to treat quite differently children who differ widely in their abilities or their motivations. Remedial learners, for example, should require both more cognitive scaffolding and assistance and more emotional reassurance and support than their more able and self-assured counterparts.

Keeping all these caveats in mind, then, let us return to our original question concerning the implications of our studies of expert human tutors for the design of more effective computer-based tutors. As we see it, there are three basic problems to be addressed in deciding how to generalize from human to computer tutors. The first we might call the "diagnosis problem"; it involves the question of whether the computer can obtain the information needed to diagnose accurately the motivational and affective state of the learner. The second involves the "delivery problem"; here, the question is whether the computer can effectively convey the subtle nuances necessary to the success of our human tutors' tactics. Finally, there is the "plausibility problem" of whether some sorts of information coming from the computer might have different effects than had the identical information been conveyed by a person.

The Diagnosis Problem

Consider, first, the problem of a computer's diagnosing the affective and motivational state of the learner. In the case of cognitive diagnoses regarding the misconceptions and lacunae in the child's understanding of an area, the evidence on which human tutors base their diagnoses rests heavily on information—overt errors and mistaken steps in attempted problem solutions—that is tangible and obvious. The material, moreover, lends itself to clear logical analysis, permitting the systematic testing of alternative diagnoses and strategies for overcoming diagnosed difficulties.

By contrast, the evidence on which expert human tutors base their diagnoses regarding the learner's motivational or affective state appears to be much more heavily dependent on less tangible and obvious sources of information. Although we have not completed the relevant extensive analyses of our tutoring sessions on this score, an initial hypothesis is that our tutors' affective diagnoses depend much more heavily than their cognitive assessments on inferences drawn from the student's facial expressions, body language, intonation, and other para-linguistic cues.

If so, then it may be much more difficult to model these affective diagnoses with the computer, since it seems likely that computers, for the immediate future, will remain unable to "read" such subtle information channels very effectively. On the other hand, it may be worth thinking about whether there are ways in which a computer tutor might explicitly request information about student affect and motivation on a regular basis and whether such information, in conjunction with analyses of overt performance errors, could be used to make somewhat reasonable diagnoses of this sort. Certainly one might imagine children being periodically asked to indicate how confident they are that they can solve an upcoming problem, or whether they feel that they would like a hint, or whether they are finding the session interesting or boring. How effectively such information might be used remains, of course, to be seen empirically.

The Delivery Problem

Despite these problems, suppose that we *assume* that the computer can obtain the information required to make the same motivational and affective diagnoses as expert human tutors. Would the computer be able to respond to the learner just as human tutors do? Could the computer, in particular, convey to the student the sorts of subtle, often implicit, messages that the strategies of our effective human tutors would seem to require? Could the computer, as our human tutors do, ask exactly the same question (e.g., "So how did you get that #?) with different intonations and accompaniments, so that the student will accurately perceive it as implicit positive feedback and a request for articulation in one case, but implicit negative feedback that the number is incorrect in another case.

For current computer tutors, in which communication takes place primarily through written text, this would seem to be a considerable difficulty. For the future, however, this does not seem like a deep or insoluble problem. Given the recent rapid advances both in speech synthesis and in technologies for hooking computers to random-access video- or audio-disks, it seems likely that computer tutors of the future can be equipped with an audible, nearly "human," voice capable of most of the nuances in speech that our analysis would require. Such a device, then, would resolve most of the delivery problems posed by current computer tutors.

The Plausibility Problem

Even if the computer could accurately diagnose the student's affective state and even if the computer could respond to that state (in combination with its diagnosis of the learner's cognitive state) exactly as a human tutor would, there remains one final potential difficulty: the plausibility, or perhaps the acceptability, problem. The issue here is whether the same actions and the same statements that human tutors use will have the same effect on students if delivered instead by a computer, even a computer with a virtually human voice. For many of the processes discussed above, of course, there would seem to be no problem. For others, especially those involving the tutor's own display of apparent affective and emotional responses, these issues may prove more difficult.

On the one hand, especially with young children, it is clear that students commonly anthropomorphize the computer (Turkle, 1984). Indeed, one often finds elementary school children applying personality terms (e.g., "friendly" vs. "mean" programs) and intentional analyses (e.g., "This guy [sic] is trying to mess me up here.") to the most straightforward and uninteresting of academic drills. Certainly a computer tutor with a virtually human voice, programmed to act as if it had empathy, confidence in the learner, and the like should heighten these responses. On the other hand, especially with older students, the receipt of seeming sympathy or emotional support from a machine may prove ineffective. Whatever the eventual outcome, the empirical questions that an "empathetic" computer will raise about "social" relationships will be interesting ones indeed.

ACKNOWLEDGMENTS

Preparation of this chapter and research it reports were supported, in part, by a research grant from the National Institute of Child Health and Human Development (HD-25258) to the first author. Requests for reprints may be addressed to Mark R. Lepper, Department of Psychology, Jordan Hall—Building 420, Stanford University, Stanford, California 94305-2130.

The authors wish to express their gratitude to Ralph Putnam, for his willingness to share his tutoring protocols, and to Ruth Chabay, for her perceptive insights during the early stages of this project.

REFERENCES

Anderson, J. R., Boyle, C. F., & Reiser, B. (1985). Intelligent tutoring systems. *Science, 228*, 456–468.

Attisha, M., & Yazdani, M. (1984). An expert system for diagnosing children's multiplication errors. *Instructional Science, 13,* 79–92.

Bandura, A. (1977). Self-efficacy: Toward a unifying theory of behavioral change. *Psychological Review, 84,* 191–215.

Bandura, A. (1986). *Social foundations of thought and action.* Englewood Cliffs, NJ: Prentice-Hall.

Berlyne, D. E. (1960). *Conflict, arousal, and curiosity.* New York: McGraw-Hill.

Berlyne, D. E. (1966). Curiosity and exploration. *Science, 153,* 25–33.

Bruner, J. S. (1966). *Toward a theory of instruction.* Cambridge, MA: Harvard University Press.

Collins, A., & Stevens, A. L. (1982). Goals and strategies of inquiry teachers. In R. Glaser (Ed.), *Advances in instructional psychology* (Vol. 2, pp. 65–119). Hillsdale, NJ: Lawrence Erlbaum Associates.

Condry, J. (1977). Enemies of exploration: Self-initiated versus other-initiated learning. *Journal of Personality and Social Psychology, 35,* 459–475.

Crandall, V. C., Katovsky, W., & Crandall, V. J. (1965). Children's beliefs in their own control of reinforcements in intellectual-academic achievement situations. *Child Development, 36,* 91–109.

Csikszentmihalyi, M. (1975). *Beyond boredom and anxiety.* San Francisco: Jossey-Bass.

Cuban, L. (1986). *Teachers and machines: The classroom use of technology since 1920.* New York: Teachers College Press.

Davis-Dorsey, J., Ross, S. M., & Morrison, G. R. (1991). The role of rewording and context personalization in the solving of mathematical word problems. *Journal of Educational Psychology, 83,* 61–68.

deCharms, R. (1968). *Personal causation.* New York: Academic Press.

Deci, E. L. (1975). *Intrinsic motivation.* New York: Plenum Press.

Deci, E. L. (1981). *The psychology of self-determination.* Lexington, MA: D. C. Heath.

Deci, E. L., & Ryan, R. M. (1985). *Intrinsic motivation and self-determination in human behavior.* New York: Plenum Press.

Deci, E. L., Spiegel, N. H., Ryan, R. M., Koestner, R., & Kauffman, M. (1982). Effects of performance standards on teaching styles: Behavior of controlling teachers. *Journal of Educational Psychology, 74,* 852–859.

Dede, C. J. (1986). A review and synthesis of recent research in intelligent computer-assisted instruction. *International Journal of Man-Machine Studies, 24,* 329–353.

Dreeben, R. (1968). *On what is learned in school.* Reading, MA: Addison-Wesley.

Dugdale, S., & Kibbey, D. (1980). *The fractions curriculum, PLATO elementary school mathematics project.* Champaign-Urbana, IL: University of Illinois, Computer-Based Education Research Laboratory.

Dweck. C. S. (1986). Motivational processes affecting learning. *American Psychologist, 41,* 1040–1048.

Dweck, C. S., & Elliott, E. S. (1983). Achievement motivation. In E. M. Hetherington (Ed.), *Socialization, personality, and social development* (pp. 643–681). New York: Wiley.

Foersterling, F. (1985). Attributional retraining: A review. *Psychological Bulletin, 98,* 495–512.

Fox, B. A. (1989). Cognitive and interactional aspects of correction in tutoring. In P. Goodyear (Ed.), *Teaching knowledge and intelligent tutoring.* Norwood, NJ: Ablex.

Gottfried, A. E. (1985). Academic intrinsic motivation in elementary and junior high school students. *Journal of Educational Psychology, 77,* 631–645.

Harter, S. (1978). Effectance motivation reconsidered: Toward a developmental model. *Human Development, 1,* 34–64.

Harter, S. (1982). The perceived competence scale for children. *Child Development, 53,* 87–97.

Hunt, J. M. V. (1961). *Intelligence and experience.* New York: Ronald Press.

Hunt, J. M. V. (1965). Intrinsic motivation and its role in psychological development. In D. Levine (Ed.), *Nebraska symposium on motivation* (Vol. 13, pp. 189–282). Lincoln: University of Nebraska Press.

Jackson, P. (1968). *Life in classrooms.* New York: Holt, Rinehart, and Winston.

Kagan, J. (1972). Motives and development. *Journal of Personality and Social Psychology, 22,* 51–66.

Kosel, M., & Fish, M. (1983). *The factory: Strategies in problem solving.* Pleasantville, NY: Sunburst Communications, Inc.

Kulik, J. A., Bangert, R. L., & Williams, G. W. (1983). Effects of computer-based teaching on secondary school students. *Journal of Educational Psychology, 75,* 19–26.

Langer, E. J. (1975). The illusion of control. *Journal of Personality and Social Psychology, 32,* 311–328.

Larkin, J. H., & Chabay, R. W. (1992). *Computer-assisted instruction and intelligent tutoring systems: Shared goals and complementary approaches.* Hillsdale, NJ: Lawrence Erlbaum Associates.

Lave, J. (1988). *Cognition in practice: Mind, mathematics, and culture in everyday life.* Cambridge, England: Cambridge University Press.

Leinhardt, G. (1987). Development of an expert explanation: An analysis of a sequence of subtraction lessons. *Cognition and Instruction, 4,* 225–282.

Lepper, M. R., Aspinwall, L. G., Mumme, D. L., & Chabay, R. W. (1990). Self-perception and social-perception processes in tutoring: Subtle social control strategies of expert tutors. In J. M. Olson & M. P. Zanna (Eds.), *Self-inference processes: The Ontario Symposium* (pp. 217–237). Hillsdale, NJ: Lawrence Erlbaum Associates.

Lepper, M. R., & Chabay, R. W. (1985). Intrinsic motivation and instruction: Conflicting views on the role of motivational processes in computer-based education. *Educational Psychologist, 20,* 217–230.

Lepper, M. R., & Chabay, R. W. (1988). Socializing the intelligent tutor: Bringing empathy to computer tutors. In H. Mandl & A. M. Lesgold (Eds.), *Learning issues for intelligent tutoring systems* (pp. 242–257). Chicago: Springer-Verlag.

Lepper, M. R., & Cordova, D. I. (in press). A desire to be taught: Instructional consequences of intrinsic motivation. *Motivation and Emotion.*

Lepper M. R., & Greene, D. (1978). Overjustification research and beyond: Toward a means-ends analysis of intrinsic and extrinsic motivation. In M. R. Lepper & D. Greene (Eds.), *The hidden costs of reward* (pp. 109–148). Hillsdale, NJ: Lawrence Erlbaum Associates.

Lepper, M. R., & Gurtner, J. (1989). Children and computers: Child development and education approaching the twenty-first century. *American Psychologist, 44,* 170–178.

Lepper, M. R., & Malone, T. W. (1987). Intrinsic motivation and instructional effectiveness in computer-based education. In R. E. Snow & M. J. Farr (Eds.), *Aptitude, learning, and instruction: III. Conative and affective process analyses* (pp. 255–296). Hillsdale, NJ: Lawrence Erlbaum Associates.

Locke, J. (1693). *Some thoughts concerning education.* London: A. & J. Churchill.

Malone, T. W. (1981). Toward a theory of intrinsically motivating instruction. *Cognitive Science, 4,* 333–369.

Malone, T. W., & Lepper, M. R. (1987). Making learning fun: A taxonomy of intrinsic motivations for learning. In R. E. Snow, & M. J. Farr (Eds.), *Aptitude, learning, and instruction: III. Conative and affective process analyses* (pp. 223–253). Hillsdale, NJ: Lawrence Erlbaum Associates.

McArthur, D., Stasz, C., & Zmuidzinas, M. (1990). Tutoring techniques in algebra. *Cognition and Instruction, 7,* 197–244.

McKendree, J., Reiser, B. J., & Anderson, J. R. (1984). Tutorial goals and strategies in the instruction of programming skills. *Proceedings of the Sixth Annual Conference of the Cognitive Science Society,* Boulder, CO.

Niemiec, R., & Walberg, H. J. (1987). Comparative effects of computer-assisted instruction: A synthesis of reviews. *Journal of Educational Computing Research, 3,* 19–37.

Ohlsson, S. (1986). Some principles of intelligent tutoring. *Instructional Science, 14,* 293–326.

Parker, L. E., & Lepper, M. R. (1992). Effects of fantasy contexts on children's learning and motivation: Making learning more fun. *Journal of Personality and Social Psychology, 62,* 625–633.

Piaget, J. (1951). *Play, dreams, and imitation in childhood.* New York: Norton.

Piaget, J. (1952). *The origins of intelligence in children.* New York: International Universities Press.

Putnam, R. T. (1987). Structuring and adjusting content for students: A study of live and simulated tutoring of addition. *American Educational Research Journal, 24,* 13–48.

Rogoff, B. (1990). *Apprenticeship in thinking: Cognitive development in social context.* New York: Oxford University Press.

Rogoff, B., & Lave, J. (Eds.). (1984). *Everyday cognition: Its development in social context.* Cambridge, MA: Harvard University Press.

Ross, S. M., & Anand, P. (1987). A computer-based strategy for personalizing verbal problems in teaching mathematics. *Educational Communication and Technology Journal, 35,* 151–162.

Ross, S. M., McCormick, D., & Krisak, N. (1986). Adapting the thematic context of mathematical problems to student interests: Individual versus group-based strategies. *Journal of Educational Research, 79,* 245–252.

Rousseau, J. (1762). *Emile.* Paris: Gallimard.

Schunk, D. H. (1983). Reward contingencies and the development of children's skills and self-efficacy. *Journal of Educational Psychology, 75,* 511–518.

Schunk, D. H. (1984). Self-efficacy perspective on achievement behavior. *Educational Psychologist, 19,* 48–58.

Schunk, D. H. (1985). Self-efficacy and classroom learning. *Psychology in the Schools, 22,* 208–223.

Seligman, M. E. P. (1975). *Helplessness: On depression, development, and death.* San Francisco: W. H. Freeman.

Shulman, L. S. (1986). Assessment of teaching: An initiative for the profession. *Phi Delta Kappan,* 38–44.

Slamecka, N. J., & Graf, P. (1978). The generation effect: Delineation of a phenomenon. *Journal of Experimental Psychology: Human Learning and Memory, 4,* 592–604.

Sleeman, D., & Brown, J. S. (Eds.). (1982). *Intelligent tutoring systems.* New York: Academic Press.

Song, M-J., & Ginsburg, H. P. (1987). The development of informal and formal mathematical thinking in Korean and U.S. children. *Child Development, 58,* 1286–1296.

Steinberg, E. R. (1977). Review of student control in computer-assisted instruction. *Journal of Computer-Based Instruction, 3,* 84–90.

Stevenson, H. W., Lee, S. Y., & Stigler, J. W. (1986). Mathematics achievement of Chinese, Japanese, and American children. *Science, 231,* 693–699.

Suppes, P. (1966). The uses of computers in education. *Scientific American, 215,* 206–221.

Taylor, R. P. (Ed.). (1980). *The computer in the school: Tutor, tool, tutee.* New York: Teachers College Press.

Taylor, S. E., & Brown, J. D. (1988). Illusion and well-being: A social psychological perspective on mental health. *Psychological Bulletin, 103,* 193–210.

Turkle, S. (1984). *The second self: Computers and the human spirit.* New York: Simon & Schuster.

Uttal, D. H., Lummis, M., & Stevenson, H. W. (1988). Low and high mathematics achievement in Japanese, Chinese, and American elementary-school children. *Developmental Psychology, 24,* 335–342.

Weiner, B. (1979). A theory of motivation for some classroom experiences. *Journal of Educational Psychology, 71,* 3–25.

Wenger, E. (1987). *Artificial intelligence and tutoring systems.* Los Altos, CA: Morgan Kaufmann.

White, R. W. (1959). Motivation reconsidered: The concept of competence. *Psychological Review, 66,* 297–333.

4

Local Cognitive Modeling of Problem-Solving Behavior: An Application of Fuzzy Theory

Sharon J. Derry
University of Wisconsin–Madison

Lois W. Hawkes
Florida State University

This chapter describes theoretical issues, basic research, and computational methodology underlying local student modeling in TAPS, an ITS for improving word-problem skills at grade-levels 4 through remedial 13. By local student modeling we refer to system capabilities that carry out on-line performance monitoring and error recognition for the purpose of informing local tutoring decisions, and distinguish these from system capabilities that focus on global evaluations of student progress for the purpose of selecting and sequencing curriculum-level instructional goals.

To some extent this chapter responds to issues raised by the introductory chapter to this volume, issues pertaining the "intractable problem of student modeling" (Self, 1988). Many criticisms aimed at the student modeling enterprise have focused on particular methods, namely model-tracing and buggy diagnostic approaches. The problem with most model tracing methods is that students' problem-solving moves must somehow be restricted to particular paths so that the system can follow what the student is doing. The basic assumption surrounding the buggy diagnostic approach is that students' buggy knowledge can be identified during performance by equating each faulty student move to a particular bug in the system's "bug catalog." Buggy diagnostics and model tracing, once seemingly promising methods, have proved to be computationally difficult for developers and (some would argue) overly restrictive for students. Moreover, recent studies of expert human tutors in action show that tutoring decisions seldom involve diagnosis at the bug level of specificity (e.g., McArthur, Stasz, & Zmuidzinas, 1990).

But even though good human tutors may not perform detailed diagnostics as they intervene to help students, they evidently do carry out a less exacting degree of error detection and interpretation. A number of researchers have recently begun to examine and model the decision-making processes by which human tutors control the timing, content, and style of tutorial intervention. (e.g., Fox, 1988a; 1988b; Lepper, 1989; Lepper et al., this volume; Lepper & Chabay, 1988; McArthur, Stasz, & Zmuidzinas, 1990; Reiser, 1989). One important aspect of the emerging picture is that good tutors neither wait for students to request assistance, nor interrupt student performance to deliver unnecessary explanations and mini-lessons. Rather, good tutors typically intervene in response to indicators that the student is experiencing difficulty with a problem-solving process. That is, good tutors give hints, helps, and motivational encouragements primarily at points where errors occur.

An error-driven approach to tutoring is highly consistent with the cognitive-apprenticeship model of instruction (Collins, Brown, & Newman, 1989). In its simplest form, cognitive apprenticeship denotes the sharing of a problem-solving experience between a student and mentor. More complex forms involve social problem solving in groups where members function in either student or mentorship roles. Brown (1987) has outlined a three-stage model of cognitive apprenticeship, based on observations of effective mentor/apprentice dialogues, that specifies different roles for mentors at each stage. In the first stage, the mentor serves as a model problem solver, thinking aloud to demonstrate the forms of executive control involved. Stage two is a complex activity whereby mentor and student work together. Control processes continue to be made public through dialogue, although the mentor guides and prompts only when the student falters or makes a query. It is in this stage that mentorship most resembles error-driven tutoring. In the final stage, the mentor cedes control to the student, functioning primarily as a supportive audience. Such cognitive apprenticeship is believed to help students development important metacognitive knowledge, knowledge about the thinking process itself and how to control it. (e.g., Baker & Brown, 1984; Palincsar, 1986).

In sum, from perspectives based on cognitive apprenticeship philosophy as well as findings of research on effective human tutors, we see that effective human tutoring appears to be neither highly controlling nor dependent on exact cognitive diagnoses. However, effective tutoring does appear to be error-driven. Thus, to the extent that a goal of intelligent tutoring research is to build computer-based systems that emulate strengths of expert human tutors, it follows that researchers must continue to seek feasible, tractable methods for monitoring performance and recognizing errors in a computer-based environment without sacrificing desired user flexibility. The work to be reported in this chapter relates to this goal. Specifically, we describe research associated with development of a fuzzy computational approach to error-driven local modeling in TAPS, an intelligent tutoring system for complex arithmetic word-problem solving. We offer the TAPS approach as an example of a feasible middle ground between specific diagnosis based on model tracing and identification of procedural bugs, on the one hand, and no local modeling at all on the other.

A Theory of Word-Problem Performance

We chose complex, multistep arithmetic word problems as the domain for our work, with particular emphasis on problems representing realistic, daily situations in which people use basic math. Although such problems are very common, many American students are very poor at solving them (e.g., Lapointe, Mead, & Phillips, 1989; National Commission on Excellence in Education, 1983; National Science Board Commission, 1983). Studies reported here show that even typical college students can experience great difficulty with multistep arithmetic word problems representing everyday situations—configuring and buying pizzas, for example. Lack of this basic problem-solving ability also is evident within our military services (see Derry & Kellis, 1986; Hechinger, 1983).

To understand the nature of the difficulties exhibited, it helps to imagine problem solving as an active construction process that involves trying to determine how all the sets of a complex problem fit together. Many researchers characterize this process as one of activating, organizing, and operating on previously learned schemas, mental abstractions that allow set-relationship patterns in problem situations to be recognized and that indicate actions appropriate for those patterns. For example, if John had 6 marbles but gave away 3 of them, this situation is recognized as an instance of a change relation, which has a start set, a transfer set, and a result set that is a later version of the start set. Although there are many possible types of relational schemas found in word problems, research by Marshall (1985; Marshall, Pribe, & Smith, 1987) indicates that a limited set of five relational schemas can account for a very large proportion of the word problems found in this country's public school textbooks and standardized adult remedial training materials.

Examples of the types of complex, multistep problems used in our research are shown in Table 4.1. Such problems require that students combine multiple relational schemas to create problem representations that may never have occurred in the past and may never again be needed in future. Our research has indicated that a persistent developmental difficulty in adult problem solving stems not from misconceptions associated with underlying arithmetic relations but rather from comprehension and memory-management processes associated with constructing representations of complex problem situations. For example, we have available test data for 81 typical 7th graders and 244 typical college students showing the percentage of students in each sample who successfully solved problems of varying complexity. Virtually all college subjects and most 7th graders were able to solve all categories of single-schema word problems, indicating basic understanding of arithmetic concepts. However, both groups

TABLE 4.1
Multischema Problems Used in Studies

Problems Used in Study 1 with College Students

1.   The gang is sending Sam out for pizza. Dominoes sells its large pizza with three toppings for 12 bucks. Extra cheese is 2 bucks, and extra sauce is another 2 bucks. Additional toppings are $1.00 each. Sam is supposed to get two large pizzas. They want one with 4 and one with 5 toppings. Both pizzas will have extra cheese. Sam has a coupon that gets him 2 dollars off per pizza for an order of two or more. So far he has collected $20.00 from the group. How much more must he collect?

2.   Dr. Smith is buying AI machnes for his lab. Xerox sells a machine with 4 megabytes of RAM for $12K each. Adding a PC board costs another $1K, and adding a 60 meg hard disk is $3K. Extra RAM is $2K per megabyte. Smith decides to buy two AI machines, one with 5 megabytes of RAM and one with 6 megabytes. He will add a hard disk to each machine. Xerox gives him an educational discount of $1K per machine. Smith has $30K in grant money. How much most be added by the dean?

3.   The PTO gave Moore Elementary School 450 dollars. The school wants to use the money to send students on a field trip to the museum. In the third grade there are 55 boys, 60 girls, and 5 teachers. The boys and girls get in for a dollar each. The teachers' tickets cost 2 dollars each. Snacks are 1 dollar each. After the third grade trip, will there be enough money for the fourth grade to go? The fourth grade has 100 boys and girls, and 4 teachers. Assume that two students will be absent on each trip.

4.   In smalltown, teenagers earn money by selling ads for the local newspaper. Together, Lee and Jamie were allowed to sell 3 pages of ads. Each page holds 15 large ads or 30 small ads. Large ads cost $200 and small ads cost $100. The girls earned fifty cents for every small ad and a dollar for every large one. Lee worked one weekend and sold 16 large ads and 17 small ads. Jamie worked the following weekend and sold all the remaining ads. How much less than Lee did Jamie make?

Problems Used in Study 3 with 5th and 7th graders

5.   Yesterday Fred drove 4 miles in the morning and 7 miles in the afternoon. Today he drove 6 miles in the morning and 10 miles in the afternoon. How many more miles did he drive today than yesterday?

6.   Alan wants to rent an apartment for 6 months. Apartment 1 costs 200 dollars a month. Apartment 2 costs $150 a month plus utilities, which are 75 dollars. Which apartment will cost him less, and by how much?

7.   George is going out for doughnuts. He has 5 dollars and wants to buy as many glazed doughnuts as he can. He also has to buy his sister 5 chocolate doughnuts. Glazed doughnuts cost 10 cents apiece or 1 dollar for a baker's dozen. Chocolate doughnuts cost 20 cents apiece or 1 dollar for half a dozen. How many glazed doughnut can George buy?

experienced increasingly greater difficulty as the complexity of word problems increased.

Are there certain categories of knowledge or skill that enable some students to conceptualize complex problems while others cannot? In agreement with Schoenfeld (1985, 1987), Salomon and Perkins (1989), Garofalo and Lester (1985) and others, we believe that an important type of knowledge underlying the construction of complex representations and solution strategies is "metacognitive knowledge" (Flavell, 1979, 1981), which refers to a cognitive system's intelligence about itself and its ability to regulate and control its own operation. For problem solving, two important metacognitive abilities are self-monitoring and planning.

Self-monitoring refers to an individual's ability to conduct on-line self-checks of the problem-solving process, a skill that is particularly important when the subject deals with an ambiguous or confusing problem. Good problem solvers behave as though equipped with ever-present monitors operating just below the surface of consciousness (Schoenfeld, 1983). If no errors or misunderstandings occur, problem solving proceeds on automatic pilot. But when the problem posed is in some way unfamiliar, difficult, or ambiguous, the proficient problem solver behaves as though a hidden monitor is active, which alerts the processor whenever the process may be going awry. The less proficient problem solver seems oblivious to warnings, such as unfamiliar concepts, unreasonably complicated reasoning, or long strings of calculations that do not converge on a goal. When such signals occur, the expert automatically interrupts processing and seeks clarification or reexamines the problem-solving strategy. The novice is more likely to continue with a faulty approach.

Planning involves breaking a complex problem down into subgoals that can be solved separately and sequentially to reach a final solution. Planning strategies enable problem solvers to determine which subgoals should be obtained in what order. The importance of planning knowledge to the process of constructing and understanding a complex problem is easily illustrated. Consider the potential role of planning knowledge in constructing a meaningful representation for the problem that follows:

(A)   John's age is 9 now. He receives an allowance of 15 cents per day. His grandmother also sends him a $100 savings bond every Christmas. Each year on his birthday, his father plans to raise John's allowance by $1.00 per week. How much will John's daily allowance be when he is 12 years old?

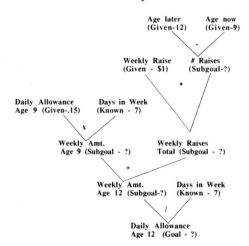

FIG. 4.1.   Tree structure resulting from working backward strategy.

One planning strategy that could help is working backward. Using this strategy, one first determines a final operation that will produce the goal. If the final operation cannot be performed immediately, then a subgoal is set to produce the precondition for the final operation. If the subgoal cannot be reached, then a sub-subgoal is set to produce the precondition for obtaining the subgoal, etc. This working backward process continues until a complete plan develops, as shown by the tree in Fig. 4.1. This tree, which makes clear the entire subgoal structure for the problem and eliminates unnecessary information, can be viewed as a particular problem conceptualization.

THE TAPS SYSTEMS

TAPS is a computer-based instructional tool programmed for the NeXT machine that is designed to serve as catalyst for helping students acquire planning, self-monitoring, and other types of metacognitive knowledge and awareness believed to be important for complex problem solving. In designing TAPS, we embraced Vygotsky's (1978) notion of cognitive tools—objects provided by the learning environment that permit students to incorporate new auxiliary methods or symbols into their problem-solving activity that otherwise would be unavailable. The major cognitive tool provided by TAPS is a graphics interface that facilitates construction of problem trees, network structures showing interrelationships among all relevant sets in a problem situation, specifying the subgoal structure of the problem, and illustrating a solution path. Tree structures such as the one illustrated in Fig. 4.1 provide a scheme for complexity management that is useful in conceptualizing many types of problems.

As shown in Fig. 4.2, a student or group working on TAPS is presented with a complex word problem to solve. Complexity and story content of each problem can be varied to match the abilities and backgrounds of system users. To make possible the construction of a tree, the system provides a menu of blank tree-node subtree diagrams ("schemas"), shown to the right of the screen in Fig. 4.2. Students proceed by selecting subtree diagrams from this menu and moving them into the workspace one at a time.

In the workspace each subtree is filled in with labels, values, and an operator so that it represents a particular set relationship from the problem. Students must select labels and operators from those supplied in menus that appear when users click at certain points on a subtree in the workspace. In this way, the system unobtrusively scaffolds students in the process of selecting subgoal sets by suggesting to them the range of possibilities available. Numerical values also appear in menus, although students may supply other numbers using the system's calculator. When filled in each subtree represents a simple equation such that the two nodes at the tope of the subtree represent two sets that can be related by an arithmetic operation to produce the set value represented by the bottom node.

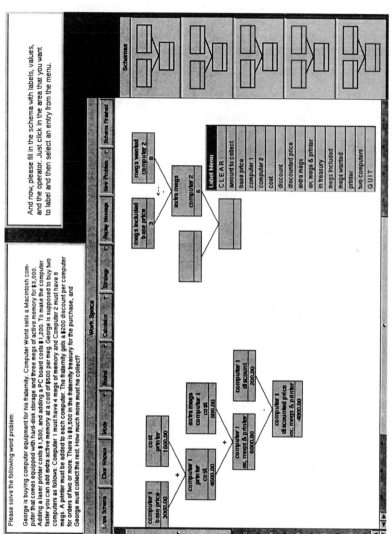

Please solve the following word problem:

George is buying computer equipment for his fraternity. Computer World sells a Macintosh computer that comes equipped with hard-disk storage and three megs of active memory for $3,000. Adding a laser printer costs $1,500, and adding a PC board costs $1,200. To make the computer faster you can add extra active memory at a cost of $500 per meg. George is supposed to buy two computers as follows: Computer 1 must have 4 megs of memory and Computer 2 must have 8 megs. A printer must be added to each computer. The fraternity gets a $200 discount per computer for orders of two or more. There is $9,500 in the fraternity treasury for the purchase, and George must collect the rest. How much more must he collect?

And now, please fill in the schema with labels, values, and the operator. Just click in the area that you want to label and then select an entry from the menu.

FIG. 4.2. TAPS screen illustrating system tools and partially worked problem.

113

Each blank schema in the subtree menu is shaded differently to indicate where it can be attached to another subtree. System users select the appropriate subtree diagram and then "click" with the mouse at the point on the problem tree (in the workspace) where the new schema will be attached. In this manner, students can chain subtree schemas together to form complex tree structures, as shown in Fig. 4.2. Each time a schema is added to the workspace and filled in with labels and set values, a step in the problem-solving process has been completed.

When a step is completed to the users' satisfaction, the button labeled "schema finished" is pressed. This is the system's signal to perform an analysis of the students' progress. Analysis of each problem-solving step is carried out by a "diagnoser" that attempts to match the students' evolving solution tree to one of the solution trees contained in the system's knowledge base. Tutorial feedback is conditional upon the diagnosis and can be provided through one of two channels: either printed visually in message windows, as shown in Fig. 4.2. Or, the visual message displays can be deactivated and system messages received aurally as voice feedback.

In the hands of an able instructor, peer tutor, or student with an exploratory bent, TAPS can serve as a powerful and flexible demonstrator of the idea that different solution paths, alternative conceptual analyses, and different search strategies can be combined to generate equally "correct" (albeit, not always equally efficient) solutions to the same problem. Another idea that can be demonstrated or discovered with TAPS is that many problems with drastically different surface features, objects, and topics are strategically and conceptually similar on a more abstract level. When appropriately deployed in a classroom environment that encourages exploration and reflective social interaction, TAPS will stimulate students and instructors to engage in planning and self-monitoring, and to discover how and why alternative problem-solving approaches work differently for different classes of problem situations.

However, the TAPS system is capable of much more than merely serving as an unintelligent cognitive tool that stimulates exploration and interaction, for it is able to monitor and trace the performance of users during problem-solving sessions. TAPS can recognize and interpret a range of different problem-solving errors and has the capability of recognizing and interpreting patterns of errors in problem-solving performance. This diagnostic capability is what makes it possible to implement intelligent tutoring strategies in accordance with the cognitive apprenticeship model. The remainder of this chapter describes research pertaining to development of TAPS's monitoring and error-recognition capability.

THE ERROR-DETECTION STUDIES

The goal of these studies was to gain knowledge about the kinds of errors students typically make while solving complex arithmetic word problems.

EXPERIMENT 1

Subjects and Procedures

Subjects in the first study were five "expert" and five "novice" problem solvers selected from a pool of 244 introductory psychology students who participated for course credit. Subjects' membership in either the novice or expert category was determined by their scores on the TAPS test, our own 2-hour experimental test of word-problem skills. The TAPS test consists of 117 multiple-choice items designed to measure students' ability to identify sets and set relationships in word problems, as well as their performance on problems representing both simple and complex combinations of five basic relational schemas representing additive, multiplicative and proportional structures.

Subjects scoring in the upper 15% range (at or above 91%) on the TAPS distribution were designated as "experts," and those scoring in the lower 15% range (at or below 75%) were designated as "novices." Five expert and five novice subjects were chosen by randomly selecting from these upper and lower groups. There were 3 females and 2 males in the lower group, with an average overall SAT score of 845. There were 4 females and 1 male in the high group, with an average SAT score of 1,198.

The methodology employed for examining students' errors was think-aloud protocol analysis (Ericsson & Simon, 1984; Schoenfeld, 1983, 1985). Each of the 10 selected subjects received individual training and practice in think-aloud procedures and then thought aloud as they solved, using pencil and paper, the first four complex word problems shown in Table 4.1. We note that three of these problems (number 1, 2, and 4) deliberately included information that was irrelevant to the problem solution and one problem (number 3) contained an ambiguous phrase requiring interpretation. One problem (number 2) dealt with world knowledge known to be unfamiliar to the subject population. Our decision to incorporate these features into the problem set was based on the assumption that such difficulties often are present in both real-word and textbook problems and that students must possess the problem-solving skills necessary for dealing with them.

Each subject was allowed to work for up to 8 minutes on each problem. If the subject lapsed into silence for more than 3 seconds during a session, the experimenter immediately tapped lightly on the subject's shoulder as a reminder to think aloud. If a problem was solved either correctly or incorrectly within the time limit, the experimenter inquired whether the subject was totally satisfied with the answer. This sometimes resulted in the subject's choosing to rework the problem. When time expired or the subject indicated satisfaction with the answer, the subject was asked to provide a verbal recap explaining what the subject thought and did while the problem was being solved. The entire problem-solving session was recorded and transcribed for analysis.

115

Coding and Analysis

As noted by Ericsson and Simon (1984), the analysis of think-aloud protocol data requires that a theoretical perspective be adopted as a basis for development of a coding system. Because our theory states that solving word problems involves the recognizing and chaining together of set relations, our approach to protocol analysis involved depicting each subject's solution as a binary tree representing the set relationships that were identified by the subject and how they were connected together arithmetically.

An example protocol with its corresponding tree coding is shown as Fig. 4.3. This particular example is a comparatively short and simple protocol chosen for illustrative purposes. As shown, the tree code explicitly represents every set and relational schema recognized by a subject, the subgoal set computed from each relational schema, the order in which the relational schemas are entered into the problem representation, and the connecting together of schemas through their common sets. The meaning and values assigned by the subject to each set in the problem representation was coded by extracting the relevant terms and phrases directly from the protocol and using them to label the sets in the tree representation of the problem-solving session. The coding was further enriched by noting points in the construction process where idle periods of more than 10 seconds occurred, where questions were asked, and where other verbalizations occurred. Checking and retracing of problem-solving steps were indicated by drawing an arrow identifying the beginning and ending points of these activities (no retracing occurred in the example protocol). Checking was distinguished from restarts, instances in which the subject abandoned a current solution strategy and made a fresh start. Restarts, whether spontaneous or prompted by the experimenter, were coded as new trials, each with a separate binary tree. Restarts also were distinguished from spontaneous corrections or changes to the current problem representation, which were indicated by drawing a line through the abandoned portion of the tree and writing in the subject's correction.

To help interpret errors in student trees, for every experimental problem we theoretically conceptualized an AND/OR tree of all possible semantically meaningful solutions. Using the AND/OR solution tree as a standard, each student tree could then be judged by comparing it to the corresponding AND/OR "expert" tree. First, the student tree was matched to the appropriate AND/OR branch to determine which strategy the subject was attempting to pursue. Once a strategy was identified, the student's and the expert's solution trees were "matched" to determine where and how the student deviated from the expert solution. To the extent that a subject had pursued an acceptable strategy, the subject's tree matched one of the expert's solution branches. But when the subject tree deviated from the path specified by the expert tree, a mistake was indicated. Each such deviation in the subjects' protocols was noted and described.

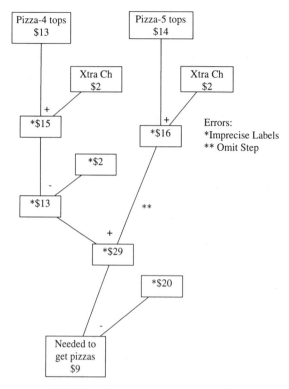

FIG. 4.3.   Example of coded protocol.

The next step in the analysis was to determine which of the coded deviations represented parent, or critical, errors. A parent error is an uncorrected source error that causes other errors to be propagated throughout a solution tree. To provide a simple example, suppose that a problem statement specifies that the cost of one doughnut is $.35, but the subject accidentally enters an incorrect value of $.25 into a calculation to determine the cost of 6 doughnuts. The resulting subgoal set (cost of 6 doughnuts) also will contain an incorrect value, as will all subsequent calculations that are derived from the incorrect subgoal set. Thus the student's tree will fail to match the expert tree at several locations. However, only one of these deviations, the original bad value, is relevant as a parent error, since if it is corrected all subsequent deviations will disappear.

Findings of Error Analysis

Eleven general categories of deviation errors were observed, accounting for more than 98% of all errors in this sample. To further enhance the potential for

TABLE 4.2
Definition of Error Categories

---

1. Bad value assignment (4 subtypes): Value for set required in solution is incorrect in otherwise correctly labeled schema.

    1.1: Transfer error. Set value given in problem and entered into solution, but subject makes incorrect transfer into problem solution.

    1.2: Inference error. Set value not given but can be inferred or easily calculated based on problem information. World knowledge may be required to infer appropriate Value. However, value determined through mental calculation or inference is incorrect and is entered into solution.

    1.3: Propagation error: Set value entered into solution has been obtained from previous bad schema-based operation (e.g., bad schema, bad calc).

    1.4: Others. All others not listed above.

Plausible interpretations: Carelessness, lack of self-monitoring. For error condition 1.2, could be due to lack of world or specialized knowledge, or ambiguous wording or problem statement.

2. Bad label (2 subtypes): Schema is correct and present in solution path, but one set is imperfectly or imprecisely labeled, *and* this leads to problems.

    2.1: Imprecise label. For example, instead of labeling a set as "Cost of apartment one month," set may be labeled "Cost of apartment."

    2.2: Other. Any labeling problem not covered above.

Plausible interpretations: There is no error, student is taking notational shortcut and has accurate representation in WM; Student has overlooked important, discriminating detail, is overgeneralizing Student is being careless with memory management, failing to make detailed notes when needed.

3. Bad schema (5 subtypes): Student constructs schema that is not on current solution path. Any schema is bad if it has at least one set that is clearly mislabled.

    3.1: Bad subgoal. Student sets subgoal to compute set that is not on current solution path. A "correct" schema may be formed for the unneeded set.

    3.2: Irrelevant data. Schema not in solution is constructed because student has failed to eliminate irrelevant problem information. This may result in extra schema, a hybrid schema that combines irrelevant with valid solution sets, or in the substituting of a wrong for a correct schema.

    3.3: Good subgoal. Student clearly has set a good subgoal that is on current solution path and is attempting to calculate that subgoal, but is combining wrong sets for calculating it.

    3.4: Strategy confusion: Student is on one solution path, but then "borrows" schema that is not on current solution path but is correct for another one. This code is used only when there is confusion between two strategies.

    3.5: Other. All schema errors that do not fit clearly in categories described above.

Plausible interpretations: Lack of planning knowledge or planning skill; opting to use a trial-and-error, data-driven strategy of working forward, with little or no prior planning. Carelessness, lack of solf-monitoring; (if error uncorrected); Unspecified comprehension difficulty, possibly resulting from difficult or ambiguous text. In case of 3.3, schema knowledge, rather than planning, would be implicated.

4. Arithmetic errors (2 subtypes)

    4.1: Calculation error. Correct schema and operation indicated but student makes arithmetic error while computing unknown set value. Error may be decimal error. Error is typically propagated through entire solution.

    4.2: Wrong attachment. Correct sets have been related but wrong operator is applied.

(continued)

TABLE 4.2
(*Continued*)

Plausible interpreations: Lack of schema knowledge; Carelessness.

5.   Omit errors (3 subtypes)

    5.1:   Omit step (schema). Student is pursuing correct solution strategy but one schema is omitted.
    5.2:   Omit branch. Student omits entire branch in problem-solving strategy.
    5.3:   Premature goal. Nearing end of basically correct path, but does not completely finish solution. May have failed to identify goal.

Plausible interpretations: Memory overload and poor memory management; Comprehension difficulty leading to overgeneralization, failing to perceive important, discriminating details; Carelessness, impulsiveness, failure to completely analyze problem, accompanied by lack of self-monitoring; Failure to develop adequate subgoal plan, due to lack of planning knowledge and/or skill.

6.   Isolated bits (2 subtypes)

    6.1:   Non-schema set. Names (writes down) or calculates set but is unable to relate it to other sets.
    6.2:   Non-strategy schema. Names or calculates schema, but is unabale to connect it to a strategy.

Plausible interpretations: Lack of planning knowledge and/or planning ability. Lack of elementary chaining skill (ability to join schemas). Unspecified reading comprehension problems, possibly due to ambiguous wording of problem statement. Lazy processing, failure to analyze in depth, lack of effort.

7.   Hesitancy: Long idle period with no action.

Plausible interpretations: Lack of effort; Distraction; Comprehension failure, can't identify suitable schema; Confusion in planning, can't identify a next step. Thinking about or checking work covertly.

8.   Wild goose chase: Three or more bad schemas connected together as solution strategy.

Possible interpretations: Lack of planning knowledge or skill; Self-monitoring failure; Miscomprehension of problem statement.

9.   Given up: Student decides to quit or make wild stab at answer without completing solution strategy.

    9.1:   Promising effort. Gives up before finishing good strategy.
    9.2:   Unpromising effort. Abandons unpromising effort.

Plausible interpretations: Motivational problem; Running out of available time, in a hurry to finish, class period possibly ending.

10.   Strategy shift: Student begins new schema and continues on a different path than one that was being pursued.

    10.1:   Unnecessary shift. Abandons promising effort.
    10.2:   Other

Plausible interpretation: Lacks subgoal plan, using trial-and-error, data-driven processing, which has led to instantiation of viable schema that is part of a different plan.

11.   Time expires.

Plausible interpretations: Difficult problem; Generally poor problem-solving skill; Poor motivation, lack of effort.

TABLE 4.3
Types of Critical Errors Observed in Eighty Protocols Obtained from Ten Experts and Ten Novices
in Two Problem-Solving Studies, Expressed in Termed of Absolute Frequencies and Percentage
of Total Critical Errors

Error Category	Experts			Novices		
	Study 1	Study 2	% of Total	Study 1	Study 2	% of Total
Bad schema	8	4	29	10	6	21
Bad set value	5	1	15	6	1	09
Lavel problems*	0	2	05	4	5	12
Omit step/branch	1	6	17	8	5	17
Isolated bit	3	4	17	0	4	05
Arithmetic error	1	1	05	1	5	08
Abandon good strat.	1	0	02	1	5	08
Hesitancies	0	0	0	4	2	08
Time expires	1	1	05	2	1	04
Gives up	1	0	02	1	3	05
Wild goose chase	0	0	0	1	1	03
Other	1	0	02	0	1	01
Totals	22	19		38	39	

*Number of protocols in which labeling errors found.

diagnostic specificity, it was possible to subdivide these error categories into a number of more specific categories. Shown in Table 4.2 is a detailed listing of major error categories. The frequencies with which each general category was observed in both expert and novice protocols are shown in the first and fourth columns (labeled Study 1) of Table 4.3. Frequencies in Table 4.3 refer only to uncorrected critical errors, that is, parent errors that were sources of all mistakes made in problem solving that ultimately led to an incorrect answer. Critical errors must be the primary focus in tutoring because when these are eliminated, all other errors disappear.

In sum, both experts and novices made critical problem-solving errors that led to incorrect answers, although experts (not surprisingly) made fewer errors. There were eleven distinctively different ways in which students' solution trees deviated from expert solutions. The most frequently seen critical deviation was the insertion of an incorrect schema into the solution strategy. Schema omissions and insertion of bad set values also occurred with relatively high frequency. Together, these three types of deviations accounted for more than 60% of all critical errors observed.

EXPERIMENTS 2 AND 3

The purpose of these studies was to estimate the validity and reliability of the error categories derived from Experiment 1 by determining their fit to protocol data collected from different subjects using different word problems.

Subjects and Procedures

In experiment 2 we employed identical procedures for both data collection and subject selection, but employed a different (although structurally similar) set of word problems and another sample of five expert and five novice subjects. Study 3 employed very similar data-collection procedures but easier word problems and a sample of 16 5th and 7th grade students from the Florida State Developmental Research School who were nominated by their teachers as representing a full range of ability levels with respect to arithmetic word problems. Examples of problems used in the study with school children are included in Table 4.1. As with the problems given to adult subjects, children's problems contained a moderate degree of both ambiguity and unfamiliar world knowledge.

Procedures for identifying errors were identical to those described in Study 1. However, in addition to the experimenters' codings, the same error-identification analysis was performed on a subset of fourteen representative protocols by an independent coder. A reliability estimate on the coding procedures was determined by dividing the total number of matching error codes for the two raters by the total number of error codes assigned by the two raters. The reliability thus represented the percentage of codings that matched and was determined to be .91.

Results

In both experiments, the error-classification system accounted for approximately 99% of all observed errors. The ability to account for almost all error conditions for both populations with only eleven basic error categories is significant, since it indicates that comprehensive error identification for multiple age levels can be accomplished with a system that recognizes only eleven basic error patterns. This is a highly feasible and tractable programming problem. Also, as suggested in Table 4.2, each error category can be associated with a set of possible instructional interpretations, although more sophisticated and accurate interpretations would likely require recognition of complex error patterns. This issue is discussed later in the chapter.

Summary findings for all three studies are provided in Table 4.4, which shows major error categories and compares their frequencies as parent errors for expert and novice college subjects, and for children. An interesting point of distinction between groups was the relatively high number of omit errors in children's protocols, indicating that a major difficulty for children is that they frequently ignore subgoal schemas that are essential for obtaining the solution.

THE PROTOTYPE SYSTEM

System Components

We have applied the findings of our error analyses to the development of an on-line monitoring and error-detection capability in TAPS. TAPS, as most ITSs,

TABLE 4.4
Critical Errors Made by Expert and Novice College Subjects and Children Expressed as
Frequency and Percentage of Group Totals

Error Type	Experts (n = 10) 40 Protocols		Novices (n = 10) 40 Protocols		Children (n = 10) 48 Protocols	
	Freq.	%	Freq.	%	Freq.	%
Bad schema	12	.29	16	.21	15	.17
Bad Set	6	.15	7	.09	7	.08
Label problems*	2	.05	9	.12	5	.06
Omit step or branch	7	.17	13	.17	40	.46
Isolated bit	7	.17	4	.05	1	.01
Arithmetic error	2	.05	6	.08	12	.14
Abandon good strat.	1	.02	6	.08	2	.02
Hesitancies	0	.00	6	.08	3	.03
Time expires	2	.05	3	.04	1	.01
Gives up	1	.02	4	.05	2	.02
Wild goose chase	0	.00	2	.03	0	.00
Other	1	.02	1	.01	0	.00
Totals	41		77		88	

*Number of protocols in which labeling problems found.

consists of four basic modules: interface, student record, domain expertise, and (still under development) teaching expertise (Wenger, 1987). In the following discussion we briefly overview the first three components of our ITS and then provide more detail on development of the monitoring and error-detection capabilities in the fourth module. We give examples to illustrate our approach rather than give technical details of the associated algorithms. Although the examples illustrate only some of the errors that can be detected, the same approach is used for all of the types of errors observed in the error studies just described.

The Interface

As previously described, the interface requires students to employ graphic tools in constructing tree solutions for given word problems. Solutions are formed by selecting, filling in, and linking simple relational schemas. Graphics tools are provided that allow the student to *build* solutions from blank schema triads, as shown in Fig. 4.4a. Each schema represents two sets from the problem that can be joined together by an operator to give a third set. The blank schemas are filled in, or instantiated, by the student using labels and operators from pop-up menus. Each problem in the system has an associated set of labels and operators stored with it. The chosen labels are inserted with a mouse into the appropriate location

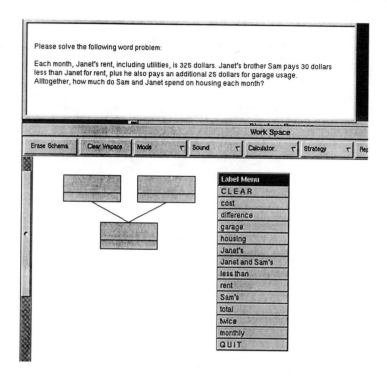

FIG. 4.4.   TAPS solutions to rent problem.
4(a).   Screen showing rent problem, blank schema and label menu.
4(b)–4(e).   Four paths representing instantiation of stored tree solutions.

in the schema. Figures 4.4(b)–4.4(e) show four possible solutions for "the rent problem" that can be built by filling in schemas and joining them together.

The Student Record

A generalized student record is being developed independently of the tutoring system and is described in Holmes (1991). The technique described next was developed for the student record and borrowed for use in the tutoring module.

Based on the observation that the presence of certain sets of attributes implies the presence of another higher-order attribute, our technique looks for *patterns* of attributes in order to draw conclusions, i.e. we use such patterns to make inferences. For example, a schema-omission error (attribute 1) appearing with an imprecise label error (attribute 2) implies an overgeneralization error (higher-order attribute). We represent a particular combination of attributes as a particular linear equation, with weights representing the importance of a specific attribute

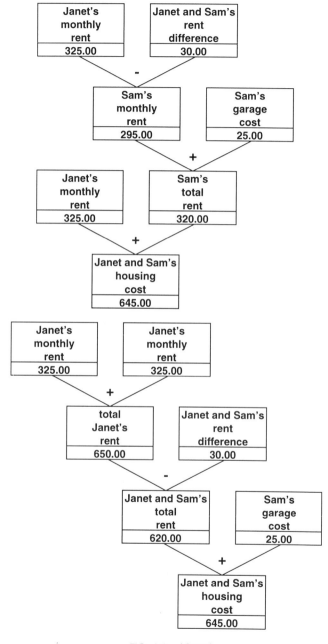

FIG. 4.4. (*Cont.*)

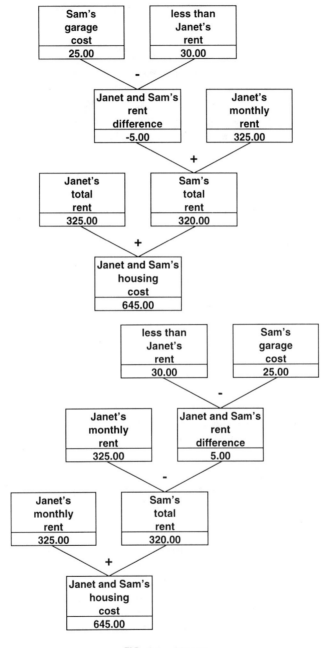

FIG. 4.4. (Cont.)

for making the desired inference. For example, the equation for overgeneralization might be:

.5 (omit schema) + .5 (imprecise label) = overgeneralization

Instantiation of the equation with observed values for constituent attributes will produce a value for the inferred attribute. (We explain shortly what attribute values means in the TAPS system and how they are obtained.) Each such instantiation can be thought of as a production rule. Thus, each pattern-matching equation represents an entire class of related production rules. These concepts are clarified further.

The Domain Expertise

The domain expertise in the TAPS system consists of, for each problem, the set of all typical solution trees, expressed as chained together schema triads (see Fig. 4.4). Associated with each stored problem is the list of labels and values and operators from which the student can choose to instantiate the schemas (see Fig. 4.4(a)). Each correct label, value, and operator in each schema has an associated weight stored with it that represents its relative importance in the schema and in the solution. The importance of these weights to monitoring and error-detection in TAPS is clarified in a following discussion of the pattern-matching algorithm.

Tutoring Module

The philosophy behind the tutoring module in the TAPS system is that this activity can be divided into two components: (1) the location of the student in the system's tree of solutions along with detection of possible errors and error patterns; and (2) the response (or non-response) associated with the tutoring strategy. We look on the former as an imprecise pattern-matching activity; the student solution is created and the system determines with a degree of uncertainty which of the system's solutions (patterns) the student is constructing. Information is then gathered on the types and locations of errors in this path. Currently we detect, to a fuzzy degree, the "primitive" errors found in the error analysis described previously (see Table 4.2). Later, but using the same techniques, we plan to add more capability for finding complex patterns of primitive errors.

The purpose of the error detection and location routine is to supply the tutoring component with knowledge of the hypothesized errors, to locate the student solution in terms of the tree of solutions, and to collect data on errors. This routine is independent of the tutoring strategy being used; a particular tutoring strategy may use knowledge of the errors, or, in fact, need no knowledge of them. Thus, if error information is needed for the tutoring strategy being used, it is passed to it. The history of these errors is kept in a trace. This trace can be used in many ways: analyzed by researchers; used as input for the tutoring strategy; input for a postsession reflective interaction with the student; input to the student record for updating purposes.

Rather than a precise description of this approach we offer a more general overview with examples. First, we introduce our informal fuzzy reasoning. We then outline the algorithm for location of the student solution in the system's tree of solutions with simultaneous error detection, and indicate how this capability provides necessary information for intelligent tutoring.

Informal Fuzzy Reasoning

In detecting student errors there are many instances where this activity is imprecise. Correspondingly, in matching a student solution to our tree of solutions, it will often not be a precise match. Thus, we use a technique that allows us to work with this inherent uncertainty. Rather than a crisp $0/1$ (does not have feature/has feature) system, we use the whole interval $[0, 1]$, with a 0 representing not having the feature, and 1 having the feature. The intervening values gives a continuum which represents degrees of membership so that 0 corresponds to nonmembership, and 1 to complete membership. This of course provides an infinite number of values which for this task is not necessary. Thus, as proposed by Schwartz (1989), we have divided the interval into 7 adjacent sections, I_1, $I_2, \ldots, I_7$. As it is often more meaningful for humans to think in linguistic terms, we give these 7 intervals linguistic labels. This allows researchers, tutors and teachers to interact linguistically with the system even though internally numeric values are used. Linguistically then, the intervals can, for some primary term X, be referred to as:

{definitely not X, not X, rather not X, neither X or not X, rather X, X, definitely X}.

In terms of our pattern-matching task, I_1 refers to definitely not a match and I_7 to definitely a match. The intervening intervals correspond to various degrees of match of the student solution to a part of the solution tree. For ease of computation we use the numerals $1, 2, \ldots, 7$, rather than $I_1, \ldots, I_7$. How this idea is used in the algorithm for location in the tree and error detection is discussed next.

Pattern-Matching Algorithm

The basis of our approach to error-detection is the presence in the system of the solution tree of all feasible or typical solutions of the given problem and an algorithm which allows imprecise matching of the student's solution to this tree. As previously mentioned, each solution is built up from schema triads chained together. Each triad consists of three nodes, represented as a set of labels and a value joined together by an operator as illustrated in figure 4. Associated with each label or set of labels, value and operator is a weight in the range $1, 2, \ldots$

, 7, with 1 indicating "very not important" to 7 indicating "very important." That is, a weight of 7 indicates the label must be included and if omitted we have error category "imprecise label," whereas a lesser value indicates that this term is not crucial for representing the concept of the schema. For example, consider the first schema in solution 4(b). One set is instantiated with labels, Janet and Sam, rent, and difference. The term difference is important for defining the concept of the set, and so it is given a high weight of 6 or 7. However, the term Janet and Sam is less critical to the definition of the concept and consequently is given a lower weight. Thus, the value of the weight gives a fuzzy approximation of the term's necessity.

The task of determining the student's position in the tree of solutions (i.e., recognizing the solution the student is building) is a fuzzy or imprecise task. We need to know the approach that the student is taking in her solution but do not require a precise match to one of our stored solutions. This imprecision is facilitated by the fact that rather than storing each possible solution, we store representations of classes of solutions. That is, in the system's tree of solutions (see Fig. 4.4, for example), each stored solution represents a class of solutions that are structurally and semantically equivalent. A particular member of a class is formed by the student filling in the blanks in the schema triads with acceptable labels, values and operators. For example, Fig. 4.4(b) is but one representation of its class; some others are given in Fig. 4.5. Table 4.5 shows the sets of labels for each schema node from which acceptable labels can be chosen for the solution path represented by Fig. 4.4(b). This illustrates an important contribution of

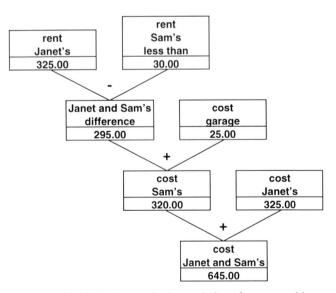

FIG. 4.5(a)–5(h). Alternative instantiations for rent problem.

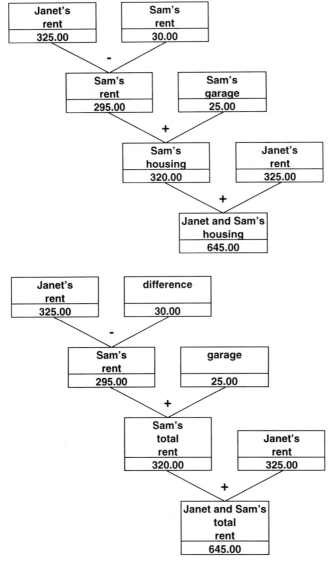

FIG. 4.5. (*Cont.*)

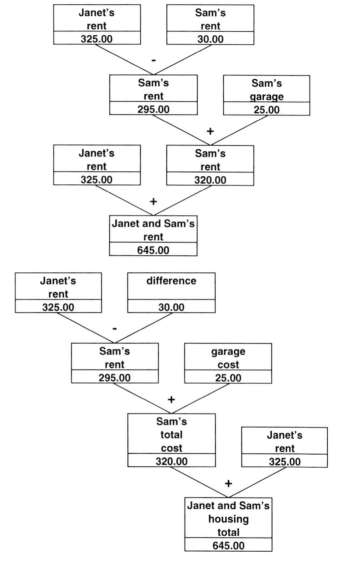

FIG. 4.5. (*Cont.*)

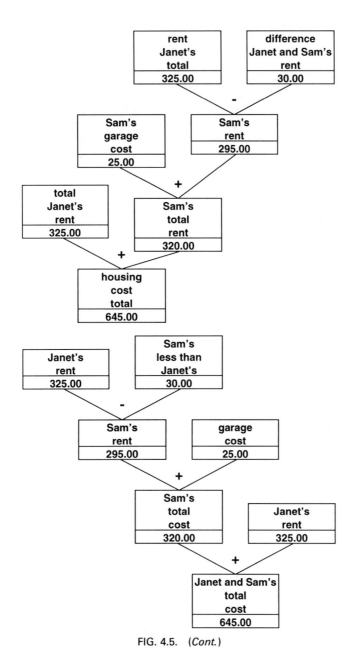

FIG. 4.5. (Cont.)

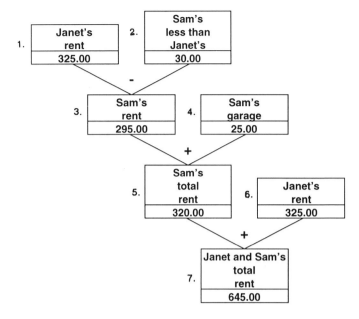

FIG. 4.5. (Cont.)

TABLE 4.5
Sets of Labels and Weights for Solution in Figure 4.4b

1. {Janet} = 7
   {rent, housing, cost, total} = 5

2. [{rent, [less than, difference] },
   *{Sam's, [less than, difference], rent, Janet's},
   { [Janet and Sam's], {difference, rent}] = 7

3. {Sam's} = 7
   {monthly, rent, housing, cost} = 4

4. {Sam's, rent, cost} = 5
   {garage} = 7

5. {Sam's} = 7
   {housing, cost, rent, total, monthly} = 4
   {garage} = 2

6. {Janet's} = 7
   {rent, housing, cost, monthly, total} = 5

7. {Janet and Sam's} = 7
   {total, cost, housing, rent, monthly} = 4

Note. Numbers on left side of table correspond to nodes in Fig. 4.5b. Numbers on right are assigned weights. A set with weight 7 is required and if missing indicates an "imprecise label." Curly brackets, { }, indicate that one or more enclosed items may be included in any order, though associated weight is added in only once. Square brackets, [ ], indicate that only one of the enclosed items or item sets is selected. An order flag (*) indicates that labels must occur in order. Sets of labels can be nested, e.g., *{Sam's, [less than, difference], rent, Janet's}.

our work: A very large number of acceptable solutions are recognized by the system while only a very small number of trees are actually stored; for example, well over 300,000 acceptable solution trees are represented by the one tree in Fig. 4.4(b)!

The matching to the tree of solutions is done using the weights. Linear equations are formed by multiplying the weight of each matching item (label, value, or operator) by "7" (to indicate a match) and summing over all matched items in the schema. Normalizing these results gives a number in the range 1 to 7 for each path (i.e., schema in the path) in the solution tree. The highest number obtained from the linear equations corresponds to the system's best estimate of where the student's current schema is in terms of solutions recognized by the system. The number 7 indicates a solution exactly as included in our tree. If the highest number calculated is less than 7 this implies that the student's solution is not identical to one of the solution classes. However, in our system, this does not mean this solution is unacceptable. Rather, the student's solution is accepted with a degree of fuzziness; certain less important labels have been omitted and/or one or more of the errors described in Table 4.3 has probably occurred. This approach gives the system dramatic flexibility in that it is able to recognize "correct" solution steps even though they are nonexact matches. If a tie occurs, that is, if the system computes an identical fuzzy value for two or more triads, just as a human might be unsure at this point of where the student is, so is the system; it awaits another schema to break the tie, again, as a human tutor might. The lower the number in the range [1, 7], the less likely it is that the solution being constructed matches this particular branch of the solution tree.

Basically, the algorithm works as follows. When the student enters her first schema the system must determine which is the most probable path, using the linear equations. The terms that are most important in making this determination have heaviest weight and hence play the biggest role in identifying the path and distinguishing it from others. Once a path has been established, with an acceptable degree of certainty, the system checks along this path as subsequent schemas are entered, as it is most likely the student will follow this path if she continues to be successful in her solution. Otherwise other paths must be checked (for example a "change of strategy" may have occurred). As the student solves the problem the system follows along identifying her path and postulating the various errors that were identified in our study. These are identified through the linear equations as illustrated in the next section of this chapter. The information on errors is saved in the form of a trace. It can be used locally together with a tutoring strategy, saved until the end of the student's attempt to solve the problem and used as input for a reflective session, and/or sent on to the student record to be analyzed and used to update the history on the student.

The system repeats this matching and error collection as the student enters schema triads. If the student continues on one solution path, the system simply follows along this path, monitoring errors. If the student should "change strategies" then the system must again search for the best match. If there is no match at an acceptable level, this can indicate the student is completely lost. In this case, the action taken by the system depends on the tutoring strategy in effect; for example, the system may select a solution and step through it with the student. Another possibility is that the student has built a solution such that no version of it is stored in the system. In this case the solution is saved in the trace and will be added to the acceptable solutions in the system later. Unfortunately, it would not have been recognized by the system as a valid solution tree at the time the student entered it. However, a new method for storing trees is now under development so that this difficulty will soon be eliminated.

After each solution session a trace will have been constructed of the student's activity, including the tree that the student builds, what errors were made, all self-corrections, etc.

Examples

We now provide some examples illustrated by screen displays generated by students actually solving problems on the system during a controlled experiment. The first word problem is given with possible labels, in Fig. 4.4(a).

One instantiation of the tree of solutions stored in the system is represented by Figs. 4(b)–4(e). We concentrate on the solution in Fig. 4.4(b) to illustrate that by using sets of labels and associated weights we can allow for much imprecision in determining acceptable solutions. In actuality, each of the four solutions in the tree given in Figs. 4.4(b)–4(e) represents a class of solutions, structurally and semantically equivalent. This is illustrated by noting that the solution in Fig. 4.4(b) is but one instantiation of the sets of labels given in Table 4.5. Some other instantiations are shown in Fig. 4.5.

To illustrate how the pattern-matching aspect of the algorithm begins, consider the student solution shown in Fig. 4.6. The student enters a schema triad with labels, values, and operator. This schema is matched against the first schema of each possible solution class in the tree of solutions, in our example, the four solution classes represented by Figs. 4.4(b)–4.4(e). This is done by calculating the corresponding linear equation for each of the four possible solution schemas. The highest number calculated corresponds to the solution in Fig. 4.4(b). Observe, however, that this is not the only acceptable solution. A large number of semantic variations to this solution are equally valid, for example, a few are shown in Fig. 4.5.

The student solution in Fig. 4.6 is built one schema at a time. Since the student is following a similar path to an accepted solution, the matching continues along the path represented by solution 4(b). In this example no error detection is necessary, so only the location aspect of the algorithm has been illustrated.

In Fig. 4.7 showing another student's work, consider the third schema triad

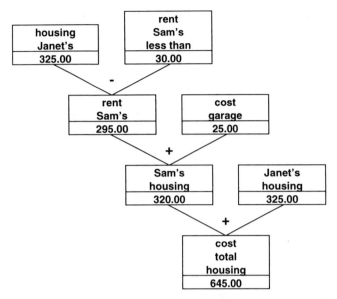

FIG. 4.6. Actual subject solution for illustrating pattern matching against stored tree.

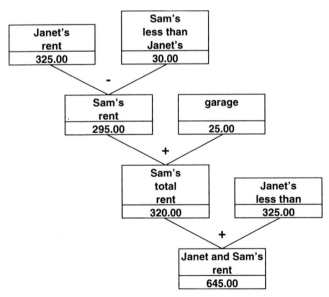

FIG. 4.7. Actual subject solution for illustrating pattern matching against stored tree.

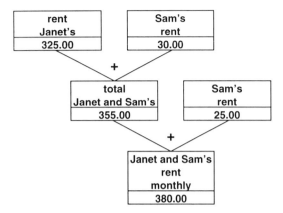

FIG. 4.8. Actual subject solution for illustrating pattern matching against stored tree.

entered, the second node, i.e., "Janet's" and "less than." The first entry is accepted as a match but the second one does not match any of the possibilities in set no. 6 of Table 4.5: "{rent, housing, cost, monthly, total} = 5." Hence "less than" would be marked in the trace as a "bad label;" however, the number calculated for the corresponding linear equation would still be highest for this path and so we identify this as an acceptable solution but one with a semantic error which may just be a slip.

In Fig. 4.8, the subject is obviously not constructing a valid solution. The linear-equation values calculated for the four solution trees in Fig. 4.4, with the labels shown in Fig. 4.8, are too low to be acceptable values for any stored solution paths or their variations. Thus, this solution would not be accepted by the system. And of course the proposed construction is indeed not a solution to the problem. The action taken at this point by the system would depend on the tutoring strategy in effect when an unacceptable solution has been entered.

Another interesting example of the kinds of errors that can be detected is seen in the partial trace (see Appendix) of the "Museum" problem:

All the third and fourth-grade classes at Kennedy Elementary are going to the museum. There are 3 third-grade classes and 4 fourth-grade classes. Every class has 30 students and one teacher. The boys and girls get into the museum for $1.50 each. The teachers' tickets cost $3.00 each. One local business donated some money for the project. The PTO provided the remaining costs. If the PTO gave $100, how much money did the business donate?

The system checks for the next schema in path 4, the solution path being followed. Checking the other possibilities, there is not a match. Then the system checks the next step (i.e., a step is skipped) in the current path. This matches, so the system correctly determines a schema has been omitted. The student at this point catches this error, and enters the omitted schema before continuing. The system correctly observes and records this sequence in the trace.

In a similar fashion the other errors in Table 4.2 are detected. This information is saved in the trace for future analysis or it can be immediately fed to the tutoring module for local use.

Use of Error Detection

Development of an error-detection monitoring system is a very important first step in designing a sensitive on-line tutor. It is important to emphasize, however, that ability to detect primitive-level errors and complex error patterns neither implies nor precludes any particular tutorial strategy or philosophy of instruction. In order to develop effective, complex intervention strategies, it will be necessary to conduct additional research leading to specific tutoring principles that will be implemented.

A variety of uses can be made of the error information collected. Most importantly, it creates a trace of the student's solution steps, both correct and incorrect. Selected information is sent to the student record at the end of the session for analysis and updating of the information housed about each student. Locally selected information from the trace is passed on to the tutor. Exactly what information is sent is dependent on the particular tutoring strategy being used for this student; different strategies may require different types of information. For example, if a reflective follow-up approach has been selected, whereby solutions are analyzed after the fact, then error information is not used at each step of the solution, but rather after the student has finished her solution.

Summary and Conclusions

The ability to identify and collect information about errors, in an imprecise way, is a significant step in the development of flexible ITSs. Rather than requiring exact matches to expert solutions, this approach gives the needed flexibility shown by human tutors in accepting variations to what would be their solution to a problem. Moreover, this is done without storing a very large number of associated solutions. In addition, the error information can be fed to the tutoring module to assist in providing the most efficacious tutoring for the particular student or group, permitting implementation of various tutoring strategies and approaches. And, as more research goes into this approach there is much promise of even more flexibility, intelligence, and individualization that is needed in such tutoring systems.

ACKNOWLEDGMENTS

This chapter is based in part on earlier papers presented at the 1989 AERA Annual Meeting, San Francisco, CA, and at the Fourth International Conference on AI in Education, Amsterdam, 1989. The authors gratefully acknowledge Harald Kegelmann, Bill Roth, Lisa Pizzuti, Kevin Dillard, and Ken Koendinger for their valuable comments and assistance during the studies and the preparation of this manuscript.

REFERENCES

Baker, L. & Brown, A. L. (1984). Metacognitive skills and reading. In D. Pearson, R. Barr, M. Kamil, & P. Mosenthal (Eds). *Handbook of reading research* (pp. 353–394). New York: Longman.

Brown, A. L. (1987). Metacognition, executive control, self-regulation, and other more mysterious mechanisms. In F. Weinert & R. Klewe (Eds.), *Metacognition, motivation and understanding.* Hillsdale, NJ: Lawrence Erlbaum Associates.

Collins, A., Brown, J. S., & Newman, S. E. (1989). Cognitive apprenticeship: Teaching the craft of reading, writing, and mathematics. In L. Resnick (Ed.), *Knowing, learning and instruction: Essays in honor of Robert Glaser.* Hillsdale, NJ: Lawrence Erlbaum Associates.

Derry, S. J., & Kellis, A. (1986). A prescriptive analysis of low-ability problem-solving behavior. *Instructional Science, 15,* 49–65.

Ericsson, K. A., & Simon, H. A. (1984). *Protocol analysis: Verbal reports as data.* Cambridge, MA: MIT Press.

Flavell, J. H. (1979). Metacognition and cognitive monitoring: A new area of psychological inquiry. *American Psychologist, 34,* 906–911.

Flavell, J. H. (1981). Cognitive monitoring. In W. P. Dickson (Ed.), *Children's oral communication skills* (pp. 35–60). New York: Academic Press.

Fox, B. A. (1988a, January). *Repair as a factor in interface design* (Tech. Report). University of Colorado, Boulder, CO.

Fox, B. A. (1988b, January). *Robust learning environments: The issue of canned text* (ONR Tech. Report). University of Colorado, Boulder, CO.

Garofalo, J., & Lester, F. (1985). Metacognition, cognitive monitoring, and mathematical performance. *Journal for Research in Mathematics Education, 16,* 163–176.

Hechinger, F. M. (1983, July 12). Report faults Army's teaching of basic skills. *The New York Times,* p. C6.

Holmes, D. J. (1991). *An informal reasoning technique and truth maintenance subsystem for global diagnosis in an instructional system.* Unpublished doctoral dissertation, Computer Science Department, Florida State University, Tallahassee, FL.

Lapointe, A. E., Mead, N. A., & Phillips, G. W. (1989). *A world of differences: An international assessment of mathematics and science.* Princeton, NJ: Educational Testing Service.

Lepper, M. R. (1989, April). *Goals and Strategies of expert human tutors: Cognitive and affective considerations.* Paper presented at the annual AERA meeting, San Francisco, CA.

Lepper, M. R., & Chabay, R. W. (1988). Socializing the intelligent tutor: Bringing empathy to computer tutors. In H. Mandl & A. Lesgold (Eds.) New York: Springer-Verlag.

Marshall, S. (1985, August). *An analysis of problem-solving instruction in arithmetic textbooks.* Paper presented at annual meeting of the American Psychological Association, Los Angeles.

Marshall, S. P., Pribe, C. A., & Smith, J. D. (1987, March). Schema knowledge structures for representing and understanding arithmetic story problems (Contract No. N00014-85-K-0661). San Diego, CA: Center for Research in Mathematics and Science Education.

McArthur, D., Stasz, C., & Zmuidzinas, M. (1990). Tutoring techniques in algebra. *Cognition and Instruction, 7,* 161–195.

National Commission on Excellence in Education. (1983). *A nation at risk: The imperative for educational reform.* Washington, D.C.: U.S. Government Printing Office.

National Science Board Commission on Precollege Education in Mathematics, Science and Technology. (1983). *Educating Americans for the 21st century.* Washington, D.C., National Science Foundation.

Palincsar, A. S. (1986). The role of dialogue in providing scaffolded instruction. *Educational Psychologist, 21,* Nos. 1 & 2, pp. 73–99.

Reiser, B. (1989, April). Pedagogical strategies for human and computer tutoring. AERA Presentation.

Salomon, G., & Perkins, D. N. (1989). Rocky roads to transfer: Rethinking mechanisms of a neglected phenomenon. *Educational Psychologist, 24,* 113–142.

Schoenfeld, A. H. (1983). Episodes and executive decisions in mathematical problem solving. In R. Lesh & M. Landau (Eds.), *Acquisition of mathematics concepts and processes* (pp. 229–258). New York: Academic Press.

Schoenfeld, A. H. (1985). *Mathematical problem solving.* Orlando, FL: Academic Press.

Schoenfeld, A. H. (1987). What's all the fuss about metacognition? In A. Schoenfeld (Ed.) *Cognitive science and mathematics education* (pp. 189–216). Hillsdale, NJ: Lawrence Erlbaum Associates.

Schwartz, D. (1991). A system for reasoning with imprecise linguistic information. *International Journal of Approximate Reasoning, 5,* 463–488.

Self, J. (1988). Bypassing the intractable problem of student modelling. *Proceedings of ITS88,* Montreal, Canada.

Vygotsky, L. S. (1978). *Mind in society: The development of higher psychological processes.* In M. Cole, V. John-Steiner, S. Scribner, & e. Souberman (Eds. and Trans.). Cambridge, MA: Harvard University Press.

Wenger, E. (1987). *Artificial intelligence and tutoring systems: Computational and cognitive approaches to the communication of knowledge.* Los Altos, CA: Morgan Kaufmann.

APPENDIX

Partial Trace for Museum Problem

Analyzing the best match, st-schema-127, with a fuzzy value of 5:
Student omitted a step! Schema museum. 423 is missing in the solution tree.

Schema st-schema-127 has been instantiated with:
fuzzy value: 5
pattern: (+ cost students total 315.00 teachers total 7 cost total 322.00)
corresp. to: museum.414

Schema st-schema-127 has been removed.

Problem schema museum.414 has been removed from the list of matched schemas.

The student created a new schema. It's internal name,
used by the diagnoser, is: st-schema-129

Matching new schema: st-schema-129.

Matching st-schema-129 with predicted schemas.

Matching student schema pattern:
(* teachers total 7 cost teachers 3.00 cost teachers total 21.00)
with problem schema museum.414, the equation yields a fuzzy value of: 3
with problem schema museum.415, the equation yields a fuzzy value of: 1

Matching st-schema-129 with remaining schemas on path.

Matching student schema pattern:

(* teachers total 7 cost teachers 3.00 cost teachers total 21.00)

with problem schema museum.423, the equation yields a fuzzy value of: 7

Matching has been terminated. Schema st-schema-129 matches with problem schema: museum.423.

Student matched the subgoal in schema: st-schema-129.

Error category 51 (omit step), has been corrected. Schema museum.423 has been inserted into the solution tree.

Schema st-schema-129 has been instantiated with:

fuzzy value: 7

pattern: (* teachers total 7 cost teachers 3.00 cost teachers total 21.00)

corresp. to: museum.423

II NONMODELERS

Tutoring Systems and Pedagogical Theory: Representational Tools for Understanding, Planning, and Reflection in Problem Solving

5

Kurt Reusser
University of Bern, Switzerland

TUTORING SYSTEMS AND PEDAGOGICAL THEORY

In designing computer-based educational systems our primary concern ought not to be with a dazzling new technology, nor should we be misguided by such romantically unrealistic goals and expectations as replacing teachers, textbooks, or even the physical and social learning activities of students through learner-machine interactions. Instead, the main object in the design of computational media as a new form of "intellectual bootstrapping" (Collins & Brown, 1988) ought to be its functional connection to a (partly normative) pedagogical and didactical[1] philosophy. The design must take into account the proper use and integration of the system into the comprehensive range of learning and teaching activities that take place in the "behavior setting" (Barker, 1978) of *schooling.*

In the first part of this chapter eight principles are suggested for designing computer-based cognitive tools for learning and problem solving. The principles, contrasting in certain ways principles outlined by Anderson, Boyle, Farrell, and Reiser (1984), or by Ohlsson (1986), are based on pedagogical theory and on cognitive research and lead to the discussion of a set of critical issues for the

---

[1]The concept of didactics is not used here in its narrow and increasingly negative sense of "spoonfeeding" students by extremely teacher-centered instructional methods which leave little of the guidance and learning responsibility to the student, but in its original and broader sense of classical Bildungstheorie (e.g., Klafki, 1963). The latter meaning includes both the question of what to teach (reflecting and constituting the object of instruction) and how to teach (designing an instructional setting of methods and media) a specific content. The two meanings of "didactics" are contained, for example, in the distinction between "product" and "process" with respect to the fundamental pedagogical goals of teaching.

design of educational software. The principles have been applied to HERON, a computerized teaching and learning environment designed to aid children in understanding and solving a wide class of complex mathematical word problems. I describe parts of HERON in the second part of the chapter, emphasizing the important role of *representational means, or formats, as conceptual tools for problem-representation, planning, and reflection.*[2]

From Cognitive Analysis to Instructional Design: Computers as Cognitive Tools

Educational software should make sense from a pedagogical point of view. Hence, four crucial considerations should govern the design of machine-supported instructional contexts: (a) a cognitive and instructionally efficient model of the task or the domain the system is designed for, (b) a sound conception of the general and content-specific learning processes associated with the domain, (c) a domain-appropriate social-cognitive concept of teaching (balancing dimensions such as explicit instruction versus discovery learning, "solo-learning" (Bruner, 1961, 1986) versus collaborative learning), and (d) a view of the active nature of the learner. With regard to the tutoring of mathematical word problems: Whoever designs a computer-based instructional system needs to know both how to effectively represent and convey the informational structures related to word problems and the processes and strategies employed by learners of different ability levels in their understanding and problem solving.

Thus work on tutoring systems should be based both on research in cognitive psychology and on research in didactical or instructional theory, two distinct fields, which still maintain few interconnections. Often enough, cognitive researchers analyze meaning structures and processes on a conceptual level, using formats that are neither translatable into instructionally efficient models of domains and tasks, nor allow inference to any normative principles (Glaser, 1987) of instruction. On the other hand, designers of textbooks and computational media, as well as (expert) teachers, are often not successful in performing microstructural cognitive task analyses, yet such analyses would be beneficial in uncovering the properties of the representational and operative "tacit" (Polanyi, 1966) knowledge inherent in the performance of a task.

This leads to the first principle:

P1: Design and use computer-based tools pedagogically, that is, as cognitive instructional tools for mindful teachers and learners in a culture of problem solving.

---

[2]Principles are fairly abstract by their nature. The reader who wants to see—while reading the first sections of the chapter—how the principles are incorporated into the tutor, might prefer to read sections of the second part of the chapter first.

In contrast to a technology-driven and opportunistic design philosophy, computers should be used in education, by judicious teachers and active, intentional learners (in the sense of Scardamalia, Bereiter, McLean, Swallow, and Woodruff, 1989) *as supportive cognitive tools in the service of explicit pedagogical goals* (Reusser, 1991). As mind-empowering prosthetic devices which belong to our overall "cultural tool kit" (Bruner, 1990), future computerized tools of learning and instruction not only act as amplifiers of our own intelligence but, beyond that, might significantly change our traditional view of the instructional setting, "redefine the natural limits of human functioning," as Bruner says (1990, p. 21). Instructional tools should be based on our best cognitive analyses of curricular tasks and processes. With regard to their status as supportive mind tools, which are always used in a specific context and with a specific purpose, they should remain a *means to a pedagogical end or goal*. As such they form a functional part of a distributed and much more comprehensive setting for pedagogical intelligence.

From the "Romantic Quest for Intelligent Machines" (Clancey, 1989) to the Activities of Virtually Autonomous Learners

The catchword "intelligent tutoring systems" (Sleeman & Brown, 1982) has come to mean that a computer functions as an intelligent, dynamically adaptive substitute for a human teacher, who is capable of performing sensitive cognitive diagnoses, which means to infer, on the basis of a constantly-retuned student model, a person's cognitive states—what the person knows, how she thinks and learns—on the basis of her overt behavior (cf. Ohlsson, 1986; van Lehn, 1988). There are good reasons to be skeptical about the feasibility—and in part even the desirability—of intelligent systems that are based on full system control and deep student modeling (Nathan, Kintsch, & Young, 1990; Resnick & Johnson, 1988; Scardamalia et al., 1989). Intelligent tutoring, in which a machine tailors its instruction to an individual student on the basis of an inferred, constantly updated, fine-grained mental model, may be seen as a long-term goal. But given the current state of the art, machine-tutoring based on *cognitive simulation* of the student is not possible across a full range of open-ended tasks and domains, where fuzzy language and qualitative world-knowledge based reasoning are required. This is especially true with regard to error modeling. As Derry and Hawkes (1989) note: "Deep modeling of procedural bugs is computationally intractable for complex problem domains, and we do not believe it is required for effective cognitive apprenticeship" (p. 33).

Even if technology based cognitive diagnosis were, in principle, a feasible goal in the distant future, it would be only one of several ways to apply advanced computing technologies to education. From a pedagogical point-of-view, there are alternative means of supporting and facilitating human learning and problem solving through interaction with a computer. The most sensible one might be to view machine-supported tutoring with the ultimate goal of developing a virtually autonomous and reflective learner and thinker. This does not require intelligent systems but flexible, didactic supports. Intelligence, on this view, is seen as being located primarily in the learner and distributed across the whole pedagogical setting, rather than being located in the computer.

Scardamalia et al. (1989) even question how useful highly intelligent systems would be: Such systems

> may also be heading in the wrong direction. For it is not the computer that should be doing the diagnosing, the goal-setting and the planning, it is the student. The computer environment should not be providing the knowledge and intelligence to guide learning, it should be providing the facilitating structures and tools that enable students to make maximum use of their own intelligence and knowledge. (p. 54)

One should therefore not conceive of computer applications in education primarily as substitutes for intelligent teachers but as tools aimed at cultivating the intelligence of the user, as didactic instruments directed, to the greatest possible extent, at fostering learner autonomy and self-regulation. One can add that there is little evidence that even expert human teachers are able to carry out extensive cognitive diagnosis (e.g., McArthur, Stasz & Zmuidzinas, 1990).

P2: Extend and empower the minds of intentional learners.

Computer environments should be seen as mind-extending or catalyzing tools for intelligent and volitional learners and virtually autonomous problem solvers. They should provide stimulating and facilitating structures in order to promote meaning construction activities, such as planning, representation, and reflection. Such an alternative view of computers can be situated within the epistemological and didactic framework of models and metaphors currently being discussed in applied metacognitive research. These include, for example, the Vygotskian-inspired models of coaching and scaffolding (Brown & Palincsar, 1989), of cognitive apprenticeship (Collins, Brown, & Newman, 1989), of procedural facilitation (Scardamalia et al., 1989), of learning through reflection (Collins & Brown, 1988), or, more generally, of autonomous and self-directed learning and problem solving (Beck, 1989; Bruner, 1986).

From this pedagogical perspective, tutoring would not be considered successful primarily with respect to the degree to which a system is able to "intelligently" force a student down some preset solution path, as human tutors very often do but, instead, to the degree to which it optimizes students sense of control, and to the degree to which student solutions are self-generated.

P3: Provide learners with some guidance according to the "principle of minimal help." (Aebli, 1961)

Making errors, or getting stuck, is an inevitable part of learning. However, in order to provide effective feedback or graduated help, a tutor does not necessarily need to perceive what the student is thinking but to know what the structure of the task is, and what the student is doing while working on it. Since learners can become highly confused and demoralized by undetected errors (Anderson et al., 1984), some feedback must be provided—either immediate, delayed, or on request. Good teachers, as well as intelligent learners, follow the didactic "principle of minimal help" (Aebli, 1961). Ideally, a tutoring system would leave it to the student, to use or seek only as much help or feedback from the system as he needs. If tutorial action appropriate for an individual learner is called for, cognitive modelling, however, is not the only way to determine its quality. An alternative basis for characterizing students' errors and making tutorial decisions can be established through a different form of behavioral diagnosis (cf. Wenger, 1987). It requires a careful conceptual analysis or decomposition of the knowledge or skill to be taught. The tutor should know mature (expert) and less mature models of the processes and representations to be taught. Feedback during problem-solving, for example, on errors, can be based on a conceptual analysis of the solution space. This makes it possible to determine when and how the observed knowledge-construction activity of a particular student deviates from a predetermined set of solution paths (Derry & Hawkes, 1989). Thus, mapping overt student performance onto powerful representations of a task can lead to effective guidance without assessing student thinking on a moment-by-moment basis. Still another type of feedback is used by Nathan, Kintsch, and Young (1990), in their tutoring of distance-rate problems. The student can run an animation (time varying computer graphics) on the basis of his problem model, enabling him to judge its correctness on his own.

From Learning through Memorization and Drill-and-Practice Routines to Learning through Active Construction, Comprehension and Reflection

Computer-based cognitive tools should be less oriented toward memorization and drill-and-practice and, instead, toward fostering meaning construction activities, like understanding, problem solving, planning, and reflection. Computers with today's direct-manipulation graphic interfaces (Hutchins, Hollan, & Norman, 1985) are best equipped to do (and undo) such things as generating icons, selecting, presenting, touching, linking, placing, storing, and retrieving information, including bookkeeping and monitoring of the user's actions. Thus they are ideally suited to providing both representational and procedural facilitation to the student's understanding.

P4: Have students construct and externalize their mental models.

Uncovering the covert, or externalizing the hidden, intermediate and compo-nent steps and products of the learner's "effort after meaning"—as Bartlett (1932) who was a constructivist far ahead of his time, framed the self-construc-tive nature of the creation of meaning—is a major cognitive function of comput-er-based instructional tools. Normally unobservable knowledge-construction ac-tivities that are reified (Collins & Brown, 1988) as accessible visual displays reduce the burden on working memory. What has been externally represented, objectified, embodied, organized, and made overt and explicit by *extracortical organizers of thought* (Vygotsky, 1978), can then be identified, inspected, ana-lyzed, discussed, communicated, further reflected and operated upon, and finally carried out consciously and deliberately by the learner (Greeno, 1987; Pea, 1987).

By proposing that students make their thinking explicit and that they actively construct their own conceptualization of a problem or domain, we do not pretend any quasi-automatic and significant improvement of knowledge organization or higher-order thinking skills. Just as an empty head cannot think, there is no effective computer-supported learning without domain-related, representational and procedural (strategic) tools supplied by the educational culture. This claim is in direct opposition to the empirically unwarranted, romantic growth optimism currently in vogue, an optimism that is inspired by Piagetian ideas of cognitive growth and maturation (cf. Aebli, 1978), by related ideas of radical construc-tivism and discovery learning, as well as by a superficial understanding of concepts proposed by Vygotsky. Proponents of this view sometimes seem to believe that the self-construction abilities of children, as well as skill and knowl-edge formation in general are simply emergent, nonintentional properties of mostly nondirective or nonauthoritarian social interactions between children and more knowledgeable others.

P5: Provide students with intelligible and effective representational tools of thought and of communication.

Efficient conceptual representation of content is a key problem for both learn-ing and teaching. Appropriate representational formats of domains and tasks, including tree structures, coordinate graphs, diagrams, data tables, conceptual networks, symbol systems (alphanumeric, algebraic . . .), and scientific nota-tions, are indispensible tools not only for thinking, problem solving, and reason-ing, but also for the *communication of knowledge.* Tutors and textbooks should provide students, as an important target of instruction, with cognitively plausible operative, iconic, and symbolic systems of representation rooted in a deep se-mantic understanding of the domain.

Finding facilitating representations for almost any (class of) problem(s) should be seen as a major intellectual achievement, one that is often greatly underestimated as a significant part of both problem-solving efforts in science (Simon, 1977)[3] and of efforts in instructional design. Teachers and designers of knowledge media, should take pedagogical responsibility for giving students the power of effective *domain ontologies* (Greeno, 1983). That is, they should supply students with carefully designed conceptualizations, symbol systems and instructional models of tasks and concepts, that are vital for the development of expertise in almost any knowledge domain.

But what are cognitively plausible and efficient systems or forms of representation? If supplying carefully designed conceptualizations of problems and domains for students is a significant cognitive issue and a major pedagogical device, questions arise about how to characterize the qualities of *good* instructional representations. There are at least two related issues involving *goodness:* One is the question of representations as *domain ontologies* (Greeno, 1983; Wenger, 1987), also called the issue of *cognitive and epistemic plausibility or fidelity* (How *faithful* is a conceptual model of a domain and what are its *ontological commitments?*). The second is the issue of representations as *pedagogical means* of looking at a topic or domain (tools of *Anschauung*), an issue, as Ohlsson (1987) remarks with respect to a proposed "pedagogy of illustrations," that is not yet well understood.

I think an answer to the question of the cognitive-didactical quality of instructional representations contains several elements. They are outlined next and are incorporated into the tutoring system[4] described later in this chapter:

1. Cognitively plausible and pedagogically useful representational systems or formats allow students, while creating and elaborating a mental representation of a problem, to capture (the) essential structural features of the problem and to differentiate the problem from classes of similar problems. Efficient representations permit one to organize a task around salient properties and invariants of its (functional or relational) deep structure, i.e., around abstract relations among components—something that, for example, experienced teachers and expert problem-solvers do intuitively. It requires breaking up a domain into *conceptual building blocks* in such a way that the natural and conceptual con-

---

[3]Scientists, especially mathematicians and logicians, always have devoted much energy to the development of useful and efficient forms of symbolization. As Simon (1977) notes, there might be only a few basic formats of representation at all in science. On the psychological level of the individuum, numerous studies show the superiority of experts in knowledge organization and problem conceptualization: Skilled problem solvers not only build rich problem representations before they start solving a problem, but good representations of problems significantly affect problem solving efficiency as well.

[4]The basic representational format and strategy of our system are solution trees. The reader may read the sections on this format in parallel with the following list of components of efficient representational systems.

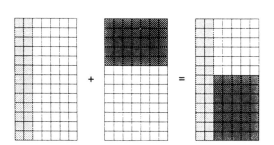

FIG. 5.1. Instructional representation designed to provide an iconic understanding the operative structure of fractions addition. The task is

$$\frac{2}{7} + \frac{5}{13} = \frac{2 \times 13 + 7 \times 5}{7 \times 13}$$

From Van Hiele (1986). Reproduced by permission of Academic Press.

straints inherent in the domain or task become explicit and easier for the learner to grasp. In a sufficient and concise representation, everything that is needed for processing is contained in it, and everthing that is contained, is relevant.

2. *Representational notations guide students' problem-solving and knowledge-construction activities by supplying operative, iconic, and symbolic forms of solutions and—more generally—of understanding.* Efficient representational formats make evident the constraints that problem spaces and solutions must satisfy. Well-defined notational formats can serve as a form of *written calculus* (Clancey, quoted from Wenger, 1987, p. 320) for a domain or a class of problems. They reflect the constraints of a task, direct students' construction of mental models in ways theoretical task analysis says are required for solving, and allow "the quality of solutions to be evaluated" with respect to its form (Wenger, 1987, p. 320).

3. *Good representational formats enforce intentional structural editing, that is, they encourage students to view their manipulations of a representation as semantically meaningful operations.* This can be encouraged (a) by supporting different ways of conceptualizing, or multiple solution paths, (b) by allowing the student to reconfigure a construction process or to refer back to prior parts of it, and (c) by discouraging referentially empty manipulations of the mere syntax of a representational format.

4. *Effective representations allow rapid recognition and retrieval of relevant information, mainly by reducing abstract problem-solving and reasoning processes in favour of processes which come closer to perceptual operations, to seeing things* (cf. Wertheimer, 1945). The great utility of computationally efficient diagrams "arises from perceptual enhancement" (Larkin & Simon, 1987, p. 95), the fact that relevant relations and conclusions can be easily computed and read off with the help of "simple, direct perceptual operations" (Reusser, 1984). Two diverse examples of efficient iconic representations are depicted in Figs. 5.1 and 5.2. Further examples include the coordinate system, or function diagrams.

5. *Effective representational systems provide a structural basis (platform) upon which, using domain-specific or general problem-solving methods or strat-*

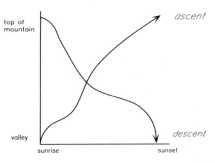

FIG. 5.2.   From Duncker (1935) stems the following problem: One morning at the time of sunrise, a monk started out to climb a high mountain. A narrow spiral path led upwards to a temple. After some days of Lent and of meditation, again at sunrise, the monk came back down to the valley following the same path downwards that he came up. Does there exist a location on the mountain path which the monk reaches at exactly the same hour of the day on his ascent and on his descent?—The visual diagram maps in a productive and unique way the problem situation onto the standard notational format of the coordinate system. To most readers, the visual representation elicits a kind of a gestalt switch, of sudden restructuring.—The problem is easily solvable if one succeeds in representing it (either externally or mentally) in a visually insightful way, for example, by assuming that two monks do the ascent and the descent on the same day. The given pictorial representation allows one to read off, with simple perceptual operations, the solution that the monks must meet each other at some place.

egies, the user can act, manipulate, and reason. Their efficiency also arises thus from *operative enhancement,* the fact that procedural formats of representation support certain kinds of actions and transformations on its objects. Examples include the widely used and fundamental procedural formats of alphanumeric and algebraic equations.

   6. *Instructionally valuable representations serve to mediate between idiosyncratic and informal analyses of problems and concepts and shared cultural and more formal analyses.* Among their most important dual function is to provide bridges from ordinary language, or the physical view of concrete objects, to canonical scientific languages and conceptualizations. That is, efficient representations inherit a dual role: They should be linkable, on the one hand, to common natural language descriptions of reality and to informal analyses of problems and domains, including learners' everyday mental models and intuitions.[5] On the other hand, they also contain conceptual elements that correspond to variables in abstract views, scientific models and formalisms, as, for example, mathematical notations.

   7. *Hence, cognitively plausible instructional representations should be parts of learning systems* (Nesher, 1989) *in which multiple representations, designed*

---

[5]Nesher (1989) makes an important point to this in saying that artificial representations should enrich, and not simply replace "the child's intuitions from his everyday experience" (p. 212). As a general principle, theoretical knowledge that can not be deeply connected with the learner's old concepts and intuitive theories, does not become instrumental or integrated into his existing knowledge base. On the contrary, it remains alien to it.

152   REUSSER

*to preserve different aspects of an invariant relational structure, are linked in a
yoked fashion* (Resnick & Johnson, 1988). Choosing "an apt combination of
situational and quantitative models for instructional purposes is a challenging
problem" (Hall, Kibler, Wenger, & Truxaw, 1989, p. 280). Connected representations allow the student to view the same object, relationship, or process, from
different representational perspectives. By fostering *mobility* between multiple
representations (Aebli, 1981; Bruner, Olver, & Greenfield, 1966; Piaget, 1947),
it should become clear to the learner "that it is not the representation on the
screen that matters in the end, but the representation built up in the students'

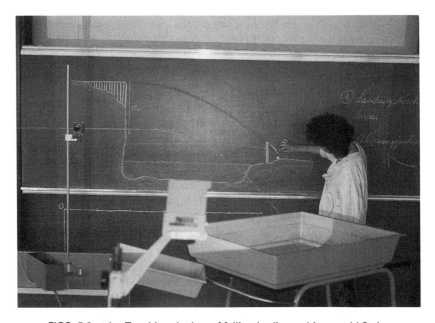

FIGS. 5.3a–d.   Teaching the law of falling bodies to 14 year old Swiss
eighth-graders with the aid of a yoked (discovery learning) system of
representations (after Hollenstein, Staub, & Stüssi, 1987). The system
was successfully used in classroom instruction and by groups of students. At the beginning, the following problem was posed to the students: A stuntman wants to jump with a motorcycle a gorge 50 meters
wide with a drop of 15 meters. What must his initial speed be?
FIG. 5.3a.   In the classroom, a simulation of the problem situation was
built up and represented with the aid of iconic, manipulative, and
symbolic elements, that is: a sketch including the gorge, the ramps for
the jump, and the ideal trajectory (1) was drawn on the blackboard; in
order to simulate the possible effects of the varying speed of the motorcycle on the trajectory, a jet of water (2), adjustable in pressure, was
projected on the wall (3); a computer graph depicting the coordinate
system, allowing to study the jet of the water as time-varying graphics,
could also be projected.

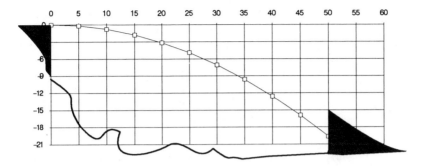

FIG. 5.3b.   The figure intimately connects to Fig. 5.3a. It represents the problem situation in a more abstract way. The representation is generated by a personal computer (where the problem is implemented with graphic and symbolic tools) which can be used by the students for setting up theoretical experiments and for mathematization.

head—their mental models" (Resnick & Johnson, 1988, p. 27). Figure 5.3 shows parts of an connected learning system of multiple, progressively more abstract instructional representations designed for teaching the law of falling bodies, starting from study of the trajectory (parabola) of horizontally thrown objects.

8. *Externalized representations supply teachers and students with a conceptual language to communicate and talk about what is to be learned.* They give referential meaning to students' thinking and discussions of the task, but also to the instructional dialogue between teachers and learners.

Representation has been a perennial issue in problem solving literature since Gestaltpsychology (Wertheimer, 1945). As a classical wisdom in problem solv-

FIG. 5.3c.   Representation of the underlying mathematical problem structure as computer-generated data tables (Columns: left = falling time; middle = horizontal distance; right = vertical distance) according to parameters that were set by the students. Comparing different tables allow the students to inductively infer the law of falling bodies: the handwritten entries refer to the comparison of the change in (falling) time with the change of the horizontal and vertical speed.

velocity	72	km/h	20	m/sec
time interval	0.5	sec		
start with	0	sec		
time (sec)		horizontal (m)		vertical (m)
0		0		0.000
0.5		10.000		-1.226
1		20.000		-4.905
1.5		30.000		-11.036
2		40.000		-19.620
2.5		50.000		-30.656
3		60.000		-44.145
3.5		70.000		-60.086
4		80.000		-78.480
4.5		90.000		-99.326
5		100.000		-122.625
5.5		110.000		-148.376

t (sec)	d: depth of drop (meters)	calculation of d
1	4.91 m	1 * 1 * 4.91
2	19.62 m	2 * 2 * 4.91
3	44.15 m	3 * 3 * 4.91
4	78.48 m	4 * 4 * 4.91
.	.	.
.	.	.
.	.	.
t	d	t * t * $g_{/2}$

FIG. 5.3d. Abstractively reduced data table from Fig. 5.3c
generated on the blackboard
during classroom discussion.

ing says: to properly understand a problem is halfway to the solution. To solve a
problem means first to *understand* it, to represent, or see its inherent structure,
which means to build an appropriate internal and/or external conceptualization or
rich data structure. Most problem-solving processes inherently consist of a repre-
sentation-construction part which is followed by problem-solving operations that
act upon the created representation. Thus, there can be no doubt that carefully
designed instructional models of tasks and domains, which facilitate the organization and (re)construction of meaning in knowledge acquisition and problem
solving, constitute vital tools and targets of both learning and teaching—both
within and outside of computer-assisted instruction.

However, the design of plausible and efficient representations as *instruments
of thought and communication* (Kaput, 1989) is more than a prerequisite pedagogical task, and far more than just ad hoc and tricky didactic art work to be
quickly replaced by canonical (symbolic) notations and standard conceptualizations of science. The issues of *computational efficiency* (Larkin & Simon, 1987;

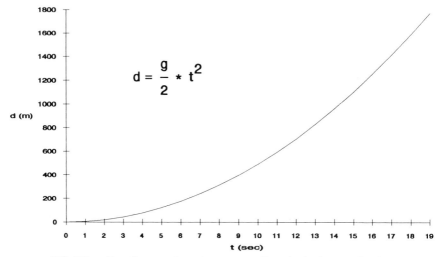

$$d = \frac{g}{2} \star t^2$$

FIG. 5.3e. Function graph and corresponding algebraic equation for
the law of falling bodies.

Winston, 1984), of *conceptual faithfulness* and *cognitive and epistemic fidelity (Roschelle, 1990; Wenger, 1987)*, or of *intelligibility (Reusser, 1984)* of effective instructional representations touches the fundamental epistemological question of what are the building blocks, the psychological forms or mediums of knowing and thinking (Aebli, 1981), and the *conceptual entities* (Greeno, 1983), out of which our most effective mental models and our most satisfying cognitive activities are made. Thus, there are questions of ontological and epistemological commitments and implications which are not beyond pedagogical design but intimately and inseparably connected to it.

P6. Promote the use of comprehension-related strategies. Together with representational formats, general and domain-specific strategies are the cognitive tools of thinking and problem solving.

Complementary to providing facilitating representational entities and formats should be procedural assistance, the facilitation of domain-specific and global strategies. While advice with respect to high-level (meta)cognitive (control) strategies like planning, reflecting, setting and maintaining attention to goals, searching (for alternative solution paths), or monitoring one's own performance, is easier to provide from computers in many cases (cf. Cumming & Self, 1990)—and also seems to be transferable to other domains (Brown & Campione, 1990), sensitive task-specific help is a far more difficult problem. Domain-specific *strategic* assistance, that is, assistance beyond simply providing solutions via "informed feedback" (Wenger, 1987), can only go as far as it is possible to formalize the semantics of a domain. And, as a corollary to this, it will be successful only in so far as cognitive or behavioral diagnosis are feasible.

P7. Encourage reflective and self-directed learning.

Pedagogically designed computer environments, which at the same time enable and force students to uncover and reify their knowledge-building activities, provide a motivating and powerful medium for self-paced reviewing, discussing, and reflecting upon one's own thought processes. Collins and Brown (1988) have framed the notion of the computer as a "tool for learning through reflection." This refers to the unique power of the computational medium to "keep track of the actions used to carry out a task" (p. 1), to display thinking paths, and to allow students to focus and reflect on the why's and how's of their own problem solving—all at their individual pace and according to their own direction. Giving students over and over again opportunities to monitor on-line the visually displayed traces of their planning and thought processes, including alternative routes taken through problem spaces, and to retrospectively analyze those traces and products by reconsidering what has been done, may eventually lead—beyond the acquisition of domain-relevant strategies and control structures—to an overall *reflectivity* which characterizes more mature and expert learners and problem solvers.

From Robinson-Crusoe-Learning[6] to Supportive Contexts of Collaborative Learning

Intelligence should not be seen as a property of the mind alone but rather as a quality that is distributed among the components of learning systems and the social-cognitive environments in which they are embedded (Bruner, 1986; Pea, 1987; Salomon, Perkins, & Globerson, 1991). Apprentices and nascent experts of almost any demanding domain don't develop professional knowledge and skill like the lonely Robinson, that is, as single and independent learners. Instead, they receive substantial expert guidance in instructional settings which supply rich knowledge sources and competent scaffolding. A significant part of learning occurs in interaction with more knowledgeable and skilled, significant others (Mead, 1934; Vygotsky, 1978). It is, in contrast, a certainly questionable feature of our traditional culture of schooling that students are treated almost exclusively as lonely, single learners—as *solo learners,* as Bruner (1986) says. It is unlikely that in the near future computers will become really good conversational partners or sensitive coaches and critics. However, as components that help foster cooperative learning, they can play an important role in classroom learning where collaborative work is supported.

P8. Extend the use of computer-based instructional tools into a supportive classroom culture of collaborative learning.

Computers should not be seen primarily as isolated tools for single learners but rather as instructional devices in classroom environments that support collaborative learning. Computers permit teachers to arrange a broad variety of collaborative learning activities around the reified conceptualizations of students:

• Small learning groups can look back over their comprehension or solution paths and mutually discuss their situation models;

• learning dyads and groups might also view (abstracted) replays or animated traces of solution paths (including those of experts), interrogate aspects that were different, and reflect by which changes they could be improved (Collins & Brown, 1988; Lajoie, this volume);

---

[6]Robinson Crusoe, the hero of Daniel Defoe's (1720) famous adventure story, who is cast up on a lonely island and condemned to reinvent and rediscover the tools of culture on his own, is the prototype of the lonely individual learner. Another romantic prototype of lonely learning is Jean Jacques Rousseau's (1762) solo learner Emile.

• study partners can collaborate in ways similar to patterns of cognitive apprenticeship, where partners alternatively assume the job of monitoring processes or of scaffolding a set of strategies;

• finally, pairs of students can engage in a dialogue while jointly planning a solution or constructing a shared situation model, thereby developing, refining, tuning, or repairing each other's mental models of the task (Roschelle, 1990; Salomon, 1990.)

HERON: A COGNITIVE TOOL FOR UNDERSTANDING AND SOLVING COMPLEX MATHEMATICAL WORD PROBLEMS

In the second part of the chapter, I describe a computer-assisted learning system called HERON,[7] developed for the domain of mathematical word or story problem solving, which was designed around the pedagogical and cognitive principles outlined above. I begin with a brief overview of the system and then describe the cognitive-pedagogical analysis of the task. In so doing I concentrate on solution trees as the representational format used for instruction in planning and problem conceptualization in this domain. Finally, I describe in some detail an example of how it can be used for instruction.

As is known from educational practice and from countless studies conducted over the past decade (for a review, see Verschaffel, in press), mathematical word problems are difficult for students at all grade levels. At critical points of students' school careers, applied mathematical problems are often used to assess situated mathematical knowledge and cognitive skills, such as planning, problem-solving, reasoning, or abstraction.

Mathematical word problems contain a description of an action, story, or process structure and an implicit or latent mathematical structure. Both textual worlds, which are interwoven with each other, are related by a problem question defining a variable, the value of which has to be determined.

The system HERON was designed to assist children to improve on this curricular task. It is related to three main lines of work: to the theory of discourse comprehension of van Dijk and Kintsch (1983), to our cognitive simulation work on problem comprehension and mathematization (Reusser, 1985, 1989a, 1990a), and to the cognitive and instructional framework of Aebli (1980, 1981, 1983), including work on solving complex mathematical story problems (Aebli & Staub, 1985; Aebli, Ruthemann, & Staub, 1986).

HERON is a *graphics-based instructional tool for facilitating and fostering*

---

[7]After the Greek mathematician HERON of Alexandria (appr. 100 BC) who created some of the first mathematical word problems, still found in modern mathematical text books, and who, in his book *De automatis,* far ahead of our time thought about the facilitation of life by building machines.

self-directed understanding and solving of complex mathematical story problems. The system is designed to assist students from grade levels 3 through 9 in understanding the language of a problem in order to construct internally a concrete episodic situation model, and to construct externally an explicit and reified mathematical problem model from which a linear equation can be derived.

The system provides the user with a basic instructional format or tool for problem representation—tree structures—and two kinds of instructional strategies that can be accessed. *Solution trees* or *planning trees* are used by the system to conceptualize mathematical problems at an intermediary, bridging stage between text-surface and underlying equation. The first kind of strategy is directed at text comprehension: the analysis of the problem-text in order to build an internal model of the problem situation (situation model). These relatively weak strategies, which the user can call on as needed, supply explanatory help with respect to the vocabulary, the syntactic and the semantic structure of complex texts. The second kind of strategy aid is directed at the constructive abstraction of the mathematical structure of a problem. It helps students to identify, analyze, and conceptualize the relevant pieces of information, and supports the reified planning and construction of a mathematical problem model, including the derivation of an equation.

HERON gives the student a fair amount of interactive flexibility and a high degree of control both in conceptualizing the problem and in planning the mathematical solution. Although HERON does provide instructional help according to students' needs, it does not perform any behavioral diagnosis on the basis of *student modeling.* Instead, our approach follows the design philosophy of *unintelligent tutoring* put forth in ANIMATE by Nathan, Kintsch, and Young (1990). However, in contrast to ANIMATE, which does not try to understand the student at all, HERON performs a behavioral analysis of what the student is doing on the basis of cognitive task analysis.

Cognitive Task Analysis I: From Text to Situation to Equation

Professional teaching should be based on a sound cognitive psychological and didactic decomposition of the curricular task at hand, including an analysis of the product and of the processes involved. As a starting point for teaching children to understand and solve mathematical word problems, one needs first a clear picture not only of the mathematical and the domain concepts involved, but also of the underlying comprehension and mathematization skills by which students of various levels of ability and practice extract mathematical information from verbal problem statements.

Understanding mathematical text problems is a complex and knowledge-intensive inferential and highly constructive process that requires skillfull interaction of more than one kind of knowledge, including linguistic, situational, as well as mathematical knowledge. In school mathematics, this interaction entails transforming natural-language problem texts into some canonical form of mathematical expression, for example, an equation. In this process, the mathematical deep structure of a word problem is merely *one* constraining factor for getting at the right arithmetic strategies. Indeed, factors other than mathematical skill are a major source of difficulty with word problems (Cummins, Kintsch, Reusser, & Weimer, 1988; Staub & Reusser, 1991). Thus, linguistically cued situational and mathematical understanding is not optional, or superfluous, but a helpful and mandatory achievement (for empirical evidence see, e.g., De Corte, Verschaffel, & de Win, 1985; Hudson, 1983; Reusser, 1988, 1989b).

By integrating work from Aebli (1980) and from Kintsch and Greeno (1985), I have developed a rule-based simulation model (Reusser, 1985, 1990a) that illuminates the role of language and situational factors in understanding and solving word problems, and that provides explicit and detailed descriptions about the tacit knowledge involved in these processes. The computational model takes elementary addition and subtraction word problems as input, understands and solves them by using various strategies (in the sense of van Dijk & Kintsch, 1983) and by creating several transient representations based on the words in the problem texts. The process includes the construction of four interrelated and mutually constraining mental representations or levels of comprehension: a *textbase* as a propositional representation of the textual input, a *situational model* as an elaborated qualitative representation of what the text is about, a *mathematical problem model* as the abstract gist of the situation, and an *equation* (Fig. 5.4).

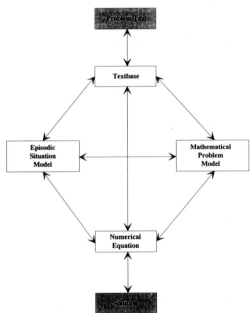

FIG. 5.4. Four interconnected levels of comprehension in solving mathematical word problems (after Reusser, 1985).

The ideal didactic sequence for learning the right *mapping between text, situation model, and equation,* is to consciously go through and elaborate these levels of comprehension. But it will be no surprise that students often deviate in characteristic ways from this pattern. There are the skilled students, on the one hand, who frequently skip a detailed qualitative modeling of the structure of the situation. Their mathematical strategies, deeply connected with rich patterns of situational knowledge, allow them to get directly at an abstract mathematical problem model or the numerical equation. When reading a problem they can almost immediately "see" the right mathematical schema, trigger a smart super-strategy and map it onto the problem situation. Weaker or novice students, on the other hand, who adopt similar strategies of "direct translation" (see Bobrow, 1964) by trying to jump from the text to an equation, fail with the same tasks. Still other students, who are severely lacking in all types of relevant knowledge and skills (linguistic comprehension skills, domain knowledge, and efficient mathematical knowledge) sometimes adopt even worse *coping* strategies that bypass the logic of mathematical sense-making activities (Lehtinen, 1989; Reusser, 1984, 1988; Schoenfeld, 1989). For example, there are students who simply plug numbers into some equations, or perform various kinds of "magic" number work. These students need the guidance of an adequate pedagogical setting. They have to learn to analyse and conceptualize a problem step by step:

• First, they need help putting the problem into a language that allows them to connect its semantic content with their everyday and intuitive concepts and experience;

• next, they must work towards constructing a mathematical understanding of the problem (by establishing the appropriate intermediary problem representations;

• finally, they must map these onto a formalized notation in a canonical format.

Cognitive Task Analysis II: Solution Trees as Representational Tools

Conceptual representation, which is related to the crucial issues of *task analysis* and of *problem space reification,* has been the major driving force for the design of HERON. Although ordinary language provides us with the single most important medium (Bruner et al., 1966) for communication and representation of meaning, there are certain kinds of information that cannot be adequately expressed linguistically. Because it lacks explicitness and because it contains many irrelevant details, ordinary language is not an efficient instructional representation for mathematical structure, for example, for the quantitative entities and relations implied by mathematical story problems. The mathematization of a word problem requires a step-by-step transformation of its textual structure into more adequate, perceptually enhanced and computationally efficient (Larkin &. Simon, 1987) forms of representation, ultimately a numeric format. A crucial step in this process is to find *auxiliary representations* (Paige & Simon, 1966) which are intermediary to both the textbase (Kintsch, 1974) and the underlying mathematical structure, that is, which mediate between language and situation comprehension and quantitative, or mathematical thinking.

HERON uses a graphical format for problem representation, planning, and reflection, called *calculation or solution trees* (Aebli, Ruthemann, & Staub, 1986; Derry & Hawkes, 1989),[8] or *conceptual planning trees.* As an analytic tool, solution trees supply a network formalism of dynamically linked entities designed to capture the operative, semantic-mathematical deep structures implied in a broad range of story (algebra) problems. As a mental modeling tool for students, the tree structures, which can be flexibly manipulated and visually inspected, provide a means for reifying both planning and construction processes and the (intermediary) products of understanding.

The semantic building blocks of solution trees are *domain-specific relational schemata,* each schema forming a subgoal in an arbitrary complex, hierarchical solution tree. Each relational schema or triad consists of a pair of qualitatively and numerically specified *situation units,* allowing the computation of a third, unknown unit. Each situation until is expressed as a box containing three sub-fields of information: a field for the *numerical value,* which may be unknown, a field for the *unit of measurement,* and a textual label field, containing semantic information about the unit's *situational role* which links the quantitative information to a qualitative situation model.

Examples of the graphical form of the situational elements composing different relational schemata are depicted in Fig. 5.5. Domain-specific relations— *Sachverhältnisse,* as Selz (1922) called them—form the basic semantic units of HERON. Their conceptual complexity is a major source of the difficulty of (algebra) word problems, requiring situated, world-knowledge-based reasoning.

Solution trees in HERON are constructed through mixed forward- or backward-inferencing activity. Forward-inferencing means that the student's solution starts by constructing triads based on the quantities given in the problem statements. Backward-inferencing means that the student starts with the goal element contained in an explicitly stated or inferred problem question and works backwards to the given elements via some intermediate calculational levels. In any case, quantitative elements of the problem text, which are recognized as solution-relevant, problem-specific mathematical relations, are combined first with local, then with progressively larger, hierarchical compositions of triadic schemata. The (sub)goal-driven construction proceeds until the mathematical solu-

---

[8]Derry and Hawkes (1989) use an almost identical concept of solution trees as a basic representational format in their system, TAPS. Both groups have developed their ideas completely independently of each other.

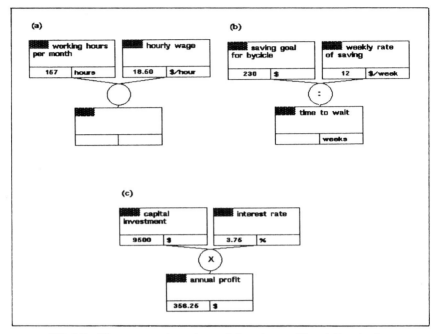

FIG. 5.5.   Three nascent versions of domain-specific relational schemata or Sachverhältnisse (Selz, 1922) as examples of the building
blocks of solution trees. (a) and (b) are incomplete, (c) is completed.
Each schema relates (R) two semantic concepts in a mathematically
meaningful way. Other examples: R (distance, speed, time); R (initial
price, discount, sale price); R (volume, mass, density).

tion, constrained by the form of the completed planning-tree, can be computed
from a final triadic schema.

Figure 5.6 shows two solution trees describing alternative mathematical conceptualizations of the same problem including different final equations. Both
solution paths can be mapped onto each other through the laws of associativity
and commutativity.

Taken together, there are many reasons to consider solution trees (ST) as
cognitively plausible and useful representational and conceptual tools in HERON
and as a goal for instruction. Solution trees incorporate most of the qualitative
features outlined earlier (see principle P5):

• they are transparent, self-explanatory, and visually inspectable cognitive
instruments for representing, evaluating, and communicating the processes of
understanding and solving of a large class of word problems;

• they are manipulable, perceptual, highly dynamic and flexible forms for
constraining knowledge-construction processes and their (intermediary) products;

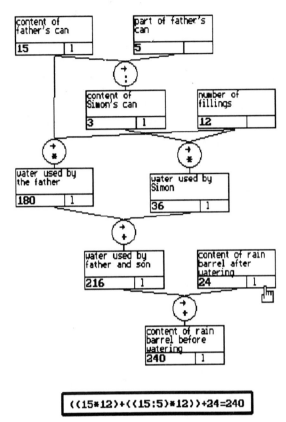

FIG. 5.6a. Two different solution trees mirroring two paths of comprehension of the same task: Little Simon and his father are watering
their vegetable garden. The father has a 15-liter watering can. Simon's
can holds one fifth of that. Both fill their cans 12 times. After that, there
are still 24 liters in the rain barrel. How much water can the rain barrel
hold? (translation from German)

- they illuminate the hidden construction processes by which the student determines the structure of problem situations;
- in so doing they make students' thinking overt and accessible to reflection and discussion;
- they encourage generative understanding, i.e., one can start constructing a tree without already having completely understood the problem;
- they provide an efficient form of written calculus that can be directly translated into informationally equivalent equations;
- they provide a bridging representation intermediate to both text and implicit mathematical structure;

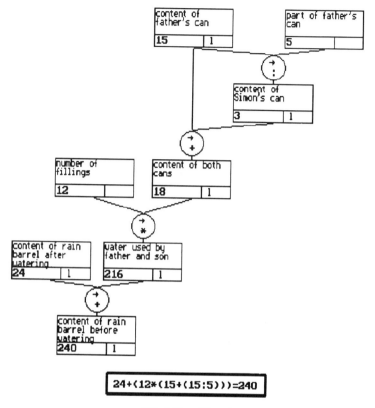

FIG. 5.6b. (Cont.)

- they facilitate movement between textual (situational) and mathematical understanding;
- they are usable for students from a very early age;
- they provide a basis for the design of feedback.

The concept of solution or calculation trees was theoretically derived from an earlier notion of *Simplex-Complex structures* (Breidenbach, 1963; Fricke, 1987), introduced as *thinking tools* (Bauersfeld, 1965) into mathematics education in the '60s. Bauersfeld defined a *simplex* as "a relational network across three mathematically relevant domain-concepts" (p. 125), whereas a *complex* is a combination of simplex structures. Solution trees are used in Swiss and German mathematics text books as an intelligible, but hardly flexible tool (with respect to pencil and paper manipulation).[9]

---

[9]A formalism similar to the framework of solution trees was proposed by Shalin and Bee (Greeno, 1987), and further discussed by Hall, Kibler, Wenger, and Truxaw (1989). In Shalin and

Solution trees allow simultaneous grasping of both the semantic (situational) and the mathematical deep structure denoted by a problem text. By following the different converging semantic and mathematical constraints propagated through the network structure of a solution tree, the corresponding problem can be understood on three levels: on a purely *semantic level of domain relations* (Sachverhältnisse); on the level of *numbers and quantitative operations* that progressively constrain the mathematical unknown; and finally, on the level of *units of measurement*.

With regard to instruction, the crucial aspect of solution trees is that they do not allow one to focus only on the latent or implicit mathematical structure of a problem; that is, they are tools of both quantitative and qualitative reasoning. By providing subfields of information describing the semantic role of every quantitative entity processed in a tree and relating these to the problem as a whole, students are forced to reconstruct a problem at its mathematical *and* semantic (linguistic-situational) level. In HERON the labels that interpret the semantic meaning of a quantity in the qualitative context of an episodic situation, or action, are called *situation concepts*. To find adequate and concise situation concepts, which give episodic meaning to any quantity employed in the construction of a tree, is not a trivial task. Good situation concepts are both products of task analysis and conceptual tools for the synthesis of the solution. While the network of quantities in a tree provides a mathematical interpretation, the network of situation concepts provides a semantic interpretation of the problem.

Solution trees and the tool kit for their construction in HERON not only give students a way to express graphically what they *think* the content-specific mathematical deep structure of a wide class of problems is, but also provide students with a constraining *schematic format* or a control structure for how the mathematical problem model ought to look. That is, by means of their schematic properties, solution trees provide a *structural form* for the planning and construction of mental models. While the mathematical understanding of a problem situation takes shape in a student's head, the schematic form of the solution tree serves as a perceptual constraint that must be satisfied by overtly constructing it on the screen of the computer.

Bee's conceptual language (which inspired also work by Thompson, 1990), networks of quantitative entities are used to describe the quantitative forms of classes of mathematical story algebra problems. Differences with the representational format used in HERON have to do with how mathematical entities and operations are treated. To my understanding, Shalin and Bees' formalism is closer to a more static and formalist view of mathematical structure, whereas solution trees, with their explicit notation of mathematical operations, are closer to an operative view of mathematical thinking (Aebli, 1980; Piaget, 1970). According to Piaget, mathematical operations are the developmental derivatives of certain classes of sensorimotor actions bearing an abstract mathematical meaning to be expressed by the set of elementary mathematical operations. However, it is beyond the scope of this chapter to provide a detailed comparison of the two conceptual approaches.

A Sample Session with HERON

HERON has been designed to facilitate the solving of any story problem that can be represented by solution trees. There are two implementations of the system: A prototype version is written in Loops and runs on a Xerox workstation (Kämpfer, 1991); another version designed for use in classrooms is written in C and runs on IBM-type machines (Stüssi, 1991).

Only a little instruction is needed to achieve almost full use of the functions in HERON. It takes third graders about 20 minutes to become familiar with the entirely mouse-driven interface of the system. Most commands and graphical tools are available as buttons displayed on the screen. Some important menus, as, for example, for filling situation concepts in solution trees, can be activated by pushing a mouse button in an appropriate, active region of the screen. In order to demonstrate the functioning of the system, the following section describes two examples of how students can use it.

The problem text of the first example is shown in Fig. 5.6. Previous to any overt construction, the student selects a problem and reads it. Following reading, the student is asked by the computer to identify relevant quantitative information in the problem text. This is done by highlighting numbers or number-placeholders in the text with the mouse-cursor. When a piece of numerical information is selected, the system creates a graphical situation unit with the selected number already filled in. The student is then asked to fill in a unit of measurement (for example *liters*) and a textual label (for example *content of father's can*). The label can be selected as a whole from a menu, or it can be constructed from a list of word elements from a menu. After the situation unit has been completed, a new piece of information is selected from the text. Depending on how the system is initialized (e.g., for weak or novice students), the student gets an error message if he or she selects a piece of irrelevant information from the text or fails to select a relevant piece. In the standard (non-novice) condition, the student decides on his or her own when to stop selecting numbers and creating situation units.

After setting up some situation elements, the student can start planning and constructing a tree-structure for the solution (Fig. 5.7). In order to create and instantiate a preliminary relational schema, for example, in order to achieve the subgoal of computing the content of Simon's can, the units labeled *content of father's can* and *part of father's can* are selected with the mouse, moved to the upper left corner of the screen and linked together. The latter is done by selecting, placing, and linking an empty operator node (circle) and two line segments. With the selection of an operator node, an empty box is automatically generated by the system. That is, for every pair of situation elements linked by an empty operator slot (circle), the system completes the nascent relational schema by creating an empty element or subgoal-slot. Before the user, with the help of menus, can fill the unit of measurement and the label into the emerging third element, he/she is asked to select the appropriate mathematical operation from a

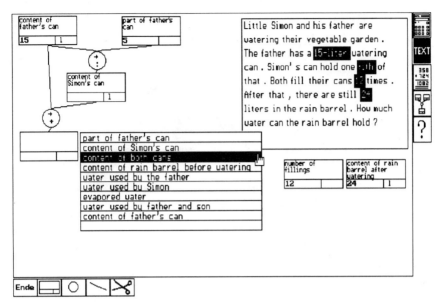

FIG. 5.7. Partial solution tree of the Simon task (for problem text see
Fig. 6; implementation on IBM AT compatible; translation from German).

menu which appears by pushing the mouse on the operator node. Now the
student can fill in the label (*content of Simon's can*) and the unit of measurement
(*liters*) and decide if he/she wants to calculate the subgoal immediately. The
calculation can be done with or without system support: for example, clicking on
the numerical field lets the system calculate and display the correct result in the
numerical field.

After each relational schema is instantiated, its resulting element can be used
to generate new schemata and to achieve further subgoals. It is up to the student
to choose which comprehension path to follow, that is, how to navigate through
the problem space. In order to determine the intermediate level subgoal of the
total amount of water carried by father and son, there are two main paths open.
In the first path (Figs. 5.7 and 5.8), an additive schema is first generated which
computes the content *of both watering cans,* and then a multiplicative schema is
instantiated computing the *total amount of water.* In a second, slightly more
complicated path (depicted in Fig. 5.6a), the order of mathematical operations is
reversed: The instantiation of two multiplicative schemata

MULTIPLY (number of fillings, content of father's can)
MULTIPLY (number of fillings, content of Simon's can)

is followed by an additive schema

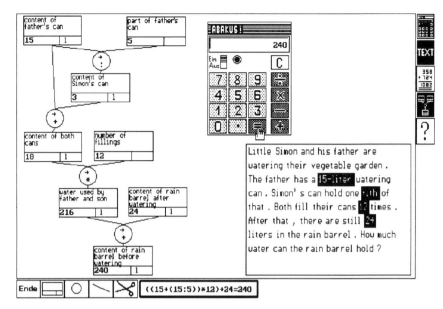

FIG. 5.8.   Complete solution tree of the Simon task.

ADD (amount of water carried by the father, amount of
water carried by the son)

leading to the same intermediate result (216 liters). Relating the *total amount of water carried* to the *amount of water remaining in the rain barrel* (24 liters) and computing the final schema leads to the final result of the *amount of water in the rain barrel before watering* (240 liters).

In order to generate equations from the solution tree, the student can click the right side of the mouse-button on any numerical value in the tree. The system then displays the equation with the selected value. For example, clicking on the value "216" in Fig. 5.6a would produce the partial equation

$$(15 * 12) + (15:5) * 12 = 216,$$

while clicking on the same value in Fig. 5.6b would produce the following equation:

$$12 * (15 + (15:5)) = 216.$$

And clicking on the final value of "240" in Fig. 5.8 will produce the goal-generating equation

$$((15 + (15:5)) * 12) + 24 = 240.$$

An example of a much more complex problem is the *Afghanistan* task. It was developed by Aebli and Staub (1985) as a new type of authentic and rich situation problems to be used in mathematics education. The elaborated story contains a nontrivial episodic, that is nonmathematical structure, describing an agent who is planning and executing a complex action leading from an initial state to an end state. The successful execution of each of its parts requires that certain situational conditions, which are either produced or encountered by the agent, be fullfilled.

Afghanistan is a mountainous country, just like Switzerland, but much drier. There are fewer springs and streams, and water is rare and valuable. From a small village a muletrack leads over a pass into a small town. To drive animals into town, one needs several days. At the end of the first day, one comes to an alp. Here a shepherd boy keeps 18 sheep and 15 goats. Above the alp, there is a snowfield which melts in the course of the summer. The water then flows towards the alp and gives 110 liters of drinking water a day for the animals. But now, the snow has not melted. Until it does, the animals drink from a waterhole below the rocks in which the water from a spring is collected. The hole is not leak-proof, so 35 liters of water ooze away every day. Each sheep drinks about 5.4 liters a day, each goat 3.8 liters.

The shepherd drinks about 2.3 liters of goatmilk a day. The spring yields 350 liters of water a day. Every day 5 liters evaporate. Each evening the shepherd drains the waterhole. He leads all the water that is left through a small canal into a basin. He has just done that this evening. He estimates that there are 90 liters of water in the basin at the moment. Another 120 liters of water ooze away as it flows to the basin. It is not lost, however. It irrigates the meadow below the small canal. As a result, more grass grows here. The shepherd can cut it 3 times a year and obtains 150 kilograms of hay each time. The hay is brought to the village and fed to the animals during wintertime. The basin is fenced with poles, so the sheep and the goats cannot drink from it. From time to time, the peasants drive some cows from the village over the pass into the town and sell them at the market. On the first day, they find water on only at the alp. When they get there, the shepherd boy takes the poles away from the basin and lets the cows drink from it. On the day on which he has estimated the available water, his father arrives at the alp late in the evening. He says to his son: "I want to bring 24 cows to the market as soon as possible. I think that they'll need a total of 320 liters of water up here." The boy says: "I can calculate when you can come." When can his father come with the cows?

As with the mathematization of any demanding word problem, the solving of the Afghanistan task requires the implicit quantitative structure to become explicit as an interconnected system of mathematical relations. However, before the underlying quantitative structure can be generated in its ultimate representational format of a solution equation, one has to understand, in a constructive effort after meaning, the problem text, the situation denoted by the text, and the implicit mathematical relations involved. The complexity of these processes of understanding, and the fact, that they require sequential and hierarchical planning,

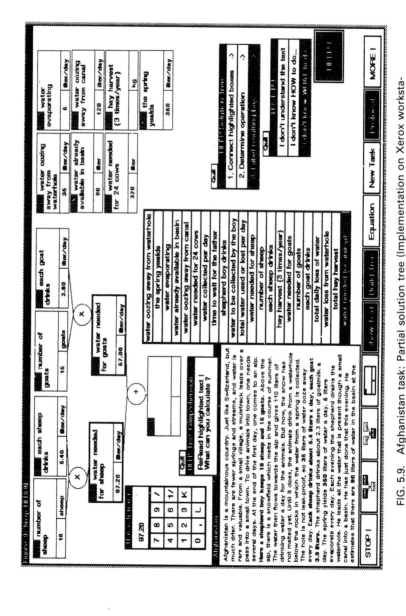

FIG. 5.9. Afghanistan task: Partial solution tree (Implementation on Xerox workstation 1186; translation from German)

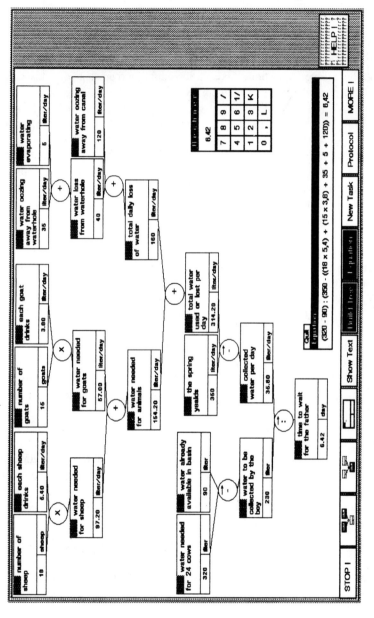

FIG. 5.10. Afghanistan task: Completed solution tree.

makes solution or planning trees especially suitable to the solving of semantically rich action problems like the Afghanistan task.

Figure 5.9 shows a solution tree (one among several possible trees) *in statu nascendi,* while Fig. 5.10 shows the same tree in its completed form as a coherent and hierarchical system of mathematical relations to be mapped onto a corresponding solution equation. From the operational perspective set up by the quantitative problem question, this solution equation represents the most concise synoptic form of the relevant mathematical aspects of the complex action.

While using HERON the student can call on a *HELP* component for both deeper comprehension of the problem text and for the construction of solution trees. *Text comprehension aids* mainly consist of explanations of words, paraphrasing of sentences, and of giving hints about which text fragments belong together and should be processed together. *Construction aids for solution trees* operate in conjunction with the aids for text comprehension, and provide help in operating the system (how to use the tools of the interface), with planning, and with constructing the trees (cf. Kämpfer, 1991; Stüssi, 1991). With the latter type of help the system provides the student (on request) with progressively more detailed hints about what to do next, ultimately offering a next operative step.

With respect to *feedback,* HERON is unintelligent, but nevertheless fairly powerful. The system does not perform cognitive diagnosis based on individualized student modeling. So far, it knows nothing about the thinking of individual students while solving a problem. However, HERON does know how to build conceptual networks, and what students are *overtly doing* when constructing their solution trees. HERON is thus able to provide feedback and customized help to the individual student on the basis of a detailed task analysis. With respect to tasks, HERON knows which quantified situation elements can or must (not) be connected in a solution tree, and which labels and units of measurement are to be attached to each quantified situation unit. HERON is able to monitor the students' overt constructive activity of planning and creating a solution tree, and to provide feedback on four types of errors: (a) mathematical operation errors (two situation units are connected by a false operation), (b) labeling errors, if an incorrect situational role concept is attached to a quantity box or situation unit, (c) errors on the selection of units of measurement, and (d) errors regarding the false inclusion or ommission of (ir)relevant mathematical information in a solution tree.[10]

Ongoing Work: The Use of HERON for Instruction

The Afghanistan task gives an impression of the constructive power and flexibility of HERON, which allows the student to decompose a problem into relational

---

[10]A different and more "intelligent" approach to error handling is used by Derry and Hawkes (1989) in the TAPS system, which is very similar to HERON in its representational format. TAPS treats errors as deviations from recognizable and preset ideal solution paths.

building blocks or subgoals and to create solution trees of almost any complexity and in any arbitrary sequence in which subgoals can be achieved. The task also illustrates the diverse and demanding *language and situation comprehension activities* that are required in solving mathematical word problems (Staub & Reusser, 1991). HERON thus can be applied as a cognitive tool to the two fundamental curricular tasks of schooling, mathematics education and reading or language comprehension instruction. Moreover, HERON can also be considered as a preparatory tool for algebra instruction: The combination of the hierarchical nature of solution trees, which are easily translatable into equations, and the system's ability to form a parameter for any given number in a problem, makes it possible to redescribe any solution tree in terms of the assigned parameters.

For the most part, the students in HERON work in pairs. After an instructional phase of 10 to 20 minutes that includes the construction of a sample solution tree, students are able to construct the solution tree for a simple problem. Complex tree, such as the Afghanistan task, may take much longer. In constructing solution trees, most students thus far have followed a *modus operandi of forward chaining* similar to the strategy described by Derry and Hawkes (1989): After a first relational unit is schematically constructed (by drawing three boxes or situation units), the boxes are numerically and situationally interpreted by filling in the numbers (one of them to be computed), the units of measurement, and the situation concepts. Then, the next schema is constructed that includes the previous result set as one of its elements. The construction—proceeding stepwise from the given information to the anticipated goal state—continues in this manner until the tree is completed.

HERON records in a log file all activities performed on the screen, including time characteristics and turn taking with the mouse. This allows *the comprehension (solution) paths to be replayed.* Pairs of students can reflect upon and discuss their solution paths. Replays are used to elicit more complete retrospective reports on what the students were thinking while solving the problem.

HERON is currently being evaluated in classroom settings that encourage collaborative problem solving in groups or pairs. It is also being tested in an empirical study comparing the solving of word problems by single users and by pairs *with and without HERON.* We think that pairs of students working together can support each other in many ways beneficial to each other. On the one hand, pairs of students share the diverse activities directly related to solving the problems, such as jointly constructing understanding of problems, monitoring and refining each other's constructions of mental models, or discussing alternative solution paths. By working together they are also able to use the system more effectively. Computer-based learning environments may still be relatively weak, compared to a sensitive human teacher, and thus require multiple and combined expertise—from the system's own (modest) intelligence and from intelligent users alike.

ACKNOWLEDGMENTS

The work in this paper was supported by the Swiss National Science Foundation (Grant No. 10-2052.86. I wish to thank the members of our research group, in which many of the ideas in this paper were shaped and discussed: Xander Kämpfer, Markus Sprenger, Fritz C. Staub, Rita Stebler, and Ruedi Stüssi. I equally appreciate the many invaluable comments on the writing of this chapter from Eileen Kintsch, as well as those of the Editors. Ruedi Stüssi's and Xander Kämpfer's assistance in preparing the figures of the chapter is also gratefully acknowledged.

REFERENCES

Aebli, H. (1961). *Grundformen des Lehrens*. Stuttgart: Klett.

Aebli, H. (1978). Von Piagets Entwicklungspsychologie zur Theorie der kognitiven Sozialisation. In G. Steiner (Ed.), *Piaget und die Folgen*. Zürich: Kindler.

Aebli, H. (1980, 1981). *Denken, Das Ordnen des Tuns* (Two vols.). Stuttgart: Klett.

Aebli, H. (1983). *Zwölf Grundformen des Lehrens*. Stuttgart: Klett.

Aebli, H., & Staub, F. C. (1985, August). *From "text comprehension" to the mathematical comprehension of text*. Paper presented at the First Convention of the European Association for Research on Learning and Instruction EARLI, Leuven, Belgium.

Aebli, H., Ruthemann, U., & Staub, F. C. (1986). Sind Regeln des Problemlösens lehrbar? *Zeitschrift für Pädagogik, 32*, 617–638.

Anderson, J. A., Boyle, C. F., Farrell, R., & Reiser, R. (1984). Cognitive principles in the design of computer tutors. *Proceedings of the Sixth Annual Conference of the Cognitive Science Society*, Boulder, Colorado.

Barker, R. C. (1978). Theory of behavior settings. In R. C. Barker (Ed.), *Habitats, environments, and human behavior*. San Francisco: Jossey-Bass.

Bartlett, F. C. (1932). *Remembering*. London: Cambridge University Press.

Bauersfeld, H. (1965). Der Simplex-Begriff im Sachrechnen der Volksschule. *Die Schulwarte, 18*, 124–132.

Beck, E. (1989). Eigenständiges Lernen. *Beiträge zur Lehrerbildung, 7*, 169–178.

Bobrow, D. G. (1964). *Natural language input for a computer problem solving system*. Unpublished doctoral thesis, MIT.

Breidenbach, W. (1963). *Rechnen in der Volksschule*. Hannover: Schroedel Verlag.

Brown, A. L., & Palincsar, A. S. (1989). Guided, cooperative learning and individual knowledge acquisition. In L. B. Resnick (Ed.), *Knowing, learning and instruction*. Hillsdale, NJ: Lawrence Erlbaum Associates.

Brown, A. L., & Campione, J. C. (1990). Interactive learning environments and the teaching of science and mathematics. In M. Gardner, J. G. Greeno, F. Reif, A. H. Schoenfeld, A. DiSessa, & E. Stage (Eds.), *Toward a scientific practice of science education*. Hillsdale, NJ: Lawrence Erlbaum Associates.

Bruner, J. (1961). The act of discovery. *Harvard Educational Review, 31*, 21–32.

Bruner, J. (1986). *Actual minds, possible worlds*. Cambridge, MA: Harvard University Press.

Bruner, J. S. (1990). *Acts of meaning*. Cambridge, MA: Harvard University Press.

Bruner, J. S., Olver, R. R., & Greenfield, P. M. (1966). *Studies in cognitive growth*. New York: Wiley.

Clancey, W. (1989). Situated cognition and intelligent tutoring systems. In H. Maurer (Ed.), *Computer-assisted learning*. New York: Springer.

Collins, A., & Brown, J. S. (1988). The computer as a tool for learning through reflection. In H. Mandl & A. Lesgold (Eds.), *Learning issues for intelligent tutoring systems.* New York: Springer.

Collins, A., Brown, J. S., & Newman, S. E. (1989). Cognitive apprenticeship: Teaching the crafts of reading, writing, and mathematics. In L. B. Resnick (Ed.), *Knowing, learning and instruction.* Hillsdale, NJ: Lawrence Erlbaum Associates.

Cumming, G., & Self, J. (1990). Intelligent educational systems: identifying and decoupling the conversational levels. *Instructional Science, 19,* 11–27.

Cummins, D., Kintsch, W., Reusser, K., & Weimer, R. (1988). The role of understanding in solving word problems. *Cognitive Psychology, 20,* 439–462.

De Corte, E., Verschaffel, L., & de Win, L. (1985). Influence of rewording problems on Children's problem representations and solutions. *Journal of Educational Psychology, 77,* 460–470.

Derry, S. J., & Hawkes, L. W. (1989). *Error-driven cognitive apprenticeship: A feasible ITS approach.* Florida State University, Tallahassee.

Duncker, K. (1935). *Zur Psychologie des produktiven Denkens.* Berlin: Springer.

Fricke, A. (1987). *Sachrechnen, Das Lösen angewandter Aufgaben.* Stuttgart: Klett.

Glaser, R. (1987). The study of cognition and instructional design: Mutual nurturance. *Behavioral and Brain Sciences, 10,* 483–84.

Greeno, J. G. (1983). Conceptual entities. In D. Gentner & A. L. Stevens (Eds.), *Mental models.* Hillsdale, NJ: Lawrence Erlbaum Associates.

Greeno, J. G. (1987). Instructional representations based on research about understanding. In A. H. Schoenfeld (Ed.), *Cognitive Science and mathematics education.* Hillsdale, NJ: Lawrence Erlbaum Associates.

Hall, R., Kibler, D., Wenger, E., & Truxaw, C. (1989). Exploring the episodic structure of algebra story problem solving. *Cognition and Instruction, 6,* 223–283.

Hollenstein, A., Staub, F. C., & Stüssi, R. (1987). Was passiert, wenn . . . Computersimulation als didaktisches Hilfsmittel. *Schweizer Schule, 10,* 10–16.

Hudson, T. (1983). Correspondences and numerical differences between disjoint sets. *Child Development, 54,* 84–80.

Hutchins, E. L., Hollan, J. D., & Norman, D. A. (1985). Direct manipulation interfaces. In D. A. Norman & S. W. Draper (Eds.), *User centered system design: New perspectives on human-computer interaction.* Hillsdale, NJ: Lawrence Erlbaum Associates.

Kämpfer, A. (1991). *Prototypische Entwicklung eines adaptiven tutoriellen Systems zum Verstehen und Lösen mathematischer Textaufgaben.* Lizentiatsarbeit. University of Bern, Switzerland.

Kaput, J. J. (1989). Linking representations in the symbol systems of algebra. In S. Wagner & C. Kieran (Eds.), *Research issues in the learning and teaching of algebra.* Reston, VA: The National Council of Teachers of Mathematics.

Kintsch, W. (1974). *The representation of meaning in memory.* Hillsdale, NJ: Lawrence Erlbaum Associates.

Kintsch, W., & Greeno, J. G. (1985). Understanding and solving word arithmetic problems. *Psychological Review, 92,* 109–129.

Klafki, W. (1963). *Das pädegogische Problem des Elementaren und die Theorie der kategorialen Bildung.* Weinheim: Beltz.

Larkin, J. M., & Simon, H. A. (1987). Why a diagram is (sometimes) worth ten thousand words. *Cognitive Science, 11,* 65–99.

Lehtinen, E. (1989). Verstehen lehren als Verändern von Lern- und Bewältigungsstrategien. *Beiträge zur Lehrerbildung, 7,* 213–219.

McArthur, D., Stasz, C., & Zmuidzinas, M. (1990). Tutoring techniques in algebra. *Cognition and Instruction, 7,* 161–195.

Mead, G. H. (1934). *Mind, self, and society.* Chicago: Chicago University Press.

Nathan, J. N., Kintsch, W., Young, E. (1990). *A theory of algebra word problem comprehension and its implications for unintelligent tutoring systems* (Technical Report 90-02). Institute of Cognitive Science, University of Colorado, Boulder.

Nesher, P. (1989). Microworlds in mathematical education: a pedagogical realism. In L. B. Resnick (Ed.), *Knowing, learning and instruction.* Hillsdale, NJ: Lawrence Erlbaum Associates.

Ohlsson, S. (1986). Some principles of intelligent tutoring. *Instructional Science, 14,* 293–326.

Ohlsson, S. (1987). Sense of reference in the design of interactive illustrations for rational numbers. In R. W. Lawler & M. Yazdani (Eds.), *Artificial intelligence and Education.* Norwood, NJ: Ablex.

Paige, J. M., & Simon, H. A. (1966). Cognitive processes in solving algebra word problems. In B. Kleinmuntz (Ed.), *Problem solving.* New York: Wiley.

Pea, R. D. (1987). Cognitive technologies for mathematics education. In A. H. Schoenfeld (Ed.), *Cognitive Science and mathematics education.* Hillsdale, NJ: Lawrence Erlbaum Associates.

Piaget, J. (1947). *La psychologie de l'intelligence.* Colin: Paris.

Piaget, J. (1970). *Genetic epistemology.* New York: Columbia University Press.

Piaget, J. (1973). *To understand is to invent.* New York: Grossman.

Polanyi, M. (1966). *The tacit dimension.* London: Routledge & Kegan.

Resnick, L. B., & Johnson, A. (1988). *Intelligent machines for intelligent people: Cognitive theory and the future of computer-assisted learning.* Pittsburgh: Learning Research and Development Center.

Reusser, K. (1984). *Problemlösen in wissenstheoretischer Sicht.* Unpublished doctoral dissertation. University of Bern, Switzerland.

Reusser, K. (1985). *From text to situation to equation* (Technical Report). Institute of Cognitive Science. University of Colorado, Boulder.

Reusser, K. (1988). Problem-solving beyond the logic of things: Contextual effects on understanding and solving word problems. *Instructional Science, 17,* 309–339.

Reusser, K. (1989a). *Vom Text zur Situation zur Gleichung. Kognitive Simulation von Sprachverständnis und Mathematisierung beim Lösen von mathematischen Textaufgaben.* Habilitation Thesis. University of Bern, Switzerland.

Reusser, K. (1989b, September). *Textual and situational factors in mathematical word problems.* Paper presented at the Third Conference of the European Association for Research on Learning and Instruction. Madrid/Spain.

Reusser, K. (1990a). From text to situation to equation: Cognitive simulation of understanding and solving mathematical word problems. In H. Mandl, E. De Corte, N. Bennett, & H. F. Friedrich (Eds.), *Learning and instruction in an international context* (Vol. II). New York: Pergamon Press.

Reusser, K. (1991, August). *Intelligent technologies and pedagogical theory: Computers as tools for thoughtful teaching and learning.* Invited address at the Fourth Conference of the European Association for Research on Learning and Instruction (EARLI). Turku, Finland.

Roschelle, J. (1990, April). *Designing for conversations.* Paper presented at the meeting of the American Educational Research Association, Boston.

Salomon, G. (1990, August). *The changing role of the teacher: From knowledge transmitter to exploration orchestrator.* Paper presented at the International Symposium on Research on Effective teaching and responsible learning. Fribourg, Switzerland.

Salomon, G., Perkins, D. N., & Globerson, T. (1991). Partners in cognition: Extending human intelligence with intelligent technologies. *Educational Research, 20*(3), 2–9.

Scardamalia, M., Bereiter, C., McLean, R. S., Swallow, J., & Woodruff, E. (1989). Computer-supported intentional learning environments. *Journal of Educational Computing Research, 5,* 51–68.

Schoenfeld, A. (1989). Problem solving in context(s). In R. I. Charles & E. A. Silver (Eds.), *The teaching and assessing of mathematical problem solving.* Reston, VA: National Council of Teachers of Mathematics.

Selz, O. (1922). *Zur Psychologie des produktiven Denkens und des Irrtums.* Bonn: Cohen.

Simon, H. A. (1977). *Models of discovery and other topics in the methods of science.* Dordrecht: Reidel.

Sleeman, D., & Brown, J. S. (1982). *Intelligent tutoring systems.* New York: Academic Press.

Staub, F. C., & Reusser, K. (1991, August). *What makes mathematical word problems difficult? The role of presentational factors.* Paper presented at the Fourth Conference of the European Association for Research on Learning and Instruction (EARLI). Turku, Finland.

Stüssi, R. (1991). *WATGRAF. Ein tutorielles System zum Lösen von handlungsbezogenen Sachaufgaben.* Lizentiatsarbeit. University of Bern, Switzerland.

Thompson, P. W. (1990). *Word Problem Analyst. Version 2.2. Tutorial I & II.* Center for Research in Mathematics and Science Education. San Diego State University.

Van Dijk, T., & Kintsch, W. (1983). *Strategies of discourse comprehension.* New York: Academic Press.

Van Hiele, P. M. (1986). *Structure and insight. A theory of mathematics education.* Orlando, FL: Academic Press.

Van Lehn, K. (1988). Student modeling. In M. Polson & J. J. Richardson (Eds.) *Foundations of intelligent tutoring systems.* Hillsdale, NJ: Lawrence Erlbaum Associates.

Verschaffel, L. (in press). A decade of research on word-problem solving in Leuven: Theoretical, methodological, and practical outcomes. *Educational Psychology Review.*

Vygotsky, L. S. (1978). *Minds in society: The development of higher psychological process.* Cambridge, MA: Harvard University Press.

Wenger, E. (1987). *Artificial intelligence and tutoring systems.* Los Altos, CA: Kaufmann.

Wertheimer, M. (1945). *Productive thinking.* New York: Harper.

Winston, P. H. (1984). *Artificial intelligence.* Reading, MA: Addison-Wesley.

6

On the Nature of Pedagogic Computer Tools: The Case of the Writing Partner

Gavriel Salomon
University of Arizona and The Haifa University, Israel

What is a tool? A tool is "an implement or device used directly upon a piece of material to shape it into desired form" (Encyclopedia Britanica, 1987, Vol. 28, p. 712). This definition needs, however, four clarifications. First, the *implement or device* need not be a real object; it can be a symbol system serving as a tool for expression and communication (Goodman, 1978), a mental strategy by means of which knowledge can be transformed, and it can be a computer program allowing the manipulation and creation of symbolic *materials*. Second, a tool is not just an implement; it entails the purposes for which it is culturally or *naturally* designed to serve, the ways in which it is used, the techniques that are necessary for its usage, and the skill and knowledge that its usage requires (Ellul, 1964). It would be difficult to conceptually distinguish between a microscope, the device, and the scientific functions it is designed to accomplish, the ways in which it is properly used, the skills its use assumes, and so on. Clearly, using the microscope as a paper weight, rather than as what is was designed for, would still render it a *tool* but it would be an entirely different kind of tool, to be judged for effectiveness and efficiency relative to bricks and old plaster sculpturines of dancers rather than relative to other instruments of magnification.

Third, implied in the definition but requiring explication is the notion that tools serve functions beyond themselves. Once an old brass microscope is used as a collector's item embedded with esthetic value it ceases to be a tool. It serves no purpose beyond itself. Tools do not have intrinsic value as their main justification. They have certain (external) purposes they are to serve, they have particular qualities or structures that allow them to serve their designated purposes, and they are based on particular rationales that explain and justify their goal-serving utility (Perkins, 1986). Last, tools need to be distinguished from machines.

Whereas machines are more or less autonomous in their functioning tools are not; they need to be skillfully operated upon throughout their functioning to achieve their purpose. Think, for example, of a car's engine as contrasted with the whole car; the former would be considered a machine while the latter—a tool (Ellul, 1964).

What makes a *good* computer tool? How do we determine that one tool, say STELLA, is *better* than another, say, the Geometric Supposer? Such a question may strike you as nonsensical for the simple reason that the qualities of all tools, and particularly versatile computer tools, greatly depend on the purposes for which they are designed and the ways in which they are used. After all, how does one compare the *goodness* of a screw driver with that of a wrench? And how does one compare LOGO when used as the subject matter of didactic instruction with its use as a language to open-endedly design time pieces with? Obviously, the quality of a tool can be judged only in light of its stated purposes, its intended and unintended effects, its structure and its rationale. Thus, the controversial issue, often discussed in this volume, concerning the design of more or less instructionally intelligent tools, tools of more or less diagnostic capability, or tools that embed a greater or lesser "understanding" of the student, may not be resolvable. The difficulty of resolution, aside of questions of feasibility, cost effectiveness, and the like, stems from the fact that different tools are designed to serve different purposes, are based on entirely different rationales, and thus have very different structures. And in the absence of common purposes, rationales, and structures, no comparing of relative effectiveness is possible.

At this point one has to distinguish between computer tools that fit the foregoing definition and those that do not and thus, are nontools. The former, genuine tools, are for example, model-builders, data sets affording manipulation, conceptual map-makers, simulations, and similarly partly or wholly open-ended instruments for the student to operate and manipulate. They are *tools* inasmuch as their operation depends on the learners' operations; they are *cognitive* inasmuch as they serve to aid students in their own constructive thinking, allowing them to transcend their cognitive limitations and engage in cognitive operations they would not have been capable of otherwise (Pea, 1985). On the other hand, many typical ITS programs, although not operating totally independently of the students, often entail sufficient artificial intelligence to make numerous important (mostly diagnostic and tutorial) decisions *for* the students. In this sense they are not really tools. Moreover, they are not really cognitive tools because, by the conception just presented, they are not designed to upgrade students' intelligent engagement. It should of course be added that not all ITS programs are of the same kind; some ITS programs come closer to being tools than others.

Why, one may wonder, is it so important to make these definitional distinctions? After all, what difference does it make whether we call one program a tool, or a cognitive tool, and another an intelligent tutor? There are two reasons for this seemingly pedantic distinction. First, underlying the differences of nature and structure are differences of theory and logic. Cognitive tools are based on the assumption best articulated by Scardamalia et al. (1989): "it is not the computer that should be doing the diagnosing, the goal-setting, and the planning, it is the student" (p. 54). This is a very different assumption from the ones underlying typical ITS. Second, and relatedly, the distinction offered suggests differences of mode of usage, and different criteria for the evaluation of quality and worth-whileness. Typical ITS are evaluated for their success in teaching and imparting knowledge structures. One does not evaluate ANGLE (Koedinger and Anderson, this volume) for the quality of hypotheses generated by the students more than one evaluates the quality of the model-builder STELLA for students' knowledge of one or another piece of information. One usually evaluates the quality of an ITS for what knowledge students have acquired from working through it and a model-building tool for the students' understanding of complex systems and their improved ability to think systemically (Mandinach, 1989). Cognitive tools are evaluated for the kinds of cognitive activities they stimulate and the kinds of abilities (even if domain-specific) which they foster.

Focusing more specifically on computer tools, we can distinguish between at least two main goals which they are designed to serve: the upgrading of intellec-tual performance, such as is afforded by the graphic program FreeHand or by any available word processor, and the acquisition and cultivation of (relatively!!) generalizable skills to be available for later employment in the absence of the tool. Following Pea (1987), we might call the former *performance-oriented* tools and the latter *pedagogical* tools. These two general classes of tools are not mutually exclusive; the facilitation of performance can have the side effect of improved skill mastery, and the facilitation of skill mastery can achieve, en route, also the improvement of performance. Nevertheless, there are, as we shall see, basic differences between tools designed for each of these purposes. A performance-oriented tool may be designed in a way that does not much facilitate skill acquisition and a pedagogic tool designed mainly for the acquisition or cultivation of skill may fail to improve performance while students work with it.

I develop here two propositions. The first proposition is that educationally useful computer tools are those that stimulate higher order thinking and guide it in a way that makes learners better and more independent thinkers. To the extent that a tool *shares* the intellectual burden with the learner, it does so only to facilitate higher order thinking by means of freeing the learner from tedious, labor and memory intensive lower level processes that often block higher order thinking. A useful tool is one that promotes thinking and cultivates it.

My second proposition is that no tool is "good" or "bad" in and of itself; its quality results from and *contributes to* the whole Gestalt of events, functions, and factors in the context of which it is being used. But since a good tool can serve as a Trojan Horse, gradually changing the nature of whole learning en-vironments, it is also changed by them. Thus, (a) its quality cannot be judged independently of that context (Salomon, Perkins, & Globerson, 1991), and (b) it can be judged only after the subversive process it has triggered reaches some level of maturity and stability in the learning environment.

PERFORMANCE-ORIENTED AND PEDAGOGIC TOOL

Computer tools, unlike most other tools, are capable of offering their users an *intellectual partnership* whereby the cognitive burden of carrying out an intellectual task becomes *shared*. The partnership with computer tools often entails two kinds of sharing. On the one hand, we have the sharing in the sense of establishing a clear division of labor: The computer tool carries out the lower level tedious computational and graphic operations, leaving to the user the task of generating hypotheses, thinking out causal links, drawing conclusions, and the like. On the other hand, tools can afford also another kind of sharing: Cognitions become "distributed" in the sense that the tool and its human partner *think jointly*. Whatever is produced is a product of the joint system, resulting from the pooling together of the intelligences of both partners (Pea, in press).

Tools differ with respect to the extent to which they offer more sharing of one or the other kind and are therefore designed accordingly. A tool needs to be rather intelligent to afford a genuine distribution of cognitive operations; it needs to be less intelligent, perhaps even deliberately so, in the case where labor is to be divided so that the human user, rather than the computer, is led to operate on a higher level of intelligence (Scardamalia et al., 1989). Thus, in the case of an intellectual partnership of the distributed cognitions type the emphasis is mainly on the joint *product;* it is a *performance-oriented tool*. On the other hand, in the case of intellectual partnership of the division-of-labor kind, the emphasis is on the changes that take place in the individual, changes that are attributed to the partnership and may result from it but are nevertheless considered those of the individual. In the latter case the tool is of the *pedagogic* kind.

All this may sound awfully abstract. Thus, consider the following example. Expert programs for diagnosis can be of either type. An expert program might be exceedingly intelligent. The joining or pooling of intelligences by a physician and that expert program may yield diagnoses that would be quite impossible for the average physician to arrive at on his or her own. We might say that the joint system, with its pooled intelligences, performs on a rather high level. But the expert program could be less intelligent in its performance offering instead some guiding help to its human partner. Rather than, say, correcting the physicians errors, offering expert-like alternatives and pointing out the most likely diagnosis, it could guide the physician to arrive him- or herself at better diagnoses thereby helping the physician to become a better *solo* diagnostician. This, then, would be a more pedagogically-oriented tool, oriented less toward the highest possible level of joint performance and more towards the cultivation of the physician's own diagnostic skills.

Which of the two is more desirable? This may, of course, depend on one's perceptions of human ability and on what would count as a worthwhile educational goal. Pea (in press), Cole (in press; Cole & Engestrom, in press) and others, have recently pointed out that most if not all human intellectual activity rather than being just a solo activity taking place in one's own head, is a distributed process between individuals and between individuals and cultural artifacts and tools. The distinction between purely cognitive and social cognitions thus becomes blurred. Indeed, one would have difficulties to separate a painter's achievements from the contribution made by canvas, brush, and paint, between the surveyor and the measuring tools he or she is using, or between one member of a planning team and the other participants. Much of the intellectual activity is downloaded onto the cultural artifacts and tools and is jointly construed by the social unit called a team. As pointed out by Olson (1986): "Almost any form of human cognition requires one to deal productively and imaginatively with some technology. To attempt to characterize intelligence independently of those technologies seems to be a fundamental error" (p. 356).

The assumption that such cognitive distribution (i.e., sharing in the distribution sense) is the rule rather than the exception and that the study of individuals' cognitions, while a time-honored tradition in psychology, ignores this social and cultural fact, has led Pea (1987; in press) to argue that computer tools should be aimed at creating powerful intellectual partnerships, aimed at upgrading joint performance, rather than aim at the cultivation of students' solo abilities. This would suggest a strong emphasis on attaining effects *with* technology, that is—upgrading students' *performance* during the partnership, as when one's diagnostic abilities improve while utilizing a medical expert system. Such an emphasis comes at the expense of its alternative—the attainment of effects *of* the tools, that is, improving solo *abilities* that result from that partnership, as when the physician becomes a better diagnostician when subsequently practicing on his or her own (Salomon, 1990; Salomon et al., 1991).

The fact that cognitions are, indeed, often socially and technologically distributed, cannot be denied. However, its implications can nevertheless be carried too far. There are at least three reasons why the strong emphasis on the distributed nature of improved performance should not be the ultimate goal of tool utilization *in education*. First, as pointed out by Salomon et al. (1991), individuals will always be faced with real-life questions, problems, and dilemmas that no partnership with any technology, intelligent and ubiquitous as it may become, will be able to assist in solving. Thus, effects *with* technology are not enough; one would want to attain also effects *of* it. Second, as pointed out by Perkins (in press), while cognitions of various types and at different levels can conceivably become distributed (the "person plus" phenomenon), there are other cognitions that—by their very nature—cannot (the "person solo" counterpart). Specifically, particular contents and procedures—representations, memory access and retrieval paths, even regulation—can be distributed between individuals and their social and artifactual surrounds. On the other hand, higher order knowledge, the knowledge of subject-matter appropriate strategies, patterns of justification, modes of inquiry, and the like, cannot. This kind of meta-knowledge of a field, rarely taught in school, is compact, is continuously needed, and is quite abstract, and thus cannot be relegated to a partnership with any technology. And since its mastery is crucial for high level intellectual activity in a field of study it needs to become part of a student's personal repertoire.

Third, as argued by Salomon (in press-a), the issue of distributed vs. solo cognitions (and hence the issue of performance vs. pedagogic tools) cannot be resolved as an either-or one. The partnership with others or with an intelligent tool is part of a longer, ongoing developmental progression. Seen in light of Vygotsky's theory, the partnership with a tool, to the extent that it does not supplant the intellectual activities of the individuals involved, can be regarded, under certain conditions, as a step en route to their growing independence of intellectual functioning. What is distributed today may become "internalized" by these individuals, allowing them not only to function on a higher level when on their own, but to later also enter increasingly higher levels of new partnership with the tool. In other words, partnerships with a tool whereby cognitions become distributed and performance is upgraded can be expected to leave some *cognitive residue* in the human partners which would be manifested, among other things, in further upgraded performance when they encounter the same tool again at a later date. They would also be expected to walk away from each such partnership with the tool with some changed understandings and better skill mastery which they can employ on their own.

The three arguments just presented lead to the conclusion that intellectual partnership with computer tools should not aim at improved performance through the distribution of cognitions as its ultimate goal. Rather, the partnership ought to be designed such that it leaves the individuals with solo cognitive residues (e.g., improved skill mastery) that would improve their autonomous higher order thinking as well as affect their subsequent partnerships with the tool. *Thus, seen in an educational context, tools ought to be pedagogic rather than just performance-oriented:* They should be designed in a way that turns effects *with* them into more lasting effects *of* them. In the following section I describe a tool, the *Writing Partner*, which was designed and studied with the foregoing considerations in mind.

THE PEDAGOGIC TOOL THE *WRITING PARTNER*

The *Writing Partner* was designed to serve as a genuine intellectual partner the effect *with* which should become effects *of* it, that is—it should improve writing performance and, through a Vygotskian-like process of internalization, ought to improve students' writing ability. The underlying psycho-logic and design-logic were presented in some detail in Zellermayer, Salomon, Globerson, and Givon (1991). The tool is based on the psychological analyses of composition writing by Bereiter and Scardamalia (1987), on their theory of procedural facilitation (e.g., Scardamalia et al., 1989), on Vygotsky's (1978) sociohistorical theory of development, and on Salomon's (1990) theory of technology and mind. In a nutshell, the purpose of the tool is to assist young writers to shift from writing compositions in the free-association, less-than-thoughtful mode of "knowledge telling" to writing better planned, self-guided, self-diagnosed, and revised compositions of the "knowledge transformation" mode (Bereiter & Schardamalia, 1987). The shift is expected to come about as a result of the employment of continuous explicit procedural facilitation (e.g., Scardamalia et al., 1989) of writing-related planning, diagnosis of difficulties, and mainly expert-like guidance. This guidance is expected to become internalized (Vygotsky, 1978) and thus turn into *self*-diagnosis and *self*-guidance. This is, then, a prototypical case of a pedagogical tool that affords an intellectual partnership of the division-of-labor kind. The program provides memory supports and the explicit guidance, contingent in large part on writers' inputs and selections, which good, "knowledge transforming" writers are known to supply for themselves. The effects *with* the tool (better performance while it is in use) are expected to become more generalizable effects *of* it when examined later on through unguided subsequent writing.

More specifically, the program affords four kinds of assistance to composition writers. First, it guides the writers through a forced process of planning their stories, in brainstorming, and outlining. Figure 6.1 shows a typical brainstorming screen where the student suggests a number of basic ideas, selects from each an appropriate keyword, and decides through the choice of an icon what status (good or bad character, a triggering event, a conflict, detail, etc.) this idea has in the planned story.

Once the writers decide to move on to "outlining," the tool, on the basis of the icons not chosen, may comment that certain elements are still missing from their idea list (e.g., "Your story has no setting. Does the story not occur in some place?"; "Your conflict does not have a resolution; wouldn't you want to resolve the conflict?"). Outlining is carried out with the icons, each representing a narrative element (character, event, setting, time, conflict) and the keyword associated with it. The writers simply drag the icons on the screen to create the desired outline of the story (Fig. 6.2). At the end of the (required) planning phase all entries can be reviewed and modified. The writers then move to the actual writing of the essay.

The second kind of procedural facilitation comes during writing. Writers can ask for ongoing assistance, which will appear on a bottom screen. This assistance appears in the form of expert-like questions that are contingent upon the keywords typed earlier into the essay. Thus, when, say, the word "accident" is entered and is identified by the tool as having been entered as a keyword part of a

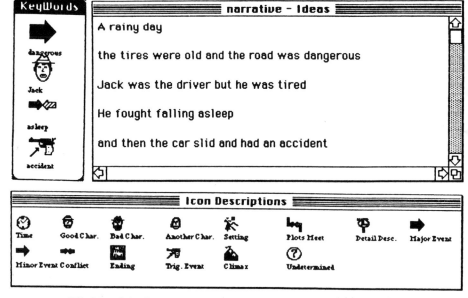

FIG. 6.1.   A brainstorming screen during planning with the Writing Partner.

particular idea and given the status of a "triggering event", it will supply guiding questions from a pool that deals with such events (Fig. 6.3).

The third kind of assistance available throughout the writing process is in the form of a pull-down screen called "I'm Stuck" and which is designed to help writers diagnose where and with what they are stuck. Each selected alternative (Opening, Lost the main idea, Plots don't met, Need a word, etc.) leads to another level of guiding questions to facilitate self-diagnosis and, in some cases

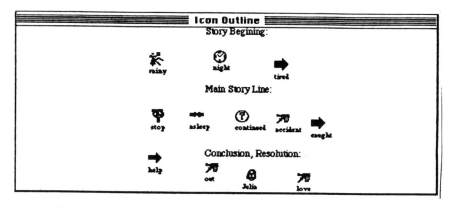

FIG. 6.2.   Dragging icons to create an outline with the Writing Partner.

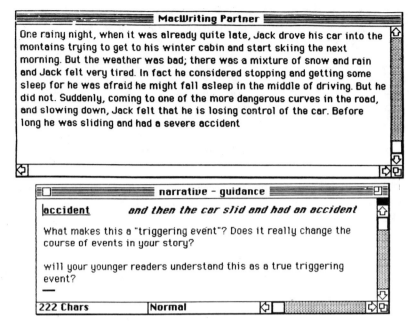

FIG. 6.3. Essay writing, including "Continuous Help" the Writing Partner.

to yet another level of specific suggestions (e.g., "If this were a movie, what would happen next? "Think of the following openings of sentences"). At each point in the writing process the writers can move on to Revision. Revision-related guidance consists of two kinds—General (concerning structure, overall interest, and flow) and Specific (geared to keywords the writers highlight or based on "Clever Questions" supplied by the tool).

Last, the tool provides memory support. At each point in the process the writers can retrieve their idea lists and outlines, thus they do not have to rely on memory of ideas that occurred to them during brainstorming or outlining.

The uniqueness of the tool lies in the expert-like guidance, itself based on relevant research, that it affords before and during the process of writing. It does not teach writing nor does it correct errors (hence it does not need to be highly intelligent). It is based on the assumption that students are the ones who need to do the thinking (planning, self-diagnosing, self-guiding) and that the tool ought only to provide them with the stimulation and guidance for doing so. In this sense this appears to be a genuine pedagogical tool. It is pedagogical because of the guidance it provides and it is a tool in the senses discussed at the beginning of this chapter.

Although the tool affords numerous kinds of guidance, each of which can potentially be used to improve the presently written essay as well as be internalized for subsequent self-guidance, the effects *with* it and *of* it are far from assured. As the theory underlying the design of the tool as well as our observations and study of it suggest, its effectiveness greatly depends on the extent to which its affordances are actually taken (Perkins, 1985). Indeed, no effects either with it or of it should be expected by a relatively mindless writer who does not try to generate a good essay plan, does not read or follow the guidance, who does not consult the "I'm stuck" screen, or who does not care to use the guidance provided for revision purposes. The tool, although "pedagogic," can do nothing to force a writer to mindfully make use of the guidance offered. The idea that support and facilitation are automatically taken is simply an erroneous myth (Perkins, 1985).

What do we know about the effectiveness of the tool and the way it is used? The first study, carried out in Israel with an early Hebrew version of the tool (Zellermayer et al., 1991) compared the effects of writing five essays by high school students over a 2-weeks period with the tool with writing on a word processor. Results were very encouraging. Students writing with the *Writing Partner* reported expending more mental effort in the process (particularly in planning), produced significantly better essays when equipped with the tool, showed evidence of internalizing its guidance (as measured by the number of metacognitive-like advise the students selected to give to a friend who is a poor writer), and wrote subsequently significantly better essays when using only paper and pencil. Importantly, partialling out guidance-internalization scores (using covariance methods) totally erased the difference in posttest writing quality between users of *Writing Partner* and the word processor. This suggested that the improvement in writing can validly be attributed to the internalization of its guidance. Later studies with a new (English) version of the tool yielded essentially the same findings. Moreover, writing with the *Writing Partner* appeared to increase middle school American students' motivation to write. Qualitative observations and interviews also showed that whereas students writing with a word processor were mentally busy with mechanical editing of their essays, those writing with the *Writing Partner* were more occupied with higher order issues such as thinking of story highlights, planning, story flow, and the like. Little wonder, then, that their essays (both the ones written with the tool and those written later on without it) were judged to be of significantly higher quality than the ones written by the word processor users.

It is also important to note that when the effects of the *Writing Partner's* guidance were compared with live guidance given by individual tutors sitting next to each adolescent writer that the latter arose visible irritation and psychological reactance, none of which were manifested when students worked with the *Writing Partner*. This is an interesting and important issue to consider: while ongoing guidance given by a computer tool is acceptable even by autonomy-minded adolescents, a similar kind of guidance is rejected when given by human experts.

NOT THE YEAST A BREAD MAKES

The foregoing conceptual discussion and description of the *Writing Partner* pertain to my first proposition, namely that educationally useful computer tools are those that stimulate higher order thinking and guide it in a way that makes learners better and more independent thinkers. But, as our experience in introducing the *Writing Partner* into English classrooms has shown us, there is far more to the use of computer tools in classrooms than the tool itself. This, then, brings me to the second proposition of this essay, namely that no tool is *good* or *bad* in and of itself; its effectiveness results from and contributes to the whole configuration of events, activities, contents, and interpersonal processes taking place in the context of which it is been used. As pointed by Cochran-Smith (1991) with respect to word processors:

> we cannot determine how word processing is most effectively used in classrooms apart from the ways particular teachers work in particular instructional contexts and that we cannot understand how word processing affects the quality, quantity, or processes of children's writing apart from the ways these are embedded within, and mediated by, the social systems of classrooms. (p. 108)

The same idea was expressed by Papert (1987) and by Newman (1990). Indeed, if you come to consider our first study of the *Writing Partner* you are bound to discover that its use had little if anything to do with classroom teaching. Students were called out of their regular classrooms to write five essays in the computer laboratory. To be sure, the study was well suited to test the theoretical proposition concerning the internalization of computer-afforded expert-like guidance and some of the conditions under which this process yields desirable results. But that study could tell us nothing about the way such a tool would affect and be affected by ongoing classroom practices. It was a study of computer tools *and* education, not a study of computer tools *in* education.

The introduction of the tool into American classrooms was a rather revealing process. Initially it entailed no more than using the tool as an *add-on* to otherwise unchanging curricula or teaching practices. And, as one could have expected, it yielded few if any positive effects. To be true, as Dwyer (1991) pointed out, the mere introduction of a critical mass of computers into a classroom exerts its own influences: Students become curious, newly emerging "experts" take a leading role, motivation increases, and the like. But these are fleeting effects, easily erased if nothing else accompanies the use of computers which are left to serve as mere add-ons. *If nothing significant changes in the classroom save the introduction of a tool, few if any important effects can be expected.* Indeed, if the *Writing Partner* is as potentially effective as the controlled study in Israel has shown then, by necessity, it cannot be treated as an add-on, isolated from all other aspects of teaching writing. *If the tool is to be effective, most everything in the classroom learning environment ought to change.*

The next phase of introducing the *Writing Partner* into 8th-grade classes involved major changes in the curriculum such that the writing curriculum and use of the tool became well orchestrated and integrated into a new configuration. This was accompanied, as it often is, by increasing team-work and communication among students, decreasing didactic instruction, writing for peers as a real audience (as contrasted with writing for the nonaudience: the teacher who grades the essays; see Cohen & Riel, 1989), and an increasing sense of autonomy by the students. Now, unlike earlier modes of introduction, it was time to assess the effects of the tool embedded within the new environment that its introduction has triggered. The assessment now pertained to the whole environment, not to the effects of the *Writing Partner* as an isolated tool nor to any other *single* component taken in isolation.

Two issues emerge in this respect: (a) the conceptual understanding of the reciprocal influences of tool and learning environment, and (b) the methodological means through which the changes in the environment can be documented and studied.

Although it is true, as the heading of this section suggests, that no bread can be baked with yeast alone (although it cannot be baked without the yeast either), and while the metaphors of the computer tool as a Trojan Horse or subversive instrument (Brown, 1990) are appealing, they leave an important element out. As much as the computer tool may trigger important curricular, activity, and interpersonal changes in the classroom, this is not a unidirectional process. As pointed out earlier, a tool is more than a technological implement; it entails also its purposes, usages, and required skills. And these—particularly modes of usage— while affecting other classroom processes *become themselves reciprocally affected by the very changes they cause* (Weick, 1979).

Consider, for example, the way the introduction of a tool such as the STELLA literally forces a shift from individual to team-work and from learning by way of recitation to learning by means of self-guided model-building and explorations of the phenomena so modeled (e.g., Mandinach, 1989). But these changes, attributable to the introduction of the tool, become themselves gradually affected by the new learning environment they trigger: As the curriculum changes and comes to deal increasingly more with authentic, complex phenomena, also the way the tool is used comes to change. What may have started out as a self-contained activity of model-building gradually becomes a more serious activity perceived by the students to serve a goal beyond itself—that of, say, socially comparing and contrasting different perceptions of the same modeled phenomena. To be sure, the tool-as-implement has not changed, but its use and the goals which its use comes to serve have drastically changed. In short, while the computer tool could have been initially seen as a powerful change agent, an independent variable if you will, gradually turns out to be itself subject to changes, that is—a dependent variable. Unfortunately, we know very little how to conceptually handle whole (learning) environments, let alone how to handle the reciprocal relations and influences among its components as they develop and change over time. And although Barker's theory of "behavior settings" (Barker, 1968) may be a starting point, it needs much development and the inclusion of other elements, such as students' perceptions and cognitions, to accommodate it to the study of tools and learning environments.

This brings me to the second issue, the one concerned with the methodological aspects of studying tool use and whole learning environment as they jointly change over time. Two assumptions need to be made here. First, in the absence of a coherent theory of learning environments we need to assume that the dimensions, variables, or parameters of the learning environment pertain to the variety of relevant behaviors, activities, contents, perceptions, expectations, cognitions, motivations, achievements, and social interrelations that can be measured and observed in a classroom over time. The more of those one captures, the fuller might the description of the environment and the changes therein be. The second assumption is that these elements, do not only *interact* with each other but that they also *define* each other in the sense of providing meaning to each other (Altman, 1988; Salomon, in press-b). For example, the use of the *Writing Partner* in the service of story writing receives its meaning from the social activity of sharing the essays and receiving peer feedback which, in turn, offers new purposes and meanings to the process of essay revision. These are not variables independent of each other but rather integrated configurations of events and processes, much like the social, personal, and economic variables the configuration of which constitutes a historical process (Altman, 1988).

While it is possible to measure or observe how specific, discrete variables such as motivation, involvement, achievement, or cooperation change over time in isolation as a function of tool introduction, the study of how the learning *environment* changes calls for the examination of changes that take place in the whole *configuration* of these. Thus, one wants to study the changes in the pattern of interrelations among the variables. (The study of changes in the pattern of configuration should not be confused with the study of the patterns in the configuration of changes—who changes more and who changes less.) The use of Small Space Analyses, a private case of Multidimensional Scaling (Guttman, 1969) turns out to serve such purposes very well. This analysis arranges the different variables in a map-like fashion whereby the stronger the relation between two variables, *all other relations taken into considerations,* the closer they are to each other.

Consider for illustrative purposes some of the findings of our latest study of the *Writing Partner*. We measured students' ITBS scores, their computer-related and writing related perceived self-efficacy (PSE), their attitudes toward writing and toward the writing project, their proclivity to be mindful, their use of specific and general metacognitions, their evaluation of the classroom social interaction and of the teaching style, and their pre- and post-project writing achievements. This collection of measures, taken both before and after the project, enabled us to

4a: CONTROL GROUP" WORD PROCESSOR ONLY

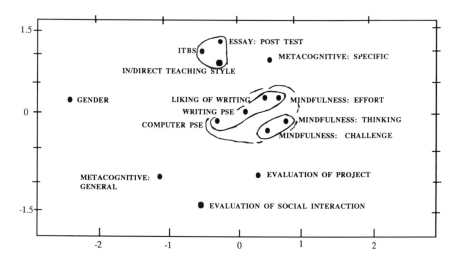

4b: EXPERIMENTAL GROUP: *WRITING PARTENR*

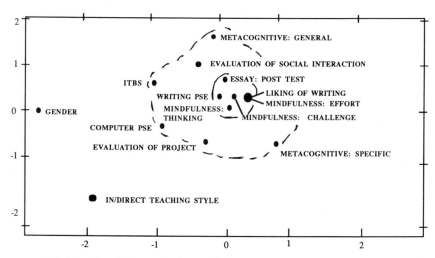

FIG. 6.4.   Small Space Analyses of the post-project configuration of variables in the control and Writing Partner groups.

examine how the interrelations among these factors change over time. The changed configuration of interrelations in the *Writing Partner* group could then be compared to that of another control group of students that wrote its essays on a word processor. The main interest concerns the interrelations among the measured variables, *not* the changes in each and every discrete one of them when taken in isolation (Salomon, in press-b).

The initial, preproject configuration of relationships among variables was quite similar to the experimental (*Writing Partner*) and the word-processor (control) groups. But as Figs. 6.4a and 6.4b show, the configuration became quite different for the two groups at postproject time. Indeed, in the control group, the *core* of the *map* consisted of perceived self-efficacy, liking of writing and mindfulness flanked on one side by the evaluation of the project and of social interaction and on the other by general ability (ITBS), posttest writing quality and evaluation of the teaching style. Importantly, the closest neighbors of posttest writing quality in the control group were ITBS and teaching style, while perceived quality of social interaction appeared to be removed, that is—far less related to it.

In the experimental group, on the other hand, postproject writing quality served as the core of the map closely aligned to students' mindfulness, attitudes toward writing, and writing-related PSE, all of which were relatively removed from ITBS. This core was flanked by students' evaluation of social interaction on the one side and with their evaluation of the project on the other. ITBS, a traditional predictor of writing quality, appeared to have lost its effect on writing quality which, in turn, had more to do with attitudes toward writing, with students' belief in their writing ability and with social interaction.

This cursory examination of the two maps suggests that writing with the *Writing Partner* had some interesting effects that would not have been captured by an examination of each and every variable in isolation or by common factor analyses. The use of this pedagogic tool made writing more a matter of volitional effort expenditure, of attitudes and of social interaction than of initial ability or of teacher's behavior. It would have been of great interest to examine in this way additional, social-interactive and teaching-style variables which, unfortunately, we did not measure. Measuring or observing such variables in addition to the ones we did measure would have given us a fuller view of the changes that have taken place in the whole learning environment due to the introduction of the pedagogic tool, the *Writing Partner*.

SUMMARY AND CONCLUSION

Two propositions were developed in this essay. The first proposition pertained to the nature of pedagogical computer tools. I argued that educationally useful computer tools are those that stimulate higher order thinking and guide it in a way that makes learners better and more independent thinkers. This proposition is based on a characterization of computer tools (as contrasted with more independently functioning programs and intelligent tutors) as not being autonomous in their operation, thus requiring the active operation by and mental involvement of students. The proposition is also based on the distinction between performance-oriented and pedagogically-oriented tools. The latter, I argue, may be (or, one might claim, *should be*) less intelligent than the performance-oriented tools because,. as pedagogic tools they ought to promote *students'* thinking, planning, self-guidance, and the like rather than do the thinking for them. Such tools *share* the intellectual burden with the students. This sharing is more a matter of a division of labor—the tool executing the lower level operations thereby freeing the student to engage in higher level ones—than a matter of distributed thinking where the product is a result of the joint rather than individual's solo thinking. The former may be very useful for performance but less so for the attainment of educationally desirable cognitive residues which allow the student improved thinking when on his or her own. Of particular interest are pedagogical tools that not only afford higher order thinking but also provide on-going expert-like guidance which can then be internalized by the student and can thus turn into *self*-guidance. The *Writing Partner,* a tool designed according to these principles and entailing internalizable procedural facilitation, is described in some detail for illustrative purposes.

The second proposition of this essay was that no tool is good or bad in and of itself. A tool's quality results from and contributes to the whole Gestalt of classroom events, functions, and factors in the context of which it is being used. It is only as a part of a whole, well orchestrated learning environment, that a tool is of any value. It follows that the design of tools can not be limited to the construction of the implement itself, intelligent and interactive as it may be. Focusing solely on the tool-as-implement would be akin to the design of a flute with little regard for the 120 piece orchestra of which it is to be part. In this light, the design of educationally-oriented computer tools is, by necessity, a meeting place for a number of areas of study and development: Curriculum, classroom management, the social psychology of team-work and collaboration, motivation, expectations, socially based learning, and more.

ACKNOWLEDGMENTS

The writing of this paper and the research reported in it were supported by a grant given jointly to the author and to the late Tamar Globerson of Tel-Aviv University by the Spencer Foundation.

REFERENCES

Altman, I. (1988). Process, transactional/contextual, and outcome research: An alternative to the traditional distinction between basic and applied research. *Social Behaviour, 3,* 259–280.

Barker, R. (1968). *Ecological psychology: Concepts and methods for studying the environment of human behavior.* Stanford, CA: Stanford University Press.

Bereiter, C., & Scardamalia, M. (1987). *The psychology of written composition.* Hillsdale, NJ: Lawrence Erlbaum Associates.

Brown, A. L. (1990, April). *Technology and restructuring: Creating a context for learning and evaluation.* Symposium paper presented at the Annual Meeting of the American Educational Research Association, Boston.

Cochran-Smith, M. (1991). Word processing and writing in elementary classrooms: A critical review of related literature. *Review of Educational Research, 61,* 107–155.

Cohen, M., & Riel, M. (1989). The effects of distant audiences on students writing. *American Educational Research Journal, 26,* 143–159.

Cole, M. (in press). On socially shared cognitions. In L. Resnick, J. Levine, & S. Behrend (Eds.), *Socially shared cognitions.* Hillsdale, NJ: Lawrence Erlbaum Associates.

Cole, M., & Engestrom, Y. (in press). A Cultural-historical understanding of distributed cognition. In G. Salomon (Ed.), *Distributed cognitions.* New York: Cambridge University Press.

Dwyer, D. (1991, April). *Technological developments and the learning environment: Points of view on the research agenda.* Symposium paper presented at the Annual Meeting of the American Educational Research Association, Chicago.

Ellul, J. (1964). *The technological society.* New York: Knopf.

Encyclopedia Britanica. (1987). *Tools* (Vol. 28, pp. 712–736). Chicago, IL: Encyclopedia Britanica.

Goodman, N. (1978). *Ways of worldmaking.* Indianapolis: Hackett.

Guttman, L. (1969). A general nonmetric technique for finding the smallest coordinate space for a configuration of points. *Psychometrics, 33,* 465–506.

Mandinach, E. B. (1989). Model-building and the use of computer simulation of dynamic systems. *Journal of Educational Computing Research, 5,* 221–243.

Newman, D. (1990). Opportunities for research on the organizational impact of school computers. *Educational Researcher, 19,* 8–13.

Olson, D. R. (1986). Intelligence and literacy: The relationships between intelligence and the technologies of representation and communication. In R. J. Sternberg & R. K. Wagner (Eds.), *Practical intelligence: Nature and origins of competence in the everyday world* (pp. 338–360). New York: Cambridge University Press.

Papert, S. (1987). Computer criticism vs. technocentric thinking. *Educational Researcher, 17,* 22–30.

Pea, R. D. (1985). Beyond amplification: Using the computer to reorganize mental functioning. *Educational Psychologist, 20,* 167–182.

Pea, R. D. (1987). Integrating human and computer intelligence. In R. D. Pea & K. Sheingold (Eds.), *Mirrors of mind: Patterns of experience in educational computing* (pp. 128–146). Norwood, NJ: Ablex.

Pea, R. D. (in press). Distributed intelligence and education. In G. Salomon (Ed.). *Distributed Cognitions.* New York: Cambridge University Press.

Perkins, D. N. (1985). The fingertip effect: How information processing technology shapes thinking. *Educational Researcher, 14,* 11–17.

Perkins, D. N. (1986). *Knowledge as design.* Hillsdale, NJ: Lawrence Erlbaum Associates.

Perkins, D. N. (in press). Person plus: A distributed view of thinking and learning. In G. Salomon (Ed.). *Distributed cognitions.* New York: Cambridge University Press.

Salomon, G. (1990). Cognitive effects with and of computer technology. *Communication Research, 17,* 26–44.

Salomon, G. (in press-a). No distribution without individuals' cognitions. In G. Salomon (Ed.), *Distributed cognitions.* New York: Cambridge University Press.

Salomon, G. (1991). Transcending the qualitative/quantitative debate: the analytic and systemic approaches to educational research. *Educational Researcher, 20*(6), 10–18.

Salomon, G., Perkins, D. N., & Globerson, T. (1991). Partners in cognition: Extending human intelligence with intelligent technologies. *Educational Researcher, 20,* 10–16.

Scardamalia, M., Bereiter, C., McLean, R. S., Swallow, J., & Woodruff, E. (1989). Computer-supported intentional learning environments. *Journal of Educational Computing Research, 5,* 51–68.

Vygotsky, L. S. (1978). *Mind in society: The development of higher psychological processes.* Cambridge, MA: Harvard University Press.

Weick, K. E. (1979). *The social psychology of organizing.* Reading, MA: Addison-Wesley.

Zellermayer, M., Salomon, G., Globerson, T., & Givon, H. (1991). Enhancing writing-related metacognitions from a computerized Writing-Partner. *American Educational Research Journal, 28,* 373–391.

7 Authors of Knowledge: Patterns of Hypermedia Design

Richard Lehrer
University of Wisconsin-Madison

At the turn of the century, Dewey advocated learner-centered but teacher-guided education built around efforts to link purpose and structure. For example, he advocated projects like designing a clubhouse because this activity embraced multiple levels of organization and placed students in the role of developing rather than receiving knowledge. Unfortunately, schools rarely have embraced this philosophy, in part because the metaphor of learning in schools is often one of knowledge transmission rather than of knowledge construction (Perkins, 1986), and in part because the construction of physical artifacts often is limited both materially and intellectually. For example, having built one clubhouse, how easy is it to revise, elaborate, or extend it to other constructions? So instead of designing clubhouses and other physical artifacts, Perkins (1986) suggests that teachers and learners design knowledge. The strength of this metaphor stems from its polysemy: Design refers simultaneously to structure and to process. In this chapter, I suggest that a new form of computer-sustained literacy, hypermedia, can be used to foster knowledge design. Accordingly, I describe the development and implementation of a hypermedia authoring environment, HyperAuthor, used by 8th-grade American history students as an instructional design tool. In the process of design, these students developed new ideas about history, and about themselves as authors of knowledge.

KNOWLEDGE AS DESIGN

Design is a ubiquitous human activity (Norman, 1988). Although it is more common to consider the design of everyday things, like toasters, VCR's, and automobiles, here I consider how the role of the designer can be extended to the

197

school. Students are typically not enfranchised as designers; here I consider the advantages of extending the franchise to students.

Components of Knowledge Design

Perkins (1986) suggests that knowledge itself results from and is a design. In Perkin's view, this metaphor implies four interrelated features of knowledge. First, knowledge is constructed pragmatically, as suggested by Dewey, incorporating human purpose and servicing human ends. Thus Perkins likens a theory to a pragmatic tool, a "mental screwdriver." Second, knowledge is structured. Purpose and structure are interwoven; structures serve purposes. Third, one's knowledge includes models or cases that exemplify its structure. This enables communication, and the development of mental models. The latter serve as springboards for reasoning (Gentner & Gentner, 1983; Johnson-Laird, 1990). Fourth, knowledge should include some means of developing and evaluating arguments. Consider, for example, the theory of evolution as a knowledge design. Its structure, the twin processes of mutation and natural selection, serve its purpose: to explain continuity and change in the fossil record. Darwin exemplified its operation in his studies of finches on the Galapagos Islands, and the theory makes a number of predictions that allow one to evaluate the strength of its arguments. In a like manner, one could consider systems that transport fluid in animals as a type of design (LaBarbera, 1990) or for that matter, human memory (Anderson, 1990). Thus, the metaphor of knowledge as design has considerable scope in application.

Schools as Contexts for Design

Treating knowledge as a process of design has several implications for schooling. First, it orients the teacher and those taught away from the image that knowledge is information, and that teachers act to transmit information, however imperfectly, to students (Perkins, 1986). Second, a teacher's role within the design tradition is to initiate a learner into the historical as well as instrumental discourse that typifies various communities such as scientists, mathematicians, or historians (Lawson, 1990). For example, good teaching of mathematics includes the establishment of classroom discourse that promotes the development of mathematical thinking (Carpenter, Fennema, Peterson, Chiang, & Leof, 1989; Lampert, 1990). Third, designing knowledge promotes the development of critical theories of knowledge because not every design accomplishes its intended purposes well (Norman, 1988).

Fourth, because design problems cannot be comprehensively stated nor solved, students must define the nature of the problem, a skill that is often lost in a world of textbook problems and examples. Moreover, "the designer's job is never really done . . . but must more often be completed in a defined period of time." (Lawson, 1990, pp. 87, 90). This encourages the development of an epistemology oriented away from dualist conceptions about the nature of knowl-edge (Perry, 1970; Ryan, 1984a, 1984b), promoting instead a view of knowledge as evolutionary and provisional.

Last, participation in discourse communities about design contributes toward the development of interest about a topic, as one discovers how one's personal identity can be extended by the activities of the community. The connection between the self and the community is maintained by what Kelly (1955) de-scribed as a "choice corollary" of personal construction: a person's choices are regulated by anticipation of the possibility for extension and definition of the self-system. For example, although one might not initially construe oneself as interested in history, one might find that trying to piece together different ac-counts of the past is like solving a puzzle, an activity that one has enjoyed in the past. By interacting with others who are similarly involved and who validate this conception (i.e., history is like problem-solving, history is fun, etc.), a possible self-as-historian evolves—an image of self that may be descriptive of the future (Markus & Nurius, 1986). If one can integrate this possible self narratively with other aspects of self, then it is likely that a portion of self-structure will be organized around the theme of self-as-historian—an "interest" (Lehrer, 1988).

Design also affords increased opportunities to identify oneself as an author and consequently to become "intrinsically" motivated to continue to develop ideas about a topic (Brown, 1988; Lepper, 1988). Because authorship implies self-agency, one is more likely to engender the direction of attention to activities and goals that validate this self-conception (Hidi, 1990; Mancuso, 1977). The result is an increased likelihood of constructing self-relevant meaning about a topic, but not total assurance—processing about oneself is apt to involve multi-ple levels of control and multiple forms of perception (Carver & Scheier, 1981). Nevertheless, on balance, design activities are likely to enhance interest in and identification with a topic.

INSTRUCTIONAL DESIGN WITH HYPERMEDIA

One way to promote design in the classroom is to place students in the role of instructional software designers (Harel & Papert, 1990). Here the goal is to develop a computer-based presentation about a topic that other students can use as a learning tool. In their efforts with Logo as an authoring tool, Harel and Papert (1990) report that this approach was marked by the "deep involvement of all participants" (p. 5). They also noted integration and flexibility in the knowl-edge developed by fourth-grade students about fractions (the subject domain in their research). In a like manner, Brown and Campione (in press) noted that having 5th and 6th grade students develop their own learning materials "led to a sea change in spontaneous activities that promote deeper understanding in the search for coherent causal explanations" (p. 21). In the research reported later, I take a similar approach, but instead of using Logo or another programming language, I decided to use a hypermedia authoring system, because such a system combines the cognitive challenges and prospects of both programming and writing (this point is discussed more fully later).

HyperComposition

Hypercomposition (also called hypertext) is a form of electronic composition that incorporates multiple forms of media: text, graphics, animation, sound, images, and video. Multiple forms of media facilitate multiple notational systems for ideas. For example, information about driving a car could be represented both by text (i.e., a set of directions) and by animations (i.e., dynamic illustration of the directions denoted in the text).

Unlike conventional text, writers of hypertext can compose multiple layers of information easily (Nelson, 1987). For example, "windows" in some computer applications can be juxtaposed, and each window can have different types of information. This layering feature reduces the mental demands on the reader— rather than integrating information across many different locations in print, readers access them concurrently in the same location (the computer screen). In contrast, readers of conventional text must rely on an index to find related information dispersed throughout the document. This indexical feature is built right into the fabric of hypertext; all related entries of an index can be available simultaneously.

Thus, hypermedia transforms the hierarchical structure of text into a network; multiple orderings of information are possible. This feature is often referred to as nonlinear text (Nielsen, 1990). The multiplicity of orderings results from the ability to connect or link any node (a node is a unit of information) in the document's network to any other node. Nodes are generally referred to as "cards" (by analogy to the more familiar index cards) and links as "buttons" that can convey information about the relationship between source and destination nodes. In practice, this feature of hypermedia accommodates individual differences in learning—it allows readers to adapt their search for information according to their preferences, prior knowledge, and so on (Bolter, 1990).

The close links between programming and hypercomposition are noted by Bolter (1990): "It puts at the disposal of writers data structures (trees and networks) that have been used for decades by programmers. Conversely, it makes us realize that the programmer's data structures are formalized versions of the textual strategies (outline and index) that writers have exploited for centuries." (p. 29, text in parentheses added). In the next section, I outline some of potential cognitive benefits of employing hypercomposition as a design tool.

HyperComposition for Design

Hypercomposition supports instructional design in several ways. First, hypermedia-based composition involves the transformation of information into an n-dimension space, in contrast to the two-dimensional space of print (Bolter,

1990). Students have the opportunity to develop a number of different links among units (nodes) of information, resulting in a new geometry of composition. In so doing, they confront decisions about (a) what information is important and what is not, (b) how to segment information into nodes (cards and/or windows), and (c) the nature of the semantic relationships among nodes, including specification of the the internodal relationship (i.e., the pathogen presented in Node A caused the disease presented in node J). Students are placed in the role of organizing information in multiple ways, and in transforming information into knowledge.

Second, because hypermedia composition involves multiple forms of media, students are confronted with decisions about the representational roles of each of the forms of media. For example, is a concept better represented as a graph or by text, or by some combination? Deciding on the nature of and the linkages between representations promotes understanding insofar as understanding involves translations among multiple and linked representations of ideas (Janvier, 1987; Mead, 1932).

Third, hypercomposition promotes a sense of authorship if students are engaged in the production of a nontrivial product (a product that others are likely to use). Thus, in the study I report later, students designed hypermedia presentations about the Civil War as sources of knowledge not found in their textbook that were intended to be used by their peers as study guides.

Fourth, hypercomposition encourages the composer to be aware of the multiple voices of his or her composition because there is always more than one path through the hyperdocument. (Readers need not cede control to the authors of hyperdocuments.) In principle, multiplicity of voice may make authors more likely to consider their audience when they design, and it may make them more likely to consider revision. Both of these activities should also promote understanding. Last, on the social plane, the hypertext focuses the interactions of the authors (the designers). This creates a new "topography of social construction" (Barrett, 1989, p. xvi) out of the diverse assumptions and understandings of the individuals involved—by working in a design team, each is required to consider the knowledge and skill developed by other team members.

A FRAMEWORK FOR COMPUTER-BASED HYPERCOMPOSITION

Figure 7.1 displays a framework for the cognitive processes involved in the fusion of designing knowledge with hypercomposition. I constructed the framework by analysis of verbal protocols (i.e., responses to questions like what are you doing now and why are you doing it?) obtained from eighth-grade students participating in the research project, by observing student behavior, and by interviewing students periodically throughout the project. The framework follows from the Hayes and Flower (1980) model of text composing processes. It

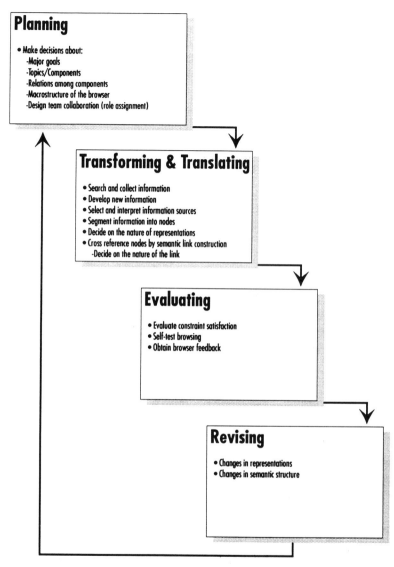

FIG. 7.1.   A framework for hypercomposition-based design.

distinguishes four primary types of cognitive processes: planning, transforming and translating, evaluating, and revising the hypermedia document.

Planning

The planning phase consists of efforts to refine the ill-structured nature of an instructional design problem like "design a presentation about the Civil War for your classmates" into a workable plan at an abstract level, including specifying major goals and deciding what subtopics to include. Novices may be expected to either leave as unspecified or to specify only very abstractly some aspects of plans that experts might develop fully, such as how users will navigate through the presentation.

Transforming

The transforming phase involves the search for, selection of, and, perhaps, development of new information, followed by its transformation into knowledge. Skills involved in searching and selecting information include the use of keywords and Booleans in electronic search, how to find information in text (i.e., use of the index and Table of Contents), how to summarize information (Day, 1986), and how to take notes (Shrager & Mayer, 1989). The creation of new information may include developing questionnaires, interviewing, using scientific instruments, and analyzing data. Skills involved in transforming information into knowledge include (a) developing an organizational framework for the information collected (perhaps by concept mapping and the like), (b) partitioning the information into nodes ("cards"), (c) deciding on how to best represent an idea, and (d) developing links among nodes. Collectively, the skills involved in this phase of the design process can be supported by a variety of computer-based knowledge-development tools, such as database managers, data analysis, graphing tools, and the like. These tools elevate skill by removing lower-order constraints on performance (Lehrer, Levin, DeHart, & Comeaux, 1987). For instance, database managers help focus attention on relations among information sources rather than on functions like information storage. Similarly, graphing tools allow attention to be focused on the relation between the type of graph selected and its intended representational function, rather than on the mechanics of constructing the graph.

Evaluation and Revision

The evaluation phase involves a test for interaction among the constraints of the design of the hyperdocument. For example, the goal of creating colorful displays (color may increase the likelihood of browser attentiveness) may detract from the goal of conveying important ideas without distracting the browser. Evaluation may also include reflection about the possible organizations of the nodes, and other audience-relevant considerations. The quality of this evaluation is constrained by one's ability to reflect on one's design actions. The last component, revision, occurs in response to the evaluation. For experienced designers, the cycle is recursive as designers typically develop provisional plans and implementations, and then evaluate and revise their design accordingly (Lawson, 1990; Schon, 1987). For less-experienced designers, the cycle may be more linear with less continuous connection between evaluation and revision and the other design phases.

HYPERAUTHOR: A TOOL FOR INSTRUCTIONAL DESIGN

I designed HyperAuthor to facilitate the design and development of hypermedia documents. It has two components: tools for construction and tools for reflection. No programming is required; students use a mouse to point and click. These authoring tools are intended to be used in an environment that includes other software tools for knowledge development, and within a classroom context where teachers initiate learners into a community of discourse.

Construction Tools

The construction tools simplify the creation of cards (nodes) and links between cards. Instead of providing a general hypertextual link facility, HyperAuthor provides students with choices about the semantic relationship between cards. This feature is designed to create increased student reflection about the nature of these relationships. Figure 7.2 displays the "Linkmaker" tool; students select (by clicking with a mouse) the source card, the *type of semantic link,* and the destination card. Different semantic links are represented by different icons.

The Linkmaker also allows students to define their own link types, and to connect cards to other media: animation, video, or sound clips. Other Hyper-Author tools (i.e., the SoundMaker) are available to create these clips. These

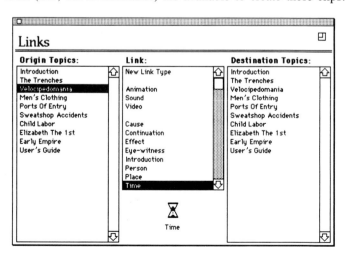

FIG. 7.2.   The LinkMaker Tool.

media are then treated by the system as another node of information; students develop libraries of these media resources over time. Other construction tools include text, drawing, and graph construction facilities. For example, the text facility allows for the choice of several different kinds of fields (regions where text can be entered), including scrolling text fields, and functions to change print size, font, and style.

Students can also take notes about any node, and these notes are linked to that node. For authors, this tool primarily serves as a reminder about information to include and other related ideas about design. For browsers, however, this note-taking facility strengthens community in that successive browsers can read the comments posted previously by others.

Reflection Tools

HyperAuthor provides four main types of reflective tools, all of which are designed to help students consider the organization of their project in different ways. The first facility, the User's Guide, is a map that is constructed by students that displays the organization of their cards. Every time a student creates a card, an icon of the card and its title is placed automatically onto the guide. Students are then responsible for arranging the icons into any desired configuration, and simple text and drawing tools are provided to assist students' efforts. Figure 7.3 displays one such guide constructed by 9th-grade students to describe relationships among topics in their presentation about World War I. The guide then serves as a navigational aid for browsers; clicking with the mouse on an icon of any node displayed in Fig. 7.3 transports the browser to that node. The User's Guide then is a means for self-reflection for authors and as a practical navigational tool for browsers.

Two other graphical displays are constructed by the system. The *scoping map* shows the number and types of links connecting any source card and its destination cards. The second, the point-of-view map displays the organization of the cards from the point of view of the particular type of link that is selected. For example, Fig. 7.4 displays the organization of a presentation about World War I according to the link of "cause." The remaining reflective tool available to students is a multimedia Table of Contents that lists the title of each card by its type (text, animation, graphics, sound).

In addition to the construction and reflection tools noted, HyperAuthor also provides standard navigational aids, such as the ability to go to the next card, the previous card, and the first and last cards in the project. These aids are supplemented by the ability to go to any card simply by clicking with the mouse on its name or icon in most of the reflective tools. Facilities are also provided for deleting links and cards, and for other forms of editing. In the next section, I describe how 8th grade students used a prototype of HyperAuthor to develop a presentation about the Civil War.

Student's Cards
User's Guide
World War I
Introduction
Intro Text
Branches
Countries
Intro to Other Countries
Maps
Most Inv. Nat.
Triple Alliance
The Alliances
Triple Entente
Balance of Power
Austria
Turkey
Germany
Germany's Flag
France
The U.S.
Causes
Introduction to Causes
Changes in Europe
Nationalism
Assassination
franz
War Plan
A.M.G INTRO
Trench Diagram
ATTRITION
ATTRITION GRAPH
SCHLIEFFEN PLAN
Leaders
Intro AMS
Douglas Haig
Joffre
Joffre photo
President Woodrow Wilson
quote
Wilson Statis
Scott
John Joseph Pershing
Weapons
Technology Goes to War!
Airplanes
Airplanes (con't)
Machine gun
Poison gas
Explosives and Artillery
Tanks

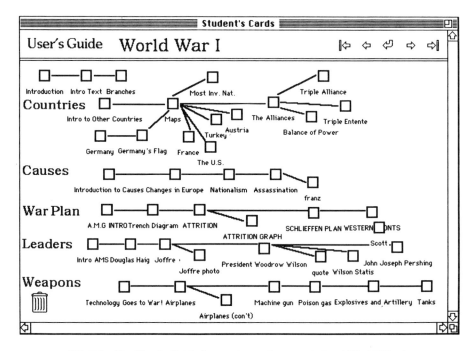

FIG. 7.3 The User's Guide from a hyperdocument about World War I.

Maps
Point-of-View Map, expanded by: Cause
Cancel
Nationalism
Assassination
Changes in Europe
Assassination
Introduction to Causes
Changes in Europe*
Balance of Power
The Alliances
Austria
Assassination

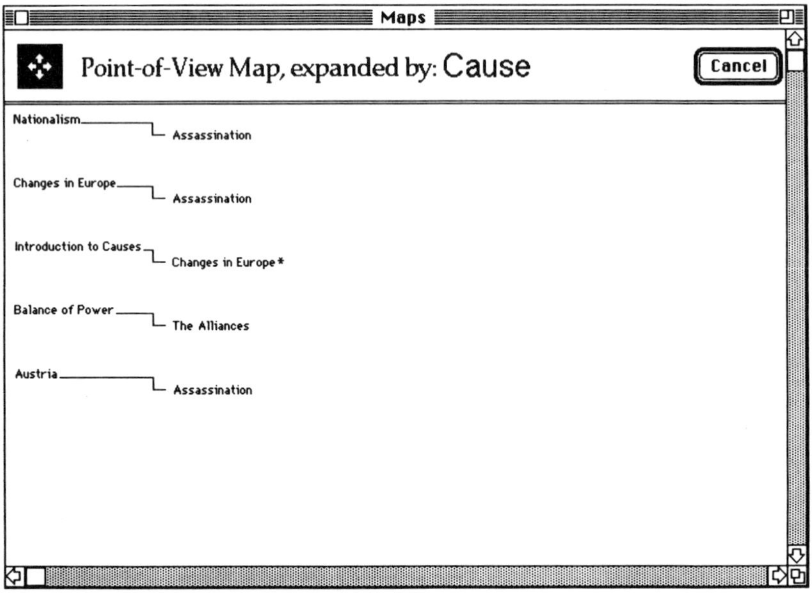

FIG. 7.4. The Point-of-View Map from a hyperdocument about World War I.

HISTORY BY DESIGN

The purposes of the study were to: (a) investigate the processes of hypermedia-based design as students developed presentations about the Civil War, (b) examine how students used a prototype of HyperAuthor with an eye toward improving its instructional utility, and (c) examine student understanding of some of the significant ideas and concepts about this epoch of American history.

Participants and Setting

Ten 8th-grade students (4 girls and 6 boys) from two American history classes participated. Students were selected by their teacher from a larger pool of volunteers. Five students were more-successful in school; they received high grades and were considered "involved and motivated" by their history teacher. These students constituted one design team. The other 5 students were less-successful in school; they received low grades (C or less) and were described as "uninvolved, disaffected, and unmotivated" by their classroom teacher. These students constituted the second design team. The decision by the teacher to allow students to participate in a new learning environment was justified for the more-successful students as "enrichment" and for the less-successful students as "they can't do any worse."

Each design team met once each day for 45 minutes in the school's library media center (The design teams met at different times, and they did not attend their history class). Either I or Annie Foong, a graduate student assistant (or both of us), was present for each session. We asked students to design a hypermedia presentation for their classmates about the Civil War. The media center contained 110 titles of books about this topic, several records of Civil War music and speeches, and other more general resources like encyclopedias. The hypermedia hardware consisted of a MacIntosh IIcx, a scanner, and a sound digitizer. Students combined these media with a prototype of HyperAuthor, but this prototype did not contain reflective tools other than the Table of Contents (the development of the reflective tools was an outgrowth of our observations of student design activity.)

Instructor Role. The role of the instructors was to coach students in the various phases of the design process outlined in Fig. 7.1. The image of teaching as coaching was drawn from the apprenticeship model of Collins, Brown, and Newman (1989), although we rarely explicitly modeled a thinking process. Instead, we tried to provoke it by asking leading questions about the subject-matter, the Civil War, and about the design of the students' presentations. Examples of content questions posed to each team were: (a) "Why did the South have slavery and the North did not? Was it a matter of moral superiority? Were there ever slaves in New York?", (b) "Why did the Civil War start in 1861? Why not 1841?", (c) "Why do we have historians? What do they do?", and (d) "Did the

Emancipation Proclamation free all the slaves?" Other content-related questions were aimed more specifically at the particular path of design chosen by each team. For example, I asked a student in the second (less-successful students) design team who was interested in battle "casualties": "In which war did more Americans die, Vietnam or the Civil War?" (He conjectured the former on the basis of superior weaponry.)

Examples of leading questions about design included: (a) "How are you going to organize your presentation?", (b) "How are you going to decide what to include and what to leave out?," (c) "Can you sketch the overall design of your project (i.e., make a map to illustrate the cards and their connections)?", and (d) "Do you see any advantages to developing some themes in your presentation? Why do we have titles in stories anyway?" These questions were intended to promote student reflection about the structure of their presentation.

We introduced students to the idea of hypermedia by modeling the organization of a document with 5×7 cards to represent nodes of information, and with pieces of string to represent links among nodes. Students also viewed several commercial hypermedia presentations, during which time we commented about the roles of multiple forms of media and multiple ways of representing a concept in the communication of ideas. We provided students with 5×7 cards that they used to plan many of their nodes, writing text and pasting illustrations before entering the node into the computer. During the course of the development of the project, students made less use of these cards and worked more often on the computer.

Sources of Data

The five major sources of data were: (a) weekly videotapes of student interactions in both design teams, (b) field notes of students' activities and conversational interactions, (c) videotapes of "design interviews" developed to probe about students' ideas about the design process, (d) two measures of knowledge organization that reflected the teacher's conceptions of important ideas and concepts about the Civil War, and (e) the presentations developed by the students (e.g., their products). The videotapes were scored by dividing each videotape into 5 minute segments and then randomly sampling 2 minutes of activity from each segment. The presence of particular categories of activities and discourse within each two minute segment was indicated by two independent raters, following the classification system presented in Appendix. A. Percent agreement between independent raters was 91. Disagreements were resolved by consensus.

Categories of observation stemmed from the depiction of the design process displayed in Fig. 7.1. Scoring categories included (a) research activities like finding and selecting information, or summarizing and interpreting information, (b) design activities like discussing the structure of the presentation or evaluating information for inclusion in the presentation, (c) collaborative activities like sharing information, (d) teaching activities like framing, and assessing knowledge or performance, and (e) off-task activities, activities that had no obvious connection to the development of the presentation.

Design Interviews. The design interviews probed for students' beliefs about the purpose and structure of their presentation, and their interest in what they were doing, as suggested by the Perkins (1986) model of knowledge-as-design (see Appendix B). Examples of questions include: (a) "What kinds of information have you found?", (b) "How does the presentation look at this point? How's it put together? Why did you use a graph (or music or other non-textual representations) here?", (c) "How are you dividing up the work?, and (d) "What do you find hard? easy? fun?"

Cognitive Structure. The first measure of cognitive structure, concept triads, presented 10 items each consisting of three concepts. Students told which two concepts were most alike and why. For example, given the concepts Gettysburg, Antietam Creek, and the Emancipation Proclamation, one student might respond that the first two were battles but another might indicate that the Union victory at Antietam Creek allowed Lincoln to issue the Proclamation. The second measure of cognitive structure, the ordering task, presented students with 20 concepts about the Civil War and asked them to indicate the degree of association among the concepts by listing like concepts contiguously, following the procedure presented by Naveh-Benjaimin, McKeachie, Lin, and Tucker (1986). Five trials were administered in all. Students' responses were converted to ordered trees to represent directional and nondirectional associations, according to the algorithm presented by Reitman and Reuter (1980).

Network Analysis. Last, the structure of students' presentations was represented as a network among concept nodes to display visually the depth and degree of concept inter-relatedness in each of the two presentations. Student presentations were also examined for the number of instances of the use of multiple representations for an idea (i.e., a graph and text, music and text, etc.).

RESULTS

Ownership and Involvement

The most striking finding was the degree of student involvement and engagement. For the more-successful students, this was immediately evident, as indicated by the high percentage of time that they were task-oriented—activities directed toward finding and selecting information, arguing about the design of the presentation, and the like. For the less-successful students, the amount of task-oriented activity gradually increased over time, with a notable decrease in off-task behavior only evident after the third week. For example, students in the less-successful group displayed off-task behavior 27% of the time during the first third of the project, 9% of the time during the second third, and less than 4% of the time during the last weeks (this percentage excludes teaching episodes where there was much less opportunity to be off-task).

What was similar between groups was the additional time they volunteered to spend on developing their presentation. Again for the more-successful students this began earlier, but for both teams it became routine during the middle third of the project, with at least two members of the team volunteering to work during their "study hall." This gradually evolved to a request to spend time after school, and finally, during the last 2 weeks, on both days of the weekend. The latter was precipitated in part by the need to meet a deadline for completion, but nevertheless, as I discuss in more detail shortly, the quality of the presentation went far beyond what one might expect from students merely trying to satisfice a goal of "completion."

Responses to the Design Interview.   Student responses to the design interviews also provided other evidence for engagement and involvement. For example, when asked to compare the development of their presentation to learning in their history classroom, students in the second group (less-successful) remarked:

"Well, you don't have to sit there and listen to lectures and stuff and read out of textbooks. You can like research it on your own and then try to get a better understanding of it and then enter it on the computer."

"You can learn on your own instead of having a teacher lecture you and saying what he thinks from his point of view. Instead you can look it up, whatever you think . . . You can put it in your own words. It's not like you have to get tested on what he thinks, instead you can tested on what you think, your point of view!"

The latter remarks indicate that students welcomed the distribution of authority from a sole locus to the teacher to a shared community of fellow interpreters of the past. Students began to believe that history was a process of interpretation, not revelation, in which students and teachers were on a more equal footing. This epistemological watershed was stated most clearly by a student from the first design team who after reading several books of eyewitness accounts of events in the Civil War commented" "And I think it's interesting that they're all different. Everybody saw a different thing . . . One person saw their loved ones and family getting killed, another saw the same people and thought that it was right (they were the enemy). So they're different and I think that's interesting because there's no real way to find out what actually went on now." This student's remarks are especially noteworthy in light of other statements that he had made earlier in the project that suggested that he viewed history as "what really happened in the past." Taken as a whole, students' comments and actions indicated a transition from receiving to authoring knowledge.

Patterns of Design

Classification of students' discourse during the first, second, and final thirds of the project indicated some common patterns: The initial phase in each group was dominated by activities and conversations related to the search and selection of information (35% of nonteacher related actions in group 1 and 25% in group 2). These search and selection activities continued in the second third of the project, but they were supplemented by more discussion of the structure of the presentation, its representations, and by evaluation of information for its inclusion in the presentation (35% of nonteacher related actions in group 1, 39% in group 2). The last 2 weeks of the project were dominated by computer entry, and further discussion of what to include or exclude in the presentation. The largest difference in the design activities of the two groups was in their pattern of collaboration and in the hierarchical nature of the design itself.

Team 1.   The first design team, comprised of more successful students, decided upon a top-down approach. In the first week of the project, they decided to concentrate on five subtopics: battles, women, not-so-famous people, slavery, and leaders. They then adopted a round-robin form of collaboration on each subtopic where each student had major responsibility for one subtopic and a minor, helping role in another. Hence, Gregory and Sue might collaborate on battles while Sue and Andy collaborated on slavery. Having assigned responsibilities and roles, the rest of the project consisted of a collaborative effort to find and select information, and to develop the structure of their presentation. Examples of collaborating on the search for information included (these are all from one session during the first third of the project):

"Here's a good map for you guys. Gettysburg!"
"Hey look, women wore skirts then too!"
"Check this out! They fought in a cornfield! It's a regiment from Wisconsin. Wisconsin? Let me see that! . . . Listen to this! (reads) Hey check this out!"
"Who's doing Blacks? Here's something! (points to a graphic about slavery)
"Oh look! unreal, it's like an advertisement!!" (the reference is to an ad for slaves)

Students in the first group also discussed the structure of their presentation in insightful ways (what we called design chatter), as indicated by the following discussion I had with them about their design during the second third of the project.

Ray: "I'll start with an introduction to Blacks. And from there maybe to individual people or maybe to leaders and then back to individuals."
Lehrer: "Which would be more interesting? How would they think about it?"
Mike: "What do you mean?"

Ray: "Well I could go to individual people like Harriet Tubman, Frederick Douglas, or I could go to bigger topics like Black Leaders, Women, Slaves, what their lives were like. ."
Mike: "I like focusing in on the people. Cause our textbook is always doing a general perspective of it. And they say bla bla did this and dee da did that. But we could provide more detail and people could find out more about people."
Michelle: "I like the general topics better. You can categorize it and still go into detail. I like that better."
Lehrer: "You mean the big categories are easier to think about?"
Mike: "Yeah, OK"
Mark: "OK"
Ray: "OK maybe that's the way" (draws a hierarchical structure on paper, compares to nonhierarchical structure)

This team also discussed the relationships among the subtopics in this session: "Frederick Douglas will have a link to leaders. "Yeah, and from Harriet Tubman to women."

Team 2. In contrast to the first team, the second team's approach to the problem was more "bottom-up." During the first week, they identified that "Civil means that . . . it's between citizens." They were uncertain about the selection of subtopics, but they agreed that perhaps they would cover "stuff on battles, weapons, how the war affected the lives of people, maybe uniforms." The first third of the project was marked for this team by a high percentage of off-task activities (at least off any task that I thought was educationally productive) and a low incidence of collaborative activities (5% in this group vs. 20% in the first group). However, during the second third of the project, the incidence of collaborative activities rose to 19% of the total number of actions coded. The pattern of collaboration was a division of labor: two students worked on battles, two on the role of women in the Civil War, and the last on weapons. Thus, the initial choices about battles and weapons were solidified, and other potential topics, like uniforms, were discarded. Students who chose to focus on the role of women in the Civil War commented: "We always read books about the Civil War and stuff and you always hear about all the men that were involved and what happened to them and no one ever says anything about the women and we think that's wrong."

These students found the resource materials in the school woefully inadequate. They then called a bookstore in the city specializing in feminist literature, wrote a letter to the principal asking for permission to go there and talk to the managers of the bookstore, and wrote a second letter to the district's Director of Curriculum asking for some funds to purchase books if any were appropriate. Some of the results of these activities are displayed in Fig. 7.5. Inspection of this figure suggests that these students developed their own voice about the role of women in the Civil War.

INTRODUCTION TO WOMEN

The civil war was a sad event. When you think of the civil war, you probably think of all the men that fought the battle. What about the women? You may not know it, but they fought their own battle. We've collected quotes on how the women feel about the Civil War.

-Shawna and Gina-

THE OTHER CIVIL WAR

AMERICAN WOMEN IN THE NINETEENTH CENTURY

-BY- GINA & SHAWNA-

FIG. 7.5. A card developed by the second group about the role of women in the Civil War.

213

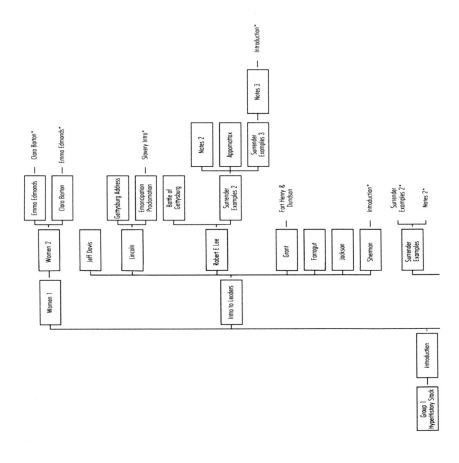

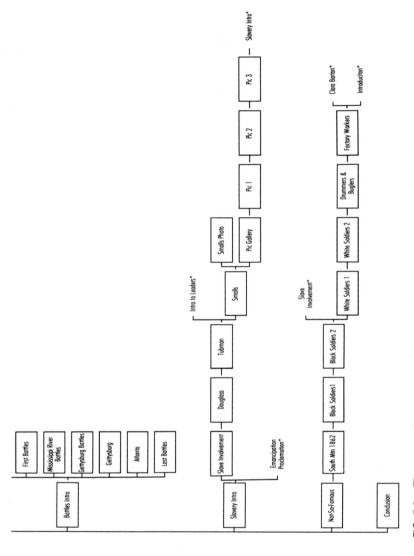

FIG. 7.6. The semantic structure of the topical nodes developed by the first design team.

First Bottles

Mississippi River Bottles

Gettysburg Bottles

Gettysburg

Atlanta

Last Bottles

Bottles Intro

Intro to Leaders*

Smalls Photo

Pic 3 — Slavery Intro*

Pic 2

Pic 1

Pic Gallery

Smalls

Tubman

Douglass

Slave Involvement

Slavery Intro

Emancipation Proclamation*

Slave Involvement*

Clara Barton*

Introduction*

Factory Workers

Drummers & Buglers

White Soldiers 2

White Soldiers 1

Black Soldiers 2

Black Soldiers 1

South Mtn 1862

Not-So-Famous

Conclusion

215

During the last weeks of the project, collaboration among the members of the second design team continued to increase, but the nature of the collaboration was akin to the modular design of a program, with little attention paid to how the different subtopics would coalesce into a coherent whole. Nevertheless, the results of this division of labor were quite elaborate, as I discuss in the next section.

Knowledge Organization

Team 1. The overall structure of the semantic relationships among the nodes in the hypermedia presentation developed by the first (more-successful) team is displayed in Fig. 7.6. The five subtopics of women, leaders, battles, slavery, and not-so-famous people serve as high-level nodes with a variety of supporting nodes following. The asterisk (*) indicates cross-topical relationships. For example, slave involvement is linked to the Emancipation Proclamation, a node also participating within the leaders section. Thus, nodes in this presentation often participated in multiple relationships, and the overall organization among the nodes was a hybrid of a hierarchy and a web. The number of links among topical nodes was high (over 50 in number), and the percentage of nodes with multiple representations (i.e., text and graphic or graphic and sound, etc.) was 76.

Team 2. Figure 7.7 displays the overall structure of the semantic relationships among the nodes in the hypermedia presentation developed by the second (less-successful) team. This structure is more strictly hierarchical, but it contains several noteworthy examples of interpretation. To illustrate, one card in this presentation compares the Civil War to the war in Vietnam in order to establish a context for the browser:

> The casualties in the Civil War were so great that it would take 66 years of fighting in the Vietnam War to equal the amount of American's that died in the Civil War. The Civil War was the largest American killing war ever to be fought.

This student came to this conclusion by constructing a graph and then extrapolating from this graph to make a projection about Vietnam. His mathematics teacher was quite surprised by this; she reported that it far exceeded this student's performance in the graphing portion of his mathematics classroom.

Another use of graphing to illustrate ideas is displayed in Fig. 7.8. Here a student uses scale to convey the difference in population between the two regions of the country at the time of the Civil War. This student's use of this graph was stimulated by his search for an explanation of how the South could suffer fewer casualties yet be defeated. Yet another example of interpretation was evident in the following explanation of the Emancipation Proclamation:

I believe that when Abraham Lincoln gave his speech he was trying to scare the Confederacy into coming back into the Union. The reason I think this is because he says if the Confederacy doesn't come back to the Union that the slaves will be freed. One thing that Abe didn't say was that the neutral states had to quit slavery, so after the Civil War slavery didn't end officially. But the 15th Amendment of the constitution gave slaves there freedom.

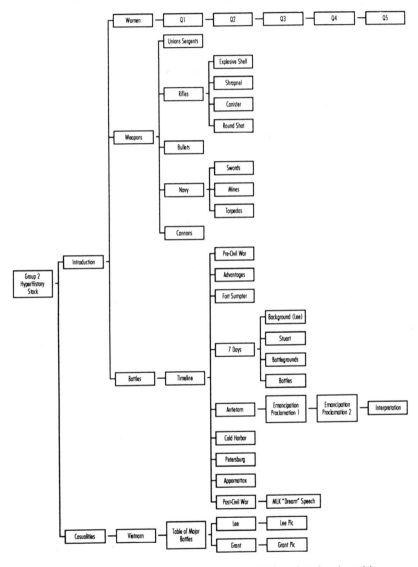

FIG. 7.7.   The semantic structure of the topical nodes developed by the second design team.

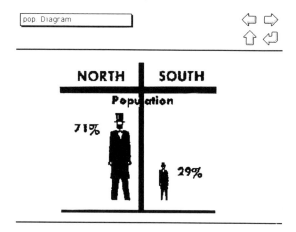

FIG. 7.8.   A representation for population of North and South developed by the second design team.

A final example of interpretation was a link from a description of the post-Civil War period to a digitized recording of Martin Luther King's "I have a dream." Hence, although the second design team's structure is not as interconnected as the first, it is nonetheless semantically rich. In this regard, the majority of the nodes in this presentation (56%) contained multiple representations.

Cognitive Structure.   Visual inspection of the ordered trees describing each student's organization of 20 concepts about the Civil War suggested a transition in knowledge organization before and after instruction for students in both groups, with a more hierarchical structure evident after instruction. Analysis of the number of possible recall orders, a measure of the degree of structure for each tree, indicated a significant decrease over time (fewer possible recall orders denote more structure, $p < .05$). However, when compared to their counterparts in the classroom (students judged to have similar aptitudes and previous grades by their classroom teacher), students participating in the design process fared no better than their peers with respect to either measure of cognitive structure (the ordered trees or the concept triads). I conjecture that these measures were not valid indicators of the extent of learning in the design teams, perhaps because much of what students developed in the design context was not anticipated by their classroom teacher. Hence, the measures, which were developed to reflect the classroom teacher's ideas about the subject-matter, did not assess adequately what the design-students learned (although it is noteworthy that these students did no worse on these measures than their counterparts who remained in the classroom.) This interpretation is supported by the results of a measure of long-term retention that I discuss later.

An alternate measure of cognitive structure was a "showcase," where students presented their hypermedia documents to their classmates. During this time, students in both design teams exhibited deep "pockets" of knowledge. For example, Fig. 7.9 displays a portion of the semantic network of propositions developed by one student as he talked about the battle of Antietam Creek. This student knew a great many details about this battle, including Lee's division of force in face of a superior strength of Union Troops, the battle's relationship to the Emancipation Proclamation, and the personalities of the generals (Lee, Mc-

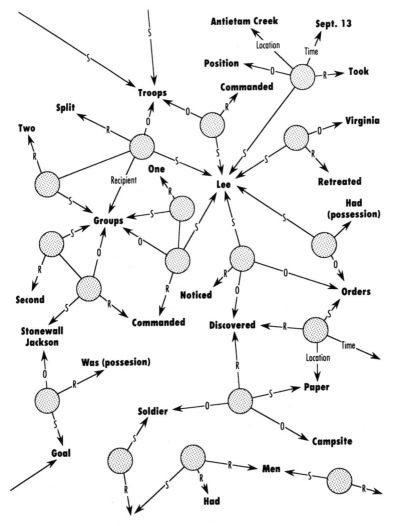

FIG. 7.9. A portion of the semantic network describing a student's propositions about the Battle of Antietam Creek.

Clelland, Stonewall Jackson, etc.). This depth of knowledge was typical of students in both design teams. Informal questioning of other students indicated that although they might know that, for example, Antietam Creek was a battle, typically that was the extent of their knowledge.

One Year Later. One year later, the ten student-designers and their classroom counterparts (8 students because 2 had moved) were interviewed about five Civil War issues: its causes, the role of slaves, notable battles, the effects of the Civil War in the present, and the role of historians. The interviewer had not participated in the previous year's work. Responses to the interview questions were scored for elaborations that went beyond surface details. For example, a response to the causes of the Civil War was scored as elaborative if it went beyond a surface cause like slavery to include notions of regional differences, industrial vs. agrarian economies, and so on. The maximum score for elaborations across issues was 5.

The results were striking: the modal number of elaborations for the design group was 4 and for the traditional group 1. A Mann-Whitney test of the difference in ranked scores between the design and traditional groups was significant: $U = 8.50$, $p < .01$. Students in the design group often applied ideas learned in the Civil War to subsequent learning. For example, one student-designer (the student who compared Vietnam and the Civil War) commented that the strategy of attrition that he had discovered in the Civil War repeated itself during the warfare of the 20th century (citing World War I as a prototype). In contrast, students in the traditional group rarely offered instances of application and instead were much more likely to include unwarranted intrusions in their recall of the Civil War. For example, one student in this group recalled that Custer was a Civil War general and went on to describe his last stand as an event in the Civil War.

Student views of the role of historians were especially revealing. All but one of the students instructed traditionally considered historians as compilers of facts, not interpreters. Representative comments included: "You . . . find as many facts as you can and present them." In contrast, all but one of the student-designers adopted an interpretive stance toward history: "Historians are people who kind of like trace things from the past, kind of put it together like a puzzle." The student-designers also often mentioned the importance of the type of source to the history constructed: "Like I said, with the diaries you're not going to lie to yourself in a diary, probably", and "When I read of things about the Civil War . . . I don't always believe exactly what he (the author) is saying. Because I could write a story about a Civil War battle too . . . you look if they (the authors) have things in the back (e.g., references) . . like even soldiers wrote a lot, they kept a diary . . . get a hold of those . . . use various ones . . . and then recreate it."

Only one student instructed traditionally indicated that the Civil War might continue to reverberate in the present. In contrast, all but two of the student-designers indicated the currency of the issues in this conflict. One student said:

"I think prejudice is the modern slavery . . . People can't get jobs, and people can't live where they want to because of what other people think . . . . there is a lot of racist acts that actually turn to violence that are in a way the little battles of the ongoing Civil War."

In summary, students' long-term recall of the Civil War suggested that the design approach lead to knowledge that was richer, better connected, and more applicable to subsequent learning and events. In contrast, students instructed traditionally failed to recall much either about the Civil War or about any higher-order application of its lessons.

DISCUSSION

This research is a preliminary effort at investigating the fusion of a new form of literacy, hypercomposition, with a new instructional metaphor, knowledge-as-design. In addition, the research is aimed at the development of a software environment to support hypercomposition-based design. Hence, I envision an interactive cycle in which, on the one hand, features of the instructional setting suggest revisions of HyperAuthor, and on the other hand, HyperAuthor makes a substantial difference in the quality of the design environment. In this regard, HyperAuthor is designed to relieve some bottlenecks and to create others. Hyper-Author removes obstacles to creating and mixing media, and it facilitates revision by providing tools for reflection on the organization of the design. On the other hand, HyperAuthor's LinkMaker facility encourages students to think about the nature of the relationship between any two nodes by requiring students to specify the type of link (its semantics) before they can link them electronically. Similarly, whenever a card is created, its title and an icon to represent it are placed into a navigational window—the "User's Guide." This places the construction of navigation for the browser squarely on the shoulders of the author(s), and encourages consideration of audience and structure as the student rearranges the icons into a format intelligible to prospective browsers.

Given its provisional nature, strong conclusions cannot be made from this research either about the utility of HyperAuthor as a design tool or about the utility of the instructional design metaphor as a means to foster conceptual change. I am, however, encouraged by the research results to date. First, students in both design teams followed their interests to develop elaborate and deep understandings of particular areas of the Civil War. For instance, although somewhat macabre, one student's focus on casualties lead him to reason proportionally about the effects of death on the populations of the two regions, North and South. He linked Vietnam to the Civil War and wondered aloud about the effects of the enormous death totals on communities during both eras. Along the way, this student explored materials about the personalities of the commanders in the Civil War (he was particularly taken with Jeb Stuart), their strategies, and the conduct of many battles. Other students developed a feminist perspective about the Civil War, a perspective not found in the resources available to them in their school's media center. Another example of understanding was the conclusion by a student that history involves a process of interpretation because "you can't really tell" about the past. His understanding of history as an interpretation evolved as he read eyewitness accounts. He was also very taken with the roles and experiences of "not-so-famous" people during the war. Reading eyewitness accounts about these ordinary people provided him with an avenue into the tapestry that must be woven from a variety of pieces and sources by practicing historians. Finally, the use of HyperAuthor to design an account of the Civil War also helped many students, particularly those who were less-successful in the classroom, change their conceptions of themselves as learners, away from receiving knowledge and toward authoring knowledge. This transition in self-conception was evident both in their actions and in their identifications of these actions as self- rather than other-directed.

Future Directions

The design approach outlined here shares much in common with the cognitive apprenticeship model of teaching and learning (Brown, Collins, & Duguid, 1989; Collins, Brown, & Newman, 1989). For instance, our use of prompts and inquiry scaffolded student learning in each design team, and over time, we faded the incidence of coaching. Moreover, the tools provided by HyperAuthor facilitated design, and the design goal of creating a resource for peers "situated" learning to a greater degree than was typical of the classroom. In addition, students worked cooperatively in teams to create their presentation ("exploiting cooperation" in the cognitive apprenticeship model). Given the emphasis of the cognitive apprenticeship approach an authentic contexts for teaching and learning, a logical amplification of our basic approach to creating fruitful contexts for authoring would involve engineering interdisciplinary settings with teams of teachers. For example, in this setting, students could develop a presentation about recycling, linking the social science of attitude, the biology of decay, the chemistry of materials, and the mathematics of data collection and interpretation. This endeavor (now implemented in two schools) connects most closely to Carver's (1991) "Discover Rochester" project. Here middle school students worked collaboratively in small groups in an interdisciplinary setting to create a hypertext document about Rochester that was used by visitors to a museum. The Discover Rochester project also explicitly tied the teaching of 17 skills to the cognitive apprenticeship model (Collins, Hawkins, & Carver, in press). Like Carver, I have discovered that engineering this type of collaborative context involves a major restructuring of the school day to allow students sufficient time to think deeply about issues.[1]

---

[1](see Lehrer, Erickson, Love, & Connell, in press).

A second future direction is the development of novel forms of assessment of student learning in design contexts (Collins, Hawkins, & Frederiksen, 1991; Frederiksen & Collins, 1989; Lajoie, 1991). To this end, I have constructed several measures of the types of skills that students may acquire in hypermedia design environments according to the framework outlined in Fig. 7.1. For example, in one task students create an annotated outline of a potential presentation about a topic (one that they have not researched previously) in approximately one and a half hours. The skills assessed include techniques for searching for information (i.e., use of electronic search techniques, use of indexes, inclusion of sources other than encyclopedias, skimming text, and so on), and techniques for selecting information (i.e., note-taking and summarization, attention to multiple forms of representation). Other forms of assessment under development include dynamic assessment of students' use of the HyperAuthor software, assessment of students' choice and justification of a particular representation for a concept, and videos of student showcases of their projects.[2] All of these efforts, however, pose formidable problems and challenges. For example, given video of student showcases, which behaviors should be evaluated and how should this information be aggregated over time by teachers? Moreover, many of the changes anticipated in student learning go beyond skill to matters of self-identity and epistemology. These areas are typically neglected in evaluation, perhaps because they often occur slowly and thus extend over the beyond the course of a typical school year. Yet these epistemological transitions are the lodestone of instruction. In this regard, hypermedia-based design promises to provide a practical context for aligning instruction and identity.

ACKNOWLEDGMENTS

Portions of this research were reported at the 1991 annual meeting of the American Educational Research Association. Thanks to Annie Foong for her role in programming the prototype of HyperAuthor, to Mark Love for his constructive role in the further development and design of HyperAuthor, and for his rendering of the figures displayed in this chapter, to Julie Albright and Tim Connell for coding the discourse reported in this study, to Michael Streibel for conversations about the nature of design, and to Sharon M. Carver for discussions about hypermedia in the classroom and the assessment of skill in this context. Thanks also to Andy Porter, Robert Clasen, and the editors for their comments on a previous version of this chapter. Parts of this work were funded by the University of Wisconsin-Madison Outreach Initiative and by the Robert M. LaFollette Institute of Public Affairs. The research reported here may not reflect the views of either organization. Copies of the HyperAuthor software may be obtained by corresponding with the author.

---

[2](see Carver, Lehrer, Connell, & Erickson, in press).

REFERENCES

Anderson, J. R. (1990). *The adaptive character of thought*. Hillsdale, NJ: Lawrence Erlbaum Associates.

Barrett, E. (1989). Introduction: Thought and language in a virtual environment. In E. Barrett (Ed.), *The society of text* (pp. xi–xix). Cambridge, MA: MIT Press.

Bolter, J. D. (1990). *Writing space. The computer, hypertext, and the history of writing*. Hillsdale, NJ: Lawrence Erlbaum Associates.

Brown, A. L. (1988). Motivation to learn and understand: On taking charge of one's own learning. *Cognition and Instruction, 5*, 311–321.

Brown, A. L., & Campione, J. C. (in press). Communities of learning and thinking or A context by any other name. *Human Development*.

Brown, J. S., Collins, A., & Duguid, P. (1989). Situated cognition and the culture of learning. *Educational Researcher, 18*(1), 32–42.

Carpenter, T. P., Fennema, E., Peterson, P. L., Chiang, C., & Loef, M. (1989). Using knowledge of children's mathematical thinking in classroom teaching: An experimental study. *American Educational Research Journal, 26*, 499–531.

Carver, C. S., & Scheier, M. F. (1981). *Attention and self-regulation: A control-theory approach to human behavior*. New York: Springer-Verlag.

Carver, S. M., Lehrer, R., Connell, T., & Erickson, J. (in press). Learning by designing hypermedia documents: Issues of implementation and assessment. *Educational Psychologist, 27*

Carver, S. M. (1991, April). *Interdisciplinary problem solving*. Paper presented at the annual meeting of the American Educational Research Association, Chicago.

Collins, A., Brown, J. S., & Newman, S. E. (1989). Cognitive apprenticeship: Teaching the crafts of reading, writing, and mathematics. In L. B. Resnick (Ed.), *Knowing, learning, and instruction. Essays in honor of Robert Glaser.* (pp. 453–494). Hillsdale, NJ: Lawrence Erlbaum Associates.

Collins, A., Hawkins, J., & Carver, S. (in press). A cognitive apprenticeship for disadvantaged students. In B. Means (Ed.), *Teaching advanced skills to disadvantaged students*.

Collins, A., Hawkins, J., & Frederiksen, J. R. (1991). *Three different views of students: The role of technology in assessing student performance*.

Day, J. (1986). Teaching summarization skills. *Cognition and Instruction, 3*, 193–210.

Frederiksen, J. R., & Collins, A. (1989). A systems approach to educational testing. *Educational Researcher, 18*, 27–32.

Gentner, D., & Gentner, D. R. (1983). Flowing waters or teeming crowds: Mental models of electricity. In D. Gentner & A. L. Stevens (Eds.), *Mental models* (pp. 99–129). Hillsdale, NJ: Lawrence Erlbaum Associates.

Harel, I., & Papert, S. (1990). Software design as a learning environment. *Interactive Learning Environments, 1*, 1–32.

Hayes, J. R., & Flower, L. S. (1980). Writing as problem solving. *Visible Language, 14*, 388–399.

Hidi, S. (1990). Interest and its contribution as a mental resource for learning. *Review of Educational Research, 60*, 289–309.

Janvier, C. (1987). Representation and understanding: The notion of function as an example. In C. Janvier (Ed.), *Problems of representation in the teaching and learning of mathematics* (pp. 67–81). Hillsdale, NJ: Lawrence Erlbaum Associates.

Johnson-Laird, P. N. (1990). Mental models. In M. I. Posner (Ed.), *Foundations of cognitive science* (pp. 469–499). Cambridge, MA: MIT Press.

Kelly, G. A. (1955). *The psychology of personal constructs*. New York: Norton.

LaBarbera, M. (1990). Principles of design of fluid transport systems in zoology. *Science, 249*, 992–1000.

Lajoie, S. P. (1991, April). *A framework for authentic assessment for mathematics*. Paper presented at the first meeting on the authentic assessment of mathematics, American Educational Research Association Presession, Chicago.

Lampert, M. (1990). When the problem is not the question and the solution is not the answer. *American Educational Research Journal, 27,* 29–63.

Lawson, B. (1990). *How designers think. The design process demystified.* Boston: Butterworth Architecture.

Lehrer, R., Erickson, J., Love, M., & Connell, T. (in press). Learning by designing hypermedia documents. *Computers in the schools, 9* (2/3).

Lehrer, R. (1988). The self as a narrative structure. In J. C. Mancuso & M. L. Shaw (Eds.), *Personal cognitive structure. Computer access and analysis* (pp. 195–228). New York: Prager.

Lehrer, R., Levin, B. B., DeHart, P., & Comeaux, M. (1987). Voice-feedback as a scaffold for writing: A comparative study. *Journal of Educational Computing Research, 3,* 335–353.

Lepper, M. R. (1988). Motivational considerations in the study of instruction. *Cognition and Instruction, 5,* 289–309.

Mancuso, J. C. (1977). Current motivational models in the elaboratuion of personal construct theory. In A. W. Landfield (Ed.), *Nebraska symposium on motivation: 1976* (pp. 43–97). Lincoln: University of Nebraska Press.

Markus, H., & Nurius, P. (1986). *Possible selves. American Psychologist, 41,* 954–969.

Mead, G. H. (1932). *The philosophy of the present.* Chicago: University of Chicago Press.

Naveh-Benjamin, M., McKeachie, W. J., Lin, Y., & Tucker, D. G. (1986). Inferring students' cognitive structures and their development using the "ordered tree technique." *Journal of Educational Psychology, 78,* 130–140.

Nelson, T. (1987). *Literacy machines.* San Antonio, TX: Project Xanadu.

Nielsen, J. (1990). *Hypertext and hypermedia.* New York: Academic Press.

Norman, D. (1988). *The design of everyday things.* New York: Basic Books.

Perkins, D. N. (1986). *Knowledge as design.* Hillsdale, NJ: Lawrence Erlbaum Associates.

Perry, W. G., Jr. (1970). *Forms of intellectual and ethical development in the college years: A scheme.* New York: Holt, Rinehart and Winston.

Reitman, J. S., & Reuter, H. H. (1980). Organization revealed by recall orders and confirmed by pauses. *Cognitive Psychology, 12,* 554–581.

Ryan, M. P. (1984a). Monitoring text comprehension: Individual differences in epistemological standards. *Journal of Educational Psychology, 76,* 248–258.

Ryan, M. P. (1984b). Conceptions of prose coherence: Individual differences in epistemological standards. *Journal of Educational Psychology, 76,* 1226–1238.

Schon, D. A. (1987). *Educating the reflective practitioner.* San Francisco: Jossey-Bass.

Shrager, L., & Mayer, R. E. (1989). Note-taking fosters generative learning strategies in novices. *Journal of Educational Psychology, 81,* 263–282.

APPENDIX A

Categories of Activity and Discourse for Videotape Analysis

Research

Searching for information (i.e., browsing texts)

Selecting information (i.e., taking notes, marking an item for later use)

Database use (i.e., creating a database, either paper or electronic)

Summarization (i.e., writing a summary of several sources)
Interpretation (i.e., restating information in one's own words)

Design

Planning (i.e., role assignment, deciding on division of labor)
Structure of Presentation (i.e., deciding on subtopics, deciding on links)
Representation (i.e., deciding, creating multiple representations)
Models/Analogies (i.e., refers to previous methods, situations)
Argument/Evaluation (i.e., justifies inclusion of a piece of information)
Audience (i.e., explicit consideration of audience)
Revision/Editing (i.e., change in response to evaluation)

Collaboration

Collaborative Construction (i.e., share information, work together)
Teaching (i.e., one student tutors another)

Teaching

Framing (i.e., ask leading question)
Knowledge Assessment (i.e., ask for information, interpretation)
Motivation (i.e., attempt to arouse curiosity)
Clarification (i.e., ask student for elaboration)
Performance Assessment (i.e., ask student to show use of scanner)
Reprimand (i.e., ask student to change inappropriate behavior)

Off-Task

APPENDIX B

Design Interview

Search/Selection

1. What kind of information have you found? Where did you find it? How did you find it?
2. How did you decide what to put into your presentation?

Structure

3. What's the status of the presentation? What's new or different since the last time we talked?

4. What are the parts? How are they related?

Purpose

5. What's the purpose of the presentation?

Arguments

6. Does it do a good job? Why did you decide to include. . . . ?
7. How else could you have done it?

Analogy

8. What else is it like?

Audience

9. How are you organizing it so someone can follow it?
10. Will someone else (like your classmates) be able to learn from your presentation? What makes you think so?

Collaboration

11. What tasks are you working on now? How are you dividing them up? Why are you doing it that way?

Interest

12. What do you like about this? dislike? What do you find hard? easy?
13. How is this experience the same as or different than learning in the regular classroom?

8

Constructing a Joint Problem Space: The Computer as a Tool for Sharing Knowledge

Stephanie D. Teasley
University of Michigan

Jeremy Roschelle
Institute for Research on Learning

This chapter presents a case study intended to exemplify the use of a computer as a cognitive tool for learning that occurs socially. We investigate a particularly important kind of social activity, the collaborative construction of new problem-solving knowledge. Collaboration is a process by which individuals negotiate and share meanings relevant to the problem-solving task at hand. The essential property of collaborative problem solving, we argue, is that it enables the construction of a shared conceptual structure which we call a Joint Problem Space. The Joint Problem Space (JPS) supports problem-solving activity by integrating semantic interpretations of goals, features, operators, and methods. We propose that the fundamental activity in collaborative problem solving occurs via the students' participation in the creation and maintenance of a JPS.

We examine learning within a computational context in order to address the question of how students construct shared meanings in model-building activities. We hold modeling to be one of the central activities of the scientific community—understanding a concept and having a model are closely related properties of cognition. We focus on qualitative modeling. Specifically, we want students to learn qualitative modeling with the Newtonian concepts of velocity and acceleration, and thereby gain deep access to key concepts of Newtonian science. The computer simulation we use, the Envisioning Machine, was designed specifically to portray a graphical, dynamic simulation of a physicists' mental model of velocity and acceleration. The design of the Envisioning Machine (see Roschelle, 1990) is intended to both enable and mediate students' learning—it enables students to construct qualitative understanding of velocity and acceleration, and mediates their discourse about the meaning of those concepts for the activity of modeling motion.

Research from a broad variety of sources has led us to consider that cognitive representations are built through social interaction and activity, in addition to individual cognition. Several prominent learning theorists have for some time argued that learning is a fundamentally social activity (e.g., Dewey, 1916; Mead, 1934; Piaget, 1932; Vygotsky, 1978). In the scientific community, concepts and models are increasingly seen as social constructions resulting from face-to-face participation in scientific activities. In particular, research in the sociology and philosophy of science has turned away from the picture of scientists as being purely objective, socially isolated, and detached from practical activity (e.g., Knorr-Cetina, 1981, Latour, 1986, Lynch, 1985). From these reports, we conclude that learning to be a scientist is as much a matter of (1) forms of participation in social activity and (2) negotiation of shared meanings, as it is of (3) internalizing scientific representations and operations.

Our work therefore views activity, communication, and representation as mutually constitutive aspects of knowing, rather than separately implemented modules. While research in the last of these areas, modeling representations, is the most familiar to cognitive scientists, there has been substantial progress in the other areas as well. Work in the fields of Conversation Analysis and Interaction Analysis are advancing the scientific understanding of how people negotiate meaning (e.g., Goodwin, 1981; Schegloff, 1991). Work in Activity Theory, particularly from Soviet scholars, is proving to be useful in analyses of learning activities (e.g., Engeström, 1987; Wersch, 1981). As a long-term goal, we see great opportunity for progress in understanding shared mental models by incorporating theory and methods of Cognitive Science, Conversation Analysis, and Activity Theory. This chapter takes a step in that direction by explicating the problem-solving activity of one of the most collaborative dyads we have studied. We add to the growing body of microanalytic research (Schoenfeld, Smith, & Arcavi, in press; Meria, 1991; Moschkovich, 1991; diSessa, Hammer, Sherin, & Kolpakowski, 1991), which shows how social activity, communication, and representation are inextricably bound together.

THE TASK: THE ENVISIONING MACHINE

Gary and Sam, the students we report on, were 15-year-old males who were taking a summer course in statistics at the University of California, Berkeley. They were comfortable working together as they had been collaborating on a computer project in the statistics course. They did not have any formal physics training. (Gary, however, had done some reading about physics on his own.) The subjects were asked to work together on an activity involving a computer simulation called "The Envisioning Machine" (Roschelle, 1986, 1991).

The Envisioning Machine (EM) is a direct-manipulation graphical simulation of the concepts of velocity and acceleration. Figure 8.1 illustrates the screen of

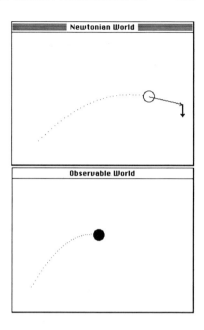

FIG. 8.1. The Envisioning Machine.

the EM. There are two windows, the "Observable World" and the "Newtonian
World." The Observable World displays a simulation of a ball moving across the
screen. This represents the goal motion. The Newtonian World displays a particle
with velocity and acceleration vectors (the thin and thick arrows, respectively).
Using the mouse, the user can manipulate the settings of these vectors. When the
simulation is run, the particle in Newtonian World moves with the initial velocity
indicated by the acceleration vector. In both worlds, the moving objects leave a
trace of dots behind them as they move. Because the dots are dropped at a
uniform time interval, the dot spacing represents speed. All the motions displayed by the EM are constant velocity or constant acceleration motions.

The specific EM activity used in this study involved matching the goal motion
displayed in the Observable World by adjusting velocity and acceleration vectors
on the particle displayed in the Newtonian World. This activity was called a
"challenge." Typically, solving a challenge requires a series of trials in which the
students watch the motions in the Observable and Newtonian Worlds, adjust the
vectors of a particle in the Newtonian World, run the simulation, and evaluate
whether the two motions were the same. Since the students had not previously
studied velocity and acceleration, they needed to experiment with the simulation
in order to learn how to adjust the vectors to produce motions that matched in the
Observable World. Moreover, since the computer did not give explicit feedback
on the correctness of a solution, students develop their own criteria for determining whether two motions were "the same." The subjects worked on the EM
activity in three sessions, each about 45 minutes long. We discuss only one

challenge from the first session of Gary and Sam's work. The session had the following format: In the beginning of this session, Gary and Sam were instructed on how to use the mouse to do the EM activity. During these instructions, the vectors were given neutral names, "the thin arrow" and "the thick arrow," rather than the more theory-laden terms "velocity" and "acceleration." The task was described as "making the motions the same," though the meaning of "the same" was not specified. Thus the instructions left the meaning of the task substantially underdetermined. After the instructions, Gary and Sam were asked to "work together" on a series of ten challenges. Each challenge consisted of matching a different Observable World motion by adjusting the arrows in the Newtonian World. When the subjects finished the challenges, about 45 minutes later, they were interviewed about what they had learned.

The Envisioning Machine Design: Fidelity and Mediation

As discussed in Roschelle (1990), the Envisioning Machine design has been characterized from two perspectives: fidelity and mediation. The fidelity perspective examines the degree of correspondence between the external display and the presumed mental model of a physics expert. Indeed, the original design (e.g., Roschelle, 1986) was inspired by the opportunity to construct an external display that corresponded to the form of experts' mental models. Roschelle and Greeno (1987) observed that experts constructed robust understanding of situations by relating two behavioral models, a commonsense model of an observable situation and a theoretical model incorporating scientific entities. The dual window design of the EM reflects the desire to have students develop similar understandings of the relationships between observable motions and Newtonian models of motion.

The fidelity perspective generally presumes a correspondence theory of representation: A better correspondence between an external display and expert mental model should support better internalization of scientific knowledge. The correspondence representation theory and the associated internalization learning theory has proved to be too simplistic to account for the relationships between physical displays and conceptual entities. In particular, students do not necessarily interpret the display that a scientist would, and therefore the crucial aspects of the display that correspond to a scientists' mental model are not necessarily available to them (Roschelle, 1991). It is a mistake to assume that students' interpretation of a high fidelity display will be isomorphic to an experts' interpretation, even after they have substantial opportunities to interact with the display as a representation system.

A mediation perspective instead focuses on the use of external displays as tools for negotiating meaning, and builds from a Pragmatic (e.g., Dewey, 1932) rather than a correspondence theory account of representation. Rather than seeking a perfect denotational relationship between external sign and internal concept, the mediation perspective accepts that interpretation is inherently uncertain, especially to newcomers to a particular community. Definitions, regardless of their degree of fidelity or their form (verbal or graphical), cannot enable a nonscientist to understand precisely what a scientist means. A mediation perspective therefore leads designers to construct external displays that will bridge the gap between commonsense and scientific interpretations by providing an enriched situation to act in and talk about. Careful attention to mediation leads to design decisions orthogonal to issues of fidelity: direct manipulation for communication, persistence, minimalism, and authentic activity. Roschelle (1990) presents a detailed report of how careful attention to the mediational properties of the display led to concrete design changes in the EM.

What is Envisioning Machine Knowledge?

As our goal is to examine the construction of *shared* knowledge in collaborative problem solving, it is necessary to discuss the nature of the physics knowledge involved in solving the EM activity. Roschelle (1991) presents a competence model of EM problem solving and shows that it accounts for key aspects of students' problem-solving performances. In this model, the EM activity is seen as a form of difference-reduction: students try to reduce the differences between the motion they control in the Newtonian World and the goal motion in the Observable World. This difference-reduction takes place in two stages: First, students set the directions of the vectors to match the overall shape of a motion. Second, students set the lengths of the vectors to match the speed at which the particle moves along the shape. The types of knowledge corresponding to these two stages are knowledge of *configurations* and knowledge of *qualitative proportionalities*.

Configurations relate the direction of the vectors to the shape of the motion produced. The velocity vector always points in the direction that the motion begins in. Depending on the angle between the acceleration vector and the velocity vector, motions with qualitatively different characteristics are produced. For example, when the velocity and acceleration vectors are collinear and opposed, the motion will go out and come back along a straight line. The Envisioning Machine motions can be categorized into four shapes with four corresponding configurations, as in Table 8.1.

TABLE 8.1
Configurations

Shape	Direction of Vectors
Straight, constant speed	no acceleration
Straight, speeding up	acceleration in sam direction as velocity
Straight, turns around	acceleration in opposite direction to velocity
Curve	acceleration at an angle to (not collinear with) velocity

TABLE 8.2
Configurations

Property of Motion		Length of Vector
Initial speed, dot spacing	proportional to	velocity
Time to reach apex	proportional to	velocity and inversely to acceleration
Height of apex	proportional to	velocity and inversely to acceleration

Within each configuration, it is still necessary to determine the proper length of each arrow. Clues for the correct lengths can be found by comparing the Newtonian and Observable World motions. For example, if the dot spacing in the Newtonian World is greater than the dot spacing in the Observable World, then the velocity vector in the Newtonian World is too long. We call relationships of this form "Qualitative Proportionalities" after similar representations developed by computer scientists investigating qualitative reasoning (see Bobrow, 1986). A qualitative proportionality is a relationship between two variables that states that an increase in one variable will result in an increase in the other. The relationship between dot spacing and length of the velocity vector could be stated as "the dot spacing is qualitatively proportional to the length of the velocity vector." Table 8.2 lists some qualitative proportionalities that students use to solve the EM task.

Roschelle (1991) argues that EM knowledge, as described earlier, is a valuable form of physics knowledge. Although it is outside the scope of this chapter to argue for this view, the line of reasoning is as follows: EM knowledge, as described before, encodes qualitative regularities in the behavior of the EM. The EM's behavior, in turn, is based on the mathematical definitions of velocity and acceleration.[1] Thus the qualitative regularities of the EM are also qualitative regularities in the concepts under their formal definitions. Learning the EM is therefore also learning specific qualitative descriptions of velocity and acceleration. Such qualitative descriptions are particularly important for understanding how physics laws apply to everyday situations.

FRAMEWORK FOR ANALYZING COLLABORATION

An examination of students' discourse and activity as they work together allows us to understand how the social interaction affects the course of learning. This necessitates a microanalysis of not only the content of students' talk, but also of how the pragmatic structure of the conversations can result in shared knowledge. In particular, it requires understanding how students use coordinated language and action to establish shared knowledge, to recognize any divergences from

---

[1]The definitions read, "Velocity is the derivative of position with respect to time and acceleration is the derivative of velocity with respect to time."

shared knowledge as they arise, and to rectify misunderstandings that impede joint work. To accomplish this aim, we draw on ideas from pragmatics (e.g., Levinson, 1983), conversation analysis (e.g., Schegloff, 1981), and protocol analysis (Ericsson & Simon, 1984) to describe how the communicative exchanges function to construct and maintain a Joint Problem Space. In coordination with an analysis of the development of students' physics knowledge, we are able to identify how social interaction promotes or inhibits learning in key segments of the problem solving process.

Recent work on the coordination of meaning in conversations has stressed that mutual intelligibility is the result of local, interactional work of the participants. Conversants establish shared meaning via the construction and accumulation of a common ground, a body of shared knowledge (Clark & Schaefer, 1989). Meaning can be coordinated and mutual intelligibility achieved because conversants provide constant evidence, positive and negative, that each utterance has been understood, and engage in repairs when it has not (Schegloff, 1991).

In our analysis of collaborative learning, we take the point-of-view that students' work is based on a shared conception of the task. We enlarge the notion of common ground, which has origins in the study of ad hoc conversations, and apply it to the study of a socially organized task-oriented activity: collaborative problem solving. In doing so, we synthesize the construct of common ground with a cognitive analysis of problem-solving activity. This enables us to apply a Conversation Analytic approach to a situation in which the topic of conversation is a structured problem solving domain.

Before we can begin to analyze the process of collaboration, it is useful to be specific about which phenomena we seek to understand. *Collaboration* is a broadly used term which serves to describe a wide variety of behaviors. In the most general sense, collaboration is said to have occurred when more than one person works on a single task. For our purposes, however, it is helpful and in fact necessary, to draw some specific parameters around what we refer to as collaboration. The following definition delineates the kind of behavior we have focused on:

Collaboration is a coordinated, synchronous activity that is the result of a continued attempt to construct and maintain a shared conception of a problem.

We make a distinction between *collaborative* versus *cooperative* problem solving. Cooperative work is accomplished by the division of labor among participants, as an activity where each person is responsible for a portion of the problem solving. We focus on collaboration as the mutual engagement of participants in a coordinated effort to solve the problem together. We further distinguish between synchronous (i.e., working together at the same time) and asynchronous activity. Although we do not propose that collaboration cannot occur in asynchronous activity (e.g., "Distance Learning "), we focus on face-to-face interactions, which can only occur as a synchronous activity.

The notion of "a shared conception of the problem" is central to our work. We propose that social interactions in the context of problem-solving activity occur in relation to a *Joint Problem Space*. The Joint Problem Space (JPS) is a shared knowledge structure that supports problem-solving activity by integrating *(a)* goals, *(b)* descriptions of the current problem state, *(c)* awareness of available problem-solving actions, and *(d)* associations that relate goals, features of the current problem state, and available actions. As the following microanalysis makes clear, we propose that the fundamental activity in collaborative problem solving occurs via engagement with an emergent, socially negotiated set of knowledge elements that constitute a Joint Problem Space.

Specifically, we hold that collaborative problem solving consists of two concurrent activities, solving the problem together and building a JPS. These activities necessarily coexist. Conversation in the context of problem-solving activity is the process by which collaborators construct and maintain a JPS. Simultaneously, the JPS is the structure that enables meaningful conversation about problem solving to occur.

The JPS is a pragmatic, rather than an ideal structure. The overlap of meaning in the collaborator's common conception of the problem is not necessarily complete or absolutely certain. Rather this overlap is sufficient to gradually accumulate shared concepts and allow convergence on certainty of meaning.

Thus to build a JPS, collaborators must have ways of:

- introducing and accepting knowledge into the JPS,
- monitoring ongoing activity for evidence of divergences in meaning, and
- repairing divergences that impede the progress of the collaboration.

There are a number of structured discourse forms that conversants use in everyday speech to achieve similar goals in the service of mutual intelligibility. These forms utilize language, bodily action, and combinations of words and actions. Our analysis shows that students can use the structure of conversation to continually build, monitor, and repair a JPS. Next, we discuss some of the categories of discourse events that have proved useful for our analysis. A complete review of discourse analysis is outside the scope of this chapter (see Levinson, 1983, for a review). Of the categories we discuss, turn-taking is the most pervasive and general. Specific turn-taking forms contribute to various aspects of joint problem-solving activity. Socially-Distributed Productions provide means for introducing and accepting problem-solving knowledge into the JPS. Narrations and Question-Answer pairs enable students to monitor each other's interpretations. Repairs offer a means to rectify divergent interpretations. Coordinations of language and action also prove important for introducing, monitoring, and repairing knowledge in the JPS.

Turn-Taking.   Communication between individuals follows a well-specified form of turn-taking that has been extensively described by linguists and sociologists (see Schegloff & Sacks, 1973). Discourse units such as questions, acceptances, disagreements, and repairs represent various specific discourse forms available for taking a conversational turn. The flow, content, and structure of turns is used as a measure of whether the participants in a conversation understand each other (see Clark & Schaefer, 1989). Similarly, in our analysis of student's collaborations, we propose that the ongoing structure of turn-taking sequences is an indication of the degree to which students share common problem representations. In analyzing collaborative work, we look for dialog in which turn transitions are smooth, and the sequence of talk follows a cooperative pattern. In periods of successful collaborative activity, students' conversational turns build on each other and the content contributes to the joint problem-solving activity.

In addition to joint work, collaborative problem solving includes periods in which partners are not fully engaged with each other. Partners occasionally withdraw from the active interaction with their partner to work on ideas that are too ill-formed or complicated to be introduced into the shared work. These periods are marked in the interaction by periods of significant next-turn deviations such as nonacceptances, disagreements, and empty turns. In a successful collaboration, such periods of withdrawal are usually followed by periods of intense interaction which serve to incorporate the individual insight into the shared problem-solving knowledge.

Socially-Distributed Productions.   One type of turn-taking structure particularly useful in understanding the production of shared problem-solving knowledge is the "collaborative completion." As described in the work of Lerner (1987) and Wilkes-Gibbs (1986), a collaborative completion distributes a compound sentence over discourse partners. That is, one partner's turn begins a sentence or an idea, and the other partner uses their next turn to complete it. One especially relevant type of compound sentence has IF–THEN form. In an IF–THEN collaborative completion, the antecedent and consequent are produced on separate turns. The distribution of the IF–THEN across turns provides an opportunity for partners to accept or repair conditional knowledge.

We call an IF–THEN collaborative completion a "Socially-Distributed Production," because its content consists of a production rule, while its form is socially distributed across turns. We also include in this category IF–THEN sentences that are delivered in installments, with the conversational partner producing acceptances in subsequent turns. An SDP may be a particularly effective means for constructing shared knowledge because it spreads the interrelated goals, features, and actions of a knowledge element across conversational turns. This provides multiple opportunities for partners to contribute to the construction and verification of the new piece of shared knowledge.

Repairs.   Because the collaboration process involves periods of individual activity, collaborative activity also produces periods of conflict in which individual ideas are negotiated with respect to the shared work. These periods of conflict usually signify a breakdown in mutual intelligibility, rather than the collaboration *per se*. In fact, the attempts to reduce conflict by resolving misunderstandings are evidence of the dyad's preference for a working style in which a shared conception of the problem is maintained. Often these attempts take the form of "repairs." Repairs are the method by which participants in talk can deal with problems or troubles in speaking, hearing, or comprehension of dialog (see Schegloff, Jefferson, & Sacks, 1977). According to Schegloff (1991), repairs are a major means for the achievement and consolidation of understanding and thereby the management of the mutual intelligibility of the collaborative problem solving activity.

Without successful repairs, breakdowns in mutual intelligibility continue longer. Both partners use justifications, counter-suggestions, assertions, and elaborations in their attempt to get their partner coordinated. Occasionally, failures to reestablish mutual intelligibility (unsuccessful repairs) lead to the students abandoning the current problem. This can be seen when partners give up on a particular challenge or give up a particular aspect of the challenge. In the course of the session, students may return to the particular challenge or problem area, and may resolve the impasse in the shared understanding or continue by working around the impasse.

Narrations.   Narrations are a verbal strategy that enable partners to monitor each other's actions and interpretations. In the EM activity, only one partner can carry out actions with the mouse at a time. These actions may be difficult for the other partner to interpret, because every action can correspond to a number of possible intentions. Narration informs one's partner of the intentions corresponding to actions. This enhances the partner's opportunities to recognize differences in the shared understanding. Continued attention to narrations and accompanying action can signal acceptances and shared understandings (Clark & Schaefer, 1989). Interruptions to narrations create an immediate opportunity to rectify misunderstandings. Narrations are also useful for the participants to signal that an action is not intended to contribute to the current shared goal; a statement like "I just want to see what this does" signals that the actor is no longer working on the task at hand, but rather is exploring a novel situation.

Language and Action.   Although there are many examples of narratives in collaborative activity, students are not wholly dependent on language to maintain shared understanding. In fact, one major role of the computer in supporting collaborative learning is providing a context for the production of action and gesture. Action and gesture can both serve as presentations and acceptances. An action or gesture can serve as an acceptance when one partner interprets the other partner's utterances by performing an action. As most of the utterances contain indexical, ambiguous references, the production of the appropriate action both accepts and confirms a shared understanding of the task. Actions and gestures can likewise serve as presentations of new ideas. Partners often use their hand or the computer mouse to demonstrate an idea. In this case, the partner's ability to successfully interpret the action through an utterance is an indication of mutual intelligibility and acceptability of the idea. The simultaneous production of matching language and action by separate partners can also produce an effective division of labor: While one partner concentrates on carrying out actions, the other concentrates on producing utterances that make the intentions behind the actions available for commentary and repair.

CHALLENGE SIX

Our goal in the remainder of this chapter is to exemplify the analysis of the process of collaborative problem solving from the point-of-view of the JPS. We look in detail at the Gary and Sam's construction of a shared conception of the task in challenge six, which was the sixth motion that they worked on. These students began challenge six about 11 minutes into their session and finished it about 8 minutes later.

In challenge six, the motion of the ball in the Observable World is analogous to that of a ball tossed straight up in the air; it starts upward, slows down, instantaneously pauses at the top, then accelerates downward (see Fig. 8.2). To construct this motion in the Newtonian World, subjects must set the direction of the velocity vector upward and the acceleration vector downward. In addition, to exactly copy the Observable World motion, the subjects must appropriately adjust the lengths of both vectors. Two earlier challenges these students investigated also required an acceleration vector, but challenge six is the first challenge that they have seen in which the acceleration opposes the velocity.

The detailed analysis that follows shows that the students progressed through challenge six in two main stages. First, they established the correct directions for the Newtonian World vectors. Second, they determined the correct lengths for the vectors. The settings of velocity and acceleration at key moments during the challenge are illustrated in Fig. 8.3. The setting in Fig. 8.3b, which the participants achieved at the end of episode 6-2, shows correct setting of the directions of the vectors, in contrast to 3a. Later, the participants adjusted the lengths of the

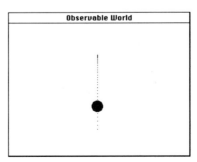

FIG. 8.2. The goal of motion in Challenge 6.

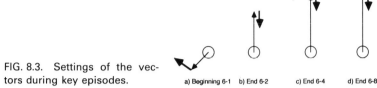

FIG. 8.3.   Settings of the vec-
tors during key episodes.   a) Beginning 6-1   b) End 6-2   c) End 6-4   d) End 6-8

vectors for a better match to the Observable World motion. Figures 8.3c and 8.3d
respectively illustrate a close approximation and the exact setting of the lengths.
The transcript[2] of language and action during challenge six will be presented
in a series of "episodes." The boundaries for each episode were chosen to be
consistent with events in the collaboration, although their exact size was determined for ease of exposition. The contents of the episodes are roughly as follows: In Episodes 6–1 and 6–2, the students constructed knowledge of the
configuration of vectors required to produce the shape of the challenge six
motion. In the remaining episodes, they focused on setting the lengths to match
the motion more closely. The problem of setting the lengths began with a considerable difference of opinions in Episode 6–3, which was resolved in Episode 6–
4. In contrast, Episodes 6–5 and 6–7 show relatively smooth elaborations of
ideas. Episodes 6–4, 6–6, and 6–8 are also interesting because of the new ideas
introduced there. In Episode 6–8, the participants negotiate a close to the problem-solving activity. The analysis of these episodes focuses on the means by
which collaborators introduce and accept ideas into the JPS, monitor emerging
interpretations, and maintain the JPS by repairing divergences in understanding.

Episode 6–1.   In the opening moments of the challenge, the subjects watched
motion in the observable world. Both partners simultaneously tried to make sense
of a kind of motion they had not yet encountered during any of the previous
challenges in the session. Although both partners were engaged, their discourse
signalled that they did not yet share the same conception of the challenge.

1	G: Challenge six.	*S reaches for mouse, G gives it up, S now has mouse for remainder of challenge*
2	S: OK.	*Runs simulation. Observable World shows challenge 6 — ball toss, straight up. Newtonian World shows random curve*
3	G: This one's gonna be a curve. No maybe not. (1.5) Oh: : : ((falling intonation)) (2.0)	

---

[2]Transcripts are presented using notation found in Suchman (1987). Appendix 1 describes the
notation.

4 S: It's the acceleration is in the
       opposite direction to start
       with.
         [
5 G: How can they make a, (.) a double   *stop simulation*
       acceleration?
6 S: See it for a second.
7 G: Oh they make it go a : : ht   *motions up then down with*
                                                finger tip
8 S: (()) the first one.   *gestures up*
         [
9 G: Let's see that again. Let's see
       that again.
    (6.0)   *S resets, runs, NW still*
                                                random curve

At the beginning of this challenge, Gary predicted what kind of motion he
thought the ball would take (line 3). Upon actually seeing the model run, Sam
correctly identified the correct relationship between the directions of the velocity
and acceleration vectors: that they should be opposite (line 4). Although his
statement is somewhat ambiguous (he could have the direction of the velocity
wrong, but the relationship between velocity and acceleration right), his later
actions clarified his intent as he set the velocity pointing straight up and the
acceleration straight down.

Gary's next utterance occurred as an overlap of Sam. By this interruption, he
did not directly accept Sam's idea that the vectors should be opposed, rather he
stated his own conception of the problem (line 5). His question about "double
acceleration" suggests that he had a different idea. Sam's statement (line 6),
instead of answering Gary's question, directed Gary's attention back to the
computer simulation. By re-stating Sam's utterance, Gary agreed to watch the
simulation a second time (line 9).

Episode 6–2. The opening episode was followed by a period in which Gary
and Sam coordinated their conception of the problem as being one in which the
velocity and acceleration arrows are in opposite directions, and set the arrows
accordingly (Fig. 8.4.).

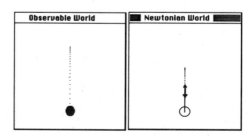

FIG. 8.4. Motion at the end of
Episode 6-2.

10	G:	Oh ok. (2.0)	*points to screen and gestures up*
			resets
11	S:	Yeah, I know what they're doing. Ok. First,	
12	G:	just need to get everything. (2.5)	
13	S:	Right about::t there::=	*sets initial position bottom center, the correct location*
14	G:	=That looks good. (2.0)	
15	S:	Ok, so we wanna be cool. (3.0) Just for now is (2.0)	
16	S:	Oh. (4.0)	*points velocity vector upwards*
17	S:	Ok. (2.0)	*sets acceleration vector downwards*
18	S:	So:: that one's pretty long. And this one right here is going (.) ba::ck (.5) like that. (3.5)	*makes velocity shorter*
			runs simulation, NW goes straight-up/down but speeds don't match
19	S:	Ooh we almost got it=	
20	G:	=Initial acceleration is too::: slow and maybe real (.5) our initial speed is too slow and maybe acceleration isn't good either.	*S stops simulation*
21	S:	Ok we, we, we got the general::	*S resets simulation*
22	G:	Hi (2.0)	*G waves at camera. Laughs.*
23	S:	Hi mom. (4.0)	*S waves at camera, laughs.*

After they watched the simulation again, Gary said "Ok, ok" (line 10) which Sam interpreted as an acceptance of his original idea that the velocity and acceleration should be set in opposition. Sam then began using the mouse to carry out this idea. Although Gary was not contributing to the discourse during this time, he was watching Sam's actions on the screen. Sam's narration as he worked (lines 11–12) allowed Gary the opportunity to comment at any point should he have disagreed. At line 19, after Sam had run the simulation with the arrows opposite, he announced "we almost got it." This utterance reflected

Sam's general satisfaction with the shape of the motion. Gary's next utterance (line 20) treated Sam's statement as an invitation to refine the standard for success; he suggested further changes that fit within the framework of setting the arrows opposite via the term "initial speed" and "acceleration." Because this utterance pushed for more detail within the context of what had already been accomplished, it is both an acceptance of past work and presentation of a proposal for future refinement. In this statement, Gary produced a "self repair" (see Schegloff, Jefferson, & Sacks, 1977) in which he corrected the initial part of the utterance, "initial acceleration" to be "initial speed." Sam's response (line 21) deflected Gary's suggestion by referring back to what they had already accomplished (getting the shape right). The episode ended with a brief period of off-task activity, in which Gary and Sam waved at the camera (lines 22 & 23). Off-task behavior was fairly rare in Gary and Sam's sessions.

These first two episodes set the context for the rest of the challenge. On one hand, the partners had agreed on the basic configuration of the arrows to match the Observable World motion (see Fig. 8.4). On the other hand, they had not agreed on how to adjust the lengths of the arrows to achieve a closer match with the target motion. In particular, their particle did not match the speed and height of the target motion.

Episode 6–3. This episode marks the beginning of a divergence of the partners' ideas about how to set the length of each arrow in order to achieve a closer match between the model and the particle. Throughout this episode, the students were working on different conceptual problems and they were talking more to themselves than to each other.

24	S:	Oh, if we could get rid of one of those things. (2.0) I'm just doing that so I can see what's in there. (2.0)	*makes velocity longer*
25	S:	Ok, this one (9.0)	*makes velocity shorter, runs*
26	S:	Ok this one's too great. Yeah. (1.5)	*stops, resets simulation*
27	G:	Initial speed isn't good enough. Aw	
		[	
28	S:	Ok (?)	
29	G:	You can't tell.	
		[	
30	S:	Now that looks fine. that's I think=	
31	G:	=Initial speed is fine?	
32	S:	Just make this one smaller.	*makes acceleration shorter*

33   G: Wait you know we could use
          particle one to (.) test the   *G points to screen, looks at*
          initial speed an::   *S, gestures up*
34   S: now this
          [
35   G: Oh we couldn't convert it to
          a particle two. (1.5)
36   S: Now ok.   *runs*
          That's slightly too much. It
          should come back.
37   G: hhh. eventually.
38   S: Ok (.) so:: (1.0) reset maybe   *stops, resets*
          make this one small
                                          [
39   G:

          It's hard to tell the difference
          between (2.0) initial speed
          an:::d acceleration.
          (4.0)   *S clicks on a vector but*
                                               makes no change, runs

40   S: Aw:: I don't think that did   *stops, resets*
          anything.

In this period of divergence, Sam continued to search for the correct solution by experimenting with different lengths for the vectors. During this search he occasionally reported on his work. Meanwhile, Gary's utterances show that he was working on a conceptual problem: distinguishing initial speed from acceleration. Both participants already understood many differences in the two concepts—they knew that each maps onto a different arrow, that the arrows did not have symmetrical effects, and that in this particular challenge the velocity arrow was up, while the acceleration was down. Thus, it seems fairly certain that Gary was trying to make a particular conceptual advance. That is, he wanted to find a principle that would determine the correct length of each vector. This is reflected in Gary's statements, "you can't tell" (line 29) and "it's hard to tell the difference between initial speed and acceleration" (line 39). His first idea of how to do this using the particle without acceleration was a good one (line 33). One could use this particle to match the *initial* motions of the Observable World and Newtonian World, because the initial motion is determined by the velocity vector alone. Then having fixed the velocity, one could focus on the acceleration. This would be a more systematic approach than Sam was following. Gary used a question (line 31), an interjection (line 33), and a comment (line 39) to try to get Sam to think about the different effects of velocity and acceleration arrow lengths. Sam's verbalizations, however, were not responses to any of Gary's comments during this time. Instead, he used his turns to report on his actions.

The lack of smooth turn-taking in this episode shows that each participant was talking out loud to himself more than to the other. The divergence between the subjects' work continued and culminated in a breakdown in the interaction. Gary eventually disengaged himself from the task (as can be seen by his verbal unresponsiveness) and began to play with the microphone:

41	S:	Ok so we're gonna try another one
		hhhere
		Oops wrong one (.) this down? (.)
		This one up.
		(4.5)
42	S:	Maybe its slightly
		(9.0)
43	S:	That's cool.

makes acceleration bigger
makes velocity smaller,
acceleration smaller

clicks on vector but no
change.
runs
G moving microphone around
stops, resets

Episode 6–4. Although Gary was disengaged with the task while he played with the microphone, his focus eventually returned to the screen and to Sam's running commentary. In this episode, Gary and Sam became re-engaged in sharing ideas through discourse and action. Through coordinated presentations and acceptances, they began to converge on a shared conception of the properties of the lengths of the vectors.

44	G:	hhh. (.5) Acceleration:: should be increased and (.) Is it going up at a good rate?	
45	S:	We could change it.	*makes velocity longer*
46	G:	Is it going up too slow or too fast?	*G turns to S*
47	S:	Too slow.	
48	G:	Ok so increase the initial speed	*G gestures up*
		[	*runs*
49	S:	I	
		did=	
50	G:	=and:::=	
51	S:	=OK, now maybe this one we might get it.	
		[	
52	G:	uh now you need to increase the acceleration too.	
53	S:	Yeah, ok. (1.0) Uh. (1.5)	*glances at G, stops resets*

In this section, Gary and Sam renewed a higher level of collaborative engagement. It is interesting to examine the structure of this successful interchange. Gary started by asking a question (line 44) that directed focus to a part of the motion using shared terminology. Sam's response (line 45), an answer to Gary's question, indicated a willingness to share the activity. This willingness contrasts sharply with his previous lack of attention to Gary's utterances. In the next two exchanges, Gary orchestrated the construction of a shared concept corresponding to initial speed. First, Gary specified a particular attribute of the motion. He again framed this statement as a question (line 46). Sam again responded appropriately and provided the value of the attribute (line 47). Gary's statement in the next turn (line 48) had two overlapping effects: it named an action to be taken (increase velocity) and named the object of that action "initial speed." In his next turn (line 49), Sam confirmed the interchange both by his verbal response and his subsequent actions with the mouse.

This discourse event has the structure of a Socially-Distributed Production. This particular SDP was presented in installments by G, with acceptances in intervening turns from S. The production could be paraphrased:

IF the Goal is to adjust the initial speed,
and the speed "going up" is too slow,
THEN make the velocity vector bigger.

The content of this SDP is a qualitative proportionality between the initial speed and the length of the velocity vector. This understanding is a breakthrough for the collaborators because it connected the length of the velocity vector to a local part of the motion: Before this SDP, Gary and Sam had used the term *initial speed,* but they consistently used it only as a name for the velocity vector. This use is distinct from the use of "initial speed" to refer to the speed at the beginning of a motion. By connecting the name of the arrow to the speed at which the motion begins ("going up"), Gary and Sam connected the length of the vector to a property of motion. They then adjusted the vector to a close approximation of the correct length (see Fig. 8.3c).

Although Gary was the first to give verbal expression to this idea (line 44), it is not clear who originated the idea. In the time period directly preceding his utterance, Sam had been engaged in extensive experiments with the lengths of the vectors. Gary could have been giving verbal expression to an idea that originated in Sam's experiments with the computer. This interpretation is supported by the fact that Sam was already adjusting the vector appropriately even as Gary was completing the SDP. However, given the nature of the data, we cannot draw definite conclusions about the originator of the idea. Regardless of originator, this episode did mark a convergence in the partners' understanding of the meaning of the length of the velocity vector. This convergence persisted throughout the remainder of the challenge, the session, and into the interview that followed.

Episode 6–5. Following the successful re-engagement in the shared conception of the problem, the partners continued a period of mutually shared activity that extended to the end of the challenge. This episode is different from the previous ones in that the students were more mutually engaged in the task. Further, they worked out simple procedural details rather than new concepts. Specifically, they worked on a shared interpretation for the length of the acceleration vector. This reflects both partners' satisfaction with the length of the velocity vector determined in the previous episode.

54	S:	Ok:: so (.5) this one goes down right there. (2.0)	*clicks on acceleration but makes no change, runs*
55	S:	That might not be enough.	
		[	
56	G:	It might take a little more than that. (.5) yeah.	
57	S:	Ok:: (4.0)	*stop, reset*
58	S:	What about there? (1.0)	*makes acceleration longer*
59	G:	OK	
60	S:	Well that's too much. Definitely. (3.0)	*makes acceleration shorter*
61	G:	hhh. here bring it down there we'll see how it is. (4.0)	
62	S:	Is it going down?	*clicks twice, but no change, clicks again makes acceleration longer*
63	G:	Yeah it is.	
64	S:	Is that good?	
65	G:	Yeah try it.	
		[	
66	S:	I:: I'm pretty sure it's gonna be way too much for (2.0)	*runs*
67	S:	Yeah, ok. (1.0)	*stops motion only part way up*
68	G:	Oh, way too much. (16.0)	*resets, makes acceleration smaller, runs*
69	G:	Oh, so close. (1.0)	*stops*
70	S:	OK (1.0) I have	*resets*
		[	
71	G:	How come it took so fa::r (.) uh so long to get back down (.) maybe (.) acceleration:: (.) (looks at S) :::up speed down. (1.0)	
72	G:	Doesn't do anything does it? (2.5) ·	*clicks but no changes, runs*
73	G:	Turn off the record hhh (5.0)	*stops, resets*
74	S:	Ok. (.) Top one make it go down. (.5) Top one. (2.0)	*clicks but no changes*

75 S: Okay::: Start.   *runs*
        (11.0)   *stop at top of screen on way*
                                                    up, makes velocity, smaller,
                                                    then larger, velocity now
                                                    unchanged from last run
76 G: That's good yeah that's good.
77 S: Good? Just gonna try it. (3.0)   *runs*
78 S: Mmm::   *stops, resets*
79 G: Maybe more acceleration?
80 S: Ok, well let's reset (mess with?)   *makes velocity shorter, runs*
        this first (3.0)
81 S: OK::: ((very low rumble))
        (6.0)

The shared nature of their work during this episode is evidenced in the data in many ways. For example, most of the conversational turns following the statement of a new idea included an acceptance. The students used questions to elicit the consent and involvement of their partner in shared decision making. The acceptances were sometimes explicit (e.g., lines 54, 57, 59) and sometimes implicit but clearly marked by the discourse structure. One such implicit acceptance was Gary's restatement of Sam's previous utterance (line 56). Furthermore, even though Sam was still in control of the mouse, the control of the activity was shared. This is nicely illustrated in the part of the dialog that begins with "Here bring it down there" (line 61). Upon hearing Gary's utterance, Sam began to move the tip of the acceleration vector downwards. While doing so, he involved Gary in the hand-eye feedback loop ("Is it going down?") enabling the pair to co-determine the setting of acceleration. (S: "Is that good?" G: "Yeah try it.")

Another difference between this episode and the preceding ones is that the content of the conversation no longer reflects differences in interpretation—the participants were now working out procedural details. This is not to say that Sam and Gary *completely* share a common understanding of the task. As evidence to the contrary, note that Sam's acceptances lack the kind of paraphrasing and elaboration that are often used to signal that participants fully comprehend each other (see Clark & Schaefer, 1989). It seems that at this point, Sam was just beginning to appreciate Gary's point-of-view. Nonetheless, as the activity unfolded, the understanding became sufficient for the partners to make two additional advances in their physics knowledge.

Episode 6–6.   In this episode, Gary interrupted the current activity to suggest a refinement to the shared understanding of the length of the velocity vector. His refinement connected the length of the velocity vector to the spacing of the dots in the beginning of the motion. This was the first time that the spacing of dots was given a local interpretation. (Roschelle, 1991, provides a detailed discussion of the difficulties that students experience in registering the features of the EM display as a scientist would.)

82	G:	Wait you know (.) you know what we c::can do we can uh stop stop. (1.5)	*G points to screen then reaches over and clicks mouse, stops.*
83	S:	Ok, now I just [	
84	G:	Now=	
85	S:	=wanna see we're off how much [	*S points to screen*
86	G:	we should compare those. (1.0) Now make it go up and compare those and:: (.) um:: hhhh. () see what the set off rate is=	*points to dots in OW* *gestures up* *slides finger to NW, gestures up* *slides finger back to OW, gestures up, brings hand to his lap*
87	S:	=Oh yeah ok. (1.0) So this is greater. ( ) This is way greater. Just look at that. Good= (())	*moves mouse so mouse-cursor is in OW and shakes it.* *((interpretation: comparing dot spacing, wider in OW than NW))*
88	G:	=So we need a higher speed?	
89	S:	Yeah. (1.0)	
90	S:	So maybe like:: (.) tha::t.	*makes velocity longer*
91	S:	And make=	
92	G:	=Maybe::=	
93	S:	=this one (.) tha::t= like::	*makes acceleration longer*
94	G:	=Now drop it ? (1.0)	*voice drops off to inaudible*
95	S:	Is that good? (.) Yeah	
96	G:	try it. [	
97	S:	maybe. (1.0)	*runs*

The discourse and the sequence of actions in this episode provide an interesting example of how partners get new ideas introduced and accepted into an established course of action. Gary marked his new idea by entreating Sam to pay attention ("wait"), and asking, "You know what we can do?" (line 82). This question was a signal to Sam that something new was to follow. However, Sam did not respond to the question. Gary then asked him directly to "stop, stop" and resorted to clicking the mouse (which had up to this point been completely in Sam's physical control). At this point, Sam was still engaged in the previous course of action and began to justify what he was doing (lines 85 & 85). Gary

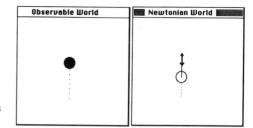

FIG. 8.5. Spacing of dots shows
difference in initial speed.

interrupted (line 86) to offer the new idea. When he said, "We should compare those," he referred to the trace dots that the particles leave behind as they move across the screen. As the spacing of the dots is an indication of speed, comparing dot spacing at the beginning of the motion is one method for determining the correct value of the velocity vector.

The idea of basing decisions on a comparison of dots was introduced by Sam in an earlier challenge, but until before this time the spacing of dots had not been given a local interpretation—Gary and Sam had compared *all the dots* in the Observable World to *all the dots* in the Newtonian World. The structure of Gary's utterances shows that he had considerable difficulty expressing his idea, as he paused, and interrupted himself several times. The gestures that accompanied the idea, on the other had, were quite clear: he pointed to the first few dots in the Observable World and gestured up, then pointed to the first few dots in the Newtonian World and gestured up, and pointed again to the dots in the Observable World (see Fig. 8.5). While his verbal expression "compare those and see what the set of rate is" (line 86) was possibly difficult to interpret, the combination of verbal expression and gesture were enough for Sam to make the correct inference. This is indicated by Sam's subsequent acceptance ("Oh yeah OK") and elaboration of the appropriate feature, the spacing between the initial dots ("this is way greater"). This elaboration leads into a SDP which expressed the qualitative proportionality between the dot spacing and the length of the velocity vector (lines 87 & 88). This SDP can be stated as:

IF   the goal is to adjust the initial speed and,
     the initial dot spacing is greater,
     THEN make the velocity vector longer.

Another important point about the interaction during this episode is that both participants were using the association between the length of an arrow and its effect transparently. For example, when Gary suggested making the initial speed *faster* (line 88), Sam took the action of making the vector *longer* (line 90). As the discourse proceeded, reference to the length of vectors dropped out in favor of references to the effect of changing the length.

The end result of Gary's interruption in this episode was the construction of a important new piece of shared knowledge: the qualitative proportionality between the local dot spacing and the local (instantaneous) speed. This shared interpretation of local dot spacing was confirmed in the interview that followed the task. The process of the construction is also important because it illustrates how participants utilize a combination of linguistic, gestural, and physical resources (the computer screen and the mouse), in order to introduce new ideas into the collaboration.

Episode 6–7. In this episode the partners continued to work together to refine the match between the Newtonian and Observable World motions. In addition, Sam introduced the idea that the vectors could only be moved in discrete amounts. This helped Gary and Sam regulate their search for the correct lengths of the vectors.

98	S:	Ok see how the acc (.) initial (1.5) oooh closer and see how much we're off=	
99	G:	=Our acceleration might be too high. (3.0)	*stops, resets*
100	S:	Ok. This is gonna be a li::bit less.	*clicks but no change*
101	G:	Didn't do anything. (14.0)	*S makes acceleration shorter, runs, stops, resets*
102	S:	Wants to be cool=((?)) =it's higher? (13.0)	*clicks four times, no changes*
104	S:	Oh.	*shakes head*
		(13.0)	*runs, stops, resets*
105	S:	Ok. (5.0)	*moves face right up against screen*
106	G:	hhh. (3.0)	
107	S:	There right about::? (1.0)	*makes acceleration longer*
108	G:	Drop it there.	
109	S:	There?	
110	G:	Yeah.	
111	S:	No, up. I can you can see the degrees if you look closely enough. (.5) One more degree. There. (4.0)	*clicks but no change* *runs*
112	S:	uh? Ok. (2.5)	*stops, resets*
113	G:	Maybe higher initial speed?	
114	S:	I'm gonna change the degree one an (.) makes the initial (.)	

115	G:	Aah::=	*falling intonation*
116	S:	=speed go up by one. (.5)	*clicks but no changes*
		Wait. (6.0)	*runs*

Like episode 6–5, this episode was marked by fluid turn taking and mutual engagement in the task and decision making. They conducted 5 runs, each time making slight changes in the vectors. Notice in particular the smooth use of the QP between length and speed (lines 113–116). Also, at one point (line 105) Sam moved physically closer to the screen to be better able to perceive the precision of the vector movements. While doing so, he made an important contribution to the task—he introduced the idea that the vectors are adjustable only in discrete units ("see the degrees," line 111) and that they could therefore adjust the vectors one unit at a time. This strategy gave the participants better control over trial and error problem solving.

Episode 6–8. This episode shows the negotiation of the challenge ending. This was typical of all challenges during this session; the successful completion of a challenge was jointly determined by the participants. Also during this episode the participants constructed a qualitative proportionality between height of a trajectory and the length of the velocity vector.

117	S:	hh Ok=	*stops*
118	G:	=It looks pretty good just (.) didn't go up high enough. (.5)	
119	S:	Yeah ok so::=	*resets*
120	G:	=maybe increase the speed.	
121	S:	Ok. (5.0)	*makes velocity longer*
122	S:	There::: (6.0)	*falling intonation, runs*
123	S:	Almost::=	*falling intonation*
124	G:	=Close enough.	*OW and NW motion match except NW initial position is one square too high*
125	S:	Wait here I want to do one thing. (2.5)	
126	S:	Reset. (4.0)	*resets, clicks but no change*
127	G:	((inaudible)) (.) There. Saw it move. (7.0)	
128	S:	Yes. We got it perfect.	*looks at G, moves face back from screen*
129	G:	Perfect.	*G puts hand on top of S's hand on mouse* *They go on to the next challenge*

Episode 6–8 began with Gary making an evaluation of the current state of the problem and what remained yet to be solved (line 118). This proposal took the form of a SDP that expressed the proportionality between the height of the ball's path and the initial speed. It is likely that Sam already recognized this relationship, because he had adopted a procedure of stopping the simulation as soon as the particle went too high. Once again, while the originator of the idea is uncertain, Gary was the first to verbalize it.

Toward the end of this episode, Sam noted (line 123) that they "almost" had a solution, and Gary responded (line 124) that he was satisfied with the degree of success that they had attained. In fact, the two motions had exactly identical velocities and accelerations, but the initial position in the Newtonian World was about a centimeter too high (see Fig. 8.3d). Sam announced that he wanted to, "do one more thing" and, receiving no objection from G, he proceeded to make one further adjustment. Although, he moved the particle downwards, he did not move it enough for the simulation to recognize the change. Nonetheless, after this change, both partners agreed that their solution was "perfect."

The challenge closed on this note of mutual satisfaction. The participants' pride in their performance during this challenge was also apparent in the interview that followed the session: Gary started out the interview by saying, "Do you wanna see number six? Probably one of our most famous ones."

CONCLUSION

Our perspective has characterized collaboration as a process of constructing and maintaining a Joint Problem Space. The JPS evolves through the coordination of communication, action, and representation use in the context of solving Envisioning Machine challenges. Our analysis of challenge six illustrated how coordinated production of talk and action by two participants enabled this construction and maintenance to succeed. The students used language and action to overcome impasses in shared understanding and to coordinate their activity for mutually satisfactory results. But as this analysis made clear, the process of collaborative learning is not homogeneous or predictable, and does not necessarily occur simply by putting two students together. Students' engagement with the activity sometimes diverged and later converged. Shared understanding was sometimes unproblematic and but oftentimes troublesome. The introduction of successful ideas was sometimes asymmetric, although it succeeded only through coordinated action. These results point to the conclusion that collaboration does not just happen because individuals are co-present; individuals must make a conscious, continued effort to coordinate their language and activity with respect to shared knowledge.

The inherent fragility of the collaborative learning process has lead us to consider the resources collaborators employ to surmount difficulties that arise in the course of working together. As our analysis has shown, the most important resource for collaboration is talk (see Teasley, 1992). Collaborators use the overall turn-taking structure of talk, as well as specific discourse forms such as narration, questions, social-distributed productions, and repairs in service of their mutual understanding. These discourse forms allowed the students to produce shared knowledge, to recognize divergent understandings, and to rectify problems that impeded joint work. Language, however, does not occur in a vacuum. Dewey (1916) put it succinctly, "Language would not be the efficacious instrument it is, were it not that it takes place upon a background of coarser and more tangible background physical means to accomplish results."

We see the "computer-supported" contribution to collaborative learning as contributing a resource that mediates collaboration. In ordinary circumstances, one cannot imagine two 15-year-olds sitting down for 45 minutes to construct a rich shared understanding of velocity and acceleration. But in the context of the support provided by the Envisioning Machine activity, our students were successful in doing just that. This leads one to ask: how do resources provided by the computer support collaboration?

Our data suggests several possible answers, all which support a mediation perspective.[3] First, we observed the use of the computer as a means for disambiguating language. Gary and Sam do not have a precise, technical vocabulary for talking about motion so they used the objects in their physical situation to support their talk. For example, in the introduction of the idea of comparing dots in episode 6–6, the students used the computer display as a means for establishing shared references. In addition, their maintenance of a shared focus of attention on the computer screen enabled efficient, but ambiguous expressions such as "make it more" to be correctly interpreted. The computer interface also provided an alternate means for producing conversational turns: actions with the mouse could be interpreted as nonlinguistic presentations and acceptances of ideas. Second, we observed the use of the computer activity as means of resolving impasses. When students had differing opinions, as in the beginning of challenge six, they resolved their differences by trying out the ideas and seeing what worked. When students had insufficient ideas to progress, as in episode 6–3, they could resort to experimentation with the computer as a means for generating new ideas. Third, we saw that the computer was a device that invited and constrained students' interpretations. The EM display was carefully designed to suggest appropriate interpretations. An instance of suggestion occurs in the beginning of challenge six, when Sam saw the new motion and leapt to the idea that the arrows should be opposite. But all the interpretations suggested by the EM representation are not necessarily appropriate, nor are the constraints embedded in the computer simulation necessarily strong enough to limit students to a single interpretation.

---

[3]These observations were first reported in Singer, Behrend, and Roschelle (1988). We thank Janice Singer for her contribution to these ideas.

Our analysis of computers as a mediating tool in collaborative learning has direct implications for student model building. Following VanLehn (1990), we find it useful to distinguish two roles for student models in learning environments: (a) student models as a conceptual resource for better understanding how students learn and (b) student models as an engineering technology for building adaptive systems. With respect to the former point, we have argued that communication, activity, and representation are mutually constitutive. Given the broad recognition among historians, philosophers, and sociologists of science that science proceeds as a social and physical activity, future work that takes a unified perspective towards communication, activity, and representation will be especially important to our understanding of how students learn science. Moreover, such unified analyses to contribute to the current interest in building learning environments to support collaborative learning. We have shown that, by drawing on existing theory and methods in Conversational Analysis, Activity Theory, and Cognitive Modeling, researchers can begin constructing analyses of collaborative learning that incorporate notions of social interaction, physical activity, and cognition.

Moreover, engineering approaches that incorporate student models will benefit from careful study of students' interaction. We suspect that the prospects for constructing adaptive student models in computers will be stronger if computer design advances from a fidelity-oriented to a mediation-oriented perspective. We have noted that fidelity in the form of correspondence between the EM display and expert's models does not sufficiently constrain students' interpretation of the display—students' interpretations of the display are diverse and often divergent from those of experts. If it is hard for students to get their own concepts in correspondence with scientific concepts, then we expect it is even harder to get a computer's internal representation in correspondence to students' concepts, at least when the topic is as rich as learning to model motion with Newtonian concepts.

On the other hand, we have noted that Gary and Sam were very successful in constructing and maintaining a shared understanding of EM. This dyad demonstrates that students have powerful resources for constructing shared knowledge, and that these resources integrally involve attunement to the strategies that are used in everyday talk: turn-taking, narratives, repairs, combinations of language and action, etc. Gary and Sam communicated using multiple conversational resources—rhythm, intonation, synchronization, body language, etc.—and not just proposition contents. Moreover, in the context provided by the EM display, Gary and Sam were able to apply their full wealth of communication resources to the problem of constructing a Joint Problem Space. The EM display supported this effort in a mediational role, by providing an enriched background for students' talk and action. Thus computers can enable students to use the powerful resources of everyday conversation to converge on robust shared meanings for technical concepts. Greater awareness of the structure of collaborative learning and the resources for negotiation of meaning should lead designers beyond the fidelity perspective, to the richer mediational perspective for the design of computer tools that enable learning in social activity.

ACKNOWLEDGMENTS

The order of the authors' names is arbitrary. Earlier drafts of this paper circulated under the first author's former name, Stephanie D. Behrend. This work was partially supported by an internship program at The Institute for Research on Learning, Palo Alto, CA, as well as the Andrew W. Mellon Foundation and an OERI grant to the Center for the Study of Learning. Substantial portions of this paper were presented at a 1989 NATO workshop on "Computer Supported Collaborative Learning" and appear as: Roschelle, J. & Behrend, S. D. (in press). The construction of shared knowledge in collaborative problem solving. In C. E. O'Malley (Ed.), *Computer Supported Collaborative Learning,* New York: Springer-Verlag.

REFERENCES

Bobrow, D. G. (Ed.). (1986). *Qualitative reasoning about physical systems.* Cambridge, MA: MIT Press.

Clark, H., & Schaefer, E. (1989). Contributing to discourse. *Cognitive Science, 13,* 259–294.

Dewey, J. (1916). *Democracy and education: An introduction to the philosophy of education.* New York: Macmillian.

diSessa, A. A., Hammer, D. M., Sherin, B., & Kolpakowski, T. (1991). Inventing graphing: Children's meta-representational expertise. *Journal of Mathematical Behavior, 10,* 117–160.

Engström, Y. (1987). *Learning by expanding: An activity-theoretical approach to developmental research.* Helsinki: Orienta-Konsultit.

Ericsson, K. A., & Simon, H. A. (1984). *Protocol analysis: Verbal reports as data.* Cambridge, MA: MIT Press.

Goodwin, C. (1981). *Conversational organization: Interaction between speakers and hearers.* New York: Academic Press.

Knorr-Cetina, K. D. (1981). *The manufacture of knowledge: An essay on the constructivist and contextual nature of science.* Oxford: Pergammon Press.

Latour, B. (1986). Visualization and cognition: Thinking with eyes and hands. *Knowledge and Society: Studies in the Sociology of Culture, 6,* 1–40.

Lerner, G. H. (1987). *Collaborative turn sequences: Sentence construction and social action.* Unpublished doctoral dissertation, University of California, Irvine.

Levinson, S. (1983). *Pragmatics.* Cambridge, England: Cambridge University Press.

Lynch, M. (1985). Discipline and the material form of images: An analysis of scientific visibility. *Social Studies of Science, 15,* 37–66.

Mead, G. H. (1934). *Mind, self, and society.* Chicago: University of Chicago Press.

Meira, L. (1991, April). *On the transparency of concrete materials: The case of learning linear functions.* Paper presented at the annual meeting of the American Educational Research Association, Chicago, IL.

Moschkovich, J. (1991, April). *Structuring peer discussion and computer exploration of linear functions*. Paper presented at the annual meeting of the American Educational Research Association, Chicago, IL.

Piaget, J. (1932). *The moral judgement of the child*. Glencoe, II: The Free Press.

Roschelle, J. (1986). *The Envisioning Machine: Facilitating students' reconceptualization of motion*. Draft manuscript, Xerox Palo Alto Research Center, CA.

Roschelle, J. (1990, March). Designing for conversations. Paper presented at the AAAI Spring Symposium on Knowledge-Based Environments for Learning and Teaching, Stanford, CA.

Roschelle, J. (1991). *Students' construction of qualitative physics knowledge: Learning about velocity and acceleration in a computer microworld*. Unpublished doctoral dissertation, University of California, Berkeley.

Roschelle, J., & Greeno, J. (1987). *Mental models in expert physics problem-solving*. (ONR Report No. GK-2). Berkeley, University of California.

Schegloff, E. A.(1981). Discourse as an interactional achievement: Some uses of "uh huh" and other things that come between sentences. In D. Tannen (Ed.), *Analyzing discourse: Text and talk. Georgetown University Roundtable on Language and Linguistics* (pp. 71–93). Washington, DC: Georgetown University Press.

Schegloff, E. A. (1991). Conversation analysis and socially shared cognition. In L. B. Resnick, J. Levine, & S. D. Teasley (Eds.), *Perspectives on socially shared cognition*. Washington, DC: APA Press.

Schegloff, E. A., Jefferson, G., & Sachs, H. (1977). The preference for self-correction in the organization of repair in conversation. *Language, 53*, 361–382.

Schegloff, E. A., & Sacks, H. (1973). Opening up closings. *Semiotica, 8*, 289–327.

Schoenfeld, A. H., Smith, J. P., & Arcavi, A. (in press). Learning: The microgenetic analysis of one student's evolving understanding of a complex subject matter domain. In R. Glaser (Ed.). *Advances in instructional psychology* (Vol. 4). Hillsdale, NJ: Lawrence Erlbaum Associates.

Suchman, L. A. (1987). *Plans and situated action*. New York: Cambridge University Press.

Singer, J., Behrend, S. D., & Roschelle, J. (1988). Children's collaborative use of a computer microworld. *Proceedings of the Conference on Computer-Supported Collaborative Work* (pp. 271–281). New York: Association for Computing Machinery.

Teasley, S. D. (1992). *Communication and collaboration: The role of talk in children's peer collaborations*. Unpublished doctoral dissertation, University of Pittsburgh, Pittsburgh, PA.

Van Lehn, K. (1990, March). *Do we need better cognitive models in order to teach better?* Presentation at AAAI Spring Symposium on Knowledge-Based Environments for Learning and Teaching, Stanford, CA.

Vygotsky, L. S. (1978). *Mind in society*. Cambridge, MA: Harvard University Press.

Wersch, J. V. (1981). *The concept of activity in Soviet psychology*. Armonk, NY: M. E. Sharpe.

Wilkes-Gibbs, D. (1986). *Collaborative processes of language use in conversations*. Unpublished doctoral dissertation, Stanford University.

APPENDIX

Notation

[Bracket indicates a point at which a current speaker's talk is overlapped by the talk of another, with overlapping talk directly beneath.

:   Colons indicate a lengthened syllable, the number of colons corresponding to the extent of lengthening.

?   Question intonation.

.   Full stop with falling intonation.

=   Equals sign indicates no interval between the end of a prior and the start of a next piece of talk.

.hh   Audible breath. Dot before indicates in breath. No dot indicates outbreath.

(–)   Words enclosed in parenthesis indicate either non-linguistic action, or transcriber's uncertain over verbatim.

((–))   Double parenthesis indicates features of the audio other than verbalization, or note from the transcriber.

(0.0)   Numbers in parenthesis indicate elapsed time in tenths of a second.

(.)   Untimed pause.

OW   Abbreviation for "Observable World."

NW   Abbreviation for "Newtonian World."

III

BRIDGING DIFFERENCES IN OPPOSING CAMPS

9

Computer Environments as Cognitive Tools for Enhancing Learning

Susanne P. Lajoie
McGill University

A current theme in the educational literature is that of "cognitive tools" (Pea, 1985; Perkins, 1985; Salomon, Perkins, & Globerson, 1991). The metaphor implies that there are tools that can assist learners to accomplish cognitive tasks. There are at least 4 types of cognitive tools that can be identified by the functions they serve. These 4 tools can: (a) support cognitive processes, such as, memory and metacognitive processes; (b) share the cognitive load by providing support for lower level cognitive skills so that resources are left over for higher order thinking skills; (c) allow the learners to engage in cognitive activities that would be out of their reach otherwise (Pea, 1985; Olson, 1988); and (d) allow learners to generate and test hypotheses in the context of problem solving. These 4 tools are not mutually exclusive. Cognitive tools that serve these functions have been incorporated into 2 computer systems that are addressed in this chapter. The first is Sherlock I, a computer-based learning environment for avionics troubleshooting (Lajoie & Lesgold, 1989; Lajoie, Lesgold, et al., 1989; Lesgold, Lajoie, Bunzo, & Eggan, 1992). The second is Bio-world (Lajoie, 1990, 1991), a computer-based learning environment that provides high school biology students with practice at diagnosing infections. My chapter describes these systems, the cognitive tools they incorporate, plus empirical evidence that such tools support learning.

COMPUTER TOOLS THAT PROMOTE LEARNING IN SHERLOCK I

Sherlock I is a computer-based environment for avionics troubleshooting. Trainees practice their troubleshooting skills in a realistic simulation of their shop where they are presented with simulations of the test equipment and technical orders.[1] Sherlock differs from the shop in that trainees can test their troubleshooting hypotheses, as to where a possible malfunction is located, in a safe and supported medium. Novices who explore multiple troubleshooting hypotheses in the real world could do damage to themselves or their equipment. However in the simulated shop Sherlock coaches novices when their actions are unsafe. Computer coaching is provided to scaffold learning. Throughout this chapter the term *scaffolding* refers to providing learners with just enough assistance to help them construct their own answer to a problem. "The metaphor of a scaffold captures the idea of an adjustable and temporary support that can be removed when no longer necessary" Brown and Palinscar (1989, p.411). The content of our *scaffolding* was designed by an avionics expert[2] and was presented in the form of textual coaching in the context of a learning impasse. The sufficiency of the scaffold was determined by the student competency and performance models. The computer assessed these models dynamically while the learner was solving a problem so that the appropriate level of assistance could be provided to the individual learner. As trainees demonstrated their competency the amount of scaffolding was decreased.

The Sherlock I treatment consisted of approximately 20 hours of instruction over a 3-week period. The instruction provided trainees with practice on realistic troubleshooting problems. The Sherlock treatment was found to be equivalent to about 4 years of additional on-the-job training (Nichols, Pokorny, Jones, Gott, & Alley, in press). Almost all trainees showed improvement in a variety of troubleshooting performance measures. Trainees were assessed dynamically by the computer while they solved problems, as well as after the training through structured interview posttests (Lesgold, Lajoie, et al., 1988). Several instructional design principles account for Sherlock's success (see Lajoie, Eggan & Lesgold, 1988; Lajoie & Lesgold, 1989; Lesgold, Lajoie, Bunzo & Eggan, 1992). The following discussion shows how the instructional design embodies the cognitive tools themes that are responsible for providing intellectual partnerships with learners.

Support Cognitive Processes

Electronics troubleshooting is a complex and time consuming task. Proficiency requires effective memory and metacognitive processes. Sherlock I supports both memory and metacognitive processes. An electronics troubleshooting problem in

---

[1]Technical orders are the technical documentation manuals used by the Air Force to describe the step by step procedures that should be followed to test an avionics unit. They include schematic diagrams and procedures for setting up the test station. These technical orders do not provide step by step procedures for troubleshooting the test station. Trainees must know how to use the technical orders to be effective troubleshooters.

[2]Gary Eggan

the avionics shop could take hours or days to complete. Because this process is often time-consuming it stands to reason that there are many steps to perform before solving a problem. Consequently, effective memory strategies can reduce the amount of time individuals waste performing steps that they had already performed earlier in the problem-solving process. Learners could support their own memory by making notes of what they had done up to a certain point in the problem space or the computer could keep track of those steps for them. Sherlock I supports the learners' memory processes by keeping track of their problem-solving activities. When a learner asks for help Sherlock I provides a recapitulation of the learner's problem-solving steps up to the point where an impasse occurred. In order to provide this type of recapitulation, the computer must be able to dynamically assess what the student has done prior to the impasse. The computer monitors each learner and in so doing is able to provide a recapitulation of the learner's activities at any point *during* the problem-solving process. This feedback serves to support the learner's metacognitive processes as well as their memory processes. Metacognitive processes are supported because the recapping of learners' problem-solving steps supplies a physical representation of the learners' internal thoughts. And, because such physical representation provides opportunities for the learners to inspect and reflect on their solution strategies, generalized metacognitive awareness is promoted. In sum, Sherlock I serves to reduce the memory load and encourages metacognitive awareness of the problem-solving process.

Sharing the Cognitive Load

There is an assumption that human cognitive capacity is limited and that we can only attend to a certain amount of information at any one time. A cognitive tool might be used to assist our attentional capacity by reducing the burden of attending to every aspect of the task. Shiffren and Schneider (1977) stated that lower level cognitive processes must be automatized before the learner has the resources available for higher order cognitive skills. Learners could be trained to learn this prerequisite knowledge before being given a more complex task. However this automatization process could be circumvented if the computer carried out lower level tasks for the learner, thereby freeing up attentional resources to accomplish other tasks. In this respect, the computer shares the cognitive load.

For a computer program to support "lower level cognitive skills" it is necessary to first identify the cognitive components of the learning task. Before designing Sherlock a cognitive task analysis of avionics troubleshooting was performed to determine exactly what skills and knowledge were involved in this task (Gitomer, 1984; Lesgold, Lajoie, et al., 1986). The cognitive task analysis consisted of several experiments that were designed to identify different levels of troubleshooting competency. Our sample consisted of airmen who were in their first term in this job specialty. The skill range in this sample was more restricted than the usual expert/novice studies and our results confirmed that we were dealing with a more homogeneous sample of high ability individuals. Instead of the usual expert/novice findings where experts are more skilled than novices on both lower level and higher level thinking tasks, our study identified skill differences on the overall problem-solving task itself rather than on discrete component skills (Lesgold & Lajoie, 1991). The key point is that skill differences were found when the cognitive load was high, as was the case when subjects had to monitor their troubleshooting strategies, trace schematic diagrams, and interpret test measurements, all in the context of troubleshooting test equipment. Skill differences were not found when trainees were tested on these skills independent of a troubleshooting problem.

Our studies confirmed the notion that humans have limited cognitive resources in the troubleshooting context. This was demonstrated by the fact that technicians were capable of performing well on tests of separate skills, such as reading schematics, but when that same skill was assessed in the context of the overall troubleshooting activity, it was no longer as effective. This finding can be explained in terms of separate cognitive skills competing for cognitive resources. Given the results of the cognitive task analysis, Sherlock I was designed to carry out some of the lower level troubleshooting processes so that learners would have sufficient attentional resources left over to carry out the higher order troubleshooting skills. One such skill is the ability to trace a signal through a circuit path. This is not a minor task since one signal might be traced through 35 pages of circuit diagrams. Sherlock I located the appropriate schematic diagram, thereby freeing up the learner's time for more complicated skills such as testing the appropriate circuit cards. Physically dismantling equipment is a lower order skill that may take hours to accomplish but little thinking time. Sherlock I can accomplish such physical tasks in seconds. By simulating these lower level operations in a condensed time frame, learners are provided with the opportunity to see the consequences of their plans and actions in a more timely manner, thus providing more immediate feedback on their performance. Put simply, learners do not have to retrieve their hypotheses from long-term memory in order to see whether the results of their actions confirm or disconfirm their hypotheses as to what part of equipment is malfunctioning. Sherlock I provides the learner with cognitive tools that reduce the amount of time devoted to lower level skills so that more resources can be allocated to higher level tasks.

Engaging in "Out of Reach" Cognitive Activities

Many cognitive activities are "out of reach" to learners simply because there are no opportunities for participating in such tasks. Computers can often bring the "real world" to the learner in a concrete and manipulable manner. Sherlock I does this by providing an artificial medium for experimenting with complex test equipment and provides a standard set of problems for technicians to solve. Several types of test equipment are provided, such as a portable digital multimeter and an oscilloscope. Technicians select the equipment they think is appropriate for the type of measurement they want to perform, and then set up the equipment to take that measurement. Once a measurement is taken, the technician must interpret the test data appropriately. Sherlock I coaches technicians in selecting the appropriate test equipment, setting up the meters correctly, and interpreting the test results.

In the avionics shop novice technicians are rarely given the opportunities to troubleshoot the test station since there is the danger that novice actions are unsafe and time consuming. Test station problems are rare and diverse, and not all technicians observe the same problems. This random assortment of diagnosis problems does not provide a shared set of learning experiences for all technicians. Unlike the shop experience, Sherlock I can provide technicians with a shared set of problems that are conducive to the instructional goals of troubleshooting performance, and provide support in an environment that provides a way to practice troubleshooting skills in a safe manner. Technicians are provided with the full problem-solving context that is in their shop environment. Sherlock I simulates the test equipment, tools, and technical documentation that technicians need for troubleshooting test equipment.

Cognitive activities may be "out-of-reach" for reasons that have nothing to do with safety or physical limitations. They may be out of reach because no assistance is available to help learners make the connections between new ideas and what they already know. In the avionics shop, novices can observe experts solving problems but often such observation does not lead to making the necessary connections between what they know and what the experts know. The avionics shop is a modern day apprenticeship setting where novice technicians can observe experts solve complicated troubleshooting problems. However, unlike traditional apprenticeship settings where physical skills can be observed, such as tailoring (Lave, 1977), the processes being modeled for troubleshooting are cognitive and consequently not as overt (Lajoie & Lesgold, 1989; Resnick, 1987). It is difficult to observe cognitive processes unless they are articulated in some manner. Expert troubleshooters may have difficulty articulating their knowledge, which would make it difficult for the novice to model expertise. This type of *cognitive* apprenticeship would not be ideal as an instructional setting since it would be difficult for a novice to make the connections between what he or she knows and what the expert knows (see Collins, Brown & Newman, 1989).

Sherlock I provides a more effective cognitive apprenticeship by providing a mechanism for making the expert's troubleshooting processes observable to the novice and consequently easier to model. Sherlock accomplishes this through coaching the learner in the context of the problem when assistance is required or requested. It is through this coaching that expert strategies are made overt. However, Sherlock is designed to offer the least hint that can enable further problem-solving progress. Much of its coaching is designed to stimulate a trainee's thinking by asking questions rather than generating answers. However, when a trainee can not construct an answer on her own, more elaborate hints are available that support the trainee's problem solving much as a shop supervisor might. The content of these hints is specific to the current work environment and to the state of the trainee's knowledge. Both general "rules of thumb" as well as specific tactics are provided when a trainee is unable to reason them out on his or her own. For instance, if a trainee has difficulty testing a circuit card, Sherlock will lead them to discover how an expert might test that card. Different levels of assistance are calculated and administered by Sherlock I that take the learner's competency and performance models into consideration. Learner's who have demonstrated high performance in the past will not need the same level of assistance as those learners with low performance models. One of the most intriguing roles a computer can play is that of a more capable peer (Vygotsky, 1978) for the learner to model (Salomon, 1988). The learner can model a computer coach just as one could model a human coach. Salomon emphasized the idea that a human learner can share an intellectual partnership with the computer (Salomon, 1990; Salomon, Perkins, & Globerson, 1991). One way the computer can best serve this partnership is to allow the learner to engage in cognitive activities that would be out of reach otherwise. When the learner reaches an impasse the computer can give advice in a way a more capable peer might, thereby stretching the learner to reach higher levels of learning. Sherlock I provides these opportunities.

Supporting Hypothesis Testing

Computers can be used to support hypothesis testing. In order to do so they must provide multiple hypothesis paths and provide support or coaching in the context of such hypotheses. Sherlock I supports hypothesis testing by providing multiple paths for technicians to explore, and by coaching the technicians in the context of their plans or actions. The technicians are not forced to conform to an expert path. Each tutor problem is associated with multiple solution paths that reflect different skill levels. These skill levels are represented as an "effective problem space" whereby a composite of novice and expert solution paths are represented in each of Sherlock's problems (Lesgold, Lajoie, Bunzo, & Eggan, 1992; Lesgold, Lajoie, Logan & Eggan, 1990). Each problem space is used as a template for programming the appropriate levels of feedback for each decision or action nodes that a trainee may traverse in the context of a problem. By incorporating the effective problem space into the programming design it was possible to monitor the learner in the context of the decisions and actions made and calculate the appropriate level of feedback required when an impasse occurred. This programming design made it possible to provide opportunities for learners to participate at a learning level they are comfortable with and still get support that scaffolds their learning and allows them to take on cognitive activities that they would not have the opportunities to engage in under other circumstances.

The technicians can select their own troubleshooting strategy for any particular problem. At the same time, precautions are taken so that technicians do not practice inappropriate strategies. For example, some hypotheses should not be pursued because they violate the assumptions provided in the technical orders. Such hypotheses were programmed as predetermined bad paths. When Sherlock identified a learner's plan as a predetermined bad path it would coach the learner accordingly. In this manner inappropriate strategies are not practiced. Another precaution is that Sherlock I assesses whether the hypotheses that are considered by the technician are confirmed by the technician's actions. If the technician's actions reflect a misinterpretation of the data, Sherlock I will intervene. For instance, if a technician reenters a hypothesis or plan that should have been rejected based on the results of his or her prior actions, Sherlock I will remind the technician about the prior action and ask the technician for a conclusion about the test equipment. Sherlock I will then coach the learner based on the appropriateness of his or her conclusion.

The effective problem space mechanism is flexible enough to provide learners with opportunities to discover effective troubleshooting strategies. However, Sherlock I is more of a *guided* discovery environment in that hypothesis generation is somewhat constrained by which options appear in the menu interface. Trainees interact with the computer by selecting menu options that correspond with their troubleshooting plans or actions. The options that appear in the menu list correspond to the hierarchical nature of the effective problem space. The menus are hierarchical in that the macro plans are presented at the beginning of the troubleshooting scenario so that trainees can inform Sherlock I as to where they want to commence troubleshooting. There is an underlying planning structure in these menus that includes both macro-level plans—such as plan to test the test station, the test package, or the unit under test—and subplans within each of these major plans, such as planning to test the circuit cards located in the unit. The hierarchical planning structure modeled in these computer menus could help constrain the problem space somewhat. Thus, the menu is a cognitive tool for identifying the hierarchical structure of the troubleshooting problem space.

A second way that the effective problem space is used to guide learning is in the way it is used to generate hints. The effective problem space is the underlying mechanism for recording the technician's problem-solving steps, and as such is used to replay such steps when necessary. Earlier, recapitulation hints were described that reduced the memory burden for the learner as well as assisted in the development of metacognitive skills. This same recording mechanism is used to generate a special purpose hint that is attached to a "panic button." The panic button is used as a last resort when the learner does not know what to try next. Sherlock I monitors the technician's solution processes and when the panic button is selected, replays the plans that the technician directly or indirectly completed prior to selecting the panic button. Sherlock I constrains the problem space by summarizing which hypotheses are no longer valid based on the learner's prior actions. This summarization process refocuses the learner on hypotheses that have not yet been considered. Thus, Sherlock I supports hypothesis generation at the same time as it supports development of self-regulatory mechanisms such as self-checking. A hypothesis must be generated as well as tested to determine if it is valid or not valid. Technicians often continue with a hypothesis or reenter a hypothesis later in the problem, indicating that they have not interpreted prior data correctly. The panic button reaffirms what the learner has generated and tested, and serves as a checking mechanism that learners later (hopefully) internalize. It is important to observe the entire problem-solving process to develop a more informative understanding of the learner's mental model. Both the recapitulation and panic button tools encourage learners to reflect on their hypotheses. Both of these computer tools are dynamic and use the learners' prior actions to help learners reflect on their problem-solving processes.

Externalizing the learner's problem-solving process can be used as a way to foster comparison between the learner's hypothesis-testing strategies and more skilled strategies. Sherlock I coaches learners by providing models of expert troubleshooting in the context of the problem. For instance, if the learner asked for assistance when testing a circuit card, Sherlock I might suggest testing pins that an expert would check if he or she were testing that card. The level of hint explicitness will vary according to the learner's competency level. A less skilled learner may need more assistance than a more skilled learner.

In summary, Sherlock I supports hypothesis testing by providing multiple solution paths and coaching in the context of these solution paths. A hierarchical structure of the problem space is modeled through the menu interface and trainees are taught the value of constraining the problem and being systematic about testing each hypothesis.

Evidence of Learning and Restructuring

Given that Sherlock I provides cognitive tools do such tools assist learning? There is evidence that those tutored by Sherlock I outperform a control group on measures of troubleshooting performance, suggesting that Sherlock I improves learning. But what is the nature of this learning? Do technicians simply solve more problems than the control group or is there a dramatic difference in the way technicians solve problems after tutoring? In the following section on evidence of learning, data is provided that supports the quantitative differences between learners. Subsequently, the section on restructuring provides qualitative evidence that mental models change as well.

The Air Force evaluation of Sherlock I found that technicians who spent 20–25 hours working with Sherlock I were as proficient in troubleshooting the test station as technicians who had 4 more years of job experience (Nichols et al., in press). Matched experimental and control groups were studied at two Air Force F-15 bases (Lesgold, Lajoie, et al., 1988). The experimental group spent on average 20 hours working through Sherlock's 34 problems. Tutoring sessions were conducted in 2–3 hour blocks that spanned an average of 12 working days. The control group subjects went about their daily activities in the avionics shop. Structured interviews were administered as pre and posttests of troubleshooting to 32 trainees. These pre and posttests posed problems based on actual failures encountered in the shop, rather than on Sherlock I problems, and Air Force technical orders were used rather than Sherlock's modified technical orders.

The pre and posttests of troubleshooting proficiency targeted the same functional areas as the tutor problems but there were some surface differences. Units, test packages, and test stations were different from our tutor, as were the schematics for test station drawers. Thus, pre and posttests measured *near transfer*, from the simulated tutoring experience, to "on the job" performance. There were no significant differences between the experimental and control groups at pretesting (X^2 (1, N = 63) = 0.00, p = 1.00) but on posttest performance (X^2 (1, N = 62) = 10.29, p < .001) the tutor group solved more problems (Mean = 30) than the control group (Mean = 21) (Lajoie & Lesgold, 1992b).

Given that the tutor group solved more troubleshooting problems than the control group, the question remained as to whether these two groups differed in the quality of their problem-solving solutions. And, if the tutor group was solving problems in a qualitatively different manner than the control group, did all tutored subjects benefit from the Sherlock I instruction in the same way? To answer these questions, a scoring template was developed that could be used to examine qualitative differences in troubleshooting performance on pre and posttest data, as well as tutor data.

Each troubleshooting problem whether it was administered as a verbal interview, as was the case in the pre and posttests, or by Sherlock I, for the tutor group, produced a problem-solving trace of the technician's plans and actions taken in the process of trying to solve the problem. The problem-solving trace (sometimes referred to as a slime trail) was the exact sequence of the plans and actions that a technician took to solve the problem. Figure 9.1 illustrates a problem-solving trace that consisted of 12 steps, 4 of these steps were plans, or hypotheses, and the remainder were actions taken to confirm specific plans. Such actions consisted of measurements, or other actions such as swapping a circuit card with a card that works, or reseating a circuit card to get a better connection.

Once we codified the problem-solving traces, each trace was blindly reviewed by our domain expert, Gary Eggan, and each step was assigned a score. However, these scores were assigned based on where the step occurred in the context of the overall solution strategies. The sequence of steps individuals select in the process of problem solving is an indicator of strategic knowledge (Snow, 1978). Changes in these sequences may be an important indicator of changes in the assembly and control processes used to organize and monitor performance pro-

Sherlock: Problem Solving Trace[1]

Steps	Level of Expertise
1. Re-run test	
2. **PIUUT**- Plan to investigate the unit under test	Completed Plan in 1 step
3. SwUUT- Swap the unit with a known good unit	Expert (1)
4. **PITP**- Plan to investigate the test package	Completed Plan in 1 step
5. SwTP- Swap the test package with a good package	Expert (1)
6. **PITS**- Plan to investigate the test station	Completed Plan in 12 steps
7. **PITestRAG** Plan to test the RAG drawer in station	Completed Plan in 12 steps
8. Test S42- Test Switch 42	
Ohms measurement on S42 pins 0 andC	Expert (1)
9. TestA1A2A2- test the A1A2A2 circuit card	
VDC test pins 41 to ground	Expert (1)
VDC test pins 34 to ground	Expert (1)
VDC test pins 14 to ground	Expert (1)
VDC test pins 17 to ground	Expert (1)
10. TestA1A1A11- test the A1A1A11 circuit card	
VDC test pins 51 to ground	Good (2)
VDC test pins 46 to ground	Expert (1)
VDC test pins 41 to ground	Expert (1)
11. TestA2A1A2- test the A2A1A2 circuit card	
VDC test pins 13 to ground	Expert (1)
OHMS test pins 15 to 13	Bad (4)
VDC test pins 14 to ground	Expert (1)
12. SwA2A1A2- swap the A2A1A2 circuit card	Expert (1)

Stimulus Data Troubleshooting Problem: Correct Solution[1]

FIG. 9.1.   Sherlock: Problem solving trace.

cesses (Snow & Lohman, 1984). Eggan developed a 4-point system for scoring different levels of troubleshooting competence: 1. expert, 2. good, 3. redundant, and 4. inappropriate steps. An expert troubleshooting step reflects efficiency, such as dividing the problem space in half by taking one measurement. Good troubleshooting steps are steps taken to collect meaningful information. A good troubleshooter might take three measurements, whereas an expert might only take one measurement to get the same information. A redundant step refers to a step that collects information that has been previously determined by a prior move. An inappropriate troubleshooting step refers to an incorrect step, such as taking a voltage measurement instead of a resistance check. An example of this scoring template is provided in Fig. 9.1 (numbers to the right of the plans or actions on the trace indicate the level of troubleshooting competency: 1–4). Problem traces were scored using this template and qualitative differences in troubleshooting competency were identified. In an independent study, two other domain experts were asked to score these traces according to their holistic interpretations of competent troubleshooting performance (Gitomer, Lajoie, & Lesgold, 1989). By holistic interpretations we are referring to the raters global rating of the overall troubleshooting performance. These raters were told to think of themselves as "Olympic judges" of excellence. They were asked to rate all the tutees on 3 problems that varied in complexity. There was a high degree of interrater reliability between these 2 judges r = .79, p < .001 (n = 39). What is particularly interesting is that the raters demonstrated a high degree of agreement in their criteria for judging troubleshooting competence.

Pre-Post Test Data.   Using this scoring system, a qualitative analysis of the types of troubleshooting steps trainees made on their pre and posttests revealed that the experimental group was significantly different from the control group on several factors that reflected emerging competence. ANCOVAs were performed that covaried the qualitative pretest variables and examined performance differences between the two groups on posttest criterion variables. The tutor group had a higher proportion of expert-like steps to solution (mean = 19.33) in the posttest than the control group (mean = 9.06) ($F(1,27)$ = 28.85, p < .01), as well as a lower proportion of inappropriate or bad moves (mean = 1.89) ($F(1,27)$ = 7.54, p < .01), than the control group (mean = 4.19) (Lajoie & Lesgold, 1992b).

Tutor Data.   The tutor group demonstrated a change in the quality of their troubleshooting moves from pre to posttest, and thus a closer examination of the nature of knowledge restructuring was made in the context of tutoring. Several analyses were performed on data from three tutor problems that examined changes over time in the types of troubleshooting steps selected (as codified in Fig. 9.1).

A repeated measures analysis of variance focused on the type of steps for three selected problems at varying time intervals early, middle, and late in tutoring. Once again the percentage of expert steps increased over the temporal course of tutoring ($F(2,45)$ = 7.20, p < .002), whereas inappropriate moves tended to decline. In general, the proportion of actions that involved making measurements, as opposed to swapping components, increased over time on tutor ($F(2,45)$ = 3.30, p < .05), as did the percentage of expert steps in the measurement areas of these problems ($F(2,45)$ = 14.56, p < .01) (Lajoie & Lesgold, 1992b).

The tutor group increased the number of expert-like troubleshooting steps as a function of time in the tutor treatment, but how similar was the tutor group's solution paths to an ideal expert solution path?[3] The technician's solution paths were compared to an ideal expert path for the same three problems mentioned earlier (early, mid-way and late in tutoring). A deviation score from the expert path was computed for each subject by using the following formula: the subject's number of solution steps minus the number of overlapping steps with the expert

---

[3] A caveat must be provided at this point. The instructional philosophy guiding the design of Sherlock is that there are multiple "expert" solution paths. However, we were interested in having at least one measure of "closeness of fit" to an expert solution path.

Deviation Scores and Number of Solution Steps as a Function of Tutoring

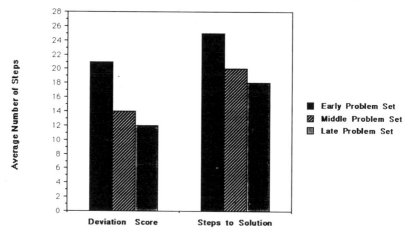

FIG. 9.2.   Deviation from the expert path as a function of tutoring.

path = subject's deviation score. A repeated measures analysis of variance that examined the effects of aptitude (high, low) and time spent in the tutoring environment (early, middle, and late tutor problem) on types of moves (deviation scores and total steps to solution) was performed. There was a significant main effect due to time spent in the tutoring environment ($F(2,42) = 4.19, p < .02$) on types of moves (see Fig. 9.2). The more problems the technician had solved using Sherlock I, the closer the technician's troubleshooting solution processes were to expert troubleshooting processes, and fewer steps were taken to reach a solution (Lajoie & Lesgold, 1989). With practice on Sherlock I, technicians became more expert-like and efficient. Both the high and low ability technicians responded in the same manner, with the low ability group showing slightly more improvement than the high ability group. Technicians demonstrated an emerging expertise in all phases of troubleshooting, including the most difficult aspects of measurement taking.

Case Study Profiles.   Case study profiles of trainees in the tutor group revealed that there are individual differences in the quality of mental models trainees have at the beginning of tutoring (Lajoie & Lesgold, 1992a). Sherlock I could adequately address these differences, demonstrating that trainees made improvements in those areas where they were weakest. Two case studies are presented that follow two learners from pretest to posttest, including performance for three tutor problems encountered early, mid-way, and late in the temporal course of tutoring (see Fig. 9.3). In Figure 9.3, profiles for two technicians, S1 and S8, are presented that consist of 5 snapshots of the types of methods, strategies, and plans these individuals developed from pre to posttest-

	Time 1 (Pretest)	Time 2 (Problem 16)	Time 3 (Problem 9)	Time 4 (Problem 23)	Time 5 (Posttest)
S1	**Methods:** Swap. **Strategies:** Random **Plans.** Incomplete tests and swaps. No solution even after redirect hints.	**Methods:** Incorrect test interpretation--reverts to swapping. **Strategies:** Serial-split between signal and data. **Plans:** Inefficient since incorrect test interpretation, serial strategy, and swaps.	**Methods:** Testing in the measurement area. Mixed testing and swapping in the stimulus data area. Requires more evidence than necessary. **Strategies:** Mainly serial: Some sign of space-splitting in measurement area. **Plans:** Complete in measurement area. Inefficient in signal data area, swaps when not confident or does not understand test results.	**Methods:** Knows where to test and interprets tests correctly. Requires more evidence than necessary. If swap instead of test will return and test the card. **Strategies:** Serial/Space split. **Plans:** Complete plans.	**Methods:** Tester. Requires minimal evidence to confirm conclusions. **Strategies:** Space-split in signal data area. **Plans:** Complete and efficient in both data and signal areas
S8	**Methods:** Swap. Performs a few simple ohmic measurements. **Strategies:** Random **Plans.** Inefficient. Does not know how to test data voltages.	**Methods:** Swap. Beginning to perform some good tests but still weak in data areas. **Strategies:** Possible space-split between measurement signal area. **Plans:** Inefficient due to not knowing how to test data voltages. Displays knowledge of where to test but does not always know how.	**Methods:** Tester. Still has some trouble tracing. Has some inappropriate test types in data areas. **Strategies:** Space-split the measurement and stimulus data areas. **Plans:** Complete.	**Methods:** Tester (expert-like). **Strategies:** Space-split the measurement and stimulus data areas. **Plans:** Complete and expert-like.	**Methods:** Tester. Knows where to test and the type to perform. **Strategies:** Space-split. **Plans:** Complete and expert-like.

FIG. 9.3. Case studies.

ing. Time 1 and time 5 refer to pre and posttests, whereas times 2–4 are data from early, middle, and late in tutoring. This chart demonstrates how Sherlock I affects different individuals in different ways.

Initially, S1 and S8 are quite different in the types of methods, strategies, and plans they use to solve problems. S1 uses a "swaptronics" methods for solving problems. Swaptronics refers to swapping a part that is suspected to be bad with an identical part that is known to be operating correctly. If the test equipment still malfunctions then that part is no longer suspected as malfunctioning. S1 uses a random strategy, which means that he swaps every part he can find, in an attempt to solve the problem. S1 does not have a complete plan and does not solve the pretest problem. S8's initial profile is somewhat better than S1's. S8 uses a combination method of swaptronics and measurement taking. Measurement taking is a more effective method for identifying the exact location of a problem. S8 demonstrated that she knew where to take the proper tests, but did not know which types of tests to perform (e.g., ohms, AC, DC). S8 was somewhat random in the types of tests taken and did not have compete plans, nor did she solve the problem.

By time 3, both subjects have demonstrated transitions from their original methods, strategies and plans. By time 3, S1 was using methods that included both measurement taking and swaptronics. Apparently S1 knew where to take measurements and knew which type of measurement to take but had difficulty interpreting the results, and reverted to swapping parts. However, S1 was no longer using a random strategy, he was using a serial strategy that implied he knew how to trace the signals to the proper circuit cards. S1 also used a space splitting strategy at one point in the solution process, which implied he knew how to divide the problem space in half to isolate the problem. However, since S1 was not as skilled at measurement taking he could not interpret the test results properly and reverted to swaptronics as a strategy. S1's plans are complete for some functional areas and not for other areas. By time 3, S8 was using a strictly measurement taking strategy but was still having difficulty in understanding which test types should be used at various locations. S8 demonstrated efficient use of a space splitting strategy for the part of the problem space where she selects the correct measurement types. S8 has complete plans.

By the time these subjects are posttested they have both tuned their knowledge and are using expert strategies. Both subjects are using measurement methods as opposed to swaptronics, and both subjects are using space splitting strategies. Furthermore, both subjects have developed complete and efficient plans. There are still some individual differences at posttesting. S8 has maintained that initial edge over S1. S1 can be categorized as using a good to expert testing strategy, whereas S8 is clearly using an expert testing strategy. S1 requires more evidence than S8 before making a decision.

These case studies illustrate that individuals can vary greatly in their methods, strategies, and plans, and that Sherlock I provides opportunities to tune the knowledge that needs to be tuned. S1 demonstrated knowledge restructuring in that he no longer used swaptronics as a method of troubleshooting. He became an efficient measurement taker. Furthermore, his strategies were no longer random trial and error, but guided by mental models of the devices in question. His strategies reflected efficiency in space splitting the problem space in an expert-like manner. Furthermore he systematically executed his plans in an efficient manner. The quality of S1's performance changed dramatically from time of pretesting to posttesting. Initially, S8 had some measurement methods but needed assistance in identifying which measurement types should be used in the context of problem solving. Over the course of tutoring S8 learned which measurement types to use at which point in the problem space and became an expert at testing the test equipment. Thus individuals with varying needs are accommodated, and transitions in different aspects of their mental models of troubleshooting performance occur.

COMPUTER TOOLS THAT PROMOTE LEARNING IN BIO-WORLD

Bio-world is presented as an example of how the cognitive tools themes can be extended into classroom instruction. Bio-world deals with a different cognitive domain than Sherlock but much of the tutoring design is built from the Sherlock experience. Bio-world is a computer coached learning environment that teaches high school students to diagnose infections. It is not intended to make physicians out of these students. Rather it is intended to provide opportunities for students to scientifically reason about the data that they have available to them in a simulated hospital environment. Bio-world is meant to foster contextualized reasoning (Resnick, 1987). In the classroom, students are taught declarative knowledge about bacterial and viral infections, how infections are transmitted, how different infections affect different parts of the body, and how our bodies have different defense systems to guard against certain diseases. Students are also introduced to concepts involving diagnostic tests that can identify the presence or absence of infection. Bio-world provides a mechanisms for putting this declarative knowledge into practice by providing opportunities for students to use such knowledge in the context of realistic problem-solving tasks, such as diagnosing a disease.

Bio-world presents students with cases to solve and with the appropriate tools to solve the cases. Students are coached in the context of diagnosing diseases. Diagnosing an infection is a dynamic problem-solving task, much like electronics troubleshooting, in that proficiency is reflected by data that are collected, the tests that are ordered, and the correct interpretation of test results. Students are presented with a patient case or a sct of cases that simply state the patients' symptoms. Students have several options available to them at any point in time: (a) they can make a diagnosis as to what they think a patient might have; (b) they can visit patients and review the information in the patient charts; (c) they can order diagnostic tests on patients to confirm their hypothesis as to what the patient may have; (d) they can visit an on-line library to read about things they do not understand, for instance, disease types, types of diagnostic tests that can be performed, and medical vocabulary, for example, gastroenteritis; (e) they can select information from patient charts that they would like to enter into their diagnostic notebook so they can review relevant information at a later time, and (f) they can consult other physicians for assistance. How do these options support the cognitive tools themes described earlier in this chapter? In the following section, Bio-World is described in terms of the four cognitive tools themes that pertain to how computers can be used to support cognitive processes, share the cognitive load, assist the learner to engage in out-of-reach activities, and provide support for hypothesis testing.

Support Cognitive Processes

One way that Bio-world supports cognitive processes is by providing students with access to declarative and conceptual knowledge through an on-line Medical Library (see Fig. 9.4). Students can select information from the library in the context of a problem. Multiple representations are available in the library, includ-

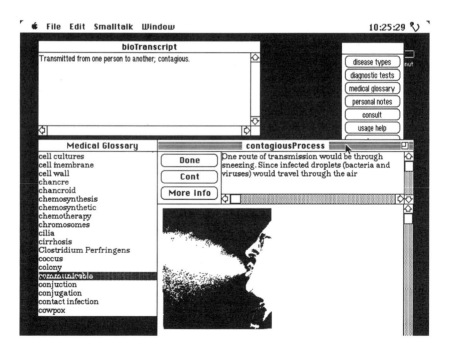

FIG. 9.4.   Bio-world medical library options.

ing textual definitions of concepts, as well as static and animated visual diagrams of complicated disease processes. Students can select the amount of information they would like to review. Figure 9.4 provides a snapshot of library usage. The table of contents is available in the upper right hand corner. Students have selected to review the glossary and have chosen the word "communicable" from the glossary menu. What follows is an explanation in the top left hand window as well as a visual diagram and further information in the middle screen. Both textual and visual information is presented in an effort to scaffold the students' declarative knowledge. At other locations in the library animated diagrams are presented rather than static diagrams. For instance, some students may have difficulty with understanding the concept of antibodies and how they protect the body against infection. Antibodies can cover the recognition proteins of the virus so the virus will not be able to infect the cell. The process by which antibodies are formed, and how they mask the receptors on host cells, may be better described visually than textually. The library provides multiple representations of knowledge to encourage learning in different contexts.

Bio-world also supports memory and metacognition. Collecting the appropriate data to confirm or disconfirm a hypothesis can be a lengthy process. The computer can review the learners' prior plans and actions and in doing so both reduce the memory burden of trying to remember all of their prior activities as well as increase the learners' metacognitive awareness of what their problem-solving processes look like. The main support mechanism for these processes is through the diagnostic notebook (see Fig. 9.5).

As mentioned earlier, the diagnostic notebook serves to support memory and metacognition. It supports memory processes by displaying the learners' previous actions, such as library searches and diagnoses that were made for a patient. Notice that the learner in Fig. 9.5 had searched the medical library for 5 terms, starting with AIDS, and entered a diagnosis of salmonellosis for Patient 1. Students enter their diagnoses for specific patients by using the hypotheses tree that appears in the bottom of Fig. 9.5. Branches in this tree represent the types of diagnoses that can be made. There are several body systems that students can explore, such as, reproduction, digestion, etc., and each body system has several types of diseases associated with it. Students must select which patients they are diagnosing under "patient names" and then select a diagnosis from the hypothesis tree and enter their diagnosis. In this example Patient 1 is highlighted and the diagnosis "salmonellosis" appears in the diagnosis column. The diagnostic notebook supports metacognition by organizing the learners' actions in a way that makes it possible for them to reflect on their overall problem-solving process rather than on one single action. This utility helps the learner check their prior plans and actions in terms of how systematic they have been in reviewing the evidence available to them. The diagnostic notebook automatically records some of the students' activities, such as what words were looked up in the library, and what diagnoses were entered for a particular patient. However, some of the data

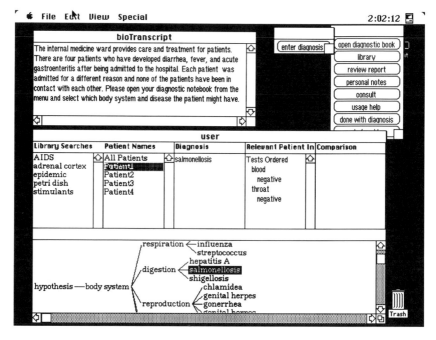

FIG. 9.5. Diagnostic notebook.

that is entered into the notebook is entered in by the students. Students generally review patient charts before making a diagnosis, and may decide to order some diagnostic tests for a patient. After reviewing the test results the learner may decide to enter the test results into the diagnostic notebook for future reference. For example, in Fig. 9.5, the students entered the test results for Patient 1. Both the blood test and throat cultures were negative. The diagnostic notebook can recap what the student has done, what domain knowledge has been requested, what patients have been seen, and what test results the learners thought were important to remember. One can see how this reduces the memory burden for students and also serves as a regulatory function in that it posts the information they collected in the process of making a diagnosis. By externalizing the diagnosis process students can reflect on their own strategies, and in doing so perhaps learn to be more systematic in their scientific reasoning skills.

Sharing the Cognitive Load

Bio-world provides tools that promote the higher-order thinking skills that are required for scientific reasoning about infections. One way to help support such higher-order thinking skills is to provide support for lower-level cognitive skills. Forming a "diagnosis" is a higher-order skill. Bio-World supports the learner in arriving at a diagnosis by performing some of the lower-order cognitive skills associated with making a correct diagnosis, such as performing diagnostic tests. Ordering the appropriate diagnostic tests for a patient is essential to making an accurate diagnosis. However performing these tests is a time consuming activity. Bio-World reduces this time to seconds, so that little time elapses between the formation of a diagnosis and collecting data that would support such a diagnosis. Rather than spend time performing tests, the students review the test data much as a physician would. Thus the diagnostic tests results are presented to the student upon request. However, the student must still interpret the test results in the context of a diagnosis. There are several types of diagnostic tests that students can examine. Descriptions of these tests are provided in the medical library and students can order tests by using the diagnostic test tree that is available in each patient chart (seen in the bottom of Fig. 9.6). This tree structure is similar to the diagnosis tree structure. Students use the tree to request which diagnostic tests they would like to order for their patient. They select the test by selecting branches and end nodes in the tree structure. There are two main branches of diagnostic tests, those that involve testing the patient (internal tests) and those that involve testing materials external to the patient, such as food cultures. Figure 9.6 presents a patient chart along with a subset of the diagnostic tests that were ordered and the test results. For this patient four microbiology tests were ordered,

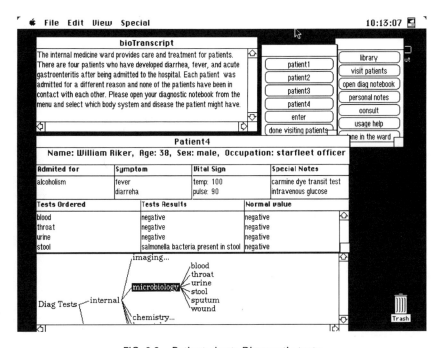

FIG. 9.6. Patient chart: Diagnostic tests.

blood, throat, urine, and stool. As noted before, learners can enter test results into their diagnostic notebook as a way to recall what data they have collected.

Engaging in "Out of Reach" Cognitive Activities

Bio-world provides learners with opportunities to perform cognitive activities that are out of their reach otherwise. Providing a modified hospital simulation presents students with safe opportunities to experiment with diagnostic test procedures without harmful consequences to patients. Students can explore theories about infections and be provided with coaching when unsafe or inaccurate procedures are attempted. Bio-world provides a context where declarative knowledge acquired in the classroom can be used in a situation that is more applicable to what may happen in a student's daily life. All students go to the doctor for one type of infection or another. Bio-world demystifies the use of biological concepts in the real world.

Supporting Hypothesis Testing

Bio-world is a safe medium in which to test hypotheses regarding infections and how they are transmitted. When students need assistance they can consult physi-

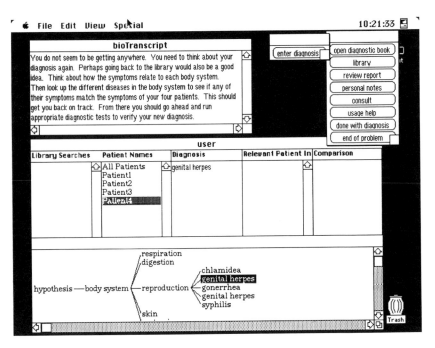

FIG. 9.7. Bio-world coaching.

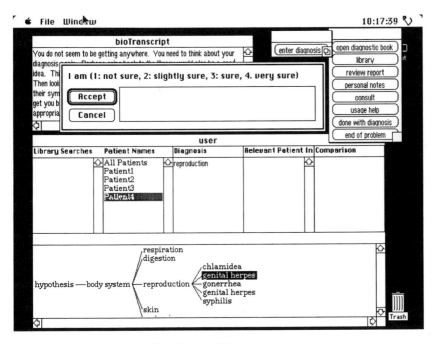

FIG. 9.8.   Confidence indices.

cians (by selecting the "consult" menu option) and assistance is provided in the context of the diagnostic problem. There are multiple diagnostic paths that can be explored and assistance is available when learners reach an impasse. An illustration of coaching is provided in Fig. 9.7. A student has entered the "reproduction system" as a diagnosis. The coach refocuses the learner's attention to the patients' symptoms and points out that such symptoms are not related to the reproduction system. In designing Bio-world two types of domain experts were consulted, physicians, and biology teachers. These experts helped identify the relevant and appropriate types of activities that should be conducted in the context of diagnosing infections. These problems are ill-defined in that there is not one best way to diagnose an infection and there are no absolutes where one action will confirm or disconfirm a diagnosis. Tutoring in this context can serve to assist students in developing efficient scientific reasoning strategies, where they are tutored to be systematic in verifying the hypotheses or diagnoses that they generate.

Bio-world records both the students' diagnosis as well as how confident students are about their diagnosis. Every time students enter a diagnosis they are asked how confident they are that their diagnosis is correct. For instance, are they not sure, slightly sure, sure, or very sure that their diagnosis is correct (see Fig. 9.8). In recording their confidence in this manner it is possible to look for the changes in confidence based on the information collected in the context of the problem.

Evidence of Learning and Restructuring

Bio-world was piloted on 84 grade 9 high school students. Students worked in groups of 3 and spent approximately 25 minutes working on a diagnosis problem. Each group consisted of one high, one medium and one low ability level student, as measured by grade. Teacher recommendations were used to ensure cohort compatibility. Figure 9.9 represents a sample problem-solving record trace stored by the computer. These record traces were scored by the researcher. These records provide information on

1. the learned states at particular points in the problem;

2. an exploration index regarding how much, as well as, what kind of information students look up in the library (this was done by recording all of the students' library entries and counting them);

3. which patients were examined and what diagnostic tests were ordered and entered into their notebooks;

4. how systematic they were in collecting data to confirm a hypotheses, that is, if they conducted a critical test for patient one did they perform the same test for the other patients?;

5. did they form their hypotheses based on data from one patient or on all patients?; and

6. how much feedback did students receive.

Preliminary analyses indicate that there is a significant difference in confidence ratings between the first diagnosis entered and the last diagnosis entered (Friedman ANOVA, test statistic $= 7.0$, $p = .01$). Confidence increases as students collect more information in the tutor. Furthermore there is a significant relationship between how confident one is and how accurate one is as judged by a set of postproblem questions that were presented on the computer (Friedman ANOVA, test statistic $= 20.57$, $p = .01$). Confidence in the group's ability to diagnosis an infection increased as a function of acquiring knowledge in the context of the problem-solving environment. Furthermore the increase in confidence was merited in that the higher-confidence groups were more accurate on postproblem questions than lower confidence groups. Confidence is an affective variable that has a relationship with the cognitive processes involved in scientific reasoning about infections and making diagnoses about such infections. These data suggest that integrating the assessment of affective variables (or motivational) with the assessment of cognitive skills may shed light on theories of learning.

Bioworld Problem Solving Recored Trace GRPID = 113

1. diagnosis = digestion   10:36:40
    confidence rating = slightly sure
    Local perform level: perhaps
    Average perm level: perhaps (2)
    Leaving diagnosis at diag book   10:37:37

2. Entering ward   10:37:43
    Starting visiting patients   10:38:04
    Viewing Patient2 chart   10:38:09
    Order test blood   10:41:38
    Order test urine   10:41:51
    Ask physician for help   10:42:34
    Ask physician for help   10:42:35

3. Viewing Patient3 chart   10:42:58
    Symptoms of Patient3 entered   10:44:22
    Leaving hospital at site   10:44:22
    Local perform level: unlearned average perform level: 1.5   10:44:56

4. Open diagnostic notebook   10:44:56
    Closing diagnostic notebook   10:47:50
    Leaving diagnosis   10:47:51

5. Entering ward   10:47:56
    Viewing Patient4 chart   10:48:06

6. Open library at site   10:49:03
    Looked up 'Hemoglobin'   10:50:56
    Looked up 'Stool'   10:52:14

7. Viewing Patient4 chart   10:53:16
    Order test stool   10:53:40
    Tests result intered into diagnostic notebook   10:54:17

8. Viewing Patient3 chart   10:54:24
    Order test stool   10:54:37
    Test result entered   10:54:52

9. Viewing Patient2 chart   10:54:56
    Order test stool   10:56:01
    Test result entered   10:56:26

10. Viewing Patient1 chart   10:56:30
    Order test stool   10:56:44
    Tests result entered   10:57:02
    Order test food samples   10:59:20
    Order test water samples   10:59:27
    Order test medical treatment samples   10:59:29
    Order test utensil samples   10:59:32
    Tests result entered   11:00:26

11. Viewing Patient4 chart   11:00:37
    Order test medical treatment samples   11:00:50
    Leaving hospital   11:01:23
    Local perform level: strong
    Average perform level: 2.75   11:01:23

12. Open diagnosis   11:01:28
    Diagnosis = salmonellosis   11:02:24
    Confidence rating = very sure
    Local perform level: unlearned
    Average perform level: 1.9   11:02:25
    Attemp exit   11:02:35

13. Question 1: Bacteria   11:03:12
    Question 2: Cultures   11:03:36
    Question 3: Digestion   11:03:46
    Question 4: Diarrhea   11:03:54
    Question 5: Medical Treatment   11:04:04

5/5 correct total time on task: 28 minutes

FIG. 9.9.   Bio-world: Problem solving trace.

CONCLUSION

Two computer systems have been reviewed in an attempt to demonstrate how computers can provide cognitive tools for learning and restructuring knowledge. Sherlock I and Bio-world are computer supported practice environments that support cognitive processes in several ways. First, each system supports memory processes by monitoring the learners' problem-solving steps and replaying these steps for learners in the context of a problem. These replays serve to reduce the memory burden for the learner, and they also serve a metacognitive function, in that they model and support self-monitoring of problem-solving performance for the purpose of helping learners internalize expert-level metacognitive processes.

Both systems provide an intellectual partnership with the learner by sharing the cognitive load. For example, both systems support the learner's attentional resources by performing lower level skills in an attempt to free up the learners' attention for higher order processes, such as, interpretation of complex data. Physical actions that are time consuming are handled by the computer system so that learners do not have as great a gap between the time they generate hypotheses and the time they observe the consequences of their actions. If one considers Anderson's (1983) stages of learning, where declarative knowledge precedes procedural knowledge, both Sherlock I and Bio-world scaffold declarative knowledge while allowing learners to practice procedural skills that they might not have access to otherwise. For example in Sherlock I, declarative knowledge such as knowledge that improper signal inputs to a circuit card will result in improper outputs from a circuit card is a declarative fact that is coached in the context of the technician's troubleshooting of avionics test equipment. In Bio-world, students may not know that salmonellosis can be caused by contaminated food sources. Bio-world directs students to library information that contains such facts, providing them with clues to determine an accurate diagnosis for their patient. Given that learners are coached in such declarative content they can resume the procedural knowledge task at hand.

Each system provides unique methods for letting learners engage in cognitive activities that would otherwise be out of their reach. A safe medium is provided for testing hypotheses and support is available when an impasse is encountered. The various levels of coaching provided by these computer systems demonstrates that individual differences can be accommodated adaptively. Furthermore, the computer as "coach" can be modeled by students in much the same way as a human coach might be modeled. In the electronics troubleshooting examples, issues of safety and efficiency in an actual shop, often preclude novices from participating in activities that are beyond their reach. In the classroom, there are not always opportunities to contextualize declarative knowledge concepts. In both the real world and in school learning situations, computer practice environments are effective ways for applying "schooled" knowledge in the context in which it may be used in the future.

Finally, each system provides an effective way to guide and support hypothesis generation. Both systems are effective in providing flexible solution paths, and support for each path. The criticism that computer tutors constrain the learner can not be made against these two systems. Sherlock I and Bio-world truly fit into what Derry and Lajoie (Chapter 1) termed the Middle-Roadie instructional camp. The instructional philosophy is middle-of-the-road with the traditional model builders on one side of the road and the iconclasts-model breakers on the other side. By model builders, we referred to researchers who share the belief that student performance can be modeled, traced, and corrected in the context of problem solving, using computers. The model breakers choose not to model student performance either because they do not believe that it is feasible to do so or because better or more cost-effective alternatives exist. Sherlock I and Bio-world capitalize on both approaches by having some modeling but not constraining the problem-solving process by forcing students down one correct path.

In addition to demonstrating the extent to which computers can be used as cognitive tools, Sherlock I was described as a test case of how such tools improve learning, in terms of performance outcomes, knowledge restructuring, and mental model building. The tutor group out-performed the control group, in terms of the number of troubleshooting problems solved, and in the quality of the processes used to solve such problems. An extensive qualitative analysis of the tutor group demonstrated that both the quantity and quality of troubleshooting steps became more expert-like as a function of experience with Sherlock I. Case studies revealed that individual differences in troubleshooting methods, strategies, and plans were accommodated by Sherlock I, providing adaptive instruction based on individual needs. Bio-world, although still in the pilot phase, adds a new dimension to computer assessment in a problem-solving domain. In addition to recording learning, Bio-world records students' confidence in their problem solving capabilities. Learning and confidence, as measured by Bio-world, go hand-in-hand.

There is sufficient evidence to support the notion that computers can be used as cognitive tools for learning, restructuring of knowledge, mental model building and promoting confidence in problem solving. Cognitive task analyses can facilitate the development of the appropriate cognitive tools for computer based learning environments in that empirical data can demonstrate what cognitive components could be addressed for a specific task. Identifying the cognitive components of a task helps both in instructional design and assessment to the learning. Instruction and assessment can be integrated. Computer learning environments can provide a mechanism for dynamic assessment that facilitates adaptive instruction. Learners have the opportunity to change their answers in the context of problem solving and get answers to their questions when they need assistance. The future is bright for bringing instruction and assessment closer together such that learners do not have delays between generating an answer and discovering if their processes are effective. Immediate feedback is not a novel idea, however, feedback that evaluates the learners prior problem-solving performance and provides adaptive feedback in a dynamic manner is a task that computers can do efficiently if provided with the appropriate student model. We also see a move toward the integration of assessing cognition and motivation in the context of problem solving activities. Again, this is not a new idea but one that psychologists return to time and time again (Lepper, 1989; Lepper et al., this volume). Perhaps student models that incorporate such indices in their assessment of learning transitions will provide us with insights into how cognition and motivation interact with each other (Snow, 1989). By building effective student modeling capabilities that fall in the middle-road camp it is possible to use computer learning environments as test beds for building better instruction and better forms of assessment such that appropriate levels of feedback are given to learners in the context of problem solving.

ACKNOWLEDGMENTS

The Sherlock project was funded through subcontracts with HumRPO and Universal Energy Systems, who were prime contractors with the Air Force Human Resources Laboratory. Sherlock was a massive undertaking led by Alan Lesgold and carried through by many key players including, Marilyn Bunzo, Gary Eggan, Jaya Bajpayee, Lloyd Bond, James Glymour, Linda Greenberg, Denise Lensky, Debra Logan, Maria Magone, Tom McGinnis, Valerie Shalin, Cassandra Stanley, Arlene Weiner, Richard Wolf, and Laurie Yengo. Equally important were Sherrie Gott and the many people that worked with her at the Air Force Human Resources Laboratory, Dennis Collins and other Air Force subject matter experts who helped us when we needed it most, and the officers and personnel of the 1st and 33rd Tactical Fighter Wings, at Langley and Eglin Air Force Bases, especially those in the Component Repair Squadrons who made room in their worlds for Sherlock and his many retainers.

The Bio-World project was funded by the Wisconsin Alumni Research Grants Office. Once again there are many people to thank including Vicki Jacobs, who managed the experiment running and worked on many aspects of the Bio-World design; Liang Yin-Yu, who was the lead programmer; Nancy Hollar, who worked on the student modeling aspect of the design, Keith Tookey who developed an animation program to accompany Bio-world, Glenn Peterson, who worked on much of the curriculum development. This project could not have been done without the assistance of Marilyn Hanson and Sue Johnson, both gifted biology teachers, and Richard Day, a physician interested in improving instruction.

REFERENCES

Anderson, J. R. (1983). *The architecture of cognition.* Cambridge, MA: Harvard University Press.

Brown, A. L., & Palinscar, A. S. (1989). Guided, cooperative learning and individual knowledge acquisition. In L. B. Resnick (Ed.), *Knowing, learning, and instruction: Essays in honor of Robert Glaser* (pp. 393–452). Hillsdale, NJ: Lawrence Erlbaum Associates.

Collins, A., Brown, J. S., & Newman, S. E. (1989). Cognitive apprenticeship: Teaching the craft of reading, writing, and mathematics. In L. B. Resnick (Ed.), *Knowing, learning, and instruction; Essays in honor of Robert Glaser* (pp. 453–494). Hillsdale, NJ: Lawrence Erlbaum Associates.

Gitomer, D. H. (1984). *A cognitive analysis of a complex troubleshooting task.* Unpublished doctoral dissertation. University of Pittsburgh.

Gitomer, D. H., Lajoie, S. P., & Lesgold, A. M. (1989, March). *Performance assessment in an intelligent tutoring environment.* Paper presented at the American Educational Research Association, San Francisco.

Lajoie, S. P. (1990, March). *Computer environments as cognitive tools for enhancing mental models.* Presented at the annual meeting of the American Educational Research Association, Boston.

Lajoie, S. P. (1991, April). *Dynamic forms of assessment using computer coached practice environments.* Presented at the National Council on Measurement and Evaluation, Chicago.

Lajoie, S. P., Eggan, G. M., & Lesgold, A. M. (1988, August). *Instructional strategies for a coached practice environment.* The Tenth Annual Conference of the Cognitive Science Society, Hillsdale, NJ: Erlbaum, 332–339.

Lajoie, S. P., & Lesgold, A. (1989). Apprenticeship training in the workplace: A computer coached practice environment as a new form of apprenticeship. *Machine-Mediated Learning, 3*(1), 7–28.

Lajoie, S. P., & Lesgold, A. (1992a). Dynamic assessment of proficiency for solving procedural knowledge tasks. *Educational Psychologist, 27*(3), 365–384.

Lajoie, S. P., & Lesgold, A. (1992b). Apprenticeship training in the workplace: A computer-coached practice environment as a new form of apprenticeship. In M. Farr & J. Psotka (Eds.), *Intelligent instruction by computer: Theory and practice* (pp. 15–36). New York: Taylor & Francis.

Lajoie, S. P., Lesgold, A. M., Eggan, G., Bunzo, M., McGinnis, T., Greenberg, L., Weiner, M., & Weiner, A. (1989). *A procedural guide for documenting the avionics troubleshooting tutor development process* (Tech. Rep.). Pittsburgh: Learning Research and Development Center, University of Pittsburgh.

Lave, J. (1977). Tailor-made experiments and evaluating the intellectual consequences of apprenticeship training. *Quarterly Newsletter of the Institute for Comparative Human Development, 1,* 1–3.

Lepper, M. (1988). Motivational considerations in the study of instruction. *Cognition and Instruction, 5*(4), 289–309.

Lesgold, A., & Lajoie, S. P. (1991). Complex problem solving in electronics. In R. J. Sternberg, & P. Frensch (Eds.), *Complex Problem Solving: Principles and Mechanisms,* (pp. 287–316). Hillsdale, NJ: Lawrence Erlbaum Associations.

Lesgold, A., Lajoie, S., Bajpayee, J., Bunzo, M., Eastman, R., Eggan, G., Greenberg, L., Logan, D., McGinnis, T., Weiner, A., & Wolf, R. (1988). *A Computer coached practice environment for the manual test station shop: Sherlock's influence on trainee job performance* (Contract No. F33615-84-C-0058). Human Resources Research Organization, Alexandria, VA.

Lesgold, A., Lajoie, S., Bunzo, M., & Eggan, G. (1992). A coached practice environment for an electronics troubleshooting job. In J. Larkin, R. Chabay, & C. Sheftic (Eds.), *Computer assisted instruction and intelligent tutoring systems: Shared goals and complementary approaches* (pp. 201–238). Hillsdale, NJ: Lawrence Erlbaum Associates.

Lesgold, A., Lajoie, S. P., Eastman, R., Eggan, G., Gitomer, D., Glaser, R., Greenberg, L.,

Logan, D., Magone, M., Weiner, A., Wolf, R., & Yengo, L. (1986). *Cognitive task analysis to enhance technical skills training and assessment* (Contract No.F41689-83-C-0029) University of Pittsburgh: Learning Research and Development Center.

Lesgold, A., Lajoie, S. P., Logan, D., & Eggan, G. M. (1990). Cognitive task analysis approaches to testing. In N. Frederiksen, R. Glaser, A. Lesgold, & M. Shafto (Eds.), *Diagnostic monitoring of skill and knowledge acquisition* (pp. 325–350). Hillsdale, NJ: Lawrence Erlbaum Associates.

Nichols, P., Pokorny, R., Jones, G., Gott, S. P., & Alley, W. E. (in press). *Evaluation of an avionics troubleshooting tutoring system* (Special Report). Brooks AFB, TX: Air Force Human Resources Laboratory.

Olson, D. R. (1988). *Mind and the technology of communication.* Paper presented at the Australian Educational Conference.

Pea, R. D. (1985). Beyond amplification: Using the computer to reorganize mental functioning. *Educational Psychologist, 20,* 167–182.

Perkins, D. N. (1985). The fingertip effect: How information processing technology shapes thinking. *Educational Researcher, 14,* 11–17.

Resnick, L. B. (1987). Learning in school and out. *Educational Researcher, 16,* 13–20.

Salomon, G. (1988, March). *AI in reverse: Computer tools that become cognitive.* Invited address at the American Educational Research Association. New Orleans.

Salomon, G. (1990). Cognitive effects with and of technology. *Communication Research, 17,* 26–44.

Salomon, G., Perkins, D. N., & Globerson, T. (1991). Partners in cognition: Extending human intelligence with intelligent technologies. *Educational Researcher, 20,* 10–16.

Shiffren, R. M., & Schneider, W. (1977). Controlled and automatic human information processing: II. perceptual learning, automatic attending, and a general theory. *Psychological Review, 84,* 127–190.

Snow, R. E. (1978). Theory and method for research on aptitude processes. *Intelligence, 2,* 225–278.

Snow, R. E. (1989). Toward assessment of cognitive and conative structures in learning. *Educational Researcher, 18*(9), 8–14.

Snow, R. E., & Lohman, D. F. (1984). Toward a theory of cognitive aptitude for learning from instruction. *Journal of Educational Psychology, 76,* 347–376.

Vygotsky, L. S. (1978). *Mind in society: The development of higher psychological processes.* Cambridge MA: Harvard University Press.

10

The Role of the Tutor in Computer-Based Collaborative Learning Situations

Sandra Katz
Alan Lesgold
University of Pittsburgh

Despite the fact that no one knows exactly how or why collaborative learning works, many learning situations that center around peer group activities have shown impressive results.[1] Well-known success stories about uses of collaborative learning methods to promote cognitive and metacognitive skills in various academic subjects include Lampert's (1986) *sense-making* approach to teaching multidigit multiplication; Palincsar and Brown's (1984) *reciprocal teaching* method to impart reading comprehension strategies; O'Donnell et al.'s (1988, 1990) *scripted cooperation,* a variation of reciprocal teaching, also designed to improve reading comprehension and to help students learn technical procedures; Schoenfeld's (1983, 1985) use of group problem solving, with the teacher playing the role of "consultant," to teach heuristics and "control strategies" for solving mathematics problems; and Scardamalia et al.'s (1989) techniques of *procedural facilitation* via prompts or "cues" to develop students' control over the writing process.[2] In each case, students assume some of the responsibility for their own and other students' learning, by working together on tasks that give them practice in using the concepts, learning strategies, and problem-solving procedures they will—it is hoped—eventually internalize.

Although not all peer learning situations are successful (Johnson & Johnson, 1985; Slavin, 1985, 1990), the overall success of collaborative learning is one

---

[1]Throughout this article, we use the term 'collaboration' as defined by Roschelle and Behrend (in press): *the mutual engagement of participants in a coordinated effort to solve [a] problem together.* Collaboration is different from cooperation, which involves a division of labor in achieving a task. Collaboration happens synchronously; cooperation is either synchronous or asynchronous.

[2]See (Collins, Brown, & Newman, 1989) for a summary of some of these approaches.

factor that has encouraged educators and designers of computerized learning systems to consider interesting ways of having students use these systems in groups (e.g., Brown, 1985). In fact, some tutoring systems have been designed with peer collaboration in mind. For example, Logo (Nastasi, Clements, & Battista, 1990; Papert, 1980) has been used extensively by teams of students in solving programming problems. There is also a practical reason for the growing interest in collaborative use of tutoring systems. Limited resources in schools often makes sharing necessary.

The few studies of the effectiveness of collaborative learning in computer-based learning environments have been encouraging (e.g., Justen, Adams, & Waldrop, 1988; Justen, Waldrop, & Adams, 1990). Roschelle and Behrend (in press) speculate on the reasons why computerized learning systems are well-suited for peer collaboration, emphasizing the opportunity that these systems afford students for communicating about things that they lack a technical vocabulary to express, and for trying out ideas and seeing what works.

Encouraging as these observations and empirical findings are, designers of computer-based collaborative learning situations, as well as the educators who use them, would do well to work in tandom with researchers who study learning in general, and collaborative learning in particular—allowing the results of their research to inform the development and use of social learning methods in computerized learning environments.[3] For example, over the past decade, research on group interaction has uncovered some of the variables that effect learning outcomes (e.g., Webb, 1985). These interaction variables could serve as criteria for automatically pairing students for collaborative activities. In addition, abundant evidence has been gathered showing that students learn by articulating their knowledge, particularly during self-explanation (Chi et al., 1989; Chi & Van Lehn, 1991). These findings suggest that computer-based collaborative learning activities should involve students in explaining their knowledge to their peers; e.g., by critiquing peer solution traces. (Shortly, we elaborate on each of these implications of contemporary research for the design of computer-based collaborative activities.) We believe that, in return, computerized learning systems can help to further theory-building about how, when, and why collaborative learning works, by making it more possible to conduct controlled studies than can often be done in classroom settings.

What are the issues that such research, and an evolving theory of collaborative learning, should help system designers and educators to address? We propose that there are three main dimensions to a design framework for computer-based collaborative learning situations: (1) the role of collaborative learning within the curriculum, (2) the instructional methods and activities used to carry out this role, and (3) the computerized tutor's function during these activities. Of course,

---

[3]Several researchers have argued the same, with respect to classroom-based collaborative learning (Azmitia & Perlmutter, 1989; Brown & Palincsar, 1989; Kellet, 1990).

with a few obvious modifications, the same framework applies to non-computer mediated collaborative learning. Following, we give a sketch of the issues that need to be considered under each of these aspects of instructional design:

1. *Role of collaborative learning within the curriculum.* Which instructional goals should be achieved through group methods, which by having students work individually on the tutoring system?

2. *Methods.* What teaching methods, and corresponding activities, should be used to achieve these instructional goals? How should these activities be sequenced to optimize learning?

3. *Role of the tutor.* What should the computerized tutor do while students work on problems together? For example, should the tutor volunteer advice, or only give advice on demand? In some computerized learning environments, the tutor acts as a coach during problem solving. What additional roles could the computer coach perform? What is the computerized tutor's role in relation to that of the classroom teacher?

It is not at all surprising that similar issues have been considered and discussed by designers of successful classroom-based collaborative learning programs, such as those cited in the opening paragraph. For example, Brown and Palincsar (1989) give detailed descriptions of the procedures and activities involved in carrying out the *reciprocal teaching* method, as well as an explicit account of the role of the teacher during these activities (see also, Palincsar & Brown, 1984). Consistent with the principles of traditional apprenticeship learning upon which *reciprocal teaching* is based, the teacher's role is to *model* the reading comprehension strategies, *support* students in learning these strategies, and *fade* support until students can carry out the strategies on their own.

Although this chapter does not speculate on why reciprocal teaching and many other classroom-based collaborative learning methods have been successful—despite the lack of a complete, empirically validated theory of collaborative learning—we suggest that one simple explanation could be that these programs are models of coherent, carefully planned and executed instructional design. Another is that they are grounded in psychological theories of learning, that have been supported by empirical research.[4] Unfortunately, the same cannot be said about many, if not most, classroom curricula. We believe that the same

---

[4]One can posit a related explanation, essentially a Hawthorne effect. Students in these programs might be highly motivated to learn in part because of the special attention they are given, and this increased willingness to learn leads to increased learning. However, 'special treatment' alone does not always lead to success. As Winter (1990) has argued, the Hawthorne effect may be more complex than has hitherto been considered. He cites evidence showing that other social, psychological, and organizational factors might play a role in determining the effectiveness of social learning—particularly, peer tutoring.

care should be taken in designing computer-based collaborative learning situations.

In this chapter, we show how contemporary views of learning, and the research in support of these views, have shaped our thinking about how collaborative activities can be successfully integrated within computer-based learning environments. We focus on the role of the tutor in a particular type of tutoring system—namely, systems that are based on principles of traditional apprenticeships. Although apprenticeships have typically been used for training in trades, motor skills (e.g., playing tennis), and physical skills (e.g., weaving), recently apprenticeship-style tutoring systems have been built and used to teach cognitive skills such as fault diagnosis in complex electronic systems, as described in Lajoie and Lesgold (1989). In computer-based apprenticeship learning environments, students work on problems with the help of the system's tutor, or coach. Like the master in traditional apprenticeships, the cognitive coach can model correct problem-solving actions and procedures, and support the student in performing complex tasks. Coached learning environments vary according to when support is given—i.e., either the system intervenes when it recognizes that the student needs help (e.g., Anderson & Reiser, 1985; Reiser, Kimberg, Lovett, & Ranney, 1992), or remains a silent observer until the student asks for help (e.g., Lesgold, Lajoie, Bunzo, & Eggan, 1992). In either case, support fades as the student comes to master the task.

More recently, some system designers have incorporated another crucial aspect of apprenticeship learning within their tutors: the opportunity to review one's performance with an expert, or "master" (Lesgold, Lajoie, Bunzo, & Eggan, 1992; Schauble et al., this volume; Reusser, this volume). Psychological experimentation (Owen & Sweller, 1985; Sweller, 1988; Sweller & Cooper, 1985) and theoretical models of case-based learning (e.g., Mitchell, Keller, & Kedar-Cabelli, 1986) indicate why a review phase is important for acquiring cognitive skills. Students often suffer from "cognitive overload" during problem-solving sessions. This can happen whether they work alone or in groups,[5] in the classroom or in computer-based learning environments. Thus, it is best to parcel out some of the instruction to a postproblem reflective or 'review' phase. During what Collins and Brown (1988) have labeled an "abstracted replay" of a student's solution, important features of the student's performance can be highlighted; insignificant details can be ignored. One system that incorporates this idea, Sherlock II (Lesgold, in press; Lesgold, Eggan, Katz, & Rao, 1992), is discussed in more detail in this chapter.

We believe that, in addition to supporting students during problem-solving tasks, the computerized coach can help students to make sense out of an expert's solution, and to explain why something a student did in a replayed solution was

---

[5]Hythecker et al. (1984) discovered that students working together become confused when a computerized tutor monitors their problem-solving activities.

inappropriate, or suboptimal. In the section entitled, Defining the Tutor's Role, we cite research that supports this view of the tutor as coach during review—in particular, the abundant evidence suggesting that student-generated explanations, and other forms of knowledge articulation, greatly facilitate learning.

Collaborative learning situations provide a natural setting for explanation, during both problem solving and review. As Collins and Brown (1988) have pointed out, during collaborative sessions, students can take turns performing the dual roles of producer (problem-solver) and critic (reviewer). These writers, and others, have suggested activities that engage students in reviewing their own and other students' work (e.g., Brown, 1985; Scardamalia et al., 1989). We take their suggestions a step further, by describing ways in which the tutor can support students in carrying out review activities, such as formulating comments that explain why a particular action was inappropriate, and/or recommending an alternative action. We suspect that this newer role for the tutor is as important as its role in supporting students during problem-solving tasks, for—as Collins et al. (1989, p. 480) have observed—review of one's own work, and that of others, appears to be an effective learning strategy.

Following a discussion of what research and classroom practice suggest about the role of the tutor in collaborative learning situations, we discuss the work we have begun on incorporating peer learning activities in Sherlock II. We describe both problem-solving and review activities. We focus on the latter—particularly, peer critiquing of student solution traces—since less attention has been paid in the literature to reflective activities than to problem-solving activities. This applies to discussions of both individual and group learning methods.

We focused our thoughts, and the discussion presented here, on the tutor's role for several reasons. First, as we mentioned earlier, several educators who have succeeded in using collaborative learning methods in the classroom have explicitly defined their role as teacher, suggesting that careful specification of the computerized tutor's role will help to ensure the success of computer-based collaborative learning situations. In addition, we believe that the computer can play a more active and important role during these situations than has yet been acknowledged, and we wish to demonstrate how this can be done. Several educators (e.g., Collins & Brown, 1988; Scardamalia et al., 1989) who have suggested innovative group activities for computerized learning environments have pointed out that technological limitations prevent these systems from doing the "individual shaping" (Collins & Brown, 1988, p. 16) that goes on in successful classroom-based collaborative learning situations. In response to these limitations, they have suggested supplementing computer-based collaborative problem solving with guidance from the classroom teacher. Although we agree that there is a ceiling on what can be achieved using tutoring systems, given the limitations of current technology, and do not deny the value of a skilled teacher's support, we believe that the computerized tutor could do more "individual shaping" than has yet been acknowledged—especially while students critique a problem-solving performance. We back this claim when we describe our plans to incorporate collaborative activities in Sherlock II.

Finally, there are also practical reasons for considering new roles that the computerized tutor can play. As the student-teacher ratio in many schools and training centers increases, and more attention is turned towards developing autonomous computerized learning systems—that is, systems that do not supplement classroom instruction—it becomes increasingly important to come up with a realistic "wish list" of what these systems should be able to do. We believe that recent views of learning, and research in support of these views, can sharpen our vision of what the tutor's role can and should be, as we will now demonstrate.

DEFINING THE TUTOR'S ROLE

We believe that the teacher, whether human or machine, has three main roles to play while students are engaged in collaborative learning activities:

1. *Provide advice on demand.* The teacher can support students in carrying out assigned tasks, much like a mentor or coach.

2. *Provide quality control over peer critiquing and other collaborative activities.* The teacher can ensure that students learn what they are expected to learn, and do not mislead each other.

3. *Manage collaborative activities.* The teacher can handle things like selecting the next task for students to work on together, and identifying students who would work well together.

In this section, we anchor our discussion of these teaching functions in a description of the collaborative activities that students can engage in while using a tutoring system. Our thoughts on this were, in turn, influenced by contemporary theories of learning—particularly theories about the facilitating role of language use in learning. The basic idea suggested by these theories is that collaborative learning requires a particular type of language use, explanatory conversation, and this type of language use promotes learning by helping students to construct elaborated cognitive structures. We thus begin our discussion with an overview of the theories that have shaped our thinking, and of the empirical evidence that supports them.

Contemporary Views of Learning

Traditionally, social interaction has taken the back seat in accounts of how learning occurs; it has been acknowledged primarily for motivational effects. Notable exceptions are the developmental theories of Piaget and Vygotsky. Both theorists acknowledged the role that social interaction plays in learning, although they differed in their emphasis on the role of social interaction in cognitive development, the theorized causal mechanisms relating social interaction to cognitive development, and other matters pertaining to the features of interactions that promote learning (Tudge & Rogoff, 1989). To summarize, Piaget placed far less emphasis on the social influence on development than on the child's interaction with the physical environment. However, followers of Piaget such as Bearison (1982) and Doise and Mugny (1984) have extended the ideas that Piaget presented in his early work (e.g., 1932) about how social interaction facilitates learning. Their research indicates that *cognitive conflicts* embedded in a social situation are more conducive to cognitive growth than is an individual's experience with conflicting viewpoints within his or her own mind. The proposed reason for this is that social situations not only bring out differences in viewpoint, as Piaget observed, but force conflict resolution; otherwise, if children fail to coordinate their ideas and actions, the interaction will simply collapse (Nastasi et al., 1990). Consistent with the ideas that Piaget expounded about how conflict resolution, or self-regulation, restores cognitive equilibrium, this "neo-Piagetian" (Kellet, 1990) view places more emphasis than Piaget did on the role of social interaction in restoring cognitive equilibrium. To both Piaget and his followers, the process of restoring equilibrium is the motivating force behind all cognitive growth.

Unlike Piaget's theory, Vygotsky's theory was "built on the premise that individual development cannot be understood without reference to the social milieu, both institutional and interpersonal, in which the child is embedded" (Tudge & Rogoff, 1989, p. 19). In addition, Vygotsky believed that social interaction plays a more sustained role in the learning process than did Piaget. To Piaget, the main contribution of social interaction to cognitive growth is the inducement of cognitive conflict. After that, the child could resolve the conflict either with his peers or independently. However, Vygotsky emphasized that learning occurs by achieving shared meaning, and the social character of arriving at shared meaning somehow becomes an inherent part of the meaning itself:

. . . arriving at a shared meaning of a gesture or word occurs in the process of actual interaction, but the social nature of the gesture or word always remains. In this way, culturally available meanings are made known to children, are taken over by them, in time to be passed on to others. (Tudge & Rogoff, 1989, p. 21)

As peers work together, they support each other in carrying out tasks that may be beyond the ability of one or both participants to accomplish alone (Vygotsky, 1978). Such social regulation is achieved primarily through dialogues in which participants adjust their language to fit within their partner's range of understanding, or "zone of proximal development." Thus, in Vygotsky's theory, language is the mediating link, or "psychological tool" (Tudge & Rogoff, 1989, p. 21) for inducing learning in social situations.

More recently, researchers such as Lave (1988), Roschelle and Behrend (in press), Greeno (1986), and others have also argued that what we know—the meanings of the concepts we have—is tied to specific social problem-solving situations in which we have operated.[6] When we encounter multiple situations that have some amount of commonality, we can learn by solving the issue of how to view those situations so that their commonalities stand out. Such viewpoints turn out to be powerful perspectives that facilitate generalization to new situations we may encounter in the future. However, two people who have experienced related problem-solving situations but in different cultural settings must overcome certain communication difficulties before they can collaborate in problem solving. Specifically, they must negotiate the meaning of the terms they use, that is, find a common language for describing and discussing the problem at hand.

The process of meaning negotiation is a powerful one for learning, because it broadens understanding and moves students closer toward full membership within a group of people who work on related problem-solving tasks and share a common language for meaning negotiation—a "community of practice," so to speak. As Sipusic, Roschelle, and Pea (1991) have pointed out, language use and learning interact in a sort of spiraling fashion within communities of practice. Talking with more skilled members of the community enables the student to acquire some of their expertise and a language for operating within the domain. Having better "language use tools" and problem-solving expertise, in turn, solidifies the student's membership within the community of practice, providing opportunities for further conversational exchanges about more advanced topics, with the same or yet more skilled members of the community.

The thread tying all of the theories we have looked at together is the idea that the conversational exchanges that occur during social interactions facilitate learning. This view has received abundant empirical support, primarily from psychological studies that show that language use is a powerful mechanism for meaning construction, for both individuals and groups of learners. Successful and unsuccessful learners differ in their tendency and ability to use language as a sensemaking tool. For example, Shuell (1988) found that these two classes of learners differ in the nature and amount of elaborations (e.g., self-explanations, questions, summaries) they produce: "Successful students are more likely than less successful students to (a) engage spontaneously in elaboration activities . . . (b) make precise elaborations—i.e., elaborations that help reduce the arbitrariness or relationships in material . . . ; and (c) recognize that precisely elaborated material is easier to remember" (p. 279).

---

[6]This statement is not intended to suggest that these researchers would admit to being adherents to Vygotskian theory. We simply wish to point out the similarity in Vygotsky's and these researchers' emphasis on the importance of the situational context in which learning occurs for the nature of what gets learned.

Explanation is one form of elaboration for which these differences stand out dramatically. For the individual learner, better self-explanations mean better performance on problem-solving tasks. Chi and her colleagues (Chi et al., 1989; Chi & Van Lehn, 1991) have shown that successful student problem solvers (in physics) generate more self-explanations that are more accurate, contain more pieces of information from distinct knowledge categories (e.g., systems, technical procedures, and concepts), and contain more justifications of actions in terms of problem-solving conditions than do less successful students. For groups of students, perhaps the most significant finding in the battery of studies on group interaction that Webb (1982, 1983, 1985) and others (e.g., King, 1989) have conducted is that students learn both from giving explanations or helpful responses to questions—with "helpful response" definable as "typically consist-[ing] of a step-by-step solution to the problem or a detailed account of how to correct an error" (Webb, 1983, p. 36)–and from receiving explanations as opposed to uninformative or "terminal" responses (e.g., "That's wrong.").

With few exceptions (e.g., Malouf, Wizer, Pilato, & Grogan, 1988; Webb, 1984), these findings hold true for computer-based group interactions (King, 1989; Webb, Enders, & Lewis, 1986). They are further validated by Peterson and Swing's (1985) research, which revealed a strong correlation between students' conceptions about what constitutes an effective explanation, the explanations students actually produce in groups, and individual achievement. The most interesting question Peterson and Swing raise about this finding is, *in which direction does the correlation operate*? In other words, do students who have a good mental model of explanations produce better explanations, or do students derive such a model by receiving good explanations from their peers?

Peterson and Swing's query represents the puzzlement that many researchers have expressed over the exact mechanisms by which explanation and other forms of knowledge articulation induce learning (e.g., Brown & Palincsar, 1989; Kellet, 1990; Tudge & Rogoff, 1989). Assuming that the research reviewed in the preceding paragraphs is valid, and effective language use does in fact promote the development of new knowledge structures and modify existing structures, we would still like to know how this restructuring takes place. Several researchers have speculated on this issue (e.g., Chi & Van Lehn, 1991), and Van Lehn is developing a system called Cascade to test Chi's and his model of the self-explanation effect (Van Lehn, 1991). We expect that controlled studies of computer-based learning situations will help to further our understanding of the mechanisms tying language use with learning.

Given the strong evidence in support of such a link that we have reviewed here, it seems to follow that one of our main jobs as designers and builders of computerized learning systems is to more fully exploit the mediating effect of language use on learning.[7] Of course, just having students work together on these

---

[7]Reusser, this volume, argues a similar point.

systems is a big step in this direction. However, peer collaboration requires us to think more explicitly in terms of developing environments that contain tools that allow students to try out different and often conflicting ideas, in order to resolve conflicts and to visually reify their plans and explanations about procedures and concepts, thereby making them public for discussion. We also need to design activities that students can engage in within these environments—particularly activities that require students to articulate their knowledge, hypotheses, and plans. Over the past few years, several system developers have been considering these issues, and an interesting repertoire of computer-based collaborative activities is evolving (Brown, 1985; Collins & Brown, 1988; Reusser, this volume; Scardamalia et al., 1989). We, too, have been exploring these ideas with respect to our system, Sherlock II (Lesgold, in press; Lesgold, Eggan, Katz, & Rao, 1992), and apprenticeship-style learning systems in general.

There are a few reasons why we believe that tutoring systems that are based on principles of apprenticeship learning are a good place to begin a close consideration of collaborative use of computerized learning environments. First, apprenticeship and peer collaboration are kindred learning methods. Peer-supported learning can be viewed as a variant of traditional apprenticeship learning, in which a "master" coaches a student in acquiring expertise. When students work together, they take over some of the master's role.[8] Computerized learning environments make it possible to create an optimal hybrid of collaborative and apprenticeship learning methods. The master in an apprenticeship setting can be there, incarnated as the computerized "expert" or "coach," in case both students need help, or seek confirmation for their hypotheses and troubleshooting plans. Of course, a human teacher could also supervise peer learning sessions, but one teacher can not work with more than one group at the same time, and the teacher's constant presence might stifle students' feeling of control over, and responsibility for, each others' learning. Furthermore, students are often better able to gauge their explanations to the level of understanding of their peers, since they may have experienced the same difficulties recently. With collaborative, coached learning systems, we end up with the best of both worlds. The opportunity for learning afforded by meaning negotiation among peers is enhanced by the availability of expert knowledge and advice.

Collaborative Activities for Computerized Learning Environments

We believe that three types of activities are ideally suited for collaborative use of apprenticeship-style learning systems. Students can:

---

[8]The degree to which this happens is one dimension along which peer learning situations vary. On one end of the spectrum, an accomplished student tutors a less skilled student, in a well-defined tutor/tutee role relationship. On the other end of the spectrum, naive learners work together, coaching each other whenever one student possesses knowledge the other(s) lack.

1. *work together on problems*
2. *pose problems to each other,* and
3. *critique each others' solutions.*

We have been developing schemes for incorporating these forms of collaborative learning in our electronic fault diagnosis training system, Sherlock II (Lesgold, in press; Lesgold et al., in press). In this section, we discuss each type of activity, illustrating our ideas in relation to Sherlock II, following a brief description of this system. More detailed discussion of the Sherlock tutors can be found in (Lajoie & Lesgold, 1989; Lesgold, in press; Lesgold, Eggan, Katz, & Rao, 1992; Lesgold, Lajoie, Bunzo, & Eggan, 1992).

Sherlock II is a coached practice environment developed to train avionics technicians to troubleshoot a complex electronic testing device—in particular, a test station that checks out aircraft modules. When the test station itself fails, locating a faulty component within it requires the technician to explore a much larger problem space than does troubleshooting a faulty module; the test station contains more than $40ft^3$ of circuitry. However, not all of this circuitry is needed to carry out each checkout procedure. So, the essential task confronting the technician is to construct a mental representation of the active circuitry—what we refer to as the *active circuit path*—and to troubleshoot this path until the fault is found. Sherlock's job is to scaffold the process of learning to construct these abstract representations and to develop effective troubleshooting strategies.

Sherlock II is a realistic computer simulation of the actual job environment. Trainees acquire and practice skills in a context similar to the real context in which they will be used. (The system is written in Smalltalk/V286, an object-oriented programming language, and runs on 386 workstations equipped with Sony videodisc hardware.) Sherlock presents the student with a series of exercises of increasing complexity. There are two main episodes in each Sherlock II exercise: *problem solving and review*. During problem solving, the student runs a series of checkout procedures to test an aircraft module suspected of malfunction, called the "Unit Under Test" (UUT). Using interactive video, the student can adjust knobs and dials on the simulated test station, take measurements, and view readings. If the student gets an unexpected reading on one of the measurement devices (i.e., digital multimeter, or oscilloscope), the student should first see if the UUT is the culprit by replacing it (or part of it) with a shop standard. If after doing this an unexpected reading still appears, the student should troubleshoot the test station. The student can test components by attaching probes to pins on a video display of an extender board, replace a suspect component with a shop standard and rerun the failed checkout test, etc. These options are available through the Troubleshooting Menu, which provides the student with choices such as Focus on component, Test component, Replace component, Get advice, etc.

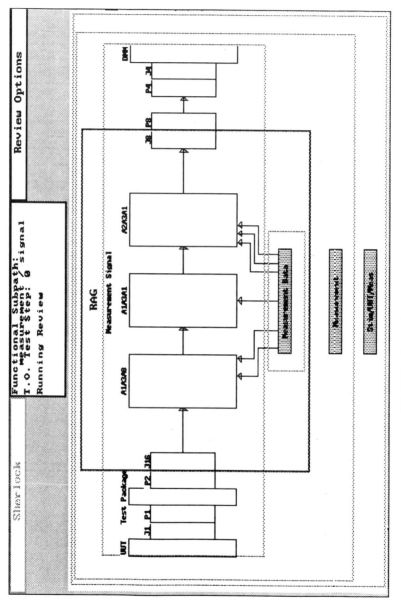

FIG. 10.1. Example of circuit path display.

Perhaps most importantly, the student can ask for help at any point while troubleshooting. Sherlock provides help at both the circuit path and individual component levels of analysis. Within each level, Sherlock offers functional/conceptual ("how it works") hints, and strategic/procedural ("how to test") hints. For example, if a student asks for strategic help at the circuit level, the student will first be told which troubleshooting goals have been accomplished, in terms of the significant functional areas of the device, such as, *You have verified the stimulus side of the test station.* Similarly, if a student asks for help with testing a component, the student will first be told which component-testing goals have been achieved, such as, *You have verified that the inputs to the A1A2A3 card are ok.*

Coaching becomes increasingly directive if the student asks for repeated help, and it is guided by the system's model of the student. (See Lesgold, Eggan, Katz, & Rao, 1992, for a description of the student modeling component in Sherlock II.) If the model suggests that the student should be able to make the next measurement with only a little help, Sherlock will give minimal support, thereby encouraging the student to interpret the hint himself, and to try to come up with the next measurement to make on his own before requesting help again. However, if the student model suggests that the student will have difficulty (e.g., the student has had trouble testing a particular type of component before), Sherlock will give several levels of help right away. More directive hints recommend a goal to achieve next, and—at the furthest extreme—information about how to achieve the next goal (e.g., by specifying a particular test on a particular component). At certain stages of circuit-level hinting, the student is shown a diagram of the active circuit path, as shown in Fig. 10.1, color-coded to indicate which circuit testing goals have been achieved or remain to be achieved. With this coaching scheme, success in solving the problem is assured, and the student is largely responsible for his own learning.

While the student is troubleshooting, Sherlock creates a record of the goals the student has achieved, and how the student achieved them, at both levels of analysis (circuit and component). This goal/test record contains a trace of the student's solution, and is the crucial input to the second "episode" of a Sherlock II exercise, review, or what we call "reflective follow-up." (The main menu for reflective follow-up is shown in Figure 10.2.) In this phase, a trainee can replay his problem solution step by step. At each step, Sherlock provides an evaluation

```
┌────────────────────────────────────────────┐
│              Review Options                  │
├──────────────────────────────────────────────┤
│ Show Sherlock's comments on my solution      │
│            Replay my solution                │
│         Replay Sherlock's solution           │
│    Compare my solution with Sherlock's       │
│           Summarize progress                 │
│          How T.O. Step #6 works              │
│           Select next problem                │
│               Exit review                    │
└──────────────────────────────────────────────┘
```

FIG. 10.2. Menu for reflective follow-up.

of what the trainee did. A number of information sources are available to the trainee as well. For example, the student can ask what an expert would have done instead. Also, the student can examine simplified diagrams of the circuitry that are organized to provide good representations of the problem as shown in Fig. 10.1. We are working on additional coaching to explain why the diagrams are structured as they are. The drawings are interactive: mousing on any drawing component produces an explanation of what is known about the status of that component given the actions (such as measurements of the circuit) carried out so far. Finally, in addition to these opportunities for reviewing one's own performance, there is also the opportunity to simply run through an expert's solution to the problem, with the same informational resources available at each step of the expert solution.

The two episodes of a Sherlock II exercise, problem solving and reflective follow-up, correspond to the dual roles that students can play during collaborative sessions—*producer* and *critic,* using Collins, Brown, and Newman's (1989) terminology. The producer performs the task at hand, while the critic evaluates the performance. Computer-based collaboration can take place during both phases. We see three kinds of socially mediated learning activities in which our electronics diagnosis trainees might participate, as introduced on p. 303. These types of activities can take place for either the producer or critic role. First, students can simply work together to solve problems, talking to each other and manipulating a simulated task environment on the computer. This can be powerful for several reasons. In addition to affording opportunities for negotiating understanding and procedural knowledge, it also might reduce the mental overload that arises during the solution of difficult problems and thus remove an impediment to learning from practice. However, there are other activities that pairs of trainees can undertake that might be even more productive.

For example, they can pose problems for each other. When one person thinks he or she has learned something important, this knowledge can be tested either by using it to solve problems or by selecting problems that the person thinks involve the new knowledge and posing them for a partner. By observing the partner's performance and, if necessary, using his new knowledge to give advice to the partner, a person can test and tune this new knowledge. Further, if the problem posed turns out not to exercise the new understanding, this itself helps in understanding the boundaries on the new knowledge. There is, of course, also a motivational side to this game of two people posing tasks to each other.

A third form of socially mediated learning takes place during the review phase. This is peer critique of problem solutions. We are now working on designs for schemes whereby one or more trainees can critique the problem solution process exhibited by another trainee (or collaborating trainees). The tools for doing this already exist for the most part, since trainees can already review their own performance and receive critique information from the computer coach. What needs to be added is a facility that permits one (or more) trainee(s) to

TASKS	COLLABORATORS	
	Individual Student and Sherlock	Students: Sherlock in background as "coach"
Problem-solving	student takes turns with Sherlock while working on problem	students pose problems to each other, or work on problems in dyads or larger groups; Sherlock provides help upon request
Review	student reviews performance; constructs explanations with Sherlock	students review a performance trace in dyads or larger groups

FIG. 10.3.   Collaborative activities in Sherlock.

generate a critique for another trainee in a sufficiently standard form, but this is a problem on the same scale as the interface tools needed to permit a trainee to work in a simulated problem solving environment altogether. We believe it is quite attainable, and describe next our preliminary design for menu-driven critiquing tools.

Of course, there are other collaborative activities that computer-based learning environments make possible, if in addition to considering the type of task involved (problem solving or review), we also consider who the collaborators are. In fact, the *nature of the task* and the *collaborators* comprise two dimensions along which to categorize the collaborative activities we plan to incorporate within Sherlock II, as summarized in Fig. 10.3. In the activities we have discussed so far, several students would work together on a problem-solving or critiquing task, while the computerized tutor looks over their shoulders, offering help only on demand. However, this "coach" could itself collaborate on tasks with a single student or group of students. For example, during problem solving, a student (or small group) could take turns with Sherlock in making troubleshooting actions. Similarly, while reviewing a student solution trace, a student critic or pane of critics[9] could ask Sherlock to generate the next comment or perform a related subtask, such as identifying what was wrong with a move. Then, the critics would take over by telling the target student (the "producer") what the student should have done instead.

The Tutor's Three Main Roles

Having presented a catalogue of collaborative activities for computer-based learning environments—particularly those designed upon principles of cognitive apprenticeship—we can now focus our attention on the role of the tutor during these activities. In this section, we discuss the three teaching functions stated at the beginning of this section and sketch out our plans to incorporate these roles

---

[9]Throughout the ensuing discussion, we will assume that there is a team of critics, but only one producer.

within Sherlock II. We justify the need for the tutor to perform these roles in light of research in educational and cognitive psychology.

The Tutor as Mentor of Collaborative Activities

The teacher can provide support to students in carrying out collaborative tasks. In apprenticeship learning situations, support can come in various guises: modeling, scaffolding, and coaching (Chi & Bjork, 1991). For example, during problem solving in Sherlock II, the tutor can tell students which goal it would achieve next, and say or model exactly how it would achieve that goal (i.e., by citing, or carrying out, the measurements it would make on a particular component); can "scaffold" the development of students' ability to construct mental models of the active circuitry by presenting abstract block diagrams, such as the one shown in Fig. 10.1; and can coach students in acquiring troubleshooting strategies via the layered hinting scheme described above. Our preference is to leave to students the responsibility for deciding when advice is needed.

The research on self-explanation and group interaction that we reviewed above suggests that availability of support is at least as necessary for review tasks as for problem-solving tasks—particularly for poorer students. To recap what we said, successful students tend to have a better mental model of what constitutes a good explanation, to generate more explanations as opposed to terminal responses, and to formulate qualitatively different explanations than do poorer students (Chi et al., 1989; Chi & Van Lehn, 1991; Peterson & Swing, 1985; Webb, 1982, 1983, 1984, 1985). Several writers have argued in favor of providing students with explicit instruction in explanation (Chi & Van Lehn, 1991; King, 1989; Mastaglio, 1990; Webb, 1983), but have not specified how this could be done. We believe that it is best done in the context of domain-specific tasks, rather than through domain-neutral exercises couched in software solely dedicated to developing explanation skills, as others have suggested (e.g., King, 1989).[10]

During review activities, as during problem solving, instructional support can also come in the form of modeling, scaffolding, and coaching. By using a rich array of hierarchical menus, such as the ones shown in Fig. 10.5, supplemented by schemes that allow trainees to draw overview sketches of circuitry and comment on them, we expect that we can provide students with a rich and adequate critiquing capability. In other words, these menus would "scaffold" the process of constructing a comment or explanation. Student critics would pace through the steps of a student solution to a problem, marking each step in terms of its suitability, selecting appropriate comments from the hierarchical menu, and perhaps adding an occasional sketch. Figure 10.4 shows the menu that helps critics pace through a solution, get help in commenting, and so on. Figure 10.5 illus-

---

[10]Glaser (1983) argues in favor of this view.

Reviewer Menu
Student's Next Step
Redisplay Move
What Would Sherlock Have Done?
What Would Sherlock Do Next?
Comment on Last Move
Register Comment
Help with Finding Error
See Sherlock's Comment
Experiment with Alternative Moves
Revise From Previous Move
Fill Out Scoreboard
Exit Review

FIG. 10.4.   Reviewer options.

trates some options for leaving commentary and critique, but it includes only a small fraction of the choices we anticipate including within the menu hierarchy.

Based on task analysis, it was determined that there are several types of errors in the electronics troubleshooting domain. We have developed a hierarchy of error types, which is illustrated by the first and third submenus (leftmost and rightmost columns, respectively) of Figure 10.5. The first submenu provides the main error categories, three of which are shown in the figure—a circuit-level strategic error, pertaining to the goal status of the functional area of the test station in which the current move was made (Functional Area); a component-level strategic error, pertaining to the problem solver's decision to test a component (Choice of Component); and a tactical error, pertaining to how the student

Comment on Last Move		
Functional Area	Describe Error	UUT not Verified First Stimulus Not Verified Measurement Signal Not Verified Load not Verified
	Suggest Fix	Verify UUT First Verify Stimulus Verify Measurement Signal Verify Load
Choice of Component	Describe Error	Tested Component Earlier Cleared by Previous T.O. Test Verified by Testing Other Component Not Central in Unverified Path
	Suggest Fix	Test Component ???
Measurement-taking	Describe Error	Probes Reversed Wrong Pin for High Wrong Pin for Low Meter not Set to Ohms Meter not Set to DC Oscilloscope not Set to DC Oscilloscope not Set to AC
	Suggest Fix	Reverse Probes Correct Pin for High Correct Pin for Low Set Meter to Ohms Set Meter to DC Set Oscilloscope to DC Set Oscilloscope to AC

FIG. 10.5.   Preliminary design of commenting menus.

carried out a measurement (Measurement-taking). Note that these options address both strategic (goal-setting) and tactical (measurement-taking) skills, thus making the curriculum goals of Sherlock II explicit to the student.

The second submenu (central column of Fig. 10.5) prompts the student critics to choose between two general functions of an explanation: describing the error, and suggesting an alternative action. After selecting one option, the student critics can select the other if they wish. The critics are given this choice because for some errors, suggesting an alternative implicitly describes the error (e.g., "reverse meter probes"). The third level of options specifies errors and associated fixes for each of the categories in the first submenu. A final level (not shown in the diagram) will prompt the critics to supply even more specific information—for example, to "click" on a particular component to test next; or to give the number of the pins to which the meter probes should be connected to make the suggested measurement. Alternately, Sherlock will automatically bring up the appropriate video display so that student critics can demonstrate a correction; for example, it will display the front panel of the oscilloscope, so that the critics can set this device correctly. Sherlock will record the critics' corrections, so that the target student can replay the suggested actions when he or she steps through the review. The important thing to observe here is that critics will actively engage in using the vocabulary of the domain, as well as a vocabulary for reviewing problems in general. Whether or not this will improve self-monitoring skills or group interaction is an empirical issue we intend to address.

When student critics indicate that they are done with a comment (e.g., by selecting the Register Comment menu option), Sherlock will assemble the pieces of the critics' menu selections into a coherent comment. Sherlock will reply upon a model of explanation, and an algorithm for generating explanations, to do this.[11] The completed comment will be displayed in a separate window.

We anticipate that students will often need more direct support than the scaffolding provided by the commenting menus. For example, critics might be unable to tell if a particular student action is appropriate or informative and, if not, why. We believe that the choice of how directive support will be should be left to the critics, and will depend upon how much control they want over discovering the knowledge necessary to complete a comment for a particular troubleshooting action; that is, should the support be mainly tutor-directed, or student-directed?

At the tutor-directed extreme, modeling, the student critics could simply ask the tutor to display an appropriate comment. In Sherlock II, the tutor would display the comment that it would generate—the one that would appear at the current point of the solution trace during our current reflective follow-up. At the other, student-directed extreme, the student critics could be allowed to experi-

---

[11]Our colleague, Johanna Moore, is working on this explanation problem now, as we will discuss presently, employing ideas previously developed in her dissertation (Moore, 1989).

ment with alternative actions (tests on particular components), until they carry out one or more informative moves—that is, actions that accomplish high-level, circuit goals such as verifying a whole functional area of the test station, for example, the signal path. In other words, Sherlock would shift the critics into problem-solving mode, at the current state of the producer's solution. System help would be available, as it is during problem solving. When the critics identify the producer's error and an appropriate alternative action, they could then ask to return to review mode, wherein they would generate a comment using the menus, and possibly create an overlay sketch of the parts of the circuitry they tested.

Somewhere in between modeling and providing tools for student-directed experimentation lies coached commenting. In Sherlock II, we plan to allow the critics to ask for help with producing a comment on a student's action. Help during review would be similar to that during problem solving; it would be increasingly directive, mirroring the increasingly directive structure of the commenting menus. For example, an initial suggestion would simply tell the critics how to go about identifying an error—"learning strategies" help, so to speak—to mouse on components to examine their goal status. More directive help would describe the type of error(s) involved—testing within a functional area at the wrong time; not satisfying a particular circuit or component testing goal—or, still more directive, what the error is. Finally, Sherlock would simply present a complete comment to the critics, as though they had requested to see it in the first place.

Even with the varied modes of support described here, some students might have substantial difficulty producing effective comments and explanations. For these students, we envision in the future having an alternative mode that would give students explicit instruction and practice in the process of generating explanations. (The hierarchical menuing scheme we have described focuses students' attention on the product, a critique; it does not highlight the *process* of generating a critique.) This is not possible right now because the current version of Sherlock lacks a model for generating explanations. Most of the hints that students receive while problem solving, and the feedback they receive during reflective follow-up, are generated by instantiating variables in templates. This requires a rich device model but its intelligence does not extend to explanation strategy. One of our colleagues, Johanna Moore, has begun work to develop a model of explanation for the domain of electronics troubleshooting, and to extend Sherlock II's explanation knowledge base and algorithms, so that hints and feedback can be tied more directly to the producer's actions, and generated using the explanation strategies that experienced trainers use.

One of the central lessons that emerged from the work of Clancey and his colleagues is that only a system that can richly model the human reasoning underlying a complex task like medical diagnosis can also teach this task (e.g., Clancey, 1982, 1987, 1988). It should follow, then, that a system that "knows" how to generate explanations in a particular domain could also guide students

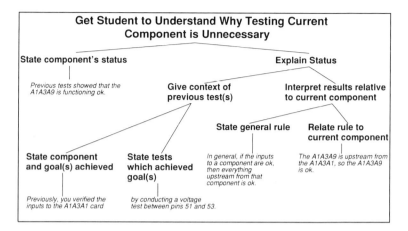

FIG. 10.6. Hierarchical plan of an explanation.

during review activities. Several expert systems contain an explanation generator. Moore (1989) developed an explanation generator for a LISP tutoring system, Program Enhancement Advisor, which was built using an expert system shell called Explainable Expert System (EES). Moore plans to extend the EES knowledge base so that it can be used to generate explanations in the domain of electronics troubleshooting.

Basically, Moore's explanation generator works by defining a discourse goal based on a user query, identifying a strategy to achieve that goal, formalizing the strategy into a hierarchically structured plan, and employing plan operators to carry out the goals and subgoals at each plan node. A top-level discourse goal in the Sherlock II context might be a complex one, perhaps consisting of two subgoals: for example, *to get the student to understand why the move was flagged as incorrect,* and to *get the student to know what to do to fix it.* Each subgoal could be further instantiated in reference to the current troubleshooting context; for example, *get the student to understand why testing the current component is unnecessary* and *suggest an appropriate component to test instead.* One strategy that a skilled trainer might use to achieve the first subgoal would be to inform the student about the component's status (i.e., good, bad, or not suspect), and then explain how that status was determined by previous tests. A simplified plan for carrying out this strategy is shown in Fig. 10.6.

These are the types of strategies that will be formalized in Moore's explanation-generation facility. The end result will be explanations that look something like the one presented below, which refers to the circuit diagram of Fig. 10.1 and addresses a hypothetical student error of testing the A1A3A9 relay card. Underlined items are instantiated variables.

Previous tests showed that the <u>A1A3A9</u> is functioning ok. Previously, you verified the <u>inputs</u> to the <u>A1A3A1</u> card by conducting a voltage test between pins <u>51</u> and

<u>53</u>. In general, if the inputs to a component are ok, then everything upstream from that component is ok. The <u>A1A3A9</u> is upstream from the <u>A1A3A1</u>, so the <u>A1A3A9</u> is ok.

The same process that Sherlock II goes through to generate this explanation could be followed, step by step, by a student critic or team of critics. The basic scheme would go something like this. Sherlock will identify the decision points in the plan and then prompt the student critics to select one of several options from menus corresponding to each decision point (plan node). For example, the first step will be to diagnose the error, using a menu of error descriptors, in order to specify a discourse goal (e.g., *get the student to understand why testing the current component is unnecessary*). Then, Sherlock will prompt the critics to select one of the strategies that it "knows" (via its model of explanation in this domain) will achieve the discourse goal. From this point on, the student critics will be asked to choose strategies for achieving subgoals of the plan, and to supply information that will instantiate explanation variables (e.g., the critics will be asked to name the previously-tested component, A1A3A1 in our example). Some stages of prompting might pass through several iterations. For example, if several component goals were achieved in order to verify a component, the student critics would be asked to describe each goal and its associated test(s). At any step during this process, the critics could request help in carrying out the current explanation step.[12] As parts of the explanation are completed, Sherlock will display the text in a separate window. In fact, we might find it instructionally beneficial to reify the process of constructing explanations with diagrams such as the one shown in Fig. 10.6.

The main objective is to provide students with tools that enable them to practice constructing the kinds of explanations that experienced trainers would produce, so that students eventually internalize evaluation criteria and explanation strategies. And, like all other aspects of cognitive strategy training in Sherlock II, direct instruction in explanation will be situated within a task—in this case, reviewing another student's solution. As we noted earlier, we believe that this is a far more effective means of developing higher-order thinking skills than is having students go through domain-neutral exercises explicitly designed to teach these skills.

One of the most difficult tasks for us will be to devise ways of making the commenting process simple and not tedious. Although we do not know exactly how to do this yet, it will probably require us to make decisions about which steps of a plan can be collapsed, and which ones can be completed for student critics without compromising instructional benefits. We might discover that the

---

[12]We have developed a hypertext-like utility that will enable students to point to terms in Sherlock II's prompts and associated menu options in order to receive an explanation about what these terms mean. For example, students could find out what a particular explanation strategy label means; that is, what this strategy does, from a rhetorical standpoint.

best scheme is a mixture of having Sherlock generate comments for some moves in a solution trace, and asking critics to generate others. Sherlock's job, then, would be to "intelligently" select moves for the reviewers to comment upon, by considering factors such as difficulty of diagnosis, and what the student model says about the reviewers' level of ability.

The Tutor as Quality Control Director
of Collaborative Activities

The second teaching function we envision is quality control, particularly during peer review activities. It is important that collaborative activity not become a *folie à deux,* and this can sometimes happen when there is no supervision of trainee activity. Research in educational psychology has shown that the effects of receiving incoherent, incomplete, or inaccurate comments can cause degeneracies (Shuell, 1983; Snow, 1977) or—at best—fail to promote learning (Webb, 1983). There are also motivational reasons to exert some measure of quality control over students' critiques. As shown repeatedly in the literature on peer tutoring, students do not respond well to tutors in whom they lack confidence (e.g., Falchikov, 1990).

The tutor's role as quality control director is related to the first teaching function we discussed, insofar as advice received from the computer coach will help to improve the quality of comments that students give to their peers. However, students may not be aware of how much support they need, and not solicit it often enough or at the right times. Consequently, in Sherlock II, we plan to have student critiques examined by Sherlock before they are passed on to another student. Our initial plan is to "filter out" only those comments that are inaccurate (i.e., contain misdiagnoses), rather than incomplete. The target student will have the option of viewing the comment Sherlock would have generated, which will, in some cases, indicate additional errors that the student critics failed to note. There are also interesting opportunities for self-review by enlarging on a peer's critique.

It is also possible to simulate peer critique situations. As suggested earlier, we could have a mode where making the critique is the primary learning activity and not all critiques are even delivered to the target student. Also, Sherlock could present simulated student solutions to a trainee for critique. Whether we maintain authentic peer interaction in these activities will depend upon what we learn about the motivational value of direct interpersonal interactions as part of the learning process. We suspect that we will want to have such interactions and that simulated peer interactions will not be as effective as real ones, but this is a matter to be resolved through empirical comparisons.

Both commenting schemes described earlier—the hierarchical menus, and the more knowledge-rich, plan-oriented approach—will permit efficient computer review of critiques. The computer would review each criticism by seeing whether it applied to the difference between an expert model's performance and the target student's performance. To deal fully with novel but enlightened alternative proposals, the system must also be able to enact the alternative move suggested by the reviewers and to see whether it is more productive than the target student's move and/or better than the expert model's move. Hopefully, we will find ways to develop this level of empiricism and humility in our systems.

The Tutor as Manager of Collaborative Activities

A final task for the computer tutor is to manage collaborative learning activities. This includes the selection of problems for students to work on, solutions for them to critique, and possibly pairing (or groupings) of students to optimize the learning opportunities each affords for a partner. Studies of group learning in the classroom show that the demands on the teacher are high, and teachers are often unqualified to carry out these demands (Nijhof & Kommers, 1985). It therefore seems desirable to offload some of the managerial work onto the computer, which has a reputation for being able to make complex decisions— involving lots of data, and/or complex interactions between variables—given suitable algorithms.

We have yet to develop plans for enabling Sherlock to carry out the managerial chores listed above, except for problem selection. We do have a scheme in which problems are ranked according to difficulty based upon certain features, such as where in the test station the fault lies, what types of measurement devices (e.g., handheld meter, oscilloscope) have to be used, etc. The system selects the next problem with reference to what the system's model of the student says about the student's ability along each of these dimensions—that is, ability to test in the region where the fault lies, ability to use the required measurement devices, etc. We also know that this scheme for mapping student ability scores to problems does not accomplish all that we would wish and are working on improved possibilities.

Intelligent pairing of students presents an interesting challenge. In response to repeatedly confirmed findings that group composition determines the effectiveness of group learning situations (as measured by individual student achievement), Webb (1985) has argued that teachers should carefully "compose" student groups. Because of the complexities involved in doing this, we expect that computers could become better suited to this task than human teachers. Indeed, the existence of computerized matchmaking services testifies for the feasibility of intelligently pairing students!

The research conducted by Webb (1982, 1983, 1985) and others has uncovered some crucial group composition variables: ability level, gender, and social orientation (extroversion/introversion), to name just a few. However, more work needs to be done to determine how interactions between these variables correlate with group effectiveness. In addition, we need to continue to develop a technology for modeling the student, so that tutoring systems can maintain and update a record of students' ability levels, learning styles, confidence, and other variables found to correlate with the effectiveness of group interaction, but that cannot always be instantiated by simply querying the student directly (as can, e.g., information about age, sex, or gender).

CONCLUSIONS

We have taken the unusual step in this chapter of describing what we plan to do next rather than what we have learned from work already completed, or so it may seem. In fact, the design work described in this chapter, when considered in light of our experiences building Sherlock II, has shown us that affording students significant opportunities for collaborative learning is not going to be substantially harder than developing effective computer-based systems for solo learning, if it will be harder at all. Both require relatively deep modeling of the task environments for which students are being trained. Both also require models of expertise sufficient to complete the tasks for which students are being trained as well as the capability for generating explanations based upon comparisons between student performance and that of the simulated expert. Both can benefit from models of student competence. In short, we expect to find that the really difficult tasks for building collaborative environments are inherent within building intelligent tutoring systems in general.

A pessimist might argue that in fact both problems are "AI complete,"not wholly solvable until all of the core agenda of the science of artificial intelligence has been completed. In a sense, this is true. Our ability to provide good learning opportunities will continue to improve, for both solo and collaborative learning, as we address and solve the core problems of artificial intelligence and become more able to build systems that behave flexibly, understandably, adaptively, and in accord with common sense. However, it is important to note that the core problems of artificial intelligence have not prevented substantial success for the prototype of our system, Sherlock I, which lacked both collaborative and reflective opportunities.[13]

A commonly held view of intelligent tutoring systems is that they consist of a set of discrete, independent modules—for example, a device simulator, student modeling component, curriculum module, and perhaps a coaching module.

---

[13]Independent field tests by the Air Force showed that 20–25 hours of training on the prototype system was roughly equivalent to 4 years of on-the-job experience (Nichols et al., in press), and retention after 6 months was about 90%. We will be field testing Sherlock II at Air Force bases during the next few months. Given our prior evaluation data, and the improvements we have made (Lesgold, Lajoie, Bunzo, & Eggan, 1992; Lesgold, Eggan, Katz, & Rao, 1992), we expect it to work extremely well.

However, our experience with the Sherlock tutors and other sophisticated systems that have been developed over the last decade show us that this view is far too simplistic. In these tutors, modules codefine each others' functions and features. For example, in Sherlock II, coaching is driven by information in the student model. We are currently working on extensions to the student modeling component which will enable it to, in turn, use students' responses to hints to further update a student record (Lesgold, Eggan, Katz, & Rao, 1992).

Similarly, once we incorporate collaborative learning activities within the Sherlock II context, we plan to further extend the student modeling routines so that students' actions during critiquing can be used to update the student model. A lot can be inferred about a student's knowledge and ability by the kinds of comments the student makes, or fails to make. The more informed student model we envision will enable the tutor to perform some of the managerial functions we outlined earlier—selecting problems for collaboration, pairing students for collaborative problem solving or critiquing, perhaps even selecting some actions within solution traces for students to critique—while leaving other actions for the computerized critic.

Once the tutor is able to perform these functions, it will be able to do more than support students in learning the primary, problem-solving task (e.g., electronics fault diagnosis) for which the system was developed. It will be able to guide students in developing the ability to monitor their own and other students' problem-solving process. As the editors of this volume have pointed out, one argument that "model-breakers" have raised against including a student modeling component in tutoring systems is that students should diagnose their errors, and monitor their problem-solving actions, themselves. We are arguing that better student models will enable tutoring systems to support activities (such as peer critiquing of student solutions) that promote these self-regulatory skills.

But the primary changes required for building collaborative learning environments are not in the realm of educational technology or, more broadly, computer science. Rather, they involve a new view of education. Education is not the dispensing of knowledge, nor are teachers the sole source of knowledge. Rather, education should be seen as the engineering of environments in which students can learn. To a significant degree, the responsibility for learning is the student's, not the teacher's. However, the teacher does have the obligation to remove obstacles to learning, to develop paths that students might—alone or in groups—follow toward learning, and to provide guidance to students when they encounter uncertainties and difficulties in following those paths.

Because learning is often stimulated by discussions among people with partial knowledge, collaborative learning paths may be of especial importance. What we have learned from the current phase of system design work is that such collaborative paths can be developed in the intelligent instructional systems world without the addition of new software technology. We need only to get down to business and try out some of the possibilities now becoming feasible.

ACKNOWLEDGMENT

The work on Sherlock II described in this article is funded by the Air Force. Sherlock II has been a collaborative effort by a team that has included (either currently or in the recent past) Marilyn Bunzo, Richard Eastman, Gary Eggan, Maria Gordin, Linda Greenberg, Edward Hughes, Sandra Katz, Susanne Lajoie, Alan Lesgold, Thomas McGinnis, Rudianto Prabowo, Govinda Rao, and Rose Rosenfeld. As with Sherlock I, Dr. Sherrie Gott and her colleagues at Air Force Human Resources, Armstrong Laboratories are active colleagues in the effort. None of our collaborators nor the funding agency necessarily endorse or agree with the views expressed. We would especially like to thank Sharon Derry, Edward Hughes, and Johanna Moore for their comments on earlier versions of this chapter, and Linda Greenberg for help with preparing the manuscript.

REFERENCES

Anderson, J. R., & Reiser, B. J. (1985). The LISP tutor. *Byte, 10*(4), pp. 159–175.

Azmitia, M., & Perlmutter, M. (1989). Social influences on children's cognition: State of the art and future directions. In H. W. Reese (Ed.), *Advances in child development and behavior* (Vol. 22, pp. 89–144). San Diego, CA: Academic Press.

Bearison, D. J. (1982). New directions in studies of social interaction and cognitive growth. In F. C. Serafica (Ed.), *Social-cognitive development in context* (pp. 199–221). New York: Guilford Press.

Brown, A. L., & Palincsar, A. S. (1989). Guided, cooperative learning and individual knowledge acquisition. In L. B. Resnick (Ed.), *Knowing, learning, and instruction: Essays in honor of Robert Glaser* (pp. 393–451). Hillsdale, NJ: Lawrence Erlbaum Associates.

Brown, J. S. (1985). Process versus product: A perspective on tools for communal and informal electronic learning. *Journal of Educational Computing Research, 1*(2), 179–201.

Chi, M. T. H., Bassok, M., Lewis, M. W., Reimann, P., & Glaser, R. (1989). Self-explanations: How students study and use examples in learning to solve problems. *Cognitive Science, 13*, 145–182.

Chi, M. T. H., & Bjork, R. (1991). Modeling expertise. In D. Druckman & R. Bjork (Eds.), *In the mind's eye: Understanding human performance* (pp. 57–79). Washington, DC: National Academy Press.

Chi, M. T. H., & Van Lehn, K. (1991). The content of physics self-explanations. *Journal of the Learning Sciences, 1*, 69–105.

Clancey, W. J. (1982). GUIDON. Applications-oriented AI Research: Education. In A. Barr & E. A. Feigenbaum (Eds.), *The handbook of artificial intelligence* (pp. 267–278). Los Altos, CA: Kaufmann.

Clancey, W. J. (1987). *Knowledge-based tutoring: The Guidon program*. Cambridge, MA: MIT Press.

Clancey, W. J. (1988). The knowledge engineer as student: Metacognitive bases for asking good questions. In H. Mandl & A. Lesgold (Eds.), *Learning issues for intelligent tutoring systems* (pp. 1–18). New York: Springer-Verlag.

Collins, A., & Brown, J. S. (1988). The computer as a tool for learning through reflection. In H. Mandl & A. Lesgold (Eds.), *Learning issues for intelligent tutoring systems* (pp. 1–18). New York: Springer-Verlag, 1988.

314

Collins, A., Brown, J. S., & Newman, S. E. (1989). Cognitive apprenticeship: Teaching the craft of reading, writing, and mathematics. In L. B. Resnick (Ed.), *Knowing, learning, and instruction: Essays in honor of Robert Glaser* (pp. 453–94). Hillsdale, NJ: Lawrence Erlbaum Associates.

Doise, W., & Mugny, G. (1984). *The social development of the intellect.* Oxford, England: Pergamon Press.

Falchikov, N. (1990). An experiment in same-age peer tutoring in higher education: Some observations concerning the repeated experience of tutoring or being tutored. In S. Goodlad & B. Hirst, *Explorations in peer tutoring* (pp. 120–142). Oxford, England: Basil Blackwell, Ltd.

Glaser, R. (1983). *Education and thinking: The role of knowledge* (LRDC Report). Pittsburgh, PA: University of Pittsburgh, Learning Research and Development Center.

Greeno, J. G. (1986). Collaborative teaching and making sense of symbols: Comment on Lampert's "Knowing, Doing, and Teaching Multiplication." *Cognition and Instruction, 3*(4), 343–347.

Hythecker, V. I., Dansereau, D. F., Rocklin, T. R., O'Donnell, A. M., Lambiotte, J. G., Larson, C. O., & Young, M. D. (1984). *Networking: Development and evaluation of a CACL module.* Unpublished manuscript. Cited in O'Donnell, A. M., Dansereau, D. F., & Hythecker, V. (1986). The effects of monitoring on cooperative learning. *Journal of Experimental Education, 54.*

Johnson, D. W., & Johnson, R. T. (1985). The internal dynamics of cooperative learning groups. In R. Slavin, S. Sharan, S. Kagan, R. Hertz-Lazarowitz, C. Webb, & R. Schmuck (Eds.), *Learning to cooperate, cooperating to learn* (pp. 103–124). New York: Plenum Press.

Justen, J. E., Adams, T. M., & Waldrop, P. B. (1988). Effects of small group versus individual computer-assisted instruction on student achievement. *Educational Technology, 28*(2), 50–52.

Justen, J. E., Waldrop, T. M., & Adams, T. M. (1990). Effects of paired versus individual user computer-assisted instruction and type of feedback on student achievement. *Educational Technology, 30*(7), 51–53.

Kellett, D. A. (1990). Peer tutoring, peer collaboration and the development of a memorisation strategy. In S. Goodlad & B. Hirst (Eds.), *Explorations in peer tutoring* (pp. 203–214). Oxford, England: Basil Blackwell, Ltd.

King, A. (1989). Verbal interaction and problem-solving within computer-assisted cooperative learning groups. *Journal of Educational Computing Research, 5*(1), 1–15.

Lajoie, S. P., & Lesgold, A. (1989). Apprenticeship training in the workplace: Computer-coached practice environment as a new form of apprenticeship. *Machine-Mediated Learning, 3,* 7–28.

Lampert, M. (1986). Knowing, doing, and teaching multiplication. *Cognition and Instruction, 3*(4), 305–342.

Lave, J. (1988). *The culture of acquisition and the practice of understanding* (Tech. Rep. No. 88–0007). Palo Alto, CA: Institute for Research on Learning.

Lesgold, A. (In press). Assessment of intelligent training systems: Sherlock as an example. In E. Baker & H. O'Neil, Jr. (Eds.), *Technology assessment: Estimating the future.* Hillsdale, NJ: Lawrence Erlbaum Associates.

Lesgold, A. M., Eggan, E., Katz, S., & Rao, G. (1992). Possibilities for assessment using computer-based apprenticeship environments. In W. Regian & V. Shute (Eds.), *Cognitive approaches to automated instruction.* Hillsdale, NJ: Lawrence Erlbaum Associates.

Lesgold, A. M., Lajoie, S. P., Bunzo, M., & Eggan, G. (1992). Sherlock: A coached practice environment for an electronics troubleshooting job. In J. Larkin & R. Chabay (Eds.), *Computer assisted instruction and intelligent tutoring systems: Shared issues and complementary approaches.* Hillsdale, NJ: Lawrence Erlbaum Associates.

Malouf, D. B., Wizer, D. R., Pilato, V. H., & Grogan, M. H. (1988, April). *Computer assisted instruction with small groups of mildly handicapped students.* Paper presented at the American Educational Research Association annual meeting, New Orleans.

Mastaglio, T. W. (1990). *User modelling in cooperative knowledge-based systems* (Tech. Rep. No. CU–CS–486–90). Boulder, CO: Department of Computer Science, University of Colorado.

Mitchell, T. M., Keller, R. M., & Kedar-Cabelli, S. T. (1986). Explanation-based generalization: A unifying view. *Machine Learning, 1,* 47–80.

Moore, J. D. (1989). *A reactive approach to explanation in expert and advice-giving systems.* Doctoral thesis. University of California, Los Angeles.

Nastasi, B. K., Clements, D. H., & Battista, M. T. (1990). Social-cognitive interactions, motivation, and cognitive growth in Logo programming and CAI problem-solving environments. *Journal of Educational Psychology, 82,* 150–158.

Nichols, P., Pokorny, R., Jones, G., Gott, S. P., & Alley, W. E. (in press). *Evaluation of an avionics troubleshooting system.* Special Report. Brooks AFB, TX: Air Force Human Resources Laboratory.

Nijhof, N., & Kommers, P. (1985). An analysis of cooperation in relation to cognitive controversy. In R. Slavin, S. Sharan, S. Kagan, R. Hertz-Lazarowitz, C. Webb, & R. Schmuck (Eds.), *Learning to cooperate, cooperating to learn* (pp. 125–145). New York: Plenum Press.

O'Donnell, A. M., Dansereau, D. F., Hall, R. H., Skaggs, L. P., Hythecker, V. I., Peel, J. L., & Rewey, K. L. (1990). Learning concrete procedures: Effects of processing strategies and cooperative learning. *Journal of Educational Psychology, 82,* 171–177.

O'Donnell, A. M., Dansereau, D. F., Hythecker, V. I., Hall, R. H., Skaggs, L. P., Lambiotte, J. G., & Young, M. D. (1988). Cooperative procedural learning: Effects of prompting and pre- versus distributed planning activities. *Journal of Educational Psychology, 80,* 167–171.

Owen, E., & Sweller, J. (1985). What do students learn while solving mathematics problems? *Journal of Educational Psychology, 77,* 272–284.

Palincsar, A. S., & Brown, A. L. (1984). Reciprocal teaching of comprehension-fostering and comprehension-monitoring activities. *Cognition and Instruction, 1,* 117–175.

Papert, S. (1980). *Mindstorms: Children, computers, and powerful ideas.* New York: Basic Books, 1980.

Peterson, P. L., & Swing, S. R. (1985). Students' cognitions as mediators of the effectiveness of small-group learning. *Journal of Educational Psychology, 77,* 299–312.

Piaget, J. (1932). *The moral judgment of the child.* New York: Harcourt Brace.

Reiser, B. J., Kimberg, D. Y., Lovett, M. C., & Ranney, M. (1992). Knowledge representation and explanation in GIL, an intelligent tutor for programming. In J. Larkin & R. Chabay (Eds.), *Computer assisted instruction and intelligent tutoring systems: Shared issues and complementary approaches.* Hillsdale, NJ: Lawrence Erlbaum Associates.

Roschelle, J., & Behrend, S. D. (in press). The construction of shared knowledge in collaborative problem solving. In C. O'Malley (Ed.), *Computer Supported Collaborative Learning.*

Scardamalia, M., Bereiter, C., McLean, R. S., Swallow, J., & Woodruff, E. (1989). Computer-supported intentional learning environments. *Journal of Educational Computing Research, 5*(1), 51–68.

Schoenfeld, A. H. (1983). Problem solving in the mathematics curriculum: A report, recommendations and an annotated bibliography. *The Mathematical Association of America,* MAA Notes, No. 1.

Schoenfeld, A. H. (1985). *Mathematical problem solving.* New York: Academic Press.

Shuell, T. J. (1983). The effect of instructions to organize for good and poor learners. *Intelligence, 7,* 271–286.

Shuell, T. J. (1988). The role of the student in learning from instruction. *Contemporary Educational Psychology, 13,* 276–295.

Sipusic, M. J., Roschelle, J., & Pea, R. (1991, March). *Talking to learn, learning to talk: Conceptual change in dynagrams and the envisioning machine.* Paper presented at the Third Biannual Workshop on Cognition and Instruction. Pittsburgh, PA.

Slavin, R. E. (1985). An introduction to cooperative learning research. In R. Slavin, S. Sharan, S. Kagan, R. Hertz-Lazarowitz, C. Webb, & R. Schmuck (Eds.), *Learning to cooperate, cooperating to learn* (pp. 5–15). New York: Plenum Press.

Slavin, R. E. (1990). *Cooperative learning: Theory, research, and practice.* Englewood Cliffs, NJ: Prentice Hall.

Snow, R. E. (1977). Research on aptitude for learning: A progress report. In L. S. Shulman (Ed.), *Review of research in education, 4, 1976* (pp. 50–105). Itasca, IL: Peacock.

Sweller, J. (1988). Cognitive load during problem solving: Effects on learning. *Cognitive Science, 12.* 257–285.

Sweller, J., & Cooper, G. (1985). The use of worked examples as a substitute for problem solving in algebra learning. *Cognition and Instruction, 2,* 58–89.

Tudge, J., & Rogoff, B. (1989). Peer influences on cognitive development: Piagetian and Vygotskian perspectives. In M. H. Bornstein & J. S. Bruner (Eds.), *Interaction in human development* (pp. 17–40). Hillsdale, NJ: Lawrence Erlbaum Associates.

Van Lehn, K. (1991, March). *A model of the self-explanation effect.* Paper presented at the Third Biannual Workshop on Cognition and Instruction. Pittsburgh, PA.

Vygotsky, L. S. (1978). *Mind in society: The development of higher psychological processes.* Cambridge, MA: Harvard University Press.

Webb, N. M. (1982). Peer interaction and learning in cooperative small groups. *Journal of Educational Psychology, 74,* 642–655.

Webb, N. M. (1983). Predicting learning from student interaction: Defining the interaction variables. *Educational Psychologist, 18*(1), 33–41.

Webb, N. M. (1984). Microcomputer learning in small groups: cognitive requirements and group processes. *Journal of Educational Psychology, 76,* 1076–1088.

Webb, N. M. (1985). Student interaction and learning in small groups. In R. Slavin, S. Sharan, S. Kagan, R. Hertz-Lazarowitz, C. Webb, & R. Schmuck (Eds.), *Learning to cooperate, cooperating to learn* (pp. 147–172). New York: Plenum Press.

Webb, N. M., Enders, P., & Lewis, S. (1986). Problem-solving strategies and group processes in small groups learning computer programming. *American Educational Research Journal, 23,* 253–261.

Winter, S. (1990). Processing and outcome in tuition for reading: The case of paired reading. In S. Goodlad & B. Hirst (Eds.), *Explorations in peer tutoring* (pp. 215–224). Oxford, England: Basil Blackwell, Ltd.

11

The Discovery and Reflection Notation: A Graphical Trace for Supporting Self-Regulation in Computer-Based Laboratories

Leona Schauble
Kalyani Raghavan
Robert Glaser
University of Pittsburgh

This chapter describes the Discovery and Reflection Notation (DARN), a graphical trace notation to support students' reflection about, evaluation of, and appropriate debugging of their search processes and strategies in the context of self-directed experimentation. Design of the notation was motivated by our studies of undergraduates' scientific reasoning with computer-based laboratories (Glaser, Schauble, Raghavan, & Zeitz, in press; Schauble, Glaser, Raghavan, & Zeitz, 1991; Shute, Glaser, & Raghavan, 1989). In these studies, students worked with one or more computer-based laboratories that simulate phenomena in various subject-matter domains (microeconomics, d.c. circuits, and geometrical optics). In each of the studies, students were set the task of trying to rediscover the laws or principles that apply within the laboratory content domains, an objective typically pursued across several sessions and over a period of weeks. Because the computer labs simultaneously serve as stimuli and recording devices (they automatically store records of all student activity), it is possible with them to study learning and complex reasoning across an extended time and also across a significant range of subject matter.

Although these laboratories are described in detail elsewhere (Glaser et al., in press; Schauble et al., 1991; Shute et al., 1989) a brief description of Smithtown, the laboratory in microeconomics, provides an example of how students interact with the laboratories and how the labs work. When working with Smithtown, a student first chooses a market to explore (markets are goods or services for production and sale, such as coffee, typewriters, gasoline, and water). In the Smithtown screen shown in Fig. 11.1, the student has been working in the ice cream market. The student makes changes in one or more independent variables (for example, the price of the good, the population of the town, or the number of

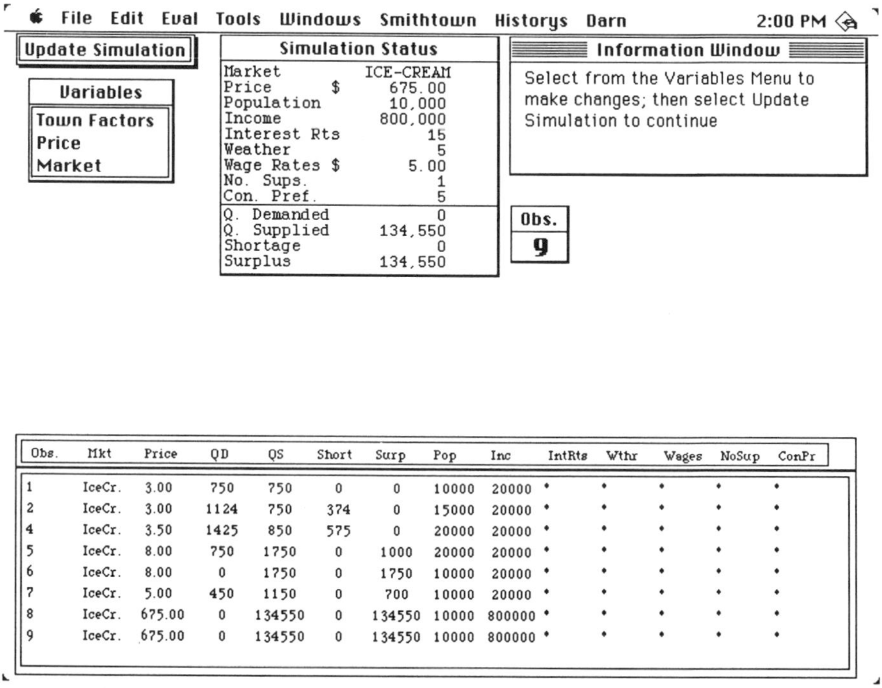

```
 É  File  Edit  Eual  Tools  Windows  Smithtown  Historys  Darn            2:00 PM 
┌──────────────────┐┌───────────────────────┐┌──────────────────────────────────┐
│ Update Simulation││  Simulation Status    ││====  Information Window  ====     │
│┌────────────────┐││Market        ICE-CREAM││                                  │
││   Uariables    │││Price      $    675.00 ││ Select from the Variables Menu to │
│└────────────────┘││Population      10,000 ││ make changes; then select Update  │
│┌────────────────┐││Income         800,000 ││ Simulation to continue            │
││  Town Factors  │││Interest Rts        15 ││                                  │
││  Price         │││Weather              5 ││                                  │
││  Market        │││Wage Rates $      5.00 ││                                  │
│└────────────────┘││No. Sups.           1  │└──────────────────────────────────┘
└──────────────────┘│Con. Pref.          5  │┌───────────┐
                    │Q. Demanded         0  ││   Obs.    │
                    │Q. Supplied   134,550  ││           │
                    │Shortage            0  ││     9     │
                    │Surplus       134,550  │└───────────┘
                    └───────────────────────┘
```

Obs.	Mkt	Price	QD	QS	Short	Surp	Pop	Inc	IntRts	Wthr	Wages	NoSup	ConPr
1	IceCr.	3.00	750	750	0	0	10000	20000	*	*	*	*	*
2	IceCr.	3.00	1124	750	374	0	15000	20000	*	*	*	*	*
4	IceCr.	3.50	1425	850	575	0	20000	20000	*	*	*	*	*
5	IceCr.	8.00	750	1750	0	1000	20000	20000	*	*	*	*	*
6	IceCr.	8.00	0	1750	0	1750	10000	20000	*	*	*	*	*
7	IceCr.	5.00	450	1150	0	700	10000	20000	*	*	*	*	*
8	IceCr.	675.00	0	134550	0	134550	10000	800000	*	*	*	*	*
9	IceCr.	675.00	0	134550	0	134550	10000	800000	*	*	*	*	*

FIG. 11.1.   The Smithtown computer program.

suppliers), and if desired, makes one or more predictions about the outcomes of the manipulations. The computer then displays the effect of these changes on a number of related dependent variables (such as quantity supplied, quantity demanded, shortage, and surplus). For each experiment, the student has the option of permanently recording as much of this information as desired into an online notebook, shown at the bottom of the screen in Fig. 11.1. He or she may also use a spreadsheet-like table package to select from, sort, and mathematically manipulate the data in various ways, or a graphing tool to graph relations in the data. When the student believes a relation has been identified, usually after carrying out several experiments, a hypothesis menu is used to state the laws or principles discovered. The computer evaluates the hypothesis for accuracy and indicates whether the student has generated sufficient evidence to support the conclusion. Thus, the laboratory provides a context for studying the full cycle of experimentation, rather than focusing exclusively on one component, for example, experimental design or hypothesis revision. The laboratory simulates about one half of the subject matter typically covered in an undergraduate course in microeconomics, providing an opportunity to observe cumulative knowledge change in an extended body of subject matter that is related to students' informal understanding of buying and selling and the motivations of consumers and suppliers. Although the other laboratories obviously vary in details, they share the same interface and have a common set of data recording and manipulation tools. In addition, each includes a simulation of some domain and provides a context for students to engage in the cycle of generating hypotheses, planning and designing experiments, making predictions, observing outcomes, recording and manipulating data, and stating observed principles.

Although the studies performed with these laboratories vary, designs typically include pre- and post-tests of content knowledge that bracket several sessions of 1- to 2-hours each, in which students engage in repeated cycles of experimentation. These tests assess changes in student knowledge, but equally important, the computer traces and audiotaped records of students thinking aloud make it possible to study the processes of learning, that is, the strategies that students use to carry out these components of experimentation activity.

SELF-REGULATORY ACTIVITIES IN SCIENTIFIC REASONING

Studies have found that good and poor learners organize their self-directed experimentation in different ways. One important difference, the focus of this chapter, is on students' self-regulatory activity, including spontaneous reflection about the evaluation of their own processes of experimentation. Our less successful students spent a disproportionate amount of time focusing exclusively on the concrete materials and procedures afforded by the laboratories. Inspection of their verbal protocols suggests that much of their attentional and processing resources were bound up in activities like choosing among lenses, deciding how many resistors to add to a circuit, or changing the number of suppliers in the tea market. Even when repeatedly asked questions to focus them on purpose, such as, "What are you trying to accomplish here?" or, "What do you think you are going to learn from this experiment?," they rarely focused on how they were going about the task, for example, by reviewing their pattern of search, evaluating the validity of the evidence generated, or considering alternative interpretations of the data.

There is now a growing literature conducted in various domains of cognitive performance, which is finding individual differences in subjects' ability successfully to monitor and control their performance by checking for comprehension, allocating processing resources and maintaining the optimal "amount" of attentionality, generating self-explanations, and engaging in other self-regulatory activities. Parallel to this work is a growing educational interest in encouraging students to engage in these activities, although it is important to note that there is as yet little consensus about the generality or domain specificity of the processes themselves, which are variously referred to as metacognitive, self-regulatory, and executive control strategies (in this chapter, we elect the term self-regulatory activities).

Writers since the time of Dewey (1933) have argued that reflective thinking plays an important role in the development of self-regulatory skills. On the one hand, reflection enables planning, which often leads to the regulation or revision of a prospective course of activity—including intellectual activity—even before it is put into play. Perhaps equally important, reflection provides a basis for evaluating activities after they have been deployed. Evaluation may be particularly important when activities fail to lead to desired outcomes, perhaps because insufficient thought or planning accompanied them. Dewey wrote about the general value of reflection as an "ingredient" of educated thinking. Contemporary researchers have taken this argument further to suggest specifically that there are likely relations between reflection, self-regulatory skills, and the development of strategies in scientific reasoning (e.g., Kuhn, 1989). The specific importance of reflection is its role in consolidating the development of new strategies. Studies show that when students invent new strategies to solve problems, it often takes considerable time and practice before the new strategies "take hold" and begin to replace more primitive, inefficient strategies (e.g., Kuhn & Phelps, 1982; Schauble, 1990; Siegler & Jenkins, 1989). Beyond consolidation of new strategies, reflection presumably plays an important role in encouraging transfer. Awareness and reflection about the advantages and disadvantages of a strategy may be necessary if regulatory skills acquired in one domain of learning are to be transferred to new domains where their use is appropriate. This kind of transfer may depend on the individual accumulating enough practice with and reflection about various kinds of problems so that he or she becomes skilled at accessing and applying the appropriate strategic approaches.

Our previous research suggests that there are two general classes of self-regulatory skills that are important in learning through self-directed experimentation. In the DARN, it is these self-regulatory skills that are depicted as objects of self-reflection. The first class are those involved in maintaining appropriate goal orientation, that is, holding in mind an organized picture of the goals and subgoals that comprise scientific discovery (cf. Klahr & Dunbar, 1988), and for each subgoal executed, performing the active inferencing that updates the relations among the subgoals. The importance of goal orientation is illustrated in a study of students working with Voltaville, our circuit laboratory (Schauble et al., 1991). In this study, the poorer students engaged in exploration that was very local and task oriented; they acted as if their objective was simply to operate the computer laboratory. When asked to explain their plan for each experiment, they typically responded with remarks like, "I'm going to choose the next circuit in the menu," or, "I guess I will go ahead and measure voltage." Thus, they appeared to focus on completing each procedural step in turn, rather than subordinating these procedures to the overall goal of finding laws and regularities. It was necessary to remind them repeatedly that the point of the activity was to try to identify principles and laws. In contrast, the more successful students stated plans that specifically mentioned objectives like finding relations, generalizing relations to new cases, or resolving anomalies in the data, for example, "I want to see if resistance works the same way in the parallel circuit as it did in the series circuit," or, "I want to figure out how the total resistance can be a smaller value than the resistance of one resistor." Our surmise is that the poorer students either did not have a clear picture of the overarching goal structure of experimentation, or they had difficulties maintaining or representing that goal so that it could effectively organize their activity.

In contrast, although the protocols of the better learners also reflected a concern with details and procedures, this was not the sole focus of their talk. In addition, they frequently mentioned purposes and goals that specified how the procedure under discussion was related to a superordinate goal, for example, a goal like discovering the mathematical relation among a subset of variables, or working to see if a principle held true in a novel case. Therefore, the first instructional objective suggested by our studies was to find a way of assisting students in developing and then maintaining a representation of the task that emphasizes its structure as a goal hierarchy.

The second class of self-regulatory activities, somewhat more frequently studied, are those involved in monitoring and evaluating one's strategies for designing experiments and interpreting data. For example, our poorer students appeared to generate a great deal of information without pausing to reflect about what the data might mean. As a consequence, their search was primarily data-driven rather than hypothesis-driven, although hypothesis-driven search is generally more fruitful (Glaser et al., in press; Shute et al., 1989). Perhaps as a consequence of holding no firm hypothesis, there was often no relation between the plan they claimed to be pursuing and the experimentation that they actually engaged in with respect to that plan. That is, what they said they were going to do was not consistent with what they actually did. Students working in Smithtown are required explicitly to state a plan for each new experiment. The ineffective students often stated a plan like, "I want to explore the relation between price and quantity demanded," and yet went on to design an experiment in which the number of suppliers was varied, but price was not. Not only did the poorer students generate experiments that were irrelevant to the current plan; they also switched plans much more frequently than the good students, jumping from plan to plan but then quickly abandoning their plans without carrying them through to a satisfactory conclusion. In contrast, the better students searched more systematically and more extensively. Their search was both broader, that is, they changed a greater proportion of the variables that could be manipulated, and also deeper, that is, they explored more values of each varied variable (Schauble et al., 1991). In contrast to the poorer students, they also appeared to understand that not all search is equally informative. For example, these more successful students were more likely to use heuristics for generating informative and valid experiments, like the control of variables strategy in which one variable at a time is varied while all others are held constant (Glaser et al., in press; Shute et al., 1989).

Our general objective, then, was to encourage students to engage more frequently and more effectively in these two kinds of self-regulatory activities. To date we have developed two experimental approaches to supporting self-regulation, both implemented interactively within the computer laboratory environment. The first approach, described in a companion paper to this one (Raghavan, Schultz, Glaser, & Schauble, 1989), involves on-line computer-based coaches that monitor student activities empirically found to be associated with effective learning. The coaches intervene with advice and coaching when a student strays sufficiently from a student model representing a "good enough" student. However, in this chapter, we focus on the second instructional approach—an interactive, computer-generated trace notation that encourages reflection by providing an on-line graphical depiction of student experimentation activity. In contrast to the computer-based coaches, the purpose of the trace is to provide students with enough support so that they will effectively become able to coach themselves, that is, to evaluate their own progress and make repairs when needed. Making students aware of their experimentation strategies and encouraging self reflection may help students improve their performance within a given experimentation task. Although it is not our direct focus in this chapter, practice in these self-evaluative activities may also encourage the generalization of strategies across domains and contexts, when it is appropriate.

COMPUTER-SUPPORTED STUDENT-INSPECTABLE TRACES

The purpose of the notation, which we call the Discovery and Reflection Notation (DARN), is to focus students' critical and reflective attention on their own behavior. In the context of computer-assisted tutors to teach algebra and geometry, Brown (Collins & Brown, 1987) and Anderson, Boyle, and Yost (1985) attempted to achieve similar objectives by including student-inspectable tree diagrams of solution paths in their intelligent tutors. The purpose of the graphs was to permit students to review their progress through the solution space. These diagrams were effective for displaying search in well-structured problems, like those in algebra and geometry. However, the challenge we faced with the computer-based laboratories was how to effectively display student activity in the complex and ill-structured problem of scientific discovery. In particular, it seemed vital to summarize and clarify the complexity for the student rather than simply mirroring it, as tree diagrams do. In trying to achieve this objective, we were influenced by Clancey's (1987) insight that it is possible to portray complex reasoning as a collection of conceptual perspectives on a stream of activity. The notion of inspecting one's problem-solving behavior from multiple perspectives seemed particular compelling, given our findings that students develop different kinds of difficulties when working in a self-directed experimentation context like Smithtown.

THE DISCOVERY AND REFLECTION NOTATION

These considerations informed the design of The Discovery and Reflection Notation (DARN), a trace generated online by the computer laboratory from its moment-to-moment records of student activity in various categories. When a student pauses in the flow of experimentation and opens the DARN menu, the current student records are parsed by the computer and displayed in three alternative views, or graphical organizations. Each of the views includes a common set of elements representing the classes of actions that can be taken within the laboratory. The way these elements are organized and patterned differs in the three views. However, before describing the organizations, we first describe the elements and the actions that they depict.

Elements and Actions

Views consist of windows containing elements that are represented as expandable buttons organized into structural patterns, one kind of pattern for each view. There are two hierarchical classes of elements. At the top level, elements are depicted as numbered observations. These observations are represented as expandable buttons, as shown in Fig. 11.2. In Fig. 11.2, the user has opened the Plan View of the DARN by selecting a menu at the top of the Smithtown screen, and has "expanded" the button for Observation 1, making it possible to review the experimentation activities that comprised this observation. The notation thus summarizes and graphically displays the sequence of experimentation activities that the student has performed within a selected observation cycle. There are five kinds of actions that can conceivably occur within an observation, and each is represented by a different kind of button: plans, variable changes, predictions, tools, and hypotheses. The action buttons can be expanded in turn, revealing more specific information about the kind of action taken. These five kinds of actions are discussed next.

Actions, therefore, are the component parts of observations. Observations, in turn, can be depicted in three overall organizations, or "views." These are called the *Student View*, the *Plan View*, and the *Expert View*. Each view arranges the windows and elements in a pattern which comprises a particular spatial array of elements and connecting lines of various kinds and colors. The patterns illustrate key issues with respect to the structure of students' experimentation activity,

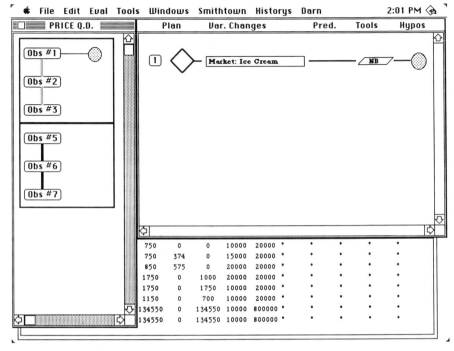

FIG. 11.2.   The Plan View.

issues identified in our studies as being particularly problematical for students. At any point during on-line work with the computer laboratory, a student may request any of the three views by selecting from a DARN window at the top of the screen.

Student View.   The purpose of The Student View is to assist the student in evaluating and reflecting upon the pattern of the experiments he or she has been generating, and to check for systematicity in changing variables, making predictions, and recording data. The Student View is a minimally edited chronological trace of the student's actions with the computer laboratory. Because it simply summarizes what the student has done in time, it is presumably the view that most closely matches the user's own initial representation of his or her search path. The Student View parses and organizes the student actions into graphical observations that include the following optional components: plans, variable changes, predictions, tool use, and hypotheses. Thus, a student can scan down the Student View and acquire an immediate impression of important factors like how frequently the plan has been changed, how many variables are being changed at a time, regularity of predictions and tool use, and the successful conclusion of the search for a principle or law.

The Student View is a large window that arrays observations in rows and columns, as displayed in Fig. 11.3. Each element in an observation can be selected and expanded to display specific information about student actions. For example, it would be possible to expand the Plan button in observation 1 to display the plan that the student formulated with respect to the first observation. Plan buttons indicate those cases where the student changes his or her plan by stating a new one to the computer. As mentioned earlier, students sometimes fail to persist with a plan until they come to a satisfactory conclusion. For example, a glimpse down the trace shows that the student has switched plans at observation 4, in spite of the fact that no conclusion has been drawn about the plan stated at observation 1.

In the next column of the Student View are Variable Change buttons, which summarize for the student all the changes made to the manipulable variables in the program simulation. A scan down this column indicates whether or not the

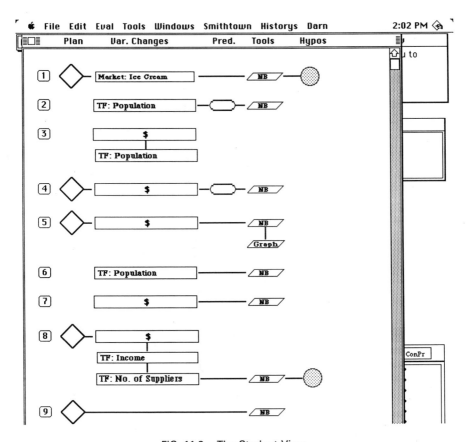

FIG. 11.3.   The Student View.

student has been using heuristics like the control of variables. In observation 3 of Fig. 11.3, this heuristic has been violated; the student has changed both price and population. Thus, the student will not know whether changes in the dependent variables are due to the manipulation of price, the manipulation of population, or both. Moreover, the Variable Changes column makes a distinction between two important classes of variables, which are referred to as *price* (denoted with a $) and *town factors* (prefixed by TF). These correspond to the distinction in microeconomics between price, which acts as a simple variable, and the determinants of demand and supply, which act as parameters. Noting this distinction is very difficult for students, and therefore, the Student View explicitly marks it.

After designing an experiment in the computer laboratories, it is optional to make a prediction about the expected outcome before observing the actual outcome. Within the Student view, the Prediction button follows an observation only if the student has chosen to make a prediction. Inspection of this trace indicates that the student has frequently opted to skip a prediction (in fact, the only predictions made are in observations 2 and 4). As with the other expandable buttons, a prediction can be reviewed by expanding its button.

The next column is titled "Tools." Referred to are the Discovery Tools included within each computer laboratory to assist students in taking, recording, and managing data. One important tool is the on-line notebook that assists students in recording and organizing numerical data. In Fig. 11.3, the button labeled NB shows that the student has recorded information from most of the observations into the notebook (it is possible to "zoom in on" the information actually recorded by expanding these buttons). However, recording was omitted for observation 3. Other tools include an on-line graphing tool (denoted by the label "Graph") and a table tool ("Table") that permits students to sort data in various ways, an aid in discerning mathematical relations. If the student has used these in the course of an observational cycle, the use is depicted in the DARN under the Tools column.

When a student discovers a law or principle in the computer laboratory, he or she states it and submits it to the computer program as a hypothesis for evaluation. At the point where a student does so, the final column in the Student View, labeled "Hypos," is marked with a small circle. The color of the circle is used to demark the correctness and generality of the hypothesis: yellow (light gray) for hypotheses confirmed only within one market (for example, if the student has generated evidence to show that the law of demand holds in the tea market), green (dark gray) for hypotheses demonstrated to hold over two or more markets, and red (medium gray) for hypotheses that are not confirmed, either because they are incorrect or because a student has not generated sufficient relevant evidence. Inspection of this column can help students identify errors like wild guessing (illustrated by strings of incorrect hypotheses that are not interspersed with additional evidence generation), failure to state any hypotheses at all (extended strings of observations never followed by hypotheses), or failure to test the

generality of a hypothesis (yellow-circled Hypothesis buttons that are not followed by green circles). For example, Fig. 11.3 shows that the student has stated
a hypothesis after just one observation. Expanding a hypothesis button permits
one to review both the hypothesis stated and the feedback that the computer
coach has given in response, and not surprisingly, if the Hypothesis button were
expanded, we would learn that the computer had provided the feedback that there
was insufficient evidence to support the conclusion.

The elements in the Student View can be inspected both horizontally, illustrating the flow of activity within an observation, and vertically within columns,
encouraging comparisons of classes of activities across observations. This ability
to quickly review classes of activities within and between observations provides
several advantages. For example, with a glance, a student can see whether she or
he has been unduly jumping from plan to plan, rather than persisting with a
particular path of investigation for a reasonable period. It is possible to see
whether he or she is systematically changing one variable at a time and then
observing the outcome, or alternatively, changing too many variables in a manner that will not support confidence about which are affecting the system. Similarly, lapses in making predictions or recording data show up as gaps in the
appropriate columns. Finally, a review of the column labeled Hypotheses reveals
problems like wild guessing or failure to bring search to closure by making a
hypothesis.

In sum, then, the Student View permits students to scan their sequence of
activity and to evaluate it for basic issues of systematicity, planfulness, and
persistence of search. It does so by showing how frequently and where in the
sequence each important kind of activity is performed. However, as noted earlier, mastering the complexity of self-directed experimentation requires the ability to consider one's own activity from alternative perspectives. As mentioned, a
problem for many of our poorer students is holding in mind their overall goal
orientation while they carry out the component processes of experimentation.
Therefore, the second perspective available in the DARN is a Plan View, which
depicts student activity with respect to its planfulness.

Plan View.   Our studies suggest that planful experimentation is more likely
to be effective than merely tinkering with the manipulable variables in a data-
driven manner (Shute et al., 1989). The second view within the DARN therefore
focuses on stated plans, and in particular, depicts whether experimentation activity is consistent or inconsistent with the current plan. In the Plan View,
elements are parsed and organized by plan. The Plan View is illustrated in Fig.
11.2. When the Plan View is opened, the computer generates a menu of all plans
stated so far. When a plan is selected from this menu, the computer displays the
observations conducted under that plan. Colored vertical links denote whether
the experiments generated are in fact relevant to the stated plan. Green lines
connect observations consistent with the plan, whereas red dotted lines denote

observations inconsistent with or irrelevant to the plan. As in the Student View, each observation button is expandable, so that if desired, the encapsulated information can be reviewed. Similarly, the convention of colored circles is maintained to depict the hypotheses that students formulate on the basis of their observations. Figure 11.2 shows at a glance that although the student has stated the plan of exploring the relation between price and quantity demanded, the first two observations are not consistent with that plan. Only starting with observation 5 does the student begin a line of inquiry that is relevant to the plan.

The purpose of the Plan View, therefore, is to graphically parse the ongoing flow of activity into units of search spent in the pursuit of a particular idea. The view permits students to review (a) how persistently they search on a given path, and (b) how much of their search is relevant to the stated objective. However, planful activity (as diagnosed by the Plan View) and systematic activity (as diagnosed by the Student View) are necessary but not sufficient conditions for successful discovery. Beyond generating systematic and planful experiments, a student must also discern the relations in the data being generated. The final view, the Expert View, addresses this issue of evidence interpretation.

Expert View. This view organizes the observations that the student has generated with respect to an "expert's" eye view based on an expert model of the domain. The purpose of the Expert View is to encourage the student to spend additional effort interpreting the data that reveal important laws he or she has overlooked. It also depicts the patterns of relations between relevant observations that comprise laws or principles within the laws of microeconomics.

Within the computer laboratory, the expert model parses student actions with respect to the concepts that it "knows," including laws specific to particular markets and laws that apply generally across kinds of markets or all markets. These concepts "known" by the expert model are summarized in Fig. 11.4, the goal history that is available in the general Smithtown program (this History is not part of the DARN). The hierarchical structure of Fig. 11.4 reflects the fact that simpler concepts toward the bottom of the figure are embedded as components in the higher order concepts that appear toward the top. These are the concepts incorporated into The Expert View, which has been selected in Fig. 11.5. The production system in the DARN parser groups together all observations relevant to a particular concept, whether or not the student has noticed it or stated it to the computer with the hypothesis menu. Inspection of the Expert View menu labeled "concepts" in Fig. 11.5 shows that the student has generated observations that are relevant to three concepts or laws that the program's expert model "knows." The student may not have yet discovered these laws, and in fact, until inspecting the Expert View, he or she may be entirely unaware that these relations exist. However, reviewing one's activity and observations through the Expert View may provide the impetus to go back and inspect portions of the data again, and in particular, to work harder to discover relations that have apparently been overlooked. The student can select any of these concepts for

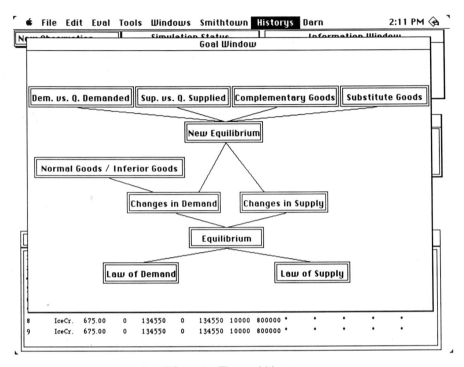

FIG. 11.4.   The goal history.

review. In this case, Law of Demand has been selected. Observations pertinent to this goal are displayed on the left within a color-coded box. The box around these grouped observations indicates that these observations are a set that comprise sufficient and valid evidence for stating the law to the computer expert. In Fig. 11.5, the student sees that there is sufficient evidence for stating the Law of Demand in the ice cream market. Note that the relevant observations are not sequentially contingent. Thus, the student might have overlooked relations among these data points unless encouraged to do so by the depiction in the Expert View. As in the other views, observations are expandable so that the student may, if desired, inspect the actions comprising each observational cycle.

In summary, we have described three views, which extend on a continuum from student-centered to expert-centered. The Student View is a sequential reflection of the student's own activities, portrayed graphically and organized in a manner that encourages the user to note important patterns in these activities. The Plan View is somewhat more evaluative, in that it calls the student to account for the relations between planned activity and the actual course of activity taken. Finally, the Expert View depicts the relevance of the student's observations to the principles and laws that can be discovered. It provides assistance both for the student who has reached an impasse in finding fruitful ways

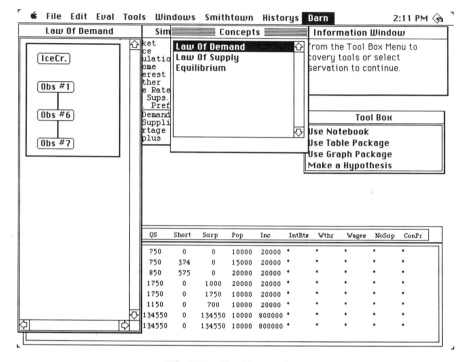

FIG. 11.5.   The Expert View.

of interpreting the evidence generated, and for the student who has not been sufficiently thoughtful about patterns that he or she may have overlooked. A student can use the DARN to evaluate his or her discovery at the close of an experimentation session. In this case, it is probably helpful to use all three views, and to explicitly reflect about the information provided by different perspectives that can be taken on self-directed exploration. However, DARN can also be used on-line during the course of discovery. We are finding in our studies that students spontaneously open the DARN window when they reach an impasse during the course of experimentation. When DARN is used as an on-line diagnostic tool in this way, the view that will be most useful will depend on the kind of difficulty being encountered. In some cases, it is helpful to consult more than one view, a simple matter if a student should decide to do so.

Study of Students' Self-Regulatory Activity

A study is now being run to learn whether the DARN provides the expected support to students working with the computer laboratories. As discussed earlier, DARN was designed with the objective of encouraging students to engage in two kinds of self-regulation. The first kind of self-regulation concerns goal-directed behavior. DARN graphically organizes important classes of student actions into units that correspond to observational cycles. Observations, in turn, are grouped with respect to plans on the one hand, and conclusions, on the other. Thus the organization of the DARN represents student activities with respect to the overall goal of discovering laws and principles. The second kind of self-regulation is to evaluate and critique one's own processes of experimentation with respect to characteristics such as their validity, informativeness, and systematicity. As we have discussed, DARN makes it easy to scan patterns of activity from alternative perspectives and notice characteristic errors: jumping from plan to plan, designing experiments without requisite baselines or the proper controls, forgetting to record pertinent data, making conclusions without sufficient evidence, and the like. The purpose of the study currently being performed is to learn whether in fact DARN encourages increased proportions of these kinds of self-regulatory activities.

The first requirement in the design of the study was to provide a context in which it would be possible to observe self-regulation. To render self-regulation observable, we asked students to work with a partner, making it more likely that self-regulatory activity would be discussed because of the need to negotiate and carry out problem solution with a peer. The task posed to the pairs is to work toward the objective of discovering as many laws or principles in Smithtown as possible within four sessions that vary in duration from 2 hrs (the first) to 1 hr (the second, third, and fourth sessions). All four sessions are typically completed within a 1-week period.

Subjects are ten pairs of undergraduates who have never formally studied economics. Each of the 20 students participates alone with an interviewer on the initial session of the study, which takes approximately 2 hours. During this session, students take a pretest of microeconomics concepts and then are given baseline training on the use of the Smithtown computer laboratory. Training consists of a 45-minute standard demonstration of the laboratory interface and tools. Then, with assistance and prompting as required from the interviewers, students engage in self-directed experimentation until they have discovered one of the three most elementary concepts: either the law of supply, the law of demand, or equilibrium. In general, students have little difficulty discovering these principles, as we know from extensive previous experience with this laboratory. After discovering their practice concept, students receive one of two forms of training in self-evaluation. Those randomly assigned to the DARN treatment group are introduced to the DARN and shown how to use it to think about the experiments that they have just conducted. Those students who are assigned to the control group are shown how to use the Smithtown notebook records, hypothesis history, and goal history to evaluate the experiments they have run during the first session. It is important here to clarify that the Smithtown records provide the opportunity to reconstruct and review a complete record of students' activities. The Smithtown screen is thus functionally equivalent to the

Student View of the DARN. However, on the regular Smithtown screen, student activities appear as changes in numerical data or as textual summaries of predictions and hypotheses; activities are not graphically depicted, parsed into major classes, or organized with respect to observations and hypotheses. Furthermore, the standard Smithtown laboratory screen contains no information analagous to the Plan View or the Expert View. In sum, then, although students in the control group pairs in principle have access to the same information as students in the DARN group, they would have to engage in a great deal of organization and inference with that information to generate the structures immediately available to the pairs working with DARN.

During the second, third, and fourth sessions, students work in pairs. All pairs spend the first 25 min of their second session in a practice evaluation session, the partners' first opportunity to work together to evaluate student discovery activity. Partners are shown the computer screen presumably produced by a hypothetical "different student." They are asked to evaluate the student's experimentation activity, and to fill out a sheet specifying the "good experimental procedures" and "poor experimental procedures" that they can identify in the student's record (of course, the record is not one produced by another student, but a standard one generated especially to portray common experimentation flaws). During the practice period, the DARN treatment groups are encouraged to use the DARN as needed to conduct their evaluation. The control groups use the regular Smithtown record facilities, including the notebook, hypothesis history, and goal history. After the practice evaluation session, the pairs begin their own program of experimentation activity, and they are encouraged to converse with each other and think aloud as they do so. Their assignment is to try to find the remaining ten principles (eight are considerably more difficult than the easiest three). After the fourth and final experimentation session, students individually take a written posttest.

As they conduct their own experiments, pairs are interrupted by a timer on two occasions during each session. At this point, the experimenter starts an "evaluation period." One evaluation period occurs after the first 25 min of the session, and the second is announced by the experimenter 5 min before the end of the session. Evaluation periods last a minimum of 5 mins, but can last for up to 15 mins, at the discretion of the students. During these evaluation periods, pairs are explicitly asked to stop and reflect about their activity to that point. They are told that during the period, they are to think about *how* they have been designing and interpreting their experiments, and to evaluate and decide whether they have been proceeding as effectively and efficiently as possible. They are encouraged to make whatever revisions to their approach that they agree are appropriate. They are asked to agree upon and generate a list of "good experimental procedures" and "poor experimental procedures" that they have been following. As during the training, the experimental groups use the DARN notation as a tool for conducting their evaluation periods. The other pairs, in the control group, use the regular Smithtown computer screen and tools.

There are three kinds of dependent variables in the study. The first is simply the amount of learning achieved, measured by gains from pretest to posttest. Although this is a rather straightforward measure of the products of learning, we expect that the DARN experimental group will learn more.

However, the major focus of the study is on processes of learning, that is, how the pairs learn. There are two classes of measures that relate to learning processes. The first class of measures concerns goal orientation. We address this question by comparing the experimental and control groups on the proportion of utterances that refer to experimentation activities in functional classes such as plans, experiments, predictions, observations, and hypotheses, in contrast to focusing on features of the laboratory itself, either variables such as markets, quantities, and interest rates, on the one hand, or on procedures, such as changing to the tea market, changing price, or adjusting wage rates. The second class of dependent variables focuses on self-evaluation. The primary measure will be the proportion of utterances spent in reviewing experimentation activity, for example, discussing whether a course of experimentation has been fruitful, talking about alternative interpretations of a set of observations, or noting that no conclusion has been reached about the relation among a set of variables. In our pilot data, we have observed that students spontaneously make self-evaluative comments about the sufficiency and validity of their evidence ("We don't have enough evidence. We didn't do more than one experiment.") their plans ("Do you want to do another product on this same price, and then with all of that, maybe we can make some more observations?"), their experimental heuristics ("Ah, $8500. Let's change price by a thousand. And let's just change one thing at a time.") the plausibility of their hypotheses ("I don't know if that makes sense, what I said, or not. Well, we will try it."), and their overall progress ("So, we are getting somewhere, then."). Analysis of the data set from the study, when it is completed, will reveal whether or not increased proportions of these comments occur from those students working with the DARN, and whether self-evaluation of this kind contributes to increased learning.

Conclusion

In this chapter we have described research on computer-based laboratories, in particular, focusing on the self-regulatory activities that differentiate successful from unsuccessful learners in these contexts of self-directed experimentation. Based on this work, we have designed a Discovery and Reflection Notation that graphically depicts students' experimentation activity with respect to three different perspectives. The purpose of the notation is to serve as a tool for encouraging students' reflection about and evaluation of their processes of learning.

In this program of research, then, computer laboratories serve as tools in multiple senses. First, the simulations in the laboratories serve both to present the discovery context that students work on, and to record data on student activity for research purposes. Thus, the computer labs serve as the instrumentation of the research. In addition to serving as research tools, the laboratories also incorporate a set of tools to scaffold students' problem solving. Each laboratory has a set of "discovery tools" that students can use for taking measurements, formulating hypotheses, and recording and manipulating data. Moreover, computer-based coaches within each laboratory evaluate student activity and provide feedback and coaching on the student's current understanding of the content domain, as well as effective ways of proceeding to learn more. Finally, as described in this chapter, the computer parses student activity with the laboratories and displays it in the Discovery and Reflection Notation, to facilitate students in reflecting on and evaluating their processes of experimentation.

We have been interested in these tools primarily as a means for studying and supporting students as they learn domain knowledge in the physical and social sciences. However, the tools themselves raise particular issues pertinent to the study of learning and individual differences. With the increasing sophistication and availability of computer-supported cognitive tools, differences in student learning will increasingly be a function of differences in students' effective use of available resources for learning, including tools like these.

ACKNOWLEDGMENTS

Preparation of this article was sponsored in part by the Center for the Study of Learning (CSL) at the Learning Research and Development Center of the University of Pittsburgh. CLS is funded by the Office of Educational Research and Improvement of the U.S. Department of Education. Additional contributors to developing the DARN were Jamie Schultz, Colleen Zeitz, and Clark Quinn.

REFERENCES

Anderson, J. R., Boyle, C. F., & Yost, G. (1985). The geometry tutor. *Proceedings of the International Joint Conference On Artificial Intelligence* (pp. 1–5), Los Angeles, CA.

Clancey, W. J. (1987). Knowledge-Based Tutoring: The GUIDON Program. Cambridge, MA: The MIT Press.

Collins, A., & Brown, J. S. (1987). The computer as a tool for learning through reflection. In H. Mandl & A. M. Lesgold (Eds.), *Learning Issues for Intelligent Tutoring Systems*. New York: Springer-Verlag.

Dewey, J. (1933). *How we think: A restatement of the relation of reflective thinking to the educative processes*. Lexington, MA: D. C. Heath.

Glaser, R., Schauble, L., Raghavan, K., & Zeitz, C. (in press). Scientific reasoning across different domains. In E. DeCorte, M. Linn, & H. Mandl, (Eds.), *Computer-based learning environments and problem solving*. New York: Springer-Verlag.

Klahr, D., & Dunbar, K. (1988). Dual search space during scientific reasoning. *Cognitive Science, 12*(1), 1–48.

Kuhn, D. (1989). Children and adults as intuitive scientists. *Psychological Review, 96*(4), 674–689.

Kuhn, D., & Phelps, E. (1982). The development of problem solving strategies. In H. Reese (Ed.), *Advances in child development and behavior* (Vol. 17, pp. 1–44). San Diego: Academic Press.

Raghavan, K., Schultz, J., Glaser, R., & Schauble, L. (1989). *A computer coach for inquiry skills* (LRDC Tech. Rep.) Pittsburgh, PA: University of Pittsburgh.

Schauble, L. (1990). Belief revision in children: The role of prior knowledge and strategies for generating evidence. *Journal of Experimental Child Psychology, 49*, 31–57.

Schauble, L., Glaser, R., Raghavan, K., & Reiner, M. (1991). Causal models and experimentation strategies in scientific reasoning. *Journal of the Learning Sciences, 1*(2), 201–238.

Shute, V. J., Glaser, R., & Raghavan, K. (1989). Inference and discovery in an exploratory laboratory. In P. L. Ackerman, R. J. Sternberg, & R. Glaser (Eds.), *Learning and individual differences*. New York: W. H. Freeman.

Siegler, R. S., & Jenkins, E. (1989). *How children discover new strategies*. Hillsdale, NJ: Lawrence Erlbaum Associates.

IV DISCUSSANTS

12 Gazing Once More Into the Silicon Chip: Who's Revolutionary Now?

Susan F. Chipman
Office of Naval Research

In the early 1980s, I gazed into the silicon chip (Chipman & Butler, 1983, 1985), seeking to give a U.S. perspective on the way that microcomputers would affect the future of education. Now that we have stepped nearly a decade into that future, it is time to reflect and to gaze into the future once again. At that time, some believed that the availability of computerized instruction would result in the withering away of schools as we have known them. Others believed that the computers which were being so enthusiastically purchased would end up locked in closets and that schools would go on as before. They believed that schools would be as little changed by computers as they have been by prior waves of educational technology (Needle, 1982). Still others saw in computers an opportunity for revitalization, an impetus to change, and a potential solution to the problems of limited individual attention, limited productivity, and shortages of technically qualified teachers that beset education (Melmed, 1984). Each of these alternative futures had not only its believers but also its active promoters. For each person who saw in technology the promise of making outstanding instruction available everywhere—in the home, in the remote rural location, in the urban classroom, there seemed to be another who considered technology as an unwelcome distraction of attention and financial resources that would be better spent attaining the traditional goals of a liberal education (Boyer, 1983).

Today it seems that the preceding paragraph could be converted right back into the present tense without serious loss of accuracy: For example, a recent report touts computer technology as a tool for bringing about radical restructuring of the schools (Sheingold & Tucker, 1990), while another (Alexander, 1991) considers technology irrelevant and unnecessary for educational reform. Except that we now know that radical change certainly did not happen quickly. Gazing

341

into the silicon chip once more, what basis do we have for deciding which alternative future will come to pass? If we decide that computer technology probably will have major effects on education, how can we predict the detailed form of that impact? There seem to be at least two major aspects to the potential impact of technology upon education. One aspect is *external.* Computer technology is changing the social environment that surrounds schooling; it is changing the nature of the work for which students are preparing in the schools. Some change in schooling can be expected, and is already occurring, as an echo of this change in the larger society. The other aspect of change is *internal:* As computers become available, or potentially available, for schooling, they may be applied to perform a wide variety of functions. Depending upon what those functions may be, there is a possibility of very profound change. The greatest uncertainty in predicting the impact of new technology lies in the difficulty of predicting the functions, especially the completely novel functions, to which it is applied (Nickerson, 1982).

The chapters of this volume represent progress reports on our investments in the development of more or less novel functions for computers in education. Examining them carefully should provide a good basis for a revised view of the likely future. First, however, let's consider the impact of the external context surrounding education.

EXTERNAL INFLUENCES

Nearly as soon as the digital electronic computer was invented, there was interest in applying computers to education. At that time, computers were exotic and expensive research devices, and little came of the efforts to apply computers in education (although some of the actual programs we can see in educational use today date from that era). By 1980, the role of computers in the larger society had changed. Computers were becoming pervasive in the workplace, and it was evident that there were and would continue to be many attractive job opportunities in computer-related work. This created a much more favorable climate for introducing computers into schools—widespread demand that they be introduced. Themselves experiencing the impact of computers in the workplace, middle class and professional parents wanted to make computer-related job opportunities available to their children through appropriate education and certainly wished that their children be prepared to meet emerging expectancies for at least minimal computer literacy. Those concerned for the welfare of less advantaged children did not wish to see them left behind either, despite those who raised doubts about the educational implications of the new technology (Levin & Romberg, 1983). A survey of teachers by the National Education Association showed that teachers also had very favorable attitudes toward the introduction of computers into the schools (Norman, 1983).

Television and print advertising campaigns by computer companies reinforced the idea that familiarity with computers is vital to one's child's future. It was not uncommon for PTA's to raise money to provide computers for their schools. The general climate of opinion was well-represented by the United States National Commission on Excellence in Education (1983), which recommended that a semester of computer science become part of the core curriculum required of all secondary students. An Advanced Placement course in computer science was codified by the College Entrance Examination Board. Local school systems moved to integrate computers and computer applications throughout the curriculum (Wierzbicki, 1983), and the states began to mandate educational computing courses (Barbour, 1984). Laws were proposed to reward with tax benefits computer companies that donate computers to schools (Mace, 1983a, 1983b). Some colleges began to mandate that every student have a computer (Wierzbicki, 1984). The initial wave of excitement over computers has passed, but providing computers for the schools is still popular. For example, grocery stores in many areas of the United States have conducted regular promotions in the last few years in which vast quantities of grocery store receipts can be collected by schools and turned in for computer equipment.

However, the real significance of this phenomenon is unclear. Even though computers of reasonable power are becoming rather cheap by the standards of the workplace, they and their software remain expensive by the standards of financially impoverished schools. My recent experience with the "community advisory committee" concerned with computers for the Arlington County, Virginia public schools is instructive, especially when one considers that Arlington is one of the most affluent communities in the country. It took 2 or 3 years to achieve the top priority goal of purchasing one classroom's supply of Macintosh computers for one (not each) of the 3 high schools in order to make it possible to teach the AP Computer Science with a Pascal compiler of reasonable speed. Merely replacing the antique and failing computers used to teach computer literacy classes and the like was an equally prolonged and gradual process. Obviously, the ratio of computers to students remains low. It seems likely that most school systems will manage to provide the computers necessary to provide computer literacy and simple programming instruction. Very low cost computers are adequate for that purpose. Educational computing applications in which one or a few computers per classroom can be used meaningfully are also likely to be practical. In contrast, sophisticated applications of computers, including sophisticated instructional applications such as those discussed in many of the chapters of this volume, tend to demand much more expensive machines. These may not be available to schools in significant numbers. This reality is beginning to be reflected in the opinions of some of the authors of these chapters, those the editors have labeled "iconoclasts."

The prevalence of computers in the larger society is bringing about redefinitions of traditional skills that have consequences for the curriculum. Obviously it is word-processing, rather than simple typing, that has become the useful vocational skill, and the schools are attempting to provide appropriate experience. (At the same time, "keyboarding" has become a computer literacy skill now seen as appropriate for every student, making some degree of typing skill attractive to many who would not have acquired it before.) Computer database search skills seem to be the obvious successor to more traditional instruction in the use of book indices and library card catalogs (which are, of course, vanishing as libraries become computerized). At least in the State of Florida, there are serious plans to provide student access to large computerized information sources, greatly expanding the potential scope of student research projects. There is serious discussion of more profound changes in the college-preparatory curriculum to reflect the impact of computer technology. In particular, it has been proposed that the standard first year college mathematics course should be changed from calculus to such topics as linear algebra, which provide the foundation for computerized computations (Conference Board of the Mathematical Sciences, 1983). Because the secondary school curriculum is designed to prepare for the first year of college, such a change would have consequences for the earlier years as well. At all age levels, there is a concern for increased emphasis on learning what computations need to be performed and on skill in approximating answers—the skills that are emphasized by the ready availability of electronic aids to perform the computations themselves. Many of these changes in the curriculum will be occurring without conscious awareness that they are attributable to computer technology: "Common sense" feelings about what should be in the curriculum will be shifting as computer technology pervades the environment surrounding the schools. Such changes will be slow and conservative, with good reason. Because the older generations who use sophisticated computer tools for mathematics were educated originally to do those computations manually, we do not know whether one can learn to effectively use the computer tools without mastering the computations first, nor do we have good ideas about how to teach direct use of the tools. It could be that comprehension of what sophisticated tools are doing requires prior personal experience with the detailed execution of those manipulations.

Already in the early '80s, the potential implications of computers for the mathematics curriculum and the related issues and concerns were quite evident. Worry that the use of calculators in schools might "rot the mind" emerged very early and led to numerous research studies on the subject. Now, it is interesting to see in the chapters of this volume how the concept of using computational power to carry out low-level aspects of tasks so that students can focus on developing higher level aspects and meta-cognitive skills has been generalized widely beyond mathematics. The difference is that the tools to execute the lower-level aspects of other tasks such as scientific reasoning may not yet exist outside the toy worlds provided by the experimental educational programs.

Noneducational software developments are a major influence on the educational applications, and this is true not merely because of associated changes in the working world for which students must prepare. The very large investments associated with widespread, popular workplace applications of computers ultimately result in good, sophisticated user-friendly programs. Consequently, these applications, or slight modifications of them, will be the ones most readily available to schools.

Word processing has been an excellent example of this phenomenon. An enormous commercial investment went into the development of useful word-processing facilities. The background provided by that investment made it possible to develop good word processing programs for microcomputers quite rapidly. Although such word processing programs are somewhat complex for instructional use with young children, subsequent modification into a useful educational too, the *Bank Street Writer* (Kurland, 1983a, 1983b), for example, was quite rapid and relatively inexpensive. Word processing is an attractive personal computer function for almost everyone. It rapidly emerged as the dominant use of personal computers (*Consumer Reports, 1983*). For young children especially, word processing offers the possibility of circumventing the very fine motor control demands of the physical writing process, a major barrier to both initial composition and later revision. More sophisticated extensions of word processing facilities that have also been successful as commercial products— spelling and grammatical checkers—are certainly attractive to teachers of writing as tools that can help to reduce the burden of paper correction. Although aids to the higher level aspects of writing—outlining and brainstorming programs— have been produced, none seems to have enjoyed a great level of success and popularity. This may be a point to consider in thinking about Salomon's chapter in this volume, describing a tool to guide the writing processes of young students.

Database programs, equation solvers, and graphic generators are other examples of sophisticated software tools that have been developed for the commercial market but may be adaptable to various educational uses. Already in the early '80s, exploration of the potential educational applications of such tools was an emerging trend (Barbour, 1984). It is interesting that the present volume highlights a variation of this view: *computers as cognitive tools*.

The point of variation is an important one because now in this volume we are talking about computational cognitive tools that have been specially created for educational use. Although there have been many benefits to the sophisticated tools that have been borrowed for educational use, there is also a dark side to that impact on education, a possible gloomy message and a somewhat arbitrary bias affecting what has happened. The long and expensive evolution of commercial tool software for the workplace—computer programs that can be used over and over again, day after day, by a very large number of users—does seem to carry a negative message about the prospects for the development of software for specifically instructional purposes. Presumably each student user would use a given lesson only once, not over and over again, and the total population of potential courseware users is both smaller and less rich in financial resources than the population of tool users. Specifically educational software tools lie somewhere in between these two extremes. It is likely, for economic reasons, that the quality of specifically educational software will be significantly inferior to the quality of generic computer tools. In the early '80s, this reality had a rapid impact on the uses to which school put the computers they were purchasing. The limitations of the computers and of the instructional software available for them tended to shift usage away from intended uses in subject-matter instruction and towards computer literacy instruction and instruction in the use of computer-based tools (Barbour, 1984; Center for the Social Organization of Schools, 1983a, 1983b; Sherman, 1983; Wright, 1982; Wujcik, 1984). Today, we need to consider whether it is possible for educational applications to take a lead role in defining and developing new computer-based cognitive tools.

INTERNAL CHANGES

The nature of the internal changes to schooling that computers will create depends greatly upon the uses to which they are put. What is the range of possible or likely uses? Where do the uses proposed by the authors of the chapters in this volume fit in the larger context of possible or likely uses? And what will be the consequences for the nature of schooling if those possible uses become prominent? Let us consider each of several major uses and their potential impact: (1) computers as a new subject of instruction, (2) computers as instructional devices, (3) computers as tools naturally integrated into such activities as writing or science laboratories, and (4) computers as tools in support of the teacher's teaching activities.

Computers as a New Subject of Instruction

For several reasons, many believed that the introduction of computers into the schools would, in and of itself, bring about significant change. There was a transitory period in which one heard speculation about radical changes to student and teacher roles because it often seemed that some of the students knew more about computers than did the teachers, so that teachers might have to defer to their students' expertise. One does not hear such speculations so often today. It did not take long for specialist teachers teaching computer-related subjects to emerge. By now, some of those early expert children have had time to become teachers themselves. Besides, the fabled phenomenon of the child computer whiz proved to be rare. A project at Bank Street in New York City, long a favorable environment for the emergence of child prodigies of all kinds, failed to find any truly expert children (Kurland, Mawbry, & Cahir, 1984). Studies of computer learning showed that many students learn as distressingly little about programming as they do about other subjects (Linn, 1985; Mayer, 1982; Pea, 1983, 1987; Pea & Kurland, 1984, 1987; Pea, Kurland, & Hawkins, 1987; Soloway, Ehrlich, Bonar, & Greenspan, 1982).

Still, whether because it is a useful way to accommodate to expert children or simply because computers were scarce, computers became known for promoting independent group work in an "activity center" while the teacher might provide instruction to another group of students. An early study showed that many teachers liked the fact that computers seemed to be conducive to cooperative group problem-solving and learning; many seemed to be more interested in this social effect than they were in computing itself (Sheingold, 1981). This same attitude seems to be reflected in Behrend and Roschelle's contribution to the present volume, with its focus on the process of interaction between two students interacting with a computer system. One assumes that the computer system is intended to teach something about Newtonian physics, but an odd game is being played. It seems that the students were not really told what the game is about, what is being represented in the graphics with which they are engaged. They may know, since we are told that one of the students has done considerable reading about physics. But it does not seem that the focus of this project is really on the learning of physics.

However, group learning activities should not be regarded as an inevitable consequence of the educational use of computers, even though continuing scarcity is likely to exert a force in that direction. The use of such group instructional strategies is a cultural matter. Group work is a fairly common instructional strategy, but attitudes vary considerably on this point. If one highly values individual performance, as many in this country do, then the orderly classroom scene of each student working separately is preferred. Some would certainly like to see each student equipped with a computer: Apple has so equipped some experimental classrooms, going so far as to equip each student with an additional home computer as well. Perhaps this vision is financially unrealistic. Alternatively, one can imagine that one computer could be used in instructing an entire class as a single group, in a rather traditional way. In brief, one should not expect a massive impact of computers on the social structure of schooling. Computer instruction will be modified to suit the demands of the school and classroom culture into which it is being introduced. At most, it may serve as a catalyst for change in unstable situations, where many already want to make a change in the style of instruction.

In the early 1980s, there was great interest in programming as a subject of instruction, and many had high expectations for widespread cognitive benefits of programming experience (Nickerson, 1983; Papert, 1980, 1987). If the chapters of this volume are indicative, that enthusiasm has faded. One problem was that there had been little time to evolve effective ways of teaching programming (Mayer, 1982). It turned out that many students—and many of their teachers—

did not master key concepts of programming such as recursion that were thought to be potentially important for general cognition (Anderson, Farrell, & Sauers, 1984; Bayman & Mayer, 1983; Kurland, Clement, Mawbry, & Pea, 1987; Kurland & Pea, 1985; Linn, 1985; Pirolli & Anderson, 1985; Pea, 1983, 1987). It began to seem that instruction must systematically identify and develop key ideas. And that students may need help in making the connections between representations of reality on the computer screen and reality itself. These issues remain open and lively. How clear is it that students would make any connection between the world of Behrend and Roschelle's computer screen and physical reality? Does the game of adjusting two vectors so as to be able to match a curve to a previously shown curve in any way penetrate to and merge with the student's intuitive understanding of the motion of real objects in the real world? We do not yet know. The contention between the believers in guided instruction and the believers in the value of free exploration continues in this volume: For example, the original drafts of chapters in this volume made several inaccurate claims that "traditional" intelligent tutoring systems rigidly force students to follow a *single* correct solution path. In fact, much of the artificial intelligence has gone into making it possible for such tutoring systems to accommodate a number of correct solution paths. Although they are not represented in this volume, it is probably worth noting that quite a few of the artificially intelligent tutoring systems that have been built teach programming languages, where one does not find single correct solutions. The broad claims for the cognitive value of learning programming seem to have faded. But perhaps we can see their echoes in the high hopes that many of the authors of the chapters in this volume have that computers will help students to make explicit and to reflect upon their own thought processes, that computers will help to develop metacognitive skills. To the extent that the computer does make thought processes explicit, students' thinking about their own thinking likely will be captured by the computer metaphor, as scientific cognitive psychology has been. This may provide a foundation for educating students to be more cognitively effective, but it will also require some education in the limits of the metaphor.

Computers as Instructional Devices

This is a complex topic because it has so many different aspects. Most of the chapters in this volume are concerned with one or another use of a computer as an instructional device. These applications should be viewed against a continuum of possibilities that can be ordered roughly according to the complexity of the programming effort required to produce them.

Drill and Practice.   This was the first major instructional use of computers, and it may well remain the dominant use. Computers are widely used for remedial drill and practice, despite considerable criticism of this use. One important reason for the early dominance is the fact that the programming of such activities is relatively easy and undemanding of creativity. The first application of any technology is likely to be to perform functions that one was already performing in other ways. It may be that teachers find computerized drill and practice an attractive aid in their work, relieving them of some dreary and demanding efforts such as the checking of papers, the maintaining and verifying of many students' attention during practice sessions, etc.

For students who seem to need extra practice, or special practice, the computer alternative may be particularly attractive and cost effective. Some have assumed that computers are intrinsically motivating, even in drill and practice applications, but it was soon appreciated that there may be important individual differences in reactions to computers and variations in the motivational value of different forms of interaction with computers (Malone, 1980, 1981). It is not obvious that interaction with a computer will be as motivationally effective as the concern and attention of a human teacher. Most experimental evaluations of computer instruction profit from the novelty of the computer and the brevity of interactions with it. To consider one extreme, it is very clear that adults who spend long hours at repetitive tasks do not enjoy the experience; children are no more likely to do so. Despite the rather early attention noted before, research on the motivational aspects of computer instruction has not been extensive. In this volume, Lepper, Woolverton, Mumme and Gurtner, one of the few groups to focus on such issues, discuss the subtle motivational dimensions of human tutorial interactions. It remains unclear whether it will be possible to emulate such interactions with a computer, or whether it will be meaningful to do so, given that students do respond differently to the knowledge that they are dealing with a computer (Fox, 1989).

Traditional Computer-Assisted Instruction. This category corresponds to somewhat more advanced instructional programming than is required for drill and practice and includes the much-maligned electronic page turner. Such software presents concepts and content in a relatively straightforward manner. The computer offers management of the student's study efforts through pacing and interspersed questions. In the more sophisticated variants, the computer may respond differentially to student responses with preprogrammed responses of its own. This mode ranges from mere computerization of a book to more substantial investment in the empirical investigation of probable student responses and appropriate instructional responses to them. We know that this can be an effective way to present instruction, but it is no more effective than traditional instruction (Orlansky & String, 1979). Except in situations where it is important to be able to provide instruction or training to small numbers of individuals at arbitrary times, it is not obvious that the production of such instruction is worthwhile. Prolonged, isolated interaction with a computer is likely to be less attractive than the more social atmosphere of the classroom. And young children require supervision from someone to ensure their safety. If only for this reason, the notion that computerized instruction of this kind could lead to greatly enhanced educational productivity and/or the withering away of traditional schools and classrooms is unrealistic, especially in a society in which it is normal for parents to leave the home for work.

Simulations. From the outset, simulations became a popular form of educational software, and they remain prominent in the projects discussed in this volume. As Lajoie points out, they make environments safe and accessible to students that would otherwise be inaccessible. They make it possible to experience an approximation of phenomena that otherwise might merely be talked about. They represent a unique contribution of computers to the educational process, or at least a contribution that would be difficult to duplicate by other means. They open up new possibilities in teaching, and a great deal of creativity has gone into the creation of simulations. Often simulations are a central component of more elaborate and sophisticated instructional systems that are discussed next.

To be effective, simulations must be integrated with a larger curricular context, whether it is also computerized or realized by the teacher in the classroom. Sheingold, Kane, and Endreweit (1983) found that successful curricular integration was rare: Often simulation software was simply played with in the guise of "computer literacy." Unless someone makes a major investment in revising standard texts to include and refer to such adjunct facilities, it is unlikely that they will be widely used. Most teachers (admittedly not the outstanding few) need supporting suggestions from teacher manuals that point out the existence of these additional facilities and describe how to use them effectively. Even with such revisions, the logistical problems of bringing in equipment, having the right software available at the right time, and so on, can present formidable barriers to use. It seems likely that the computer would have to be a permanent feature of the classroom to make such uses likely and frequent. Additional capabilities such as the possibility for a teacher to key in the topic of a planned lesson, to ascertain that there is available software relevant to that topic, and to have instant access to the software, would seem to be necessary in order to support these applications. Stronger evidence of educational value than we now have is likely to be required to convince anyone to make these investments. Consequently, it seems most likely that such applications will be effectively realized in specialized courses in mathematics or science, where a sufficient density of computer applications may be developed to make the use of the computer a regular part of the classroom routine and to justify the constant presence of computer facilities.

It is striking that still, today, so few of the projects in this volume attend to the larger curricular and school context in which their products might be used. Will they fit in? One of the few mentions of this larger context is Salomon's effort to explain away the fact that the writing aid that seemed to be effective in Israel was not effective in a similar experiment in the United States—this difference must have had something to do with the context of use.

Intelligent Computer-Assisted Instruction

In the early '80s, the brightest promise of computers in education seemed to be offered by programs that employ artificial intelligence techniques (Anderson, Boyle, & Reiser, 1985; Sleeman & Brown, 1982). The earliest artificially intelligent tutoring systems with the possibility of practical educational use were then being developed (Anderson, 1984), notably the LISP Tutor (Anderson & Reiser, 1985), which began to be used in courses at Carnegie-Mellon University, and the Geometry Tutor (Anderson, Boyle, & Yost, 1985) that was soon to see a practical trial in a Pittsburgh high school (Schofield, Evans-Rhodes, & Huber, 1990). Today, quite a number of such experimental tutors have been built or are under development. The attraction of such systems has been the prospect of providing each student with individualized tutorial interaction, approximating what an individual human tutor might provide. In addition to academic tutors of mathematics and programming and scientific reasoning, tutors of maintenance diagnosis skills—a practical application of interest to military research sponsors—have received considerable development effort (Behavioral Technology Laboratories, 1988; Gott, 1989; Town, 1987). The most thorough and careful evaluation of an artificially intelligent tutor yet done was the evaluation of one of these maintenance tutors, the SHERLOCK tutor described in the chapter by Katz and Lesgold. The tutor was found to be impressively effective (Nichols, Pokorny, Jones, Gott, & Alley, in press). The Air Force is currently planning to build an entire family of such maintenance tutors at considerable expense. It seems that the promise of intelligent tutoring systems may be coming to fruition. However, with the exception of the programming tutors that Anderson uses in courses for which he personally has instructional responsibility at Carnegie-Mellon University, intelligent tutors remain research and development experiments and demonstrations; none is in widespread use for instruction or training.

In this volume, we have several examples of such projects, a second generation geometry tutor described in the chapter by Koedinger and Anderson and a tutor of algebra word problem-solving described in the chapter by Derry, as well as the Sherlock maintenance tutor described in two of the chapters. At a recent meeting of the grantees of an NSF Science Education program concerned with applications of advanced technology to Science Education, a number of grantees were heard to say that they were "doing a standard Anderson-style tutor" to teach some aspect or other of their scientific subject (cf. Anderson, Boyle, & Reiser, 1985). Even a textbook of sorts (Wenger, 1987) has been written that provides a description of what is expected in an intelligent tutoring system and describes most of the projects that contributed to our present capability to produce intelligent tutoring systems. Thus has the *icon* of the editors' introduction been created, provoking a swarm of *iconoclasts*. But at the same meeting of NSF grantees, Anderson himself finally stood up and began his presentation by saying, "I guess I'm trying to figure out what a standard Anderson-style tutor is." The counter-revolution seems a bit premature.

What do the chapters of this volume, mostly reports of work in progress with their denouements yet to come, tell us about the gradually coalescing form that is the *icon* of intelligent tutoring systems?

In its complete form, an artificially intelligent tutoring system is a very complex program incorporating many of the features of less complex forms of instructional computing. At its core, there is likely to be a simulation if the tutor is teaching about the operation of some dynamic system—be it the economy or the circulatory system or Newtonian physics or the operation of a ship steam power plant. Typically, a tutor incorporates an expert system so that it has the capability to solve problems in the domain of the tutor in a flexible variety of ways, to match the many correct solutions that a student might have. Like a human tutor, an artificial tutor must know the subject matter. A tutor must have pedagogical knowledge and strategies to guide interaction with the tutee. A central concept of the intelligent tutoring approach is that instructional interaction should be sensitively adapted to the needs of the individual student, determined by detailed estimates of the state of student knowledge at the moment of the instructional interaction. This last feature, modeling the student's state of knowledge, is probably the most challenging task that faces the builder of an intelligent tutoring system: not so long ago, this aspect alone constituted a major AI project (Brown & Burton, 1978; Johnson & Soloway, 1985). And it is likely to require the greatest on-line computational power. These facts have made student modeling a target of the *iconoclasts* who question its value.

The chapter by Koedinger and Anderson reports on a second try at the building of a tutor of geometry proof-making. Although the original version of the tutor was instructionally successful, Koedinger and Anderson revised their beliefs about the fundamental nature of the cognitive skill being taught, and therefore about the character of the expert system representing that skill. One would like to know more about what caused this revision in the theory of geometry skill than is told in the chapter. They say they took a closer look at the behavior of skilled geometry problem solvers and found that it differed from the approach in the original tutor. That tutor modeled geometry problem solving as heuristic search in an *execution space* defined by the kinds of steps that students are taught to write down in proofs as presented by conventional geometry texts. A significant innovation of the original Geometry Tutor was to make that problem space overt with a graphic representation. This model of geometry problem solving was not the a priori effort of an AI researcher; it was based on research examining the learning of geometry proof skills that was conducted by both Greeno (1982) and Anderson.

However, it must be that what the researchers saw was heavily influenced by the available approaches to cognitive modeling. For now, they see something quite different. Skilled geometry problem solvers do not seem to make the local heuristic decisions within the execution space that are presumed by the original model. Instead, perceptual recognition of configuration schemas that are matched by the diagram of the problem sets off an abstract planning process. A global solution plan is developed within a problem space that is more abstract and more compact than the execution space of the original model. Formal details are filled in only at the end. Neither traditional instruction nor the original Geometry Tutor instructs or provides support for this kind of thinking. Undoubtedly, this evolution of the theory of geometry skill is just a typical example of the process of change in scientific theories: the formalization and application of the theory brings out and makes noticeable the ways in which the theory is inadequate. The Geometry Tutor was one of the very first serious intelligent tutors; no doubt this recognition of a need for change in its representation of geometry skill foreshadows what will happen with many other tutors. Each, afterall, incorporates what is likely to be the first attempt at a detailed and complete cognitive theory of the knowledge in the domain of the tutor. Because the original Anderson Geometry Tutor was instructionally successful, it will be particularly interesting to see how successful this new approach proves to be. Anderson has said that the artificial experts in his tutors characteristically model ideal students rather than true experts, but this new tutor does attempt to teach real expertise directly.

Intelligent tutoring entails a serious and continuing investment in cognitive research on the nature of the skill being taught. Practitioners of intelligent tutoring are becoming convinced that the quality and accuracy of this model of skill is the most critical factor in the success of tutoring. This fact points to several limits on the potential of intelligent tutoring. The knowledge or skill to be taught must be of a type that we understand well enough to be able to model it. And it must be important enough, and/or taught to enough people, to justify the associated research investment. The central role of the expert system in an intelligent tutoring system points to a paradox that may be embedded in the act of developing intelligent tutors. If we achieve sufficient understanding of an area of knowledge or skill to be able to produce a computerized tutor, that implies that we can have a computer perform the task. Then, will we still want to teach people to perform it? This issue has certainly been raised in military maintenance training, where many believe that it is expert system job aids, rather than tutors, which should be produced. It seems possible that we may experience a transitional period in which computerized tutors will be used, followed by a questioning of traditional curricular goals and a shift to education in the use of computer tools to deal with these domains. On the other hand, the hope of tutor builders is that human learners will generalize beyond the scope of the expert systems that teach them, once they have been started on the correct path.

The chapter by Derry and Hawkes reports on another tutoring project that is based on substantial cognitive research into the skill it teaches, algebra word problem solving. Here the emphasis is on a novel, fuzzy logic approach to modeling the state of student knowledge and on the associated determination of pedagogical moves. Obviously, these aspects of intelligent tutoring technology have not yet attained the status of solved problems. Today we feel quite confident that the quality of the knowledge or skill representation underlying intelligent tutoring is critical. It is less certain whether there is a significant effect of a detailed student model and the associated tailoring of instructional moves. This is an issue for current research. It is an issue complicated by the lack of direct implications from the student model to instructional acts: There are many options which must be considered and empirically evaluated. By overcoming some of the difficulties associated with the uncertainty of the student modeling process, the approach that Derry and Hawkes take may make it possible to realize the imagined potential of individually adapted instruction. We must wait to see the results of instructional experiments with the tutor.

Shute's chapter is directed at a major point of controversy concerning pedagogical strategies: whether the tightly monitored "standard Anderson-style tutor," which permits no digressions from some correct path, is preferable or whether free exploration of the problem-solving environment produces better learning. Shute makes the question still more complex by considering the possibility that the best pedagogical strategy may vary depending upon characteristics of the individual student. Shute examined learning in two variants of a tutor of basic electric circuit theory. One learning environment provided feedback on the correctness of the student solution, followed by a statement of the relevant rule, whether or not the student was correct. The other environment also provided feedback on correctness but merely drew attention to relevant features of the problem, leaving it to the student to induce the relevant rule. Shute did obtain some statistically significant effects of the type expected. Students who were inclined to exploratory behavior did somewhat better in the environment that required them to induce rules, whereas students who were not so inclined did better in the environment that provided rules. Exploratory behavior increased the amount of time required to learn but did not improve posttest performance. The inclination to explore was unrelated to measures of student cognitive ability or to incoming level of electronics knowledge. But *caveat lector*. The effects discussed in this chapter are quite small. It is uncertain how much these students learned during the brief instruction (7 hours) provided: incoming electrical circuit knowledge accounted for most of the variance in outgoing electrical circuit knowledge.

Lajoie's chapter touches on several features of intelligent tutoring while discussing the Sherlock tutor of avionics test station diagnosis, an Air Force application of intelligent tutoring, as well as a related tutor she is developing to teach biological subject matter in the schools. She emphasizes the value of the simulation aspect of intelligent tutors, that they make interesting and possibly dangerous problem-solving environments safe and accessible to students. The simulated test station will not electrocute the trainee. The Bio-World would be too complex and expensive to make available to students as a real experimental environment.

The Sherlock tutor was designed to support hypothesis testing by providing multiple solution paths for diagnosis of electronic faults and coaching in the context of these solution paths. The memory load on the student was reduced by graphic representations and replays of the information being developed in the problem solution. The coaching style was less aggressive than in a typical "Anderson-style" tutor, providing help mainly upon request. A hierarchical representation of the problem space was modeled via the menu interface, and students were taught to constrain the problem and to be systematic about testing each hypothesis. Expert problem-solving processes were overtly available to the student. Lajoie's chapter provides an example of the detailed study of learning processes that intelligent tutoring systems make possible through their capacity to collect data on every detail of trainee performance. Lajoie was able to go far beyond mere evaluation by posttest performance. She could trace detailed changes in the diagnostic strategies being used by trainees. Intelligent tutoring systems offer boundless opportunities for instructional research that could never have been done before. The instructional actions of an automated tutor can be programmed and controlled in the way that the actions of human tutors never can be. The actions of the student can be tracked and recorded in a detail that would not otherwise be possible, although sophisticated analysis techniques are needed to assimilate and make sense of such unprecedented masses of data. As noted earlier, there were many design decisions involved in building the Sherlock tutor as it was; in most cases, there was no research basis for the decision. Exploration of the consequences of different pedagogical decisions is a wide-open area for research.

In Sherlock, it was possible for the trainee to get a replay of the diagnostic process, with commentary. Katz and Lesgold elaborate on these features of Sherlock, attempt to integrate Sherlock with current enthusiasms for group learning, and speculate well beyond the state of the art about possible further development of the tutor component of Sherlock into a much more sophisticated metacognitive critic and intellectual collaborator. The related chapter by Schauble, Glaser, Raghavan, and Schultz explores rather elaborate facilities which aim to promote student reflection within a scientific reasoning task. For example, the student can see a "Plan View" of his or her actions, indicating whether or not the actions contribute to carrying out the planned exploration of variables and their effects. An "Expert View" provides an expert treatment of what can be concluded from the data collected. The experiment exploring the instructional effectiveness of this rather elaborate apparatus was just beginning as the chapter was written. Interpreting the displays may prove non-trivial for the students.

Finally, the chapter by Lepper, Woolverton, Mumme, and Gurtner provides some cautionary discussions about the extent to which we can expect success in automated emulation of human tutors. They point out that human tutors have been studied very little so that the tutorial behavior of current intelligent tutoring systems is often ad hoc. However, they are not the only ones to have studied human tutors (see, for example, Fox, 1989; Litmann, 1990), and some study of human tutors was done during the development of many existing systems. The present chapter gives particular emphasis to the affective aspect of tutorial interaction and to the tutor's monitoring of the affective state of the tutee. It rightly points out that computers would have difficulty interpreting such data as the tutee's facial expression, but grants the possibility that a computer might use alternative indicators. Still, the authors wonder whether an effective affective response to the student could be generated by the computer. The point is well-taken, but we already know that intelligent tutors can be well-received by students (Schofield, Evans-Rhodes, & Huber, 1990) and can be highly effective instructionally (Anderson, Boyle, Corbett, & Lewis, 1990; Anderson, Conrad, & Corbett, 1989; Nichols et al., in press). Perhaps greater attention to the affective dimension of instructional interaction will improve the effectiveness of artificially intelligent tutors. On the other hand, students may not expect or require affective sensitivity from a computer tutor.

In summary, intelligent tutoring technology has reached the point of being a feasible approach for teaching a wide range of skills. But it is scarcely an established, complete, and frozen technology. The options and unknowns are many. Only from the peculiar perspective of a small research in-group could it be regarded as an establishment ripe for overthrowing. From a financial point of view, intelligent tutoring may not be a practical option for most schooling situations. This is no doubt a primary cause of current interest in less computationally demanding forms of computer use in education.

Computers as Tools for Learners

In the early '80s, it seemed evident that computerized changes in the way writing, laboratory experimentation, and drafting were being done outside the school would gradually transfer, without much drama, into the way that these skills are taught within schools. The possibility of using word processing computers for writing instruction coincided with rising concern over the neglect of writing instruction in United States schools (Edwards, 1982; National Institute of Education, 1984). Little writing instruction existed, but there was widespread public support for a major reform of writing instruction. It seemed possible that a computerized approach to writing instruction might emerge as the primary mode of that reform. Computerized prompting of the writing process, word processing support, and correction facilities of varying sophistication were already available as likely elements of an instructional package. Innovative computer-based approaches to writing instruction were being developed for the elementary school classroom, notably Bolt, Beranek and Newman's project Quill (Bruce & Rubin, in press; Collins, Bruce, & Rubin, 1982; Rubin & Bruce, 1985). These involved the use of the computer in such classroom projects as the production of a newspaper, the recording of scientific data or sharing of movie reviews written by individual students. Levin's experimental project emphasized the development of writing as out-of-context communication by putting students in San Diego into network communication with students in Alaska (Levin, Boruta, & Vasconcellos, 1982). Innovations like these are compatible with some styles of classroom organization and not with others; it seemed likely that they would be adopted in places where the style of classroom organization was favorable to them, and ignored elsewhere.

Today, the picture seems much the same as before. Many experiments have been undertaken, but as of 1990, Becker (1990) was still reporting that programming and computer literacy dominated secondary school use of computers while drill and practice in basic skills dominated elementary school use. Significant use of applications—word processors, databases, spread sheets, graphics programs—was still being reported as a recent phenomenon.

Among the chapters of this volume, we have one by Salomon that describes an innovative tool for writing instruction, *The Writing Partner*. This tool prompts the writing process in a way that was guided by the research of Bereiter and Scardemalia. The hope is that this guidance will both improve the quality of student writing done with its aid and lead to internalization of the guidance, its transformation into self-guidance of writing. It is unclear whether this hope has been realized. A sketchy report of an initial study in Israel suggests that the tool did have the effects that were hoped for, but in the chapter we do not have enough evidence to evaluate the claim. It is rather unclear whether these results continued to hold true in the American school environment. On the one hand, there is a data-less claim that they did. On the other hand, the chapter indicates that when the tool was used initially as an add-on, it had no positive effects. The statement is made that a total curricular restructuring was necessary and that the evaluation became an evaluation of a total changed instructional environment rather than an evaluation of the tool. (This leaves us puzzled as to why an isolated pull-out program approach appeared to be effective in the Israeli study.) Generally, efforts to improve writing by teaching or guiding students in what appears to be a more expert writing process have not been very successful, even though research has yielded some interesting insights into the nature of more expert writing processes. The Salomon chapter does not make a convincing case that *The Writing Partner* has been more successful than other efforts. Often when improved writing is found, sheer increase in amount of writing practice is a likely explanation, rather than any special feature of the writing instruction or the writing tools.

It is probably worth noting that tools for the prompting of writing, "idea processors" and aids to brainstorming or outline construction, already existed in the early '80s. None of them seems to have enjoyed the large-scale success of the popular word-processing, database, and spreadsheet programs. Perhaps this means that the real nature of composition processes remains poorly understood so that we do not know how to aid them in an adept, functional manner. Perhaps it means that composition processes, however expert and effective, are quite idiosyncratic so that no one tool is likely to please and assist many users. In attempting to use computers to aid student composition, educators are going beyond what has evolved as a successful tool in the commercial, adult market. Perhaps that is risky.

An interesting development of the last few years is educators' great interest in using and teaching a new form of composition: hypermedia. This trend was not yet evident in the early '80s, although both the general concept of hypermedia and some specific implementations have a rather long history. The chapter by Lehrer represents this trend. Lehrer's project can be viewed in two ways. It may teach a modern form of composition, hypermedia composition. Alternatively, it could be seen as a version of the *concept-mapping* approach to instruction most actively promoted by Novak and Gowin (1984). Lehrer describes an experiment in which students constructed hypermedia presentations about topics in the Civil War; many similar experiments have been going on in the past few years. One might view this as a new form of the more traditional project-based approaches to instruction. Again, the report of evaluation results is vague and anecdotal. We are told that students became very engaged in their work, and that they often developed "pockets" of intensive knowledge. It appears that attempts to generate quantitative evidence of instructional value were unsuccessful. Chances are that hypermedia projects share the benefits and drawbacks of more traditional projects as educational tools. Researchers exploring these new technology-based projects as instructional devices would do well to examine what may have been learned in past rounds of enthusiasm for project-based instruction.

Obviously, hypermedia composition is more complex than ordinary written composition. Furthermore, we have no long tradition to show us how it can be done well. We are uncertain whether it can be done well at all; the art of hypermedia composition is as yet undeveloped. "Readers" can become lost in hyperspace; we know that already. One of the few investigations of many of these issues in hypermedia is the ongoing research project of Spoehr (1991). Students constructing hypermedia presentations could end up with knowledge that has no structure beyond vague associations—the links in a typical hypermedia system are not constrained to represent any particular type of relational information. (One might contrast them, for example, with the links in George Miller's WordNet (Miller, Beckwith, Fellbaum, Gross, & Miller, 1990) that represent the major semantic relations which organize mature knowledge of the English lexicon: synonymy, antonymy, subordination, part-whole, etc.) The attraction of hypermedia is that it seems to provide a direct representation of the knowledge networks that we develop as we acquire expertise in a subject, that it breaks free of the limits of linear presentations. However, we do not yet have a good theory of the way that knowledge networks—if that is indeed what we possess—are actually structured. Hence, hypermedia networks may not represent them well. Furthermore, it could be that a well-designed linear presentation is the best way to communicate a network. If hypermedia presentations become popular in the larger society, then their preparation will become a valued skill that we will want to teach, but it may be a skill as specialized and exceptional as film-making. In hypermedia use, even more so than in aids to composition, educators are attempting to move ahead of the larger society. Most likely, these experiments will not have widespread impact.

Two additional chapters present "cognitive tools" that are pieces of what might be present in a complete, canonical intelligent tutoring system. Reusser presents a system that provides a graphic representation for arithmetic word problems that can be used to construct and display the student's understanding of the situation presented in the problem. In addition, the system can provide feedback when students neglect important problem information or select irrelevant problem information for entry into their representation. That is, the instruction in this system is based primarily on a cognitive analysis of the skill being taught. As such, it provides a potential and partial test of the view that most of the potential gains in tutoring arise from a good cognitive analysis of the skill. This simpler system, without complex student modeling functions, might prove just as successful as a more complex and more expensive tutorial system such as the one presented by Derry and Hawkes. As of the writing of this chapter, however, the evaluation results were not in. Whatever they may be, one must then try to assign credit or blame to the multiple present or absent components: the task analysis, the graphic representation, the simple instruction, the absent sophisticated student modeling. Ideally one would like to be able to examine the added value of student modeling and correspondingly adaptive instruction while the skill analysis, graphic representations, and other features are held constant.

Behrend and Roschelle present a still more fragmentary experience that lies at the extreme of the discovery approach. For reasons that are not explained, their subjects were given a graphics world which represents Newtonian physics but that fact was somewhat concealed. Subjects were given "thick arrows" and "thin arrows" to manipulate in order to try to match a given trajectory in an adjacent display; they were not told that these represented velocity and acceleration. This seems to reduce the task to a surface computer game, with little potential educational value. The particular research subjects discussed in the chapter may have been clued in, because we are told that one of them had done considerable reading of physics on his own. For the researchers this environment had some value as a tool that provoked the social interaction they chose to analyze, but whether or not this sort of graphic environment has any value for teaching students to understand physics remains an enigma. How should the students even know that this has any relation to physics or that the rules of the graphic world are those of the real world, rather than any of the other rules that might have been programmed? Even under the best of circumstances, one must worry about getting students to make appropriate connections between computer simulations and the phenomena they are meant to represent. Here the problem was exacerbated by extreme lack of curricular integration, an isolated experience in an experimental chamber.

As in the early '80s, it still seems probable that "cognitive tools" which have received intensive investment, trial, and improvement in the worlds of adult work are a promising direction for the educational use of computers. Efforts to create new, almost unprecedented tools for exclusively educational use are likely to suffer from insufficient investment in their development and refinement.

There is no doubt that "unintelligent" instructional systems will remain an attractive alternative to intelligent instructional systems, largely because the complexity and cost of both development and implementation are likely to be lower, within the limits of fiscal feasibility for the schools. For this reason, determining when and if there is substantial benefit in the full power of student modeling and associated highly individualized instructional treatments is a priority research issue in educational technology.

Computers as Tools to Support Teaching Activities

Reviewing all the possible ways in which computer technology might have an impact on education in the early '80s, we (Chipman & Butler, 1983, 1985) realized that there was a major, neglected possibility. Computers might be tools for teachers, rather than tools for students or teachers of students. There was little discussion then of such uses. We suspected that this reflected the low value our society places on teachers: just as their pay is relatively low, little thought is given to providing teachers with tools to facilitate their work. The computers that were purchased for schools were and are thought of as being for the children, not for the teachers. This seemed strategically unfortunate. Teachers who have access to computers as tools to facilitate their daily work—in preparing work sheets or keeping records—are more likely to appreciate the potential value of computers for their students and to think of ways in which the computer can be incorporated in their classroom teaching. No doubt there are many teachers who have purchased computers for themselves, especially as prices have come down, and no doubt many teachers do use classroom computers for their own work, probably feeling slightly illicit when they do so (because the computers were intended for the students).

As seen in the chapters of this volume, innovations in educational technology continue to ignore the teacher, and there is no reason to believe that this sample misrepresents the general situation. Some early experiments did indicate that teachers appreciate computer networking facilities that break down their isolation in the classroom and provide access to help from others (Newman, personal communication). It is evident from more general experience in the computerized academic and scientific communities that this enhancement and facilitation of human communication is one of the more attractive applications of computers. It is possible that computer networks could expand teaching resources by making it easier for the teacher to draw upon members of the larger community to enrich the school environment. In the early '80s, the Educational Technology Center then funded at Harvard University was planning to link high school science teachers with each other and with scientists in universities and other settings, in an effort to upgrade the quality of instruction by increasing teacher participation in the larger scientific community. But, it is important to recall that few schools have classrooms wired for the necessary telephone lines, despite the age and pervasiveness of telephone technology in our society: Major infrastructure investments are required even for such seemingly simple innovations.

In the early '80s, we envisioned the possibility of an enhanced, dynamic blackboard that the teacher could use to illustrate ideas and concepts being presented. Computers could greatly facilitate the presentation of visual models of concepts, providing depth and motion, as well as easier production of conventional diagrams that are commonly drawn on blackboards. This would provide better communication between students and teachers who happen to think more effectively in visual terms and would provide more effective teaching of subjects in which the visual content is inherently important.

There have been great advances in computer graphics. Certainly, prepared computer graphics presentations have become common in business. Many examples of computer instruction with high-quality graphics exist. Object-oriented programming techniques are beginning to enable the generation of dynamic simulations by a user who simply constructs a visual diagram of a device from a library of parts (Hollan, Hutchins, & Weitzman, 1984; Towne, 1987), an important step in this direction. However, our expectation that computer graphics would become as easy to use as a blackboard—dynamically integrated with oral expression "in real time"—has not yet been fulfilled. We thought that by now enhanced computer graphics equivalents might be replacing the blackboards that are so common in scientific and technical offices. We thought that educators then might be able to share in this expressive technology. It took about 15 years for the vision of the powerful, highly portable personal computer (Kay, 1977) to be realized; perhaps this graphic capability will not be too far behind.

Would such a technology be used if it were available, when it seems that teachers do not often use even overhead projectors? Eventually, they may. An overhead projector largely duplicates the function of the blackboard or calls for advance preparation. Truly novel capabilities are likely to have a greater attraction. Either is much more likely to be used if it is a built-in normal feature of the classroom. We would not make much use of blackboards either if we had to make a special effort to haul them in from a closet somewhere else in the building. Certainly expense will be a barrier to any such computerized enhancement of normal classroom facilities, but one-per-classroom technology is more within reach than one-per-student technology. Why aren't we paying more attention to possible computerized enhancers of the teacher's performance?

SUMMARY PREDICTIONS

It seems likely that classrooms will continue to look strikingly similar to the way they look now. Instruction in computer literacy and computer programming have been added to the curriculum without significant changes in the organization or appearance of the school. Of course, there are computers in the schools to support such teaching, mostly in specially designated classrooms or laboratory facilities. As the years pass, replacing and maintaining the necessary equipment becomes an increasing problem, even for relatively affluent districts. Instruction in or with computers does not automatically bring about radical change; it has been and can continue to be assimilated to the dominant model of teaching, whatever that happens to be in a particular school and community.

In the early '80s, it seemed likely that the juxtaposition of the desire for curriculum reform in high priority areas such as mathematics, science, and writing with the advent of relatively affordable computer technology would result in investments in curriculum developments that integrate the use of the computer. This has happened at the R&D level. NSF Science Education and other sources of support have financed, for example, the development of intelligent tutors that relate to most of the high school mathematics and programming curriculum, as well as to some important topics in science. In addition, DOD investments in tools for building tutors of equipment maintenance skills could be applied to vocational education. Yet, it is questionable whether the potential of these technological advances will be realized in widespread school use of them. Expense remains a major barrier, particularly for intelligent tutoring technology. The required computers are much less expensive than they once were, of course, less than a quarter of the cost of comparable computing power in the early '80s, but still, it seems, too much in relation to what our society is willing to invest in education.

Because the application of technology to education is lagging its penetration elsewhere in society, not leading as it was in the first attempts at computer instruction in the 1960s, the prognosis is more favorable than it was the first time around. But the slow pace of change since the early '80s must make us more pessimistic than we were then. As I have already suggested, the "model-breaking iconoclasts and revolutionaries" of this volume might be simply responding to economic realities of schooling.

Furthermore, expense is not the only problem to be overcome. Thoroughgoing revision of the curriculum is needed to integrate technology effectively. Even the most substantial examples of technological innovations, such as the LISP Tutor or the Geometry Tutor, do not teach the entire course. Isolated simulations or other special activities, however attractive when examined in isolation, are even more problematic. Without curriculum revision that integrates them and points to them in the teacher guides, the logistical difficulties of integrating such activities into the curriculum will discourage most teachers. As the novelty value declines, the use of these activities in the belief that they provide a valuable "computer literacy" experience will decline. In this volume, this major issue finds only rather faint mention in the problems experienced with Salomon's *Writing Partner.*

It seems possible, though not quite as likely as it did in the early '80s, that inexpensive computer facilities will be used increasingly for drill and practice, eventually becoming an unnoticed change in the nature of the "seatwork" that now occupies so much of student time. Built-in correction and monitoring features may make this time somewhat more instructionally effective. In contrast, we cannot foresee that computers will take over a great deal of instructional delivery. Because human beings are very social beings, and because young children in particular require human attention and human supervision, there will be great resistance to the idea of children spending large proportions of their time in isolated interaction with a computer. Lepper, Woolverton, Mumme, and Gurtner may exaggerate the extent to which the unique qualities of human interaction are essential for every instructional interaction, but at a more global level they are certainly correct.

For essentially social and emotional reasons, it seems unlikely that large increases in the "productivity" of teachers (cf. Melmed, 1984) are either desirable or possible. Therefore, the prospects of reduced human labor costs are not there to justify large expenditures on computer equipment and correspondingly large R&D investments to produce high-quality instructional software. The promise of technology lies primarily in the prospects of improved educational results, either through its direct effects or through a shift in the allocation of teacher resources to students most in need of individual help (Schofield et al., 1990). Do we care enough about the quality of education to make big investments? Unfortunately, the evidence suggests that as a society we do not. For this reason, it seems likely now, as it seems likely in the early '80s, that the primary impact of computer technology on education will come through the adaptation to educational uses of sophisticated computer tools developed in the commercial marketplace for adult users. As mass production brings the price of these tools downward, they will become more and more common in the schools.

This prediction could be wrong. The view through the silicon chip is clouded. But the challenge to would-be revolutionaries is clear. The challenge is not breaking the "icons" of colleagues in educational R&D. The challenge is to develop innovative instruction that is actually used in the nation's schools and has a significant positive effect on the learning of a significant number of students.

ACKNOWLEDGMENTS

This chapter draws heavily on two prior papers entitled, "Gazing into the Silicon Chip: The Impact of Microcomputers on Teaching and Learning," S. F. Chipman and P. A. Butler (1983, 1985). The first paper was prepared at the request of OECD-CERI to give a U.S. perspective on educational computing. At that time, Dr. Susan Chipman was Assistant Director for Learning and Development of the National Institute of Education, and Dr. Butler worked with her as the primary person responsible for research on educational technology. In 1985, an updated version of the paper was made available as Learning Technology Center Report #85.2.3 of Peabody College of Vanderbilt University. Susan Chipman is now the Program Manager for Cognitive Science at the Office of Naval Research. The opinions expressed herein are the personal opinions of the author and do not necessarily represent the official policy or position of the Office of Naval Research. Insofar as the chapters of the present volume are discussed, these comments are based on the versions of the chapters that were made available for discussion; in some cases comments may refer to points that do not appear in the revisions.

REFERENCES

Alexander, L. (1991). *America 2000: An education strategy* (April 18, 1991). Washington, DC: U.S. Department of Education.

Anderson, J. R. (1984). *Proposal for the development of intelligent computer-based tutors for high-school mathematics.* Carnegie-Mellon University.

Anderson, J. R., Boyle, C. F., Corbett, A., & Lewis, M. (1990). Cognitive modeling and intelligent tutoring. *Artificial Intelligence, 42,* 7–49.

Anderson, J. R., Boyle, C. F., & Yost, G. (1985). The geometry tutor. In *Proceedings of the International Joint Conference on Artificial Intelligence-85* (pp. 1–7). International Joint Conference on Artificial Intelligence. Los Angeles.

Anderson, J. R., Boyle, F. C., & Reiser, B. J. (1985). Intelligent tutoring systems. *Science, 228,* 456–462.

Anderson, J. R., Conrad, F. G., & Corbett, A. T. (1989). Skill acquisition and the LISP Tutor. *Cognitive Science, 13,* 467–505.

Anderson, J. R., Farrell, R., & Sauers, R. (1984). Learning to program in LISP. *Cognitive Science, 8,* 87–129.

Anderson, J. R., & Reiser, B. J. (1985). The LISP Tutor. *Byte, 10,* 159–178.

Anderson, R. E. (1982). National computer literacy, 1980. In R. J. Seidel, R. E. Anderson, & B. Hunter (Eds.), *Computer literacy: Issues and directions for 1985.* New York: Academic Press.

Barbour, A., & Editors of Electronic Learning. (1984, October). Computing in America's classrooms 1984—EL's fourth annual survey of the states. *Electronic Learning,* 39–44.

Bayman, P., & Mayer, R. E. (1983). Diagnosis of beginning programmer's misconceptions of BASIC computer programming statements. *Communications of the Association for Computing Machinery, 26,* 667–670.

Becker, H. J. (1990). *Computer use in United States schools: 1989 An initial report of U.S.*

participation in the I.E.A. Paper presented at the annual meeting of the American Educational Research Association, Boston.

Behavioral Technology Laboratories. (1988, September) *The intelligent maintenance training system.* Redondo Beach, CA: Behavioral Technology Laboratories, University of Southern California.

Boyer, E. L. (1983). *High school: A Carnegie foundation report on secondary education.* New York: Harper & Row.

Brown, J. S., & Burton, R. R. (1978). Diagnostic models for procedural bugs in basic mathematical skills. *Cognitive Science, 2,* 155–192.

Bruce, B., & Rubin, A. (in press). *Electronic Quills: A situated evaluation of using computers for writing in classrooms.* Hillsdale, NJ: Lawrence Erlbaum Associates.

Center for Social Organization of Schools. (1983a). *School uses of microcomputers: Report from a national survey* (Issue No. 1, April). Baltimore, MD: Center for Social Organization of Schools, Johns Hopkins University.

Center for Social Organization of Schools. (1983b). *School uses of microcomputers: Report from a national survey* (Issue No. 2, June). Baltimore, MD: Center for Social Organization of Schools, Johns Hopkins University.

Chipman, S. F., & Butler, P. A. (1983). *Gazing into the silicon chip: The impact of microcomputers on teaching and learning.* Unpublished paper, written at the request of OECD-CERI. Washington, DC: National Institute of Education.

Chipman, S. F., & Butler, P. A. (1985). *Gazing into the silicon chip: The impact of microcomputers on teaching and learning* (Learning Technology Center Tech. Rep. #85.2.3). Nashville, TN: Peabody College of Vanderbilt University.

Collins, A., Bruce, B., & Rubin, A. (1982). Micro-computer-based writing activities for the upper elementary grades. In *Proceedings of the Fourth International Learning Technology Congress and Exposition.* Warrenton, VA: Society for Applied Learning Technology.

Conference Board of the Mathematical Sciences. (1983). *The Mathematical Sciences Curriculum K-12: What is still fundamental and what is not.* Report to the National Science Board Commission on Pre-college Education in Mathematics, Science and Technology.

Consumer Reports. (1983, September). How our readers are using computers. *Consumer Reports, 48*(9), 470–471.

Edwards, K. (1982). Problems related to the teaching of writing in the public schools. In B. Cronnell & J. Michael (Eds.), *Writing: Policies, problems, and possibilities.* Los Alamitos, CA: SWRL Educational Research and Development Center.

Fox, B. A. (1989). *Research on Human Tutorial Dialogue* (Final Report on N00014–86–K–0105). Boulder, CO: Department of Linguistics, University of Colorado.

Gott, S. P. (1989). Apprenticeship instruction for real-world tasks: The coordination of procedures, mental models and strategies. In E. Z. Rothkopf (Ed.), *Review of Research in Education* (Vol. 15, pp. 97–169). Washington, DC: American Educational Research Association.

Greeno, J. (1982). Forms of understanding in mathematical problem solving. In S. Paris, G. M. Olson, & H. W. Stevenson (Eds.), *Learning and Motivation in the Classroom* (pp. 83–111). Hillsdale, NJ: Lawrence Erlbaum Associates.

Hollan, J. D., Hutchins, E., & Weitzman, L. (1984). STEAMER: An interactive inspectable simulation-based training system. *AI Magazine, 5,* 15–27.

Johnson, W., & Soloway, E. (1985). PROUST. *Byte, 10,* 179–192.

Kay, A. C. (1977). Microelectronics and the personal computer. *Scientific American, 237,* 230–244.

Kurland, D. M. (1983a). Educational software tools: The rationale behind the development of the *Bank Street Writer.* The Conference on Writing Through Technology, Stonebridge, MA, January 1983.

Kurland, D. M. (1983b). *Software for the classroom* (Tech. Rep. No. 15). New York: Center for Children and Technology, Bank Street College.

Kurland, D. M., Clement, C. A., Mawby, R., & Pea, R. D. (1987). Mapping the cognitive demands of learning to program. In R. D. Pea & K. Sheingold (Eds.), *Mirrors of Minds: Patterns of Experience in Educational Computing* (pp. 103–127). Norwood, NJ: Ablex.

Kurland, D. M., Mawbry, R., & Cahir, N. (1984, April). *The development of programming expertise in adults and children.* Paper presented at the annual meeting of the American Educational Research Association, New Orleans.

Kurland, D. M., & Pea, R. (1985). Children's mental models of recursive LOGO programs. *Journal of Educational Computing Research, 1,* 235–243.

Levin, H., & Romberg, R. W. (1983). *The educational implications of high technology.* Institute for Research on Educational Finance and Governance, Stanford University.

Levin, J. A., Boruta, M., & Vasconcellos, M. T. (1982). Microcomputer-based environments for writing: A writer's assistant. In A. C. Wilkinson (Ed.), *Classroom computers and cognitive science.* New York: Academic Press.

Linn, M. C. (1985, May). The cognitive consequences of programming instruction in classrooms. *Educational Researcher, 14,* 14–29.

Littman, D. C. (1990). *Strategies for tutoring multiple bugs.* Unpublished doctoral dissertation, Yale University.

Mace, S. (1983a). Firms continue computer giveaway. *Infoworld, 5,* 38.

Mace, S. (1983b). Road to U.S. computers in schools paved with bills. *Infoworld, 5,* 39.

Malone, T. W. (1980). *What makes things fun to learn? A study of intrinsically motivating computer games.* Palo Alto, CA: Xerox Palo Alto Research Center.

Malone, T. W. (1981). Toward a theory of intrinsically motivating instruction. *Cognitive Science, 4,* 333–369.

Mayer, R. E. (1982). *Diagnosis and remediation of computer programming skill for creative problem solving.* Final Report to the National Institute of Education. University of California at Santa Barbara.

Melmed, A. S. (1984). Educational productivity: The teacher and technology. *T.H.E. (Technological Horizons in Education) Journal, 11,* 78–82.

Miller, G. A., Beckwith, R., Fellbaum, C., Gross, D., & Miller, K. J. (1990). Introduction to WordNet: An on-line lexical database. *International Journal of Lexicography, 3,* 235–244.

National Commission of Excellence in Education. (1983). *A nation at risk: The imperative for educational reform.* Washington, DC: U.S. Government Printing Office.

National Institute of Education. (1984). *What you always wanted to know about research findings: Writing.*

Needle, D. (1982). Group fights growing use of micros in schools. *Infoworld, 4,* 23.

Nichols, P., Pokorny, R., Jones, G., Gott, S. P., & Alley, W. E. (in press). *Evaluation of an avionics troubleshooting tutoring system* (Tech. Rep.). Brooks AFB, TX: Air Force Human Resources Laboratory.

Nickerson, R. S. (1982). Information technology and psychology—A retrospective look at some views of the future. In R. A. Kasschau, R. Lachman, & K. R. Laughery (Eds.), *Information technology and psychology: prospects for the future.* New York: Praeger Press.

Nickerson, R. S. (1983). Computer programming as a vehicle for teaching thinking skills. *The Journal of Philosophy for Children, 4*(3&4), 43–48.

Norman, C. (1983). *Computers in the classroom: National Educational Association Survey Report.* Washington, DC: National Educational Association.

Novak, J. D., & Gowin, D. B. (1984). *Learning how to learn.* Cambridge, England: Cambridge University Press.

Orlansky, J., & String, J. (1979). *Cost-effectiveness of computer-based instruction in military training* (P-1375). Alexandria, VA: Institute for Defense Analysis.

Papert, S. (1980). *Mindstorms: Children, computers and powerful ideas.* New York: Basic Books.

Papert, S. (1987, January). Computer criticism vs. technocentric thinking. *Educational Researcher, 16*(1), 22–30.

Pea, R. (1983). *Programming and problem solving: Children's experience with LOGO. Paper presented at a symposium entitled "Chameleon in the classroom: Developing roles for computers"* (Tech. Rep. No. 12). New York: Center for Children and Technology, Bank Street College.

Pea, R. (1987). The aims of software criticism: Reply to Professor Papert. *Educational Researcher, 16*(5), 4–8.

Pea, R. D., & Kurland, D. M. (1984). On the cognitive and educational benefits of teaching children programming: A critical look. *New Ideas in Psychology, 2,* 137–168.

Pea, R. D., & Kurland, D. M. (1987). On the cognitive effects of learning computer programming. In R. D. Pea & K. Sheingold (Eds.), *Mirrors of minds: Patterns of experience in educational computing* (pp. 147–177). Norwood, NJ: Ablex.

Pea, R. D., Kurland, M. D., & Hawkins, J. (1987). LOGO and the development of thinking skills. In R. D. Pea & K. Sheingold (Eds.), *Mirrors of minds: Patterns of experience in educational computing* (pp. 178–197). Norwood, NJ: Ablex.

Pirolli, P. L., & Anderson, J. R. (1985). The role of learning from examples in the acquisition of recursive programming skills. *Canadian Journal of Psychology, 39,* 240–272.

Rubin, A., & Bruce, B. (1985). QUILL: Reading and writing with a microcomputer. In B. A. Hutson (Ed.), *Advances in reading/language research* (Vol. III) (pp. 97–118). Greenwich, CT: JAI Press.

Schofield, J. W., Evans-Rhodes, D., & Huber, B. (1990). Artificial intelligence in the classroom. *Social Science Computer Review, 8,* 24–41.

Sheingold, K. (1981). *Issues related to the implementation of computer technology in schools: A cross-sectional study* (Memo No. 1). New York: Center for Children and Technology, Bank Street College.

Sheingold, K., Kane, J. H., & Endreweit, M. E. (1983). Microcomputer use in schools: Developing a research agenda. *Harvard Educational Review, 53*(4).

Sheingold, K., & Tucker, M. S. (Eds.). (1990). *Restructuring for learning with technology.* New York: Center for Technology in Education, Bank Street College.

Sherman, M. (1983). *Computers in Education: A Report, Recommendations, Resources.* Concord, MA: Bates Publishing Co.

Sleeman, D., & Brown, J. S. (Eds.). (1982). *Intelligent tutoring systems.* New York: Academic Press.

Soloway, E., Ehrlich, K., Bonar, J., & Greenspan, J. (1982). What do novices know about programming? In B. Schneiderman & A. Badre (Eds.), *Directions in human-computer interactions* (pp. 27–54). Norwood, NJ: Ablex.

Spoehr, K. (1991, April). *The ACCESS Project in American history and literature.* Paper presented at Annual Meeting of the American Educational Research Association, Chicago.

Towne, D. M. (1987). The generalized maintenance trainer: Evolution and revolution. In W. B. Rouse (Ed.), *Advances in man-machine systems research* (Vol. 3, pp. 1–63). Greenwich, CT: JAI Press.

Wenger, E. (1987). *Artificial intelligence and tutoring systems: Computational and cognitive approaches to the communication of knowledge.* Los Altos, CA: Morgan Kaufman.

Wierzbicki, B. (1983). Boston revolutionizes its public-school system. *Infoworld, 5,* 37.

Wierzbicki, B. (1984). College students learn to live with computers. *Infoworld, 6,* 35–36.

Wright, D. (1982). *Instructional use of computers in public schools* (NCES Report No. 82–245). Washington, DC: National Center for Education Statistics.

Wujcik, A. (1984). *Report to the task force on the status of technology use in schools.* Washington, DC: National Institute of Education.

13

Information Technology and the Future of Education

Alan Lesgold
University of Pittsburgh

With such a rich mix of chapters in this volume and such a careful and thorough discussion from Susan Chipman, perhaps there is room for something a bit more radical and preliminary. In this chapter, prompted by the kinds of tools discussed in this volume (and by my own experiences with the Sherlock technical training system), I want to consider some specific possibilities for educational technology that could help reorient American educational practice. Specifically, I see the need for more effort to build tools to support much more substantial student and teacher originated learning activities than are common today. As I am suggesting possibilities for radical change, my argument has two parts. The first is that schools might change in radical ways over the next decade and the second is that these potential changes pose a particular kind of research and development agenda.

Why should we expect change? It has been argued that schools are extremely stable entities, barely moving in the direction of the enticing tidbits we researchers place before them and unable to afford any kinds of significant costs. When people look at such technology as the Sherlock system my colleagues and I have developed for the Air Force, they admire its instructional potential and then note that it is irrelevant to schools, which cannot afford the standard high-end office computers it requires. Although it is quite conceivable that it is adaptive for schools to ignore most educational technology innovation, it simply is not true that change, even financial change, cannot occur.

Over the past few decades, there have been major changes in school expenditures. An example is school transportation. In many cities, school bussing was initially motivated by a concern for racial equality. Soon, though, others got into the act. Today, a student in my home state has the legal right to be transported, at

369

no cost, to any school within ten miles of the boundaries of his district. Sometimes a single student is carried daily by cab to a small religious school perhaps 20 miles from home (in a major urban area!). A few students yield annual costs for transportation of close to $10,000—enough for three or four systems that could run Sherlock! A school bus costs tens of thousands of dollars and lasts 5 to 10 years. Drivers also cost money. Perhaps the expenditure per bussed student is a few hundred dollars a year—surely of the same magnitude as the annual cost of a computer system sufficient to run an intelligent tutor and lasting perhaps 5 years.

Similar arguments could be made about nutritional programs in schools. School lunches will cost $1.25 this year in my son's school, or $225/year if we assume the minimum 180 day year. That amount is covered by Government programs for all who cannot afford it. Again, this is an amount of the same magnitude as might be needed to support a personal computer of some sort at every student's desk. Other areas where specific communities will sometimes make investments of similar magnitude include sports facilities, asbestos removal, building renovation, etc. All of these are potentially worthwhile investments. At higher levels of finance, I note that the Pittsburgh schools now pay many teachers over $50,000, and three or four suburban districts pay even more. At the same time, top salaries in the local Catholic system remain in the low twenties. My point is only that communities often will make real investments in schools if they believe that such investments are needed, but not always. Further, the large changes tend to be major programmatic shifts.

It is tempting to argue that an even larger revolution in education may soon occur. Because of our decentralized approach to education, many things happen at the same time. So, we have some school districts doing an excellent job, some with mediocre outcomes but relative parental acceptance, and some ripe for revolution. Let me focus briefly on this latter group without in the slightest meaning to imply that it is universal. Many good things are happening in scattered locations in the United States. At the same time, though, a peculiar closed system controls much of education.[1] Responding to public pressure, school systems set, and sometimes fail to meet, rather general goals, such as higher mean achievement test scores. In response, tests are edited to eliminate classes of items too rich and complex to show rapid improvements, and teachers focus on the minimalist items that current tests contain.

Entry to the system is also controlled. No one can be a teacher, in most places, without first going through an education school where much emphasis is placed on teaching methodology and much less on subject matter content. Students, and even their parents, have little voice in the content of what is taught. Instead, public debate focuses on control battles over the fringes of education, such as

---

[1] I realize that some schools in some places are moving beyond the situation I describe, but it is still a good account of much of education.

knowledge about sexually transmitted disease, birth control, comparative religion, or death. I know of no major fights over whether and how to teach calculus. Strangely, polls tend to show that people think their own local school is good, though they complain about some aspects of public education in general.

Special elite programs exist, and there is much infighting by parents to get their kids into such programs. The quality of the programs is often suspect, though. We all fight to get our kids into calculus classes, but they still have trouble with college math and few become scientists or engineers—largely because they are ill equipped to pursue such careers. As in eastern Europe, the commissars of education include colorless bureaucrats, dedicated patriots, and a few shameless opportunists. Efforts at reform often hit the rocky shoals of state requirements, bureaucratic forms, and turf wars. As in Eastern Europe, motivational weaknesses may be a function of the current system and not of enduring characteristics of teachers. Systemic change may well release the considerable effort and productivity needed for real improvements in learning to occur.

The system has its refuseniks. Home education is an increasingly visible practice. Here and there, major leaders confess that they never graduated from high school. Quite a number of parents believe that their children get most of their education from summer programs and from college courses taken after school. More significantly, the business world, which once emulated the world of precollege schooling with courses, credits, certifications, etc., is now beginning to move away from the traditional approach. Instead, they look for ways to facilitate small work groups to handle their own training needs, emphasizing minimal manuals, just-in-time training, and tools for facilitating learning and performance.

Against this backdrop, federal leaders have mounted a conservative resistance. We will improve the system by having more and better tests, along with vouchers or other mechanisms to permit parents to choose the schools their children attend. If we reward the right outcomes, they believe, change will naturally occur. As others have noted, the primary contribution of top leadership has been a program to assure that should education improve, we will be able to measure the improvement. All that is needed for success, we are told, is to be ready to announce it. There is a chance that this plan will work. That is, we may, while discussing new standards and new tests, achieve a better understanding as a society of our educational goals, teach those goals to ourselves and our teachers, and focus on them until they are achieved.

On the other hand, school systems, with their taxing power and with limited external incentives toward improvement, may be the wrong size for the adaptation that is required. They may be too small to conduct extensive research on their own and too big to take the risks needed if there is simply to be a free market of new approaches in the absence of extensive research. Consequently, there is a chance that what we are seeing in the current testing movement is not a real freeing up of the marketplace in education but rather a conservative educational establishment working feverishly on a new 5-year plan while the system continues to crumble irreversibly.

What would an educational revolution look like? It would probably consist of movements to force state financing of alternative schools. The Dutch model, in which groups of parents can create a school provided that they meet minimal standards, accept all who want to attend (or provide an unbiased selection procedure), and have at least enough students to be moderately efficient, might foreshadow the new educational system here. The issue of separation of church and state will probably preclude an exact replication of the Dutch scheme, of course. What is important is only that a situation might arise in which being willing to invest heavily in new approaches to learning might be necessary in order for a school to attract students or in order for a person to get a teaching job.

The Role for Technology

Should there be an opportunity for substantial educational change, how might we think about technology for education? Presumably, there would be both a stronger consumer movement, in which educational products would have to prove themselves, and economic flux, with more money potentially available for products with demonstrated value. My personal belief is that schools would begin to look to industry for ideas. What might they find? Industry does make a major investment in training. Traditionally, most of this training has followed the schooling model. However, disenchantment with the schooling model has led to several kinds of changes. First, there is a continuing pressure to cut costs. Training departments get phased out, and the work gets contracted out to specialized companies that use lower-paid staff and cut a few corners on the traditional training models while not really changing them.

A second movement is minimalist training. Instead of making a complete list of what a worker needs to know and then working through the list creating lessons for each subgoal, we see some innovators asking whether everything that characterizes journeyman competence needs to be taught. In the print realm, this shows itself as the minimal manual approach (Carroll, Smith-Kerker, Ford, & Mazur-Rimetz, 1987–1988), a systematic research effort to develop a scheme for determining the smallest amount of content that can enable efficient, safe on-the-job learning. Other manifestations of this approach are seen in various "just-in-time" learning schemes that combine job aids and bursts of explanation that occur in the context of work.

A third approach, partly allied with the second, is the focus on "performance support tools." As Marc Rosenberg (Puterbaugh, Rosenberg, & Sofman, 1989; as summarized in Rosenberg, 1991) defines it,

> A performance support tool is software designed to improve worker productivity by supplying immediate on-the-job access to integrated information, learning opportunities, and expert consultation, with scope and sequence controlled by the user.

Everything a worker needs to perform competently, including learning and information resources, would be part of the job environment. Using such tools, the worker (or groups of workers), not a trainer, would decide when to seek additional information, and would seek it from intelligent and supportive information systems. Some system components might include intelligent tutors, though they would probably have a different form from those discussed so far. Equally important, there would be rich information bases with intelligent front ends to support inquiries from students. Finally, there would be schemes for providing expert coaching, explanations, feedback about recent performances, and assistance in learning how to use the learning resources being made available.

It is useful to distinguish tools for supporting work and worker improvement from earlier ideas about automation. In the past, efforts were made to design systems that took over the hard cognitive work from humans. Training was to be primarily the learning of rote algorithms for "operating" those systems. The alternative now gaining acceptance both recognizes the limitations of computer intelligence as a substitute for human intelligence and realizes that computer systems can be powerful tools that people can use to enhance their learning efforts as well as their skilled work performances.

Also implicit in the world of performance support tools is a social model of learning. Most work is done by teams. Consequently, performance support tools will be supporting team activities. It is unlikely that this support will be solely via one-on-one enhancement of individual efforts. The Katz and Lesgold chapter in this volume discusses one small effort in the direction of supporting collaborative work. However, it does not address an issue that has recently emerged in field trials of Sherlock II. In the real world, not only do people start out at different levels of capability in a "course," they also have differing needs. The person who will be in charge of a function within a work group needs to become very expert. Another person may need moderate expertise so he or she can fill in when the expert is on vacation. A third person may need an overview so he can discuss the needs of the job intelligently in administrative meetings. Individualization with respect to student entering ability was the goal of the early intelligent tutoring system movement, and it has not been wholly achieved. Individualization with respect to student learning goals has yet to become a clear goal of the intelligent tutoring systems agenda.

From the viewpoint of a free market, the move toward performance support tools for training is worthy of special consideration. The place for individual and group initiative is preserved. However, the right tools are made available to support these initiatives. High-quality, individualized training is attainable by the groups that are asked to do it. The job of a higher-level organization is to provide tools that facilitate the training schemes that individual work units develop for themselves. And, there are external criteria for success—do the work groups function productively for the company?

For education, one can envision a similar scheme. The federal government would support research and development of performance support tools, including extensive testing of those tools. It would also have a special role in determining what constitutes success of educational efforts, by providing good data correlating student performance in different states and districts to later performance levels in workplace and in civic life. Some of the new standards and new testing schemes now being discussed attend to this part of the task. My focus is on the other part, developing a set of performance support tools that can be adapted by local school systems to support a variety of teacher and student-led activities, including targeted learning, student projects, and self-assessment. There are two key requirements for such tools:

1. The tools must be readily modifiable by students and teachers to support learning and self-assessment activities that they choose and/or design.

2. The tools must be tested sufficiently to promote confidence among teachers, school leaders, and educational policy makers that using them pays off.

Student-Centered Learning and Self-Assessment Tools

Note that the primary claim lying behind these requirements is that we should be considering what educational technology should be if scope and sequence are to be controlled by the learner. At first glance, this seems silly. After all, haven't we just come out of decades of educational rot due to letting students (at least older ones) choose basket weaving courses instead of the classical trivium and quadrivium? Telling students that it doesn't matter what they study or what they learn is not what I have in mind at all. Rather, I think it is time to consider providing students with a variety of indicators of their progress but letting them select individual learning tasks, with guidance from teachers or other support systems.

Basically, I propose that we move toward a free economy of learning, just as we have a free economy of commerce. Such an economy works best with something close to perfect information. That is, it must be possible for individual students to have a clear sense of what competences are currently being valued, or expected to be valued by the time they finish school. They also need consumer guides. That is, they need a plurality of suggested means for achieving those competences, a review of learning activities and learning tools with the same character as the reviews of mutual funds in *Money* or *Business Week*. Finally, they need learning summaries, the equivalent of the financial summaries that financial institutions now provide to customers or the outputs of the home computer ledger programs that many of us use—what knowledge have I acquired and what opportunities does it afford?[2]

---

[2]I note that some of the faults of current education are associated with ledger-like artifacts, notably transcripts of credits and lists of courses. The scheme I have in mind would provide models of opportunities for future learning and directions to follow, not a list of satisfied prerequisites or requirements for other schools or for jobs. It would be a tool for the student to use in charting future efforts, not a "bank" of tickets needed to pass through artificial turnstiles.

Learning Summaries: A New Assessment Technology

Before returning to the list motivated by Rosenberg, let's consider this issue of learning summaries. Where would these come from? A lot will be needed from the business world. Employers will need to establish patterns of competence that are associated with success in jobs. It is likely that in order to do this efficiently, they will resort to some externally verifiable demonstrations for performance. That is, instead of asking about scores on a test or diplomas, employers will want samples of real job performances. Much of this already happens, when it matters. For example, to get a license as a pilot, a nuclear power plant control room operator, or a radio operator, one needs to demonstrate a variety of job competences. To get a job as a secretary, competences such as typing speed must also often be demonstrated. Selection as a manager may involve the use of assessment centers, which often include job simulations. The drive for equal job opportunity, combined with the current testing movement, will likely produce more such specifications, since they provide more equality of opportunity than degree requirements.

However, in order for education to be readily valued, it needs to be denominated in something more closely approximating a currency. That is, there needs to be some scheme for translating between demonstrated achievements in learning and competence requirements for social roles (jobs). I believe that a variety of translation services will become available in the future, providing predictive links between records and products of learning activities on the one hand and job requirements on the other. Some of this will leverage existing psychometrics, but it will also involve new levels of cognitive task analysis and new approaches to computer-assisted and computer-based scoring of performances. The scheme I have in mind would look something like this.

A student (younger students at least would do this partly with their parents) would access a tool that allowed him or her to build a personalized set of learning goals. In response to interest inventories, public requirements, and other sources of information, the tool would build a goal structure of alternative plans for achieving the desired competences. These desired competences would include the student's personal goals and also some publicly mandated goals, such as being able to participate effectively as a citizen in decision making and perhaps national service. In early grades, the goals would be broadly diffuse, keeping every option open, while in later grades, a student might focus on being absolutely sure that certain final goals are achieved in a preplanned amount of time. Given the recommendations of such a tool, the student would prepare a plan of learning activities in which he or she expected to engage over some time period—perhaps a week for a young child up to a year or longer for a high school student. The tool would help the student assess the effect of the planned activities. That is, it would predict whether the student will be on course toward the goals he/she has set if the proposed activities are completed (taking account of any predictions of the student's likely performance, based on past work). Each student would end up with a personally selected work agenda that was "reality-tested" against his/her goals and some social constraints.[3]

Note that I have not proposed a scheme in which students do whatever they please. Rather, I have suggested that it is within the sights of the R&D world, given what we already know how to do, to let students develop, revise, and maintain their own personal plans for learning. Like personal financial plans, these plans would be good only to the extent that they are reality-based, and we will need tools that help students understand the implications of their plans. In particular, the business world will need to contribute well-founded studies of the kinds of skills really required for various job roles and of the prior knowledge needed to efficiently learn on the job. I think this is possible, and I think the results will be extremely healthy.

From a personal viewpoint, the vision I have sketched is particularly appealing. Most children, my own included, have learning experiences that go beyond school. Currently, these represent nice little extras that only occasionally influence the directions that schooling then takes. If we were to create a world in which students really could control the scope and sequence of their learning, then extracurricular learning experiences, whether running a small business, taking a three-week intensive Latin course, taking care of a disabled family member, or working as an aide in a scientist's laboratory, would become part of a student's portfolio and thereby influence the advice he or she gets in developing a plan for further learning. The very notions of plans for learning and of outside-school activity as part of such plans will be helpful for some children, too.

Many technical issues remain to be resolved, and much research needs to be done. For example, how shall the tools we envision evaluate the learning that results from an activity such as caring for a disabled family member? No machine will be intelligent enough to handle this task. With human judgments, there is a danger of translating good deeds into good evaluation outcomes. What I have in mind is not a program of credits for life experience like that currently used in night schools. Rather, I suspect that we will end up with search tools that help a human teacher match a child's special experiences to some normative ones that have been carefully analyzed and for which appropriate evaluation guidance has been developed. Then, the best matching exemplars would yield questions to be asked in deciding what might have been learned (and what could yet be learned) from the student's special experience and might even propose additional activities to confirm what had been learned.[4]

---

[3]For example, society would probably not permit a seven-year-old and his/her family to choose goals that precluded a wide range of adult roles. Equal opportunity would translate, in part, into keeping options open quite late into the school career.

[4]I am reminded of my all-too-frequent experiences in dealing with automated systems for tracking down lost luggage. When my suitcase fails to follow me on a trip, I am shown a set of pictures of luggage and asked which one my own case is most like. I buy perfectly ordinary luggage, but it never looks like any of the pictures. Still, I pick the closest match, answer a few questions, and my luggage

Information Resources

I turn now to the three kinds of resources Rosenberg mentioned: information resources, learning resources, and guidance resources, taking them in that order. We begin with information and the tools for processing it. Many of the more powerful experiences in schools today involve personal searches for and integration of information. However, students have access only to impoverished information banks. Often, the only resource is a municipal or school library. As a result, each assignment triggers a rush to the library. The winner takes out all the books on the assigned topic and the losers confabulate or ask someone for help. A more inspired teacher may give each child a different assignment. This solves the information allocation problem but still removes most opportunities for peer collaboration in getting, organizing, presenting, and critiquing the information. Simple improvements are possible today. In principle, a class could have a subscription to an information service such as Prodigy™. This would permit redundant access to information sources, but the sources remain impoverished— an encyclopedia and some extremely specialized databases but nothing like the New York Public Library or the U.S. Archives.

While it is becoming commonplace to have projects that construct online information bases for students, the tools for building and accessing such databases remain weak and ill-suited to optimal learning. Surely we can do better. Indeed, some of the experimentation by researchers such as Scardamalia and Bereiter (Scardamalia, Bereiter, McLean, Swallow, & Woodruff, 1989) shows the power of student-built information resources. A broad view of information resources for learning will recognize the learning that goes into building such databases and the possibility that at least some of them or parts of them might be student-developed in addition to being used by other students. We need tools for organizing knowledge, entering it into information systems, and extracting it from such systems. We also need research, building on some of that in this volume such as the work of Salomon and of Roschelle and Behrend, to establish how such tools should be built and how they are best used to facilitate learning. A number of projects in Europe and the U.S. are aimed at providing working adults with tools for managing and accumulating complex information, including multiple viewpoints on a complex problem (cf. Conklin & Begemann, 1988; Halasz, 1988; Marshall & Irish, 1989; Schuler & Smith, 1990; Smolensky, Fox, King, & Lewis, 1988; Streitz, Hannemann, & Thüring, 1989; Thüring, Haake, & Hannemann, 1991). We should be actively following these efforts and trying to move them toward the education world.

---

re-appears in a few days. This is partly because there are additional clues for the system to use, like my luggage tags. However, it is also partly because perfection is not required. Once there is a moderately decent match between my luggage and the computer-based description, the system works just fine. Similarly, the goal for computer-facilitated individual choice in education should not be perfection in stating exactly which competences a student has but approximate guidance about where he/she stands and what kinds of things make sense as next steps.

Learning Resources

The second educational technology area mentioned by Rosenberg, learning resources, comes closest to my own work and to much of that in this volume. I have already suggested that virtually all extant learning resources that encompass knowledge about curricular goals lack the ability to respond to student decisions about which of those goals to address and how. This shortcoming can be addressed rather easily, in some cases. We are finding, for example, that with a little bit of field testing we can develop schemes that allow students more choices in the learning tasks that Sherlock II puts before them. However, significant changes are required in our models of tutoring when we do this.

In the standard ITS paradigm, there is a student model. By comparing the student model either to an expert model or, as in Sherlock, to a curriculum goal structure, the system determines what subgoals should next be addressed and consequently what tasks should be assigned. When students are given the opportunity to request nonstandard assignments, some problems arise. Sometimes it is impossible to specify a task without specifying its solution. So, for example, it would be counterproductive for a student to be able to ask Sherlock for a problem in which the fault to be discovered is in Switch S53 of the test station, since the whole point of a problem would be for the student to find the fault.

What ends up being required, at some level, is for the system to build a model of how the student sees himself. That is, the system must know which competences the student is trying to achieve and which he (or she) thinks are already mastered. A simple example shows why this is necessary. We decided to add to Sherlock II the ability for the trainee to ask for a harder problem than Sherlock would otherwise have provided.[5] Sherlock, like most human teachers, is conservative in assessing student capability. It needs to see repeated evidence of a student's knowledge in order to credit that knowledge. Consequently, it is quite conceivable that a student might believe that he or she can handle more challenging work than Sherlock prescribes. This could easily happen at the beginning of training, when Sherlock is moving from default assumptions about a student to empirically-supported evaluations. It can also happen later, if a student gains a sudden insight that allows much-improved performance—Sherlock takes a while to notice and credit such changes. So, students may well understand their capabilities better than Sherlock does.

It is not very difficult to let a student request a more challenging problem than Sherlock would otherwise provide. Given one or more difficulty orderings for a

---

[5]A Sherlock problem is a simulation of a task that would take perhaps eight hours in real life and which is accelerated to require about a half hour of simulator time. Time savings result from not having to carry out physically a number of simple actions that can readily be described to the simulation program, such as exposing a part of the circuitry to permit testing. Actually doing this might take 10 min, but it can be simulated instantly. Usually, trainees solve one or two Sherlock problems a day, in a course of training lasting about a month.

set of problems, if our student model would ordinarily pick a problem with difficulty s, we might, in response to a student request for harder problems, have it select a problem with difficulty $s+\delta$. However, we might also want to adjust the student model that led to the originally selected difficulty level, if it turns out that the student really is ready for harder problems. My colleagues and I now think that we should take account of the student's inputs to the extent that they match his or her subsequent performance. Equally important, since he or she will be getting a problem that is not matched to the system's model of his or her ability, changes to the student model based on how the problem is solved may need to be adjusted. If a trainee asks for a harder problem and does well, this is really worthy of note in our modeling, but if he or she asks for a hard problem and does poorly, we may not want to decrease our competence estimates too much.

All in all, we need a scheme that will push the student model toward a trainee's self-appraisal (expressed by asking for easier or harder problems), within certain constraints. The model should move towards the self-appraisal when it is supported by reality and should move the residue of the expressed self-perception toward the student model when it is not supported by subsequent performance. Here is such a scheme. Assume that we have a sequence of problems and that trainees are placed into that sequence on the basis of some of their student modeling variables. Let the placement of a trainee in the problem sequence[6] for his or her ith learning opportunity be denoted by s_i. Note that s_i is not part of the student model. It is the placement in the problem sequence that would normally have resulted from the student model. When a trainee asks for harder problems, we will add δ to his or her placement standing. So, the revised placement in the problem difficulty sequence will be $s_i+\delta$.

$$s_{i+1} = \hat{s}_{i+1} + \epsilon\delta \qquad (1)$$

We will want to compute a new value s_{i+1} after the trainee solves the problem. This value will be compared to the value generated by the student model and will be the basis for changing the student model. Now, after the trainee solves the next problem, suppose his or her new student model placement is closer to $s+\delta$ than to s. We will then want to correct the student model as shown in (1), where $\hat{s}_{i+1}$ refers to the problem placement level corresponding to the system's new student model appraisal of the trainee, and where ϵ is less than 1.

On the other hand, if a trainee does not do well on the new problem, then the corrected student model should not be reduced too much, since the problem was inappropriately hard, but the trainee's self-appraisal trace should be forced toward the level corresponding to the student model. More specifically, if $\hat{s}_{i+1}$ is the problem level corresponding to the system's new estimate of the student

---

[6]So far, we have assumed that there is a primary difficulty ordering of all problems. In fact, problems may have multiple dimensions of difficulty, but we have not yet attacked this case.

model, then the corrected level should be only ϵ of the distance down from s_i, as shown in (2). The actual placement, for problem selection purposes, should probably also be $\epsilon\delta$ above s_{i+1}.

$$s_{i+1} = (1 - \epsilon)s_i + \epsilon\hat{s}_{i+1} \qquad (2)$$

It would then be necessary to back-propagate the corrections to the problem selection in order to actually adjust the student model, and this might involve considerable qualitative inference as well as possible quantitative manipulations. Choices in "blame assignment" for the needed corrections (deciding which parts of the student's specific knowledge were inaccurately modeled) might be handled by simply asking the student how he thinks he is doing on various learning subgoals. My point in presenting this bit of detail is simply to indicate that the kinds of thinking required to take account of student inputs in the process of student modeling are relatively small. The claims by a student that he or she really understands how to do something (or really does not), when substantiated by performance on significant tasks, are simply another form of evidence to be considered in arriving at an overall student model. (The accuracy of a student's self-appraisals may itself be worthy of note.)

The foregoing example is extremely primitive and meant only to help convey the possibility of developing tools that have the important property of being under the control of students and their teachers. Part of control, but not the only part, is the ability to base activity on self-assessments of competence. Self-assessment must not become self deception, so whatever scheme is developed to take account of student self-assessments must have means for deciding whether the student's self-appraisal matches his performance. However, the need to be careful should not obscure the positive side of involving students and teachers in making choices about learning projects.

Another aspect of user control in learning resources is shaping of the resource itself. Here extant educational technology seems to fall at two ends of a continuum. At one end, one finds tools that are meant to be shaped to user needs, such as spreadsheets, microcomputer-based laboratory packages, LOGO, etc. At the other end, one tends to find systems that take on themselves the task of adapting to user requirements. This is a tremendous responsibility, and one way to interpret my message is that it may be better to temper intelligent adaptability in a system with direct user control. Task prescription is only one area where this is the case; there are many others. Further, students and teachers often have needs and modes of usage for tools that are not anticipated by their users.

As an example of the kinds of adaptability issues I have in mind, consider the many bulletin board systems that proliferate in university Unix™ environments. One can readily imagine a school world in which many student projects were energized by such bulletin boards, and some such efforts already exist (e.g., Levin, Riel, Rowe, & Boruta, 1984; Newman & Goldman, 1987; cf. Newman, Griffin, & Cole, 1989). The best developed are in university environments and not formally part of the instructional system, but they readily could be. These networks are meant to be proliferated. A student migrates from one university to another, finds his favorite bulletin board missing, and arranges for it to be added. Other students therefore are seeing it for the first time long after a community of readers has developed. It is as if new people are constantly joining a long-ongoing discussion group. This creates certain stresses.

New people sometimes find it difficult to join electronic bulletin board groups. Consider, for example, a new Microsoft Windows™ user who discovers a bulletin board dedicated to that system. Stereotypically, such a new user will broadcast through the bulletin board system a variety of questions that have been answered many times already. This will be followed by a number of complaints about overloading the mail system. On a good day, someone will point the user toward an archive of oft-asked questions and their answers.

How can we do better? A solution that is pretty low tech has developed on some of the commercial information utilities like Compuserve™. There, a user must "join" a new forum. This involves a 15 second ritual of specifying your name, something the system already knows, of course. However, it also results in one's being alerted to libraries of old conversation "threads," answers to common questions, names of people willing to help newcomers, etc. In addition, some systems may screen new submissions to help with the redundancy problem.

Can we do better than this? Quite probably. It is possible for an intelligent system to shadow usage and intervene with suggestions based upon inferences about the likely goals of the user. For example, Fischer's Kaestle system (Fischer & Lemke, 1988) will intervene to help a Unix™ user become more efficient. However, there is a danger in being too helpful. Sometimes a user simply does not want to be bothered learning to be more efficient at something he doesn't plan to do very often. A good performance support tool for learning should be like a butler, magically smoothing the way but never imposing its views or approach on the user.

Guidance Resources

The last area Rosenberg points to is expert consultation. Here, there are many opportunities. One thing that is becoming clear, though, is that giving advice is not so easy. As Moore (1989) has noted, in human interactions, requests for advice almost always involve follow-up questions by the advice seeker, and sometimes these questions are extremely vague ("Huh?," "Why?," etc.). When an initial explanation is offered, for example, we often don't fully grasp it but are uncertain what to ask about. Part of the further interaction is the clarification of the original information request. Between humans, the necessary attunement of helper to requester can be quite subtle and graceful, though it is not guaranteed to be so. Between people and machines, this subtlety remains largely a topic of research. It is, however, very important research, since it is absolutely necessary to producing technology that can function broadly as support for student and teacher initiative in learning.

Summary

I am excited by this volume, because it indicates great progress in harnessing information technology to support learning. The projects, by and large, are aimed in a helpful direction, and progress is being made. Further, I am optimistic that if good tools for learning are produced, they will be used, and eventually they will be used widely. This may well happen as part of a major revolution in our ideas and institutions for learning. Whether or not one agrees with my predictions, I think it is possible to agree that the field will be advanced most by designing tools that can help groups of people who work together, including teachers and students, design and carry out learning projects that achieve goals they value.

REFERENCES

Carroll, J. M., Smith-Kerker, P. L., Ford, J. R., & Mazur-Rimetz, S. A. (1987–1988). The minimal manual. *Human-Computer Interaction, 3,* 123–153.
Conklin, J., & Begemann, M. L. (1988, October). gIBIS: A hypertext tool for argumentation. *ACM Transactions on Office Information Systems, 6,* 303–331.
Fischer, G., & Lemke, A. C. (1988). Constrained design processes: Steps toward convivial computing. In R. Guindon (Ed.), *Cognitive science and its applications for human-computer interaction.* Hillsdale, NJ: Lawrence Erlbaum Associates.
Halasz, F. G. (1988). Reflections on Notecards: Seven issues for the next generation of hypertext systems. *Communications of the ACM, 31,* 836–852.
Levin, J. A., Riel, M. M., Rowe, R. D., & Boruta, M. J. (1984). Muktuk meets jacuzzi: Computer networks and elementary school writers. In S. W. Freedman (Ed.), *The acquisition of written languages: Revision and response.* Norwood, NJ: Ablex.
Marshall, C. C., & Irish, P. M. (1989, November). Guided tours and on-line presentations: How authors make existing hypertext intelligible for readers. *Proceedings of the 2nd ACM Conference on Hypertext (Hypertext '89).* Pp. 15–26. Pittsburgh, PA.
Moore, J. D. (1989). *A reactive approach to explanation in expert and advice-giving systems.* Unpublished doctoral dissertation. University of California, Los Angeles.
Newman, D., & Goldman, S. V. (1987). Earth Lab: A local network for collaborative classroom science. *Journal of Educational Technology Systems, 15*(3), 237–247.
Newman, D., Griffin, P., & Cole, M. (1989). *The construction zone: Working for cognitive change in school.* Cambridge, England: Cambridge University Press.
Puterbaugh, G., Rosenberg, M., & Sofman, R. (1989, November/December). Performance support tools: A step beyond training. *Performance & Instruction, 28,* 1–5.
Rosenberg, M. J. (1991, July). *Performance support tools: Repositioning training in the 90's.* Presentation at the Conference on Second Generation Instructional Design. Logan, UT: Utah State University, Instruction Technology.
Scardamalia, M., Bereiter, C., McLean, R. S., Swallow, J., & Woodruff, E. (1989). Computer-

supported intentional learning environments. *Journal of Educational Computing Research, 5,* 51–68.

Schuler, W., & Smith, J. B. (1990, September). *Author's argumentation assistant (AAA): A hypertext-based authoring tool for argumentative texts* (Working paper 470). Darmstadt, Germany: Gesellschaft für Mathematik und Datenverarbeitung mbH, Institut für Integrierte Publikations- und Informationssysteme [Institute for Integrated Publication and Information Systems].

Smolensky, P., Fox, B., King, R., & Lewis, C. (1988). Computer-aided reasoned discourse or, how to argue with a computer. In R. Guindon (Ed.), *Cognitive science and its applications for human-computer interaction* (pp. 75–82). Hillsdale, NJ: Lawrence Erlbaum Associates.

Streitz, N. A., Hannemann, J., & Thüring, M. (1989, July). *From ideas and arguments to hyperdocuments: Travelling through activity spaces* (Working paper 402). Darmstadt, Germany: Gesellschaft für Mathematik und Datenverarbeitung mbH, Institut für Integrierte Publikations- und Informationssysteme [Institute for Integrated Publication and Information Systems]. Also published in *Hypertext '89: Proceedings* (Special Issue-SIGCHI Bulletin). New York: Association for Computing Machinery.

Thüring, M., Haake, J. M., & Hannemann, J. (1991, May). *What's Eliza doing in the Chinese Room? Incoherent hyperdocuments—and how to avoid them* (Working paper 533). Darmstadt, Germany: Gesellschaft für Mathematik und Datenverarbeitung mbH, Institut für Integrierte Publikations- und Informationssysteme [Institute for Integrated Publication and Information Systems].

Author Index

Subject Index

394 SUBJECT INDEX

37
as a tutorial goal, 81–87
Children
anthropomorphizing the computer, 102
requiring supervision while using computers, 349–350
Coaching, 146, 284, 292–293, 298, 304, 355
Bio-world, 280, 281
computerized, 292–293
Sherlock I, 266–268
Sherlock II, 301–302, 303
Cognition
engaging in out-of-reach activities of, 284
using Bio-world, 280
using Sherlock I, 264–266
processes of
Bio-world's support of, 276–278
Sherlock I's support of, 262–263
situated, 6
structural organization of
in hypermedia presentation, 218–221
tool usage and ability regarding, 67
Cognitive apprenticeship, 6–7, 9, 145, 146
provided by Sherlock I, 265–266
three-stage model of, 108
Cognitive load, 284, 292, 355
Bio-world's sharing of, 278–280
Sherlock's sharing of, 263–264
Cognitive tools, 5–6, 6, 7, 8–9, 359, 360
computer-based, 6–7
eight principles for designing, 143–157
computer environments as, 261–286
distinguished from computer tools, 180–181
four types of, 261
Collaboration
analysis of
challenge six, 239–253
framework for, 234–239
categories of discourse events, 253–254, 255
language and action, 238–239
narrations, 238
repairs, 237–238
socially-distributed productions, 237
turn-taking, 236–237
computer-supported, 239–255
definition of, 229, 235
distinguished from cooperative work, 235
peer, 290, 298, 377
Collaborative learning/problem solving, 156–
157, 173, 236
computer-based, 239–255
apprenticeship, 292
coaching, 292–293
effectiveness of, 290
role of tutor in, 289–313
three main dimensions to design a frame-

work for, 290–291
Joint Problem Space (JPS) and, 236–237,
239–255
Colleges. *See Schools*
Comprehension aids, text, 172
CompuServe, 381
Computer-assisted instruction, 15, 349–350, *see
also Computer-based tutors*
drill and practice, 348–349
intelligent, 351–356
simulations, 350–351
traditional computer-assisted instruction,
349–350
Computer-based collaborative learning. *See Collaborative learning/problem solving*
Computer-based hypercomposition. *See
Hypercomposition*
Computer-based learning environments. *See
Learning environments*
Computer-based tutors, *see also Intelligent tutoring system (ITS); Tutoring sys-
tems; Tutors*
delivery problem of, 101–102
design of
motivational techniques of human tutors
and the, 75–102
diagnosis problem of, 100–101
intelligent pairings of students by, 311
plausibility problem of, 102
Computer graphics, 361
Computers
anthropomorphization of, 102
courses on, 343, 346–348
high costs of, for schools, 343, 363
Computer tools
distinguished from cognitive tools, 180–181
pedagogic, 179–194
Conceptual representations, 148–155
Confidence, 80
Bio-world and, 281–282, 285
strategies for enhancing, 82–84, 87
attributional inoculation techniques, 88–
89
avoiding direct negative feedback, 87–88
direct maximization of success, 89–90
direct minimization of failure, 90
as a tutorial goal, 81–82
Configuration, 20, 233–234
Conflict resolution, 295
Construction
HyperAuthor's tools for, 204–205
Constructivist theory, 6
Control, 80
illusion of, 98
intrinsic motivation and, 92
strategies for enhancing, 92–93

SUBJECT INDEX 399

episode in Sherlock II, 299, 301
in geometry, 17–18, 40–41
group, 289, 304
local cognitive modeling of, 107–137
skipping steps in, 18–20, 40, 42
social, 296
TAPS system and, 112–114
error detection studies for, 114–121
prototype for monitoring and error detection, 121–137
traces
of Bio-world, 283
of Sherlock I, 269–270
Problem space, 17, 18, 160, 355
effective, 266–268
Problem trees, 111, 112, 114
Procedural facilitation, 146, 185–187, 289
Prodigy, 377
Program Enhancement Advisor, 308
Programming, 357
hypercomposition and, 200
teaching, 347–348
Project Quill, 357

Q, R

Qualitative proportionalities, 233–234
RAND Algebra Tutor, 41
Reciprocal teaching, 289, 291
Reflection, 146
HyperAuthor's tools for, 205
role of, in developing self-regulatory skills, 322
Reflective follow-up
episode in Sherlock II, 301–302
Remedial students, 100
human tutors working with, 77–78
responding to errors, 79–80
Repairs, 237–238
Representations, 148–155
graphic, 359
Revision phase
of hypercomposition-based design, 203
Rule-application vs. -induction learning environments, 65–72
learning outcome, 56–59
method of study for, 49–56
number of problems required, 60–62
time spent on tutor, 59–60, 70
total number of problems, 70
within-tutor analyses regarding, 62–65
feedback provided, 49, 51

S

Sachverhaltnisse, 161, 162, 165

Scaffolding, 146, 262, 304
Schema justification hints, 30–31
Schema, 27, 29–30, 34, 36–37, 109, 110, 112, 116, 165, 166–167
diagram configuration, 20–23
domain-specific relational, 161, 162
search, 20
Schema selection hints, 30
Schools, *see also Education; Teaching*
changes in
cutting costs, 372
minimalist training, 372
performance support tools, 372–374
as context for design, 198–199
expenditures of, 369–370
impact of computer technology on, 1, 341–363
information technology and the future of, 369–382
Scripted cooperation, 289
Self-assessment, 374, 378–380
Self-confidence
Bio-world and, 281–282, 285
strategies for enhancing, 82–84, 87
attributional inoculation techniques, 88–89
avoiding direct negative feedback, 87–88
direct maximization of success, 89–90
direct minimization of failure, 90
as a tutorial goal, 81–84, 87–90
Self-construction, 148
Self-explanations, 297, 304
Self-guidance, 188, 194
Self-monitoring, 111
Self-regulation, 6, 268, 295
Discovery and Reflection Notation (DARN) and, 319–336
experimental approaches supporting, 324
research study on students' activities involving, 332–335
two general classes on skills in DARN
goal orientation, 322–323, 332–333, 335
monitoring and evaluation, 323–324, 333, 335
Sense-making approach, 289
Sherlock I, 284, 285, 351, 355
definition of, 261–262
engaging in out-of-reach cognitive activities with, 264–266
evaluation of, 268–275
evidence of learning and restructuring in, 269–275
functions of, 262
problem-solving traces of, 269–270
providing hints, 267–268
sharing the cognitive load in, 263–264